A MANY-COLORED TOGA

The Diary of

Henry Fountain Ashurst

A MANY-COLORED TOGA

The Diary of
Henry Fountain Ashurst

Edited by
GEORGE F. SPARKS

Drawings by
H. BEAUMONT WILLIAMS

THE UNIVERSITY OF ARIZONA PRESS

TUCSON   1962   ARIZONA

CONTENTS

PROLEGOMENA

An Assessment

When one writes an introduction to a book, and particularly an introduction as limited in length as this is to be, the choice lies between attempting a critique of what the author has written or some discussion of the author himself.

The diary of Henry Fountain Ashurst needs no critique. It will speak for itself. Indeed it would be presumptuous to dissect or attempt to illuminate the matchless prose that flows from his lips or is etched by his pen.

I shall, therefore, confine myself to Henry Ashurst, the man. Him I have known well, perhaps I should say intimately, for a half-century. And since his diary, unlike Pepys', speaks mostly of others and modestly refrains from self-advertisement, I owe its readers a word about this remarkable man. The facts of his life help to make understandable the development of the character and the attainments that are uniquely his among American statesmen.

In my six decades of public life I have known in a most personal way perhaps a thousand public figures who have achieved prominence of one degree or another. They number Presidents of the Republic and Premiers of foreign states; senators and congressmen, governors and legislators, mayors and sheriffs, authors and educators, artists and actors, business leaders and labor leaders, farmers and cowpokes. In none was combined so well as in Henry Ashurst the humility of greatness, the passion for justice, the devotion to his native land, and the loving kindness that the prophets of old commended man to show to his fellow man.

Royalty is born from royalty but greatness may be achieved from the humblest beginnings. Henry Ashurst is living proof of this. He was born in a camp at Winnemucca, Nevada, in the year 1874. The University which now publishes his diary was then no more than a thought in man's mind. The following year his parents settled near what is now the present site of Flagstaff and there he had his first schooling. He was still a boy when he rode the range, trying to earn what he whimsically describes today as an overpaid twenty dollars a month. But his companions — the solitude of the range and the life under summer sun and winter stars, helped mold a philosophy of life, just as isolation or imprisonment helped mature the thought and character of many great men. The range and solitude encouraged reading and reflection, and stimulated the burgeoning of ideas. It made him, incidentally, the most literary of our modern-day senators and compelled his contemporaries to remember that he, like the Websters and the Clays, the Calhouns and the Madisons, the Henrys and the Jeffersons of an earlier day, was something more than a mere politician and officeholder.

His early love was the law and he remains as proud of his identification with it as ever were Hammurabi or Napoleon of their codes. He saw how basic law is to the needs of civilized man, even when he lived as a part of the raw frontier, and its precepts have remained to this day his guiding stars.

He became northern Arizona's best-known lawyer, both as a fair and patient prosecutor and a warmly sympathetic and wondrously successful pleader. His election in 1912 as one of Arizona's first two United States senators was a foregone conclusion.

In electing Henry Ashurst and continuing him for thirty years as its United States senator, the youngest state of our Union earned the admiration, the respect, and I suspect even the envy in a few instances, of some of its older sisters. No longer could it be suggested that erudition and wisdom, legal knowledge and prudence, urbanity and wit could not be found west of the Alleghenies. In the Senate, in the Capitol, in Washington, and in the capitals of the world Henry Fountain Ashurst had proved that he stood with equals. Arizona and its people basked in the reflected admiration and respect that were his.

This is no place to enumerate his accomplishments as a senator and as chairman of the great Committee on the Judiciary where he played a leading role in maintaining the independence of the Republic's judiciary. Nor is there room to recite from his great speeches, which will some day make a book of their own. It is enough to say that when he was about to speak, the press galleries filled to capacity, and that his farewell address as a senator has become a classic.

He was defeated for his sixth-term nomination, but those who know will affirm that the loss of his beloved wife a few months before had made him a reluctant candidate and an even more reluctant campaigner. I suspect that secretly he may have welcomed the change from political life. It gave him the opportunity to devote himself fully to the pursuit of his treasured literature — to the poets he loved so well and whose words he could recite so rapturously. For him, Aristotle and Tacticus, Aristophanes and Homer, Dante and Chaucer, Byron and Keats, Whittier and Longfellow, were the companions of his waking hours.

On the occasion of his eightieth birthday, Henry Ashurst said that at that age a man has atoned, or tried to atone, for the wrongs he has committed and has forgotten the wrongs, if any, against himself. Of Henry Ashurst it can be said that he did not have to reach eighty to make such an affirmation. The concluding words in his diary declare "it a comforting assurance [to him] that nothing in this diary will cause pain to any living person or bring reproach to the memory of anyone who is dead."

That is indeed the epitome of Henry Ashurst. It might well be his epitaph.

Carl Hayden,
United States Senator

An Appreciation

Emerson, in his essay, *Nature* remarks that "a third use which Nature subserves to man is that of language," and in the section of this essay touching on language he points out again and again the closeness of Nature to the words of man. This is true, for we find honesty of expression coming from people whose lives have been in contact with Nature.

His years in the saddle as a cowboy carried Henry Ashurst into the remote places of Arizona where he must have found Nature — such a true source of expression, likewise a source of inspiration. While Henry has delivered more than five thousand speeches of varying types to various audiences, undoubtedly in his youth he directed thousands more to the redness of a canyon wall, or the blueness of a juniper tree, and his words surely have carried high into the sighing pines and across the waters of the lakes of his County of Coconino — words that no one but his horse and himself heard; words which are now floating around in space, mingling with those words of other men who have become beacons of expression, who, likewise, inspired by Nature's closeness and by the loneliness of the saddle, orated, or sang, or spoke verse to an inanimate world of beauty. Such men all attest to the wisdom of the words of Emerson, who wrote, "That picturesque language is at once a commending certificate; that he who employs it is a man in alliance with the truth and God."

Ashurst's speaking was a many-faceted diamond among the jewels of eloquence this era has produced, and the brilliance of this warm stone is but a total of all its facets, his speeches comprising some five thousand of them all shining temptingly in their own bright and brilliant way, each providing the diamond with a new and unusual lustre.

Ashurst's has been a dedicated life in which hard work has been the keystone. The thought of it reminds me of the stories my uncle used to tell about boat trips up the Colorado River. Large iron rings would be set into the stone faces of the canyon walls, or secured to the trunks of great trees along the shores. Through these rings the Captain would pass ropes, and then by a series of heaves and hos from those on board, including passengers and crew alike, the boat would pass over the sandy shoals and into deeper and more navigable waters.

As Ashurst encountered shoals on his journey up the changeable river of life, he would not sit waiting for the fates to release him, but he would look hard for some strong point to which to fasten his rope, and then pull himself through to better water. His has been an exemplary life for that reason alone, if none other existed, for he is a living example of the benefits that come to men who live with freedom and independence of thought, and it is fitting to extol this life which will serve as a growing example to the generations which follow.

Epitome of a tribute to those who pioneered our state, the record in this diary of Ashurst's public life spreads as the two tips of a draftsman's compass across the day of the old and the day of the new.

It is fitting and proper that the University of Arizona Press pay the tribute of publication to the diary of a man who was one of our first United States senators and who remains today a great American and a great Arizonian. I am honored to have been asked to write an introduction for the diary of Henry Ashurst.

Barry M. Goldwater,
United States Senator

Introduction

Henry Fountain Ashurst began his diary in 1910 when he was thirty-four. Two years later, with Arizona's statehood, he assumed the figurative toga of a senator of the United States — a garb which he came to wear with all the honor, pride, dignity, and prestige which traditionally accrued to the wearer of the classic Roman garment. Few individuals indeed have worn more fittingly or nobly the ancient gown. Few have come by it more deservedly as Americans, either by way of birthright or of purposeful and dedicated labor.

Ashurst's early years represent a life sometimes hard and rigorous; sometimes adventurous, and prophetic of a many-sided future. Growing up on one of the last frontiers of America, his lifetime spans the coming of age of the nation and its forceful strides into a position of world leadership. The bare and simple facts of Ashurst's origin and early years are both propitious and dramatic in the manner in which they established the foundations of his career as senator and enriched his background.

The settlement of the West as a process of the migration of races, culture, and families to new lands is a fascinating part of the history of American development. Taking part in this dramatic movement, the Ashurst family was among those hardy and adventurous groups of pioneers in northern Arizona, one of the last frontiers of the American West. It is interesting to trace the backgrounds and the movements of the people who were to determine an important aspect of Henry's future. His parentage was similar to that of many another westerner of that period. He was the son of William Henry Ashurst and Sarah Elizabeth Bogard Ashurst, both of whom had been brought as children to California during the early 1850's following the Gold Rush. William's grandfather, of English ancestry, had been a Baptist preacher in Kentucky and then settled for a time in Missouri before taking the long and arduous journey to California. Henry's mother, of French background, was orphaned as a child shortly after she arrived in the West. The paths of the two young people, William and Sarah, crossed in Redbluff, California, and they married in 1871.

William inherited as part of his father's estate a band of sheep and a piece of land near Redbluff. One spring in search of pastures he took his small family and his sheep into the Sierra Nevada Mountains. Although he intended to return in the autumn, he wandered on to the plains and deserts of Nevada and established a camp near Winnemucca. Here Henry Fountain Ashurst was born on September 13, 1874. Soon the family moved southward by covered wagon to cross the Colorado River at Stone's Ferry, and down to the Big Sandy River in northwestern Arizona. In 1875–76 the little group settled a homestead nine miles south of what is now the town of Williams, Arizona. The drought of 1877, however, proved a deadly blow to the Ashurst stock business, and again the family moved, this time to a ranch in the high pine region near Mormon Lake, south and east of the present town of Flagstaff. Here Henry grew to young manhood in a rugged but magnificent land. Within a radius of one hundred miles were the scenic wonders of the Southwest — the Painted Desert, the Petrified Forest, and the Grand Canyon.

That the elder Ashurst gained respect and standing in the neighborhood is shown by the fact that in 1887 he served in the Fourteenth Territorial Legislature as a representative from Yavapai County. Feeding and educating a large family, however, placed a severe strain on parents who struggled to gain a living in harsh country under difficult conditions. Therefore, when the ranch proved unprofitable, Ashurst turned to mining a claim in the Grand Canyon. There he died alone in an accident in 1901. Young Henry was the second in a family of ten children; and it was the problem of educating children plus the hardships of winter on the ranch, that brought the Ashurst family to Flagstaff. Up to this time the youngsters had been given the rudiments of an education by ranch hands who possessed various backgrounds.

Besides going to school, young Ashurst held a number of jobs. From the age of twelve, he worked on the home ranch and hired out as a range rider. Later, when he was only nineteen, Sheriff Donahue appointed him turnkey in the county jail at Flagstaff at the generous wage of sixty dollars a month. Ashurst immediately took charge of about thirty-five prisoners. Soon he was employed in a lumber yard in Flagstaff and in the evenings began to study law. His first opportunity to travel was to California in the winter and spring of 1895. In San Francisco the law courts fascinated him, and he spent much time observing their processes. Upon his return to Arizona, he worked again in the lumber yard in Flagstaff, saved his money, and in the autumn returned to California to study stenography at Stockton Business College and to try his hand at newspaper reporting in his spare time. He went back to Arizona to be a stenographer in Salzman's Store in Williams, and shortly was appointed Justice of the Peace. In November 1896, at the age of twenty-two, came election to the Territorial House of Representatives of the Arizona Legislature. This event marked the beginning of an active political career which was to be forty-four years long; marked also the conclusion of a youth full of educative experiences. One final year of law at the University of Michigan in 1903-04 was to round out Ashurst's formal education, but by that time he was already an established lawyer and politician in Arizona.

During the early years Ashurst became enamoured of the joys of public speaking — oratory as it was called in those days. He took every opportunity to practice and to improve his real talent in speaking by addressing audiences of all kinds, and thus gained considerable reputation and skill in this ability — so much so that he was later to be widely known as the Silver-Tongued Orator of Arizona. No doubt, this helped to provide a springboard for prominence, first in legal and then in political activities. The love of public speaking became a dominant and lifelong enthusiasm. He once estimated that he had delivered five thousand speeches.

In 1904, Ashurst married Elizabeth McEvoy Renoe, a widow, who had come to Flagstaff to take charge of the recently established United States Weather Station. She was to be his constant companion and co-worker in all his political endeavors until her death in 1939. Ashurst became a second father to John Renoe, her son, who was seven years old at the time of the marriage.

Sometime after he started his diary, Ashurst sensed that someday this record of events might be of interest and value to others. As time went on, he recorded his impressions with special care and used the same precise and colorful language that characterized his other writings and his speeches. In view of the fact that he wrote for a possible public audience, one may conclude that the diary was not intended to be secret or confidential. There is much here that is, nevertheless, personal and intimate, much that was recorded without consideration of how it would sound or what reaction it might cause many years later. Ashurst pulled no punches as he observed world-shaking events and famous personages. However, his is always a kindly, albeit discerning and penetrating eye. Here we find the sweep, the panorama, the ironies, and the disillusionments of recent history recorded. True, much of the same information may be found in the daily newspapers of the period. Ashurst, however, adds that vital personal touch as his mind ponders keenly the events of great significance in which he participated. Few professional historians or journalists can bring alive these same happenings more vividly.

Ashurst placed the diary in my hands to arrange for publication several years ago, shortly after I completed my doctoral dissertation, *The Speaking of Henry Fountain Ashurst,* a study which gratified him and which was completed partly through his cooperation and willingness to answer many questions. I met and conferred with the former senator numerous times both in Washington and in Arizona. His charm of manner, his distinguished figure, and the brilliance of his repartee dominated every social gathering. Above all, his keenness of intellect and his never-failing, encyclopedic memory for dates, personages and places made conversation with him a delight.

After Ashurst's defeat for the Arizona senatorial seat by Ernest W. McFarland in September, 1940, he delivered in the Senate words of farewell — a final gracious bow of defeat to the will of the people and at the same time an expression of his great confidence in the electorate:

" . . . It is the undoubted right of the people to change their servants, and to remove one and displace him with another at anytime they choose, for a good reason, for a bad reason, or for no reason at all . . . The American people have that transcendent attribute which I believe is superior to the other things I have mentioned — the determination to remain free."

The good sportsmanship, distinction, and gracefulness of this farewell speech called forth a tremendous ovation from the press.

Upon relinquishing the senatorial toga, Ashurst served for two years on the Board of Immigration Appeals in the Department of Justice and then retired to a private life of leisure. It was then that he wrote to an old friend and another former senator, Henry L. Myers of Billings, Montana: "I am existing in undistinguished humility and am too humble to be of interest even to a zoologist."

The facts seem to belie the statement, however, for Ashurst has continued to gain interest as a public figure by delivering numerous speeches notable for their well-turned phrases, their grandeur of expression and their clarity of diction; by appearing delightfully on radio and television; and finally by accepting, at the age of eighty-seven, the role of a senator in a Hollywood film based on the political novel, *Advise and Consent*.

Ashurst once said that if there were a career he could have enjoyed more than that of senator, it might have been that of actor. As Shakespeare said: "All the world's a stage, and all the men and women merely players, they have their exits and entrances; and one man in his time plays many parts . . ." Ashurst played many roles, but one role he loved, honored, and acted consummately — that of a senator of the United States.

Sincere appreciation is expressed to Henry Fountain Ashurst for the privilege of preparing the diary for publication, to Jack L. Cross, Editor of the University of Arizona Press, for suggesting the title, arranging the format, and the organization pattern; to Elizabeth H. Shaw of the Press, for assistance in editing; to Gustav L. Seligmann, Jr., for research connected with the list of personages in the appendix; to Donald M. Powell, for indexing; and to The University of Arizona Alumni Association for the encouragement provided by a faculty research grant.

George F. Sparks,
Tucson, Arizona

Foreword to the Diary

In writing a foreword many years after the last entry was made in this diary, pride and modesty seem to disrelish the all-too-frequent appearance of the unwelcome personal pronoun "I," but as this is a book by myself about myself, it is not clear how first person singular could have been well avoided.

Moreover, the reader does not seek for literary excellence in a diary but does expect to find spontaneous unlabored compositions reflecting the diarist's impressions contemporaneous with the happening of the event.

Diary entries were written whilst I was in the court room, in the Senate chamber, on political campaigns, on lecture tours, on steamships, on railroad trains, in foreign lands, and some during stormy parliamentary contests. I admit that in committing these entries to print I am almost tempted to suppress a vagrant entry here or there and that I have ached from impulse to amplify some of them but have decided that the diary must go forth "as is," and thus reflect my impression and opinion at the time I wrote the entries. Nothing has been altered. Nothing has been omitted except repetitious entries and some entries of no historical value and of no interest to anyone.

In looking over these pages, it is observed that numerous events with which I was connected are not recorded and that mention has not been made of many persons who played important parts during the space of time between the beginning and the conclusion of this diary.

Many of the unrecorded events and many of the unmentioned persons were important, but they did not happen to be in my attention when I wrote.

The gaps between the various dates are not excisions; there were many days when I made no entry.

Henry Fountain Ashurst
Washington, D.C.

1

New State, New Senators

> Political science does not make men,
> but takes them from Nature and uses them.
>
> Aristotle

I   June, 1910–December, 1912

The entry of a state into the federal union
is a majestic event.

Prescott, Arizona, June 17, 1910. Received telegrams advising that the House bill for the admission of the Territories of Arizona and New Mexico into the Union as separate states passed the Senate yesterday. The Senate proposal requires the direct approval of the constitution of the new states by both the Congress and the President before they shall be admitted into the Union. Senator Beveridge, chairman of the Senate Committee on Territories, said yesterday: "The nation is as vitally interested in the form of government of the states as are the states themselves. It is not only a measure of justice, but of safety. It will prevent unsound provisions in the Constitution."

Prescott, June 19, 1910. The House of Representatives yesterday concurred in the Senate amendments to the statehood bill and only President Taft's signature is now needed to make the bill a law. Dispatches, from Hon. Ralph H. Cameron, Arizona's delegate to Congress, arrived, announcing the progress of the bill and an impromptu celebration was held in the Plaza last evening.

The Democrats here criticized that provision of the statehood bill, which requires that the Constitution to be framed must be affirmatively approved by the President *and by the Congress.* The Democrats argue that if the people of Arizona are capable of setting up a state government they are also capable of framing their own organic law for the new state without dictation or censorship from Washington. Nevertheless, many telegrams of congratulations were sent to Delegate Cameron and to Senator Beveridge.

June 21, 1910. Dispatches say that President Taft signed the statehood bill yesterday. Prescott, not satisfied with her tame celebration Saturday evening, attempted a more enthusiastic

jollification and there was much band-music and oratory. It is
remembered that in 1891 a Constitutional Convention was held
in Arizona whereat a constitution was framed which was ratified
by the voters, but Arizona was denied admission into the federal
Union because the proposed constitution provided that *silver*
as well as gold should be legal tender for the payment of any
and all debts, public and private. Telegrams were received today
by Territorial officials from Senator Beveridge, in part as follows:

> Arizona will be among the first on the roll call of the
> states and I know that Arizona people will see to it that she
> will be among the first to stand for noble ideals.

> I like good and clean fighters and I have never known
> cleaner or better fighters than you have proved yourselves
> to be.

Douglas, June 26, 1910. Last evening I spoke at a banquet
under the auspices of the Douglas Democratic Club. All the
speakers urged that the coming Constitutional Convention frame
such modern constitution as will suit Arizona and submit same
for approval or rejection, as the President and the Congress may
choose. There was no sentiment at this meeting toward framing
a constitution with a view of obtaining admission without regard
to what should or should not be Arizona's fundamental law.
Amongst the speakers at the banquet was Hon. Robert F. Broussard, representative in Congress from Louisiana.

On yesterday Marcus A. Smith, formerly Arizona's delegate
to Congress, spoke at Tucson and warned that the provision in
the statehood bill requiring the approval of the constitutions of
Arizona and of New Mexico by the Congress and also by the
President is taken seriously at Washington and that should an
objectionable constitution be framed by Arizona, neither the
Congress nor the President would hesitate to reject the document. The sentiment of this Territory is forming into two camps:
namely, one which urges that our constitution be framed so as
to insure its approval at Washington, whilst the other camp
urges that the constitution should be an expression of the people
upon their proposed organic law without regard to whether it
shall be adopted or rejected by the federal authorities.

August 2, 1910. Copy of manifesto I wrote is published today.
It reads in part as follows:

The Constitutional Convention should not attempt to make a constitution such as was desired by the illustrious Titbat Tettlemouse, who wanted "a law giving everybody everything." In framing this constitution care should be taken to avoid placing legislation in the constitution. Let us manfully make a constitution for Arizona and her people, manfully submit it to Congress and the President, and if it be not approved we shall at least maintain our self-respect and retain that noble peace of mind which always comes as the rich reward of courageous rectitude.

Los Angeles, August 19, 1910. Last evening I spoke at banquet of the Hassayampa Club at the Hollenbeck Hotel here. The toastmaster, Judge Nave of Arizona, asserted that four Democratic candidates for the United States Senate (in event of statehood) were present at the speakers' table, viz., Mr. Mark Smith, Mr. Reese M. Ling, Colonel H. L. Pickett and myself.

September 7, 1910. I spoke at Tucson last night in support of Democratic nominees for delegates to Constitutional Convention, who are urging that a constitution be framed without regard to the wishes of the Congress or the President. Some authorities at Washington advise that if the Constitution shall contain the initiative, referendum, recall, the guarantee of bank deposits, etc., the Constitution will be vetoed by the President and disapproved by the Congress.

September 13, 1910. The elections yesterday resulted in a Democratic majority in the coming Arizona Constitutional Convention. The state of Maine yesterday elected Democratic state officials and also a Democratic legislature which will elect a Democratic United States senator. The insurgent revolt in the National Republican party has swollen to such extent that the Republicans may not carry the Congressional elections next November.

October 11, 1910. Constitutional Convention assembled yesterday at Phoenix and chose Mr. George W. P. Hunt to be president of the Convention.

November 9, 1910. Results of elections held throughout the nation yesterday indicate that the National House of Representatives has been carried by the Democrats, and that New York, New Jersey, Massachusetts, Connecticut, and Ohio have elected

Democratic governors. It is obvious that the Republican party (supreme in the federal government since March 4, 1897) is now torn with dissension, its leaders are denouncing one another, and its prospects are gloomy.

December 10, 1910. The Constitutional Convention adopted a Constitution and adjourned yesterday. The entry of a state into the federal union is a majestic event. Under our federal system it is a symmetrical creation of political authority. Although attempts are frequently made to weaken or absorb the states by the federal government, statehood is the most beneficent plan yet devised for America.

Prescott, January 1, 1911. My wife, my stepson, John Russell Renoe, and I came here from Flagstaff two years ago today and are now living at 114 North Alarcon Street in a commodious frame house (rent twenty-five dollars per month) in which, tradition says, General John C. Frémont and his family lived for a time whilst he was Governor of the Territory of Arizona and Prescott was the capital.

In the year 1878 and for many years thereafter, my parents were ranchers about one hundred miles north of Prescott in the Mogollon Mountains. In the autumn of the year 1878 they came here in a wagon to get supplies, and six days were required to reach here from their ranch. They put up at the Dan Hatz Hotel and found the citizens here eager and astir over the news that the new Governor of the Territory, General John C. Frémont would soon arrive. I remember that the General, grizzled and dusty, came into Prescott in a horse-drawn or mule-drawn vehicle at the head of a cavalcade; but as he arrived on a Sunday (no festivities on a Sunday) the reception was held a few days later. The General did not come to this house but was lodged in the home of Attorney Tom Fitch, "the Silver-Tongued Orator of the Pacific Coast." In his speech at the reception Mr. Fitch aroused applause by declaring that he was present not so much to "see the General" but to honor "Jessie," the Governor's queenly wife who was the daughter of the famous Missouri Senator, Thomas Hart Benton.

January 14, 1911. The all-absorbing topic of conversation is: Shall the proposed Arizona Constitution be ratified? What with my law practice, with attending meetings of the "Statehood League," preparing speeches, studying *The Federalist* and *Elliott's Debates* and the decisions of the Supreme Court of the United States, as well as studying the history of the republics of antiquity, to learn what is a "republican" form of government, I am busy indeed.

Kingman, April 3, 1911. Waiting anxiously but with outward composure two contingencies; viz., 1. What action will President Taft and Congress take upon the Arizona Constitution? 2. What will be the verdict of the jury in the Dempsey Powell homicide case? I am leading counsel defending Mr. Powell.

Kingman, April 5, 1911. Defended Mr. Dempsey Powell, charged with murder. Attorneys Elias S. Clark and Colonel John F. Wilson, both of Prescott, are associate counsel for defense.

April 6, 1911. Verdict of jury in Powell case: "Not Guilty." The defendant, Mr. Powell, and his father, mother, sisters, brother, attorneys and witnesses, making in all about fifty persons, started for Prescott on the noon train from Kingman, Mohave County, whither we went from Prescott, Yavapai County, on a *change* of *venue*. This Powell case was tried before Judge Edward M. Doe, Associate Justice of the Arizona Supreme Court, sitting at *nisi prius*.

Judge Doe was born in Cabot, Vermont, in 1850 but the traditions of that thrifty commonwealth had little to do with forming his habits or directing his career. He is a bon vivant, bohemian, and gourmet. Fishing and hunting attract him, and all things gustatorial engage his attention. He has an intellectual and epicurean slant. At a tender age he had a cockney nurse and as a result his diction is like the speech of one who was reared within range of the sound of the bells of Bow Church, London, which renders him of doubtful value here as a political speaker. At the age of fifteen years he ran away from his father's house and spent a handful of months in Germany where he patronized the gaming-tables and gymnasiums.

He was graduated from the University of Iowa; practiced law in Iowa; thence he went to western Texas where amidst

gun-men and gamblers he maintained his self-respect. In one
encounter he fired in self-defense and killed a man. He came
to Flagstaff in 1887 and at once took a leading place at the
Arizona bar.

The sumptuousness and frequency of his formal dinners,
his wide searches for choice foods and rare vintages, the varying
styles of his apparel, his courtliness of manner, and the thralldom in which he was held by the gambling habit aroused much
interest in that (then) new community, but woe to the man
whose temerity led him to make unseemly comment upon Mr.
Doe's habits for he carried a sword-cane and was a not contemptible fencer. He is subtle and ingenious, is six feet tall and
is erect. When he came to Flagstaff in 1887 he had a high top-
knot of reddish hair and a heavy carnelian moustache both now
turned to gray. In recent years his habit of keeping his mouth
filled with huge quids of masticated cigars, interferes with his
articulation.

He was appointed District Attorney of Coconino County in
1891 and was elected to the same office in 1902 and 1908, but
resigned in 1909 to accept his present judicial office from President Taft. I defeated him for District Attorney of Coconino
County in 1904 and 1906. As a specimen of his strange habits,
I saw him in attendance in the Territorial Supreme Court at
Phoenix in 1893 wearing a cutaway coat and a crimson Tam
o'Shanter.

Prescott, April 7, 1911. Today Attorney John F. Wilson died
from heart failure. Thus passes one of my strong friends. He
was a colonel in the Confederate Army and was Delegate to
Congress from Arizona for four years. He was associated with
me in the defense for Mr. Powell at Kingman, and we all arrived
in Prescott at three o'clock this morning.

Prescott, September 1, 1911. The glory of the summer has
come and gone since I last wrote in this diary. My failure to
write herein is because I have been hard-pressed with my law
cases, especially the Marley cases, wherein Mr. J. W. Marley and
his four sons are charged with the larceny of cattle in Navajo
County. The cattlemen's associations are driving hard to con-

vict Marley of felony and also to recover heavy damages from the Marleys.

The late session of Congress adopted a resolution providing that if Arizona, at an election soon to be had, votes to omit from her constitution the recall of the judiciary, statehood will be granted. We are therefore now commencing a campaign to elect a representative in Congress, a governor and other state officers, and a legislature which will choose two United States senators.

This evening I spoke to a large audience assembled on the Plaza here, and formally opened my campaign for the U.S. Senate. The speech evinced little wisdom or profound thought but it was charged with repartee, color, and action and was filled with imagination, that is to say, those qualities that affect the senses and emotions; hence it was a successful "stump" speech.

Prescott, October 24, 1911. Primary Election Day. Messrs. Mark A. Smith, Eugene S. Ives, Reese M. Ling, Eugene B. O'Neill, H. L. Pickett, A. F. Parsons, and myself are all trying to secure nomination for U.S. senator on the Democratic ticket. I have made no entry herein since September 1, but since that date I have conducted a campaign of immense energy. I have travelled by automobile, by steamcars, buckboard, stagecoach and on horseback and have been a peripatetic bifurcated volcano in eruption. I quoted poetry, good and bad. I hurled tropes, metaphors and similes. I am now too fatigued to read the returns.

October 25, 1911. Doubt existed as to my nomination for U.S. Senator until I received telegrams advising that I had carried Gila County by large majority. Former Delegate Mark A. Smith of Tucson is also nominated for U.S. senator on the Democratic ticket whilst Mr. Hoval A. Smith, of Bisbee, and Delegate Ralph H. Cameron, of Flagstaff are each nominated on the Republican ticket for U.S. senator.

December 12, 1911. General Election Day. Mr. John Birdno, Chairman of Democratic Territorial Central Committee, announced all Democratic nominees elected.

December 13, 1911. The judicial recall was eliminated from the Constitution by the voters yesterday and we are advised that

President Taft will sign the Proclamation of Statehood. During the campaign it appeared, for a time, as if the "opponents of any kind of statehood" might coalesce with those who demand the "judicial recall or no statehood" and refuse to eliminate the judicial recall from the Constitution. Such refusal might have defeated statehood.

December 14, 1911. I have published a letter of thanks saying: "I am very humble and very grateful." This letter has softened many harsh critics.

December 28, 1911. Telegram from Mr. Ed Rainey of San Francisco inviting me to attend a banquet to be tendered to Mr. William R. Hearst in recognition of Mr. Hearst's services in promoting the Panama Pacific International Exposition to be held in San Francisco in 1915.

San Francisco, California, January 2, 1912. Mr. Ed Rainey, Mr. Calvin Brower of Panama Pacific International Exposition, Mr. Al (Blinker) Murphy, a reporter, and I motored several hours inspecting grounds of the Panama Pacific Exposition. To the theatre in evening with Mr. and Mrs. Rainey.

January 3, 1912. At invitation of Mr. A. Lenord Hall, whom I knew in New York City twelve years ago, I spoke to the Advertisers Association. At the banquet this evening at the Palace Hotel, Mr. Hearst's facility as a public speaker surprised me not a little.

January 5, 1912. Spent day with Mr. Charles Stanley, my comrade of cowboy days. Twenty years ago he worked for my father on the "Old Ashurst Ranch," and since he left our ranch he has been around the world with Buffalo Bill's Wild West Show.

Flagstaff, January 25, 1912. Attorney Thomas A. Flynn and I dined at the home of Mr. T. A. Riordan. In the evening a reception was tendered to me at the County Court House. Felicitous speeches were made by Judge Edward M. Doe, Attorney J. E. Jones and Attorney Flynn. In response, I tried to say something worthwhile, but the eagle would not fly. I was taken aback by glowing things the speakers said of me. I had spent màny years in Flagstaff and it seemed grotesque to hear myself eulogized before persons who had known me as a "gawky" kid.

February 8, 1912. Attorney Nicholas Vyne told me that some persons in Washington were assembling my recent campaign speeches, but for what purpose Mr. Vyne could not learn. I had hoped that charitable history would not perpetuate those speeches.

Prescott, February 14, 1912. Dispatches announced that President Taft had signed the Statehood Proclamation and Arizona is thus the forty-eighth state admitted into the federal Union. Governor and all other state officers inaugurated today. The Territory of Arizona was created in 1863; President Lincoln signed the bill. Arizona has made much progress within the past twenty years, that is, if comfortable living be "progress." In 1875, when my parents came to Arizona the transportation of persons and supplies in bull-teams and buckboards was precarious and difficult and the life of a white person was in peril from Indians. Comfort and ease have now supplanted the early hardships.

Arizona is now the leading copper producing state. Irrigation systems pour their waters upon the deserts; vegetables, cotton, citrus fruits, flowers, melons, potatoes and grains now grow abundantly; and a movement is gathering momentum, which, ere it runs its course, will criss-cross this state with roads and bridges.

To the "tenderfoot" the desert presents nothing attractive, but these deserts at times are gorgeous with the sensuous poppy and are regal with the scarlet glory of the blossoming cactus, whilst the pungency of the wild sage is pleasant to the nostrils. The prevailing hue of the desert is far from monotonous for there are the ever-changing color-tones of the sky and the rich purples in the distant sandhills.

The prophets of old drew inspiration from the deserts. But the desert is cruel; her heated sands and scorching winds, her flail of heat, her scarce and alkali waters and bitter dust, her mirages and similarity of topography confuse the wanderer and bring raging thirst, exhaustion, delirium and death when the canteen leaks, the trail is lost or the horse "plays out." A hole in the boot of the pedestrian on the desert, and within a few miles the sharp sand grains cut the foot so severely that further walking is well-nigh impossible.

Prescott, March 4, 1912. Represented Mr. J. P. Rhode in the Superior Court who had been sued by the estate of Lee Murphy for $5,000 damages for killing Mr. Murphy. It was a dreary case. I had not a "leg to stand on" in court. The jury promptly returned a verdict against Mr. Rhode for the full $5,000. Mr. Rhode was not present but was at the state prison at Florence.

March 20, 1912. The state legislature is now in session and will ballot on next Tuesday, the 26th instant, in separate houses for the U.S. Senators and will meet in joint session Wednesday, the 27th, to declare the result. On October 24th last at the primary and at the general election on December 12th last, Mr. Mark A. Smith and I were *endorsed* by our party and by the people for the U.S. Senate. The state legislature considers itself morally bound to elect Mr. Smith and myself, as we secured this endorsement.

Phoenix, March 21, 1912. My wife and I left Prescott yesterday. A number of friends came to the depot to say goodbye.

March 25, 1912. Arrived in Yuma and went down the Colorado River on the old steamboat "Searchlight." Examined levee and river-front work of Yuma Reclamation Project.

March 26, 1912. Hon. Marcus A. Smith and I were today elected to the U.S. Senate by unanimous vote in both houses of the legislature, the House voting separately, and we were invited to address the joint session tomorrow where the votes will be canvassed. In the nominating speeches presenting Mark Smith's name in the Senate and the House, high praise was given to Mark for his able services whilst he was Arizona Delegate. My name was presented in the Senate by Senator Homer R. Wood of Yavapai County, and Hon. H. H. Linney of Yavapai County presented my name in the House.

March 27, 1912. Mark Smith and I each addressed joint session of the Legislature after the canvass of the vote. My speech did not flow fluently, for when there comes to one, as there comes so seldom and to so few, the realization of a high ambition, it is difficult to make proper expression of one's feelings. The entire membership of the legislature escorted Mark Smith and myself and wife to the Southern Pacific depot where a large concourse of citizens gathered to bid us Godspeed as we left for Washington.

At the train I was called upon for a speech but I responded with the following lines only:

There are billows far out in the ocean
That will never break on the beach
There are waves of human emotion
That can find no expression in speech.

March 31, 1912. Arrived in Washington early this morning with my wife and Mr. M. I. McKelligan, of Bisbee, my secretary, Senator Smith and his secretary, Mr. Paul Kreuger, are quartered at the Hotel Ebbitt. My wife and I are quartered at the Raleigh. The question as to the length of terms we are to draw is of interest here and is a subject of discussion in Arizona. I am anxious to draw a "long term" for I have just had an exhaustive and, to my slender purse, an expensive campaign. Representative Hayden of Arizona called at our hotel and said my mileage will be $1,000.

April 1, 1912. To Senate Chamber with Representative Hayden. The Senate convened at 2:00 P.M. Senator Luke Lea of Tennessee announced death of his colleague, Robert L. (Bob) Taylor, whereupon the funeral committee was appointed and the Senate adjourned out of respect to his memory. Senator Martine of New Jersey introduced me to Senator Page of Vermont. I observed that Senator Page did not use blotting paper but employed the old-time sandpots to take up ink from the inky paper. I met also Senators Culberson of Texas, Cullom of Illinois, Root of New York and O'Gorman of New York. So the new senators from Arizona and New Mexico were not sworn in today. Is it chance or is it design that prevented our being sworn in on All Fools Day?

April 2, 1912. Senate convened at 2:00 P.M. Senator William Alden Smith of Michigan, chairman of the Committee on Territories, announced that the two territories, Arizona and New

Mexico, "have been admitted into the Federal Union in appropriate form and constitutionally;" he then presented the credentials of Mr. Albert Bacon Fall of New Mexico. Senator Warren of Wyoming presented the credentials of Mr. Thomas Benton Catron of New Mexico, Senator Shively of Indiana presented credentials of Mark A. Smith and Senator Charles A. Culberson of Texas presented mine. Escorted by these senators to the Vice-President's rostrum, we were sworn in by the Vice-President, James S. Sherman, whose urbanity has earned him the sobriquet of "Sunny Jim," whereupon in conformity to a resolution of the Senate dated May 14, 1789, the Senate proceeded to ascertain into what classes the four new senators should be assigned.

A separate box from which to draw numbered paper slips was provided for each state; Mr. Catron from the New Mexico box and I from the Arizona box respectively drew a slip bearing simply "Number One;" hence he and I were assigned to Class No. 1, and our terms will expire March 4, 1917; Mr. Fall from the New Mexico box drew a slip marked "Number 2," and his term will expire March 4, 1913; Mark Smith from the Arizona Box drew a slip marked "Number 3," and his term will expire March 4, 1915. Thus occurred a drawing which will not take place again unless and until some new state is admitted. Mark Smith was disappointed because he did not draw a "long term," and as we walked from the Vice-President's rostrum to our seats, he asked to see the card I drew, and said, "I wish I could have drawn it." My wife witnessed the drawing from the Senate gallery.

Mark Smith and I received from a local florist, upon order from Messrs. T. A. Riordan and M. J. Riordan of Flagstaff, many dozen American Beauty roses of the brave red with stems five feet long. After the drawing the following letter was brought to me in the Senate Chamber from Governor Wilson of New Jersey, who is seeking the Democratic nomination for President.

Trenton, New Jersey
April 1, 1912

My dear Senator:

I am expecting to be in Washington on Thursday next the fourth of April, and am wondering if I might have the pleasure of seeing you at my rooms in the New Willard Hotel sometime in the afternoon before one-half past three o'clock.

Unfortunately I am bound to take a train at 3:40 for Chicago, but although I am sharply limited in time, I do not want to forego the advantage of seeing you while I am in the city, if it is possible for me to do so.

Cordially and sincerely yours,
Woodrow Wilson

April 3, 1912. The following telegram was received from Mr. George Babbitt who had known me since my boyhood.

Flagstaff, Arizona
April third

Hon. Henry F. Ashurst
Washington, D.C.

Heartiest congratulations. You deserve the Senatorship as a fitting reward for your zealous efforts in behalf of Arizona. It was her good fortune that you drew the long term and we are all overjoyed. I trust you will live long in the service of the people and that your life will be full of happiness.

George Babbitt

Amidst these felicitations I am depressed, as I cannot (no man could) measure up to the dizzily high standard which my friends have set for me. To fall below their high estimate of myself is to disappoint them poignantly and to live up to such a high standard is not within the domain of speculation.

Here is one of the felicitous telegrams. It is signed by one hundred Democratic leaders, viz.,

Phoenix, Arizona
Third April

Hon. Henry F. Ashurst
U.S. Senator, Washington, D.C.

Warmest congratulations and highest esteem from all Arizona and your loyal constituents. Our love for you and faith in your ability, integrity and sincerity of purpose are a few of the attributes which will put Arizona on the highest pinnacle of progressiveness where God and our manhood has ordained and which we will attain under your able leadership.

April 5, 1912. Governor Woodrow Wilson was in Washington yesterday, but I did not see him as my engagements at the Senate were such that I could not leave the Senate Chamber. I sent Mr. McKelligon, my secretary, to assure him of my confidence.

April 15, 1912. The sub-committee (Senators Dillingham, Brandegee, and O'Gorman) of Senate Judiciary Committee today heard arguments for and against Hon. Richard E. Sloan, nominated by President Taft for district judge for Arizona. Judge Sloan was present with his counsel, Mr. Ernest Lewis of Phoenix, and Mr. William Seabury of New York, whilst Mr. Robert Morrison of Prescott argued against confirmation.

In the evening I addressed the Young Men's Democratic Club at New Willard Hotel and there learned of the sinking of the steamship "Titanic" with over a thousand lives lost.

April 17, 1912. Attended a meeting of the Senate Committee on Indian Affairs and observed how committee work is done.

April 20, 1912. With Mr. E. Dana Durand, Director of the Census, and Hon. George A. Loud, representative from Michigan, I acted as a judge in a debate between George Washington and Washington and Lee universities.

April 30, 1912. Wife and I dined with Interstate Commerce Commissioner and Mrs. Franklin K. Lane. I met Mr. Lane in Arizona in my campaign in October, 1911, when I boarded the passenger train at some flag station on the Southern Pacific and after brushing off the dust, I spent an hour with him in the dining car.

May 1, 1912. Senator Mark Smith has many friends. He is one of the best storytellers in Congress; and of all the senators, his company is the most sought. His repartee and learning make him welcome everywhere. He is of such vast experience in Congress that my unsophistications nettle him and tax his patience. He is opposing the confirmation of Judge Sloan.

May 17, 1912. This fight Mark Smith and I are making against the confirmation of Judge R. E. Sloan, nominated for the district bench, is difficult. I do not dislike Judge Sloan; I have tried many cases before him at *nisi prius*. In his later years on the bench, he became cross and sour. If Sloan comes to grief, it will be upon that age-old rock upon which many judges have been wrecked, viz., he rides, hunts, fishes, dines, and fraternizes with a *few* but not with *all* the lawyers at his bar. Those with whom he does *not* ride, hunt, fish, or dine are filled with jealousy and rage. He is assailed with a fury which he cannot understand.

May 26, 1912. To St. Patrick's Church with Senator O'Gorman; thence to luncheon with Monseigneur Russell and Uncle Joe Cannon, sometime Speaker of the House of Representatives.

May 27, 1912. Attended court as a witness against one H. A. W. Page indicted for libeling Representative H. D. Clayton of Alabama. Thence to War Department to urge General Leonard Wood, Chief of Staff, not to abandon Fort Whipple, an army post near Prescott.

June 1, 1912. Senator Clarke of Arkansas spoke in Executive Session against Judge Sloan's confirmation. Senators Root of New York and Clark of Wyoming spoke for Sloan. Senator Bailey of Texas defended Sloan when Sloan's debts were discussed. Bailey said that Sargeant S. Prentiss, the eloquent orator, left the state of Mississippi full of unpaid promissory notes. I agreed that Judge Sloan's debts are no evidence of his unfitness for the bench. He has lived modestly and his salary as Judge has been small.

June 8, 1912. Mr. Ober B. Frye, now of Terre Haute, Indiana, called. He was my chum at Flagstaff when we were boys.

June 10, 1912. Senate considered the conference report on the army appropriation bill whereupon Senator Lodge opposed the item in the form of "new matter" which the conferees on the disagreeing votes of the two houses have inserted into the conference report. Senator Lodge argued that the "new matter" if enacted into law would make it impossible for General Leonard Wood to be Chief of Staff again and impossible for either General Funston or General Goethals ever to be Chief of Staff. Senator Francis E. Warren, one of the conferees who had inserted the "new matter," defended the "new matter" upon the hypothesis that four years was long enough for one man to serve as Chief of Staff, and that after four years of such service the officer should resume service in the line.

Senator Root entered the debate and as he was sometime Secretary of War, his remarks were listened to with interest. After criticising the bad practice on the part of conferees of inserting "new matter" into conference reports, he concluded his remarks with the following: "You might as well adopt a provision saying that after the 5th day of March no man whose initials are L. W. should ever be detailed as Chief of Staff." Upon roll call the conference report was agreed to.

I voted against the adoption of the conference report as it was a discrimination against General Wood, whom I knew to have rendered conspicuous service in the "early days" of Arizona when the Apache Indian raids were frequent. Friction exists between Brigadier General John J. Pershing (son-in-law of Senator Warren) and Major General Wood; but whatever may have caused the "new matter" to be inserted into the conference report, it was obvious that Senator Warren was anxious to disqualify General Wood from further service as Chief of Staff.

June 17, 1912. President Taft vetoed army appropriation bill because of item therein which would have disqualified General Leonard Wood for reappointment to position of Chief of Staff.

June 20, 1912. For the past sixty days politicians have watched with varying emotions the contest between President Taft and Colonel Roosevelt for the Republican presidential nomination. If but one-half of what each says against the other be true, then neither of them should be President.

June 21, 1912. Mr. Reese Ling, the newly elected Democratic national committeeman, came in today from Arizona exuding amiability.

June 23, 1912. My wife and I visited at Arlington Cemetery the grave of Captain Buckey O'Neill, an Arizona hero, who fell in the Spanish American War in July, 1898.

June 25, 1912. Wife and I attended a session of the Democratic National Convention at Baltimore, where we saw W. J. Bryan defeated for temporary chairman. The Champ Clark men feared that if W. J. B. were made temporary chairman his oratory would stampede the convention and secure the nomination for himself. Bungling managers are in charge of Mr. Clark's campaign.

June 27, 1912. My wife, two secretaries, and I attended Democratic National Convention at Baltimore where everything was smooth as alabaster until W. J. B. presented his anti-Ryan-Belmont-Morgan resolution; then chaos reigned. His resolution threw the convention into bad humor and its tumult so impressed him that he withdrew some of the injudicious words of his resolution.

July 1, 1912. Governor Woodrow Wilson now in lead at Baltimore convention. The convention hall is filled with the shouting of the captains and with curses of W. J. B. for his "betrayal" of Champ Clark.

July 6, 1912. Sent the following letter to Governor Wilson:

Hon. Woodrow Wilson,
Governor of New Jersey,
Seagirt, New Jersey.

My dear Governor Wilson:

> *Flippity-flop, goes the brim of my hat,*
> *Hippity-hop the sole of my shoe;*
> *From shoe to hat, I am certain that*
> *Every western state will vote for you.*

Just a line to tell you that it is the unanimous consensus of opinion that you will not only be elected but will make a good and great president.

I am, dear sir, with kind personal regards and sentiments of esteem,

Cordially yours,
Henry F. Ashurst

July 12, 1912. Received the following from Governor Woodrow Wilson:

Trenton, N.J.
July 11, 1912.

To Honorable Henry F. Ashurst,
Washington, D.C.

My dear Senator:

That was a very delightful letter of yours of July sixth. The simile that was in it had also the energy of conviction and I enjoyed it particularly. Thank you very much.

Cordially yours,
Woodrow Wilson.

July 13, 1912. Senator Lorimer of Illinois whose election, it is alleged, is tainted with fraud, concluded his three-day speech in his own defense. He spoke bravely. Large numbers in the galleries in tears when he concluded. On the vote he was excluded by almost two to one.

July 20, 1912. Senate considered Sundry Civil Appropriation Bill. When the item making appropriations for National Parks was reached, various Senators described the scenic grandeur of their respective states; whereupon I turned loose some superlatives as to the scenic grandeur of Arizona.

August 2, 1912. Senate sat at a court of impeachment. The managers from the House of Representatives were announced and were conducted to the seats arranged for them in front of the secretary's desk. The respondent, Judge Archbald, Associate Judge, U.S. Commerce Court, accompanied by his counsel, entered the chamber and took the seats provided for them; whereupon a number of senators, who had not been sworn in as judges in the impeachment trial, took the requisite oath.

After debate between the House managers and the counsel for the respondent, Senator Clark of Wyoming, the chairman of the Senate Committee on the Judiciary, announced that he anticipated that a decision as to a date upon which the trial of the respondent should begin, would lead to much debate; whereupon the galleries were cleared, the Senate doors were closed, and the question was up as to what date should be set for commencing the trial. Some senators insisted that the trial should proceed immediately, others urged that the trial should not be commenced until the summer was over. After two hours of wrangling, Senator Root, of large capacity for solving practical difficulties, suggested an expedient so simple that every senator wondered why he himself had not hit upon that particular plan for setting the day of trial.

Senator Root moved that the secretary call the roll of the senators and that as each senator's name was called, instead of voting "Aye" or "No," the senator should respond by naming a date on which he desired the trial to commence. Upon roll call over a score of dates were voted for; but the third day of December, 1912, received the highest number of votes, whereupon the Senate went into open session and the eligible order was entered directing that the trial of the respondent should begin on December 3 next.

August 7, 1912. The Senate considered the House bill providing for the opening, protection, and operation of the Panama Canal and the sanitation and government of the Canal Zone, which bill provides amongst other things, that "no tolls shall be levied upon vessels engaged exclusively in the coast-wise trade of the United States."

The motion of Senator Burton of Ohio, to strike this free transit provision from the bill, brought an animated debate which lasted until midnight, but before adjournment Senator

Burton's motion was decided in the negative — yeas eleven, nays forty-four. Every Democratic senator present voted to reject the Burton amendment, that is to say, voted for free transit through the Canal for American ships engaged exclusively in our coastwise trade.

Learning that a number of Democratic senators were on the point of voting for the Burton amendment, I took a copy of the National Democratic Platform adopted at Baltimore not two months ago, went to the respective senators and pointed out to them the following pledges in our platform: "We favor the exemption from toll of American ships engaged in coastwise trade passing through the Canal." And again: "Our pledges are made to be kept when in office as well as relied upon during the campaign." I asked them how the Democratic party in the coming campaign expected to earn the esteem of the people if we violate our pledges *during* the campaign?

August 8, 1912. Senate passed the bill providing for the opening, protection, and maintenance of the Panama Canal, with free transit through the canal for American ships engaged exclusively in our coast-wise trade.

Prescott, September 30, 1912. Spent this month preparing the Marley cases and other law cases which I had pending in the courts when last March I left Arizona to take up my duty in the Senate. When these pending cases are disposed of, I shall abandon law practice. The public is entitled to all my time.

October 19, 1912. Attorney Thomas A. Flynn of Flagstaff and I returned today to Prescott from Southern Arizona whither we were speaking for Wilson electors. If no candidate for President (Wilson, Roosevelt, or Taft) shall receive a majority in the Electoral College, the duty of choosing the President will be transferred to the House of Representatives where each state, under the Constitution, would cast one vote. It is possible that a deadlock may ensue in the House of Representatives; its membership is now made up of forty-eight state delegations, of which twenty-two state delegations would vote Democratic, twenty-two would vote Republican and four delegations are evenly divided.

October 29, 1912. Finished trial of the Marley cases here at Holbrook before Judge Sidney Sapp and a jury. Hon. Reese M.

Ling and Hon. E. S. Clark were leading counsel for the prosecution and were well prepared. All Marleys are convicted. Judge Sapp granted certificate of "probable cause" which will stay execution of the sentence of the Marleys and thus keep them from prison until Supreme Court decides their appeal.

Washington, December 2, 1912. Congress convenes and Senate adjourns out of respect to memory of Vice-President Sherman, Senator Rayner, Maryland, and Senator Heyburn, Idaho, who died during adjournment.

December 22, 1912. Yesterday I went to Princeton, New Jersey, and met the President-designate, Governor Woodrow Wilson. I called at his residence in the evening, was admitted by Mrs. Wilson who said the Governor had just arrived from Trenton, and within a minute, in he walked. We exchanged salutations. He laid down an armload of papers and removed his cap and greatcoat. Our conversation touched public questions but it was obvious to me that he had not forgotten his controversy with some of the trustees and faculty of Princeton University during his presidency thereof as he referred to the subject. This controversy began with and involved Wilson's plan of reconstructing the campus into quadrangles where students, men of all classes together in each building, could take meals and lodgings. This Wilson plan seemed to call for the elimination of clubs, an old institution at Princeton which bound the students in fellowship.

During our discussion of this episode of his Princeton career, he referred to the contest against his Princeton plans, waged by Dean Andrew West and Trustee Moses Taylor Pyne; I suggested that he offer them consulships in Madagascar or Haiti. It was in my mind seriously to say to him that he should be content to know that while the efforts of Dean West and Mr. Pyne brought outward elegance to the University, his own labors in the intellectual and moral realm gave to the University a new dignity, fresher tone, and a grander soul, but discretion warned me not to pursue the subject and I took my leave. Went to Waldorf-Astoria Hotel, New York, to a public dinner in honor of Governor-Elect William Sulzer and at midnight left for Washington with W. J. B.

A silence has fallen
upon the world...

January 2, 1913. Senator Joseph W. Bailey of Texas spoke three hours bidding farewell to the Senate. He denounced William R. Hearst and assailed the initiative, referendum, and recall. Senator Bailey was, in 1896, a delegate to the Democratic National Convention which nominated W. J. B. for the Presidency, and although four years previously he had tutored W. J. B. in Bimetallism, he reluctantly supported Bryan's nomination, alleging that Bryan by his advocacy of government-owned railroads and telegraphs, was not a Democrat.

Senator Bailey is tall, of Adonic beauty, of golden voice, and is a tremendously attractive orator. He came to the Senate in 1901 after ten years service in the House of Representatives. He is a colossal engine of majestic colloquial expression, has specialized on the federal Constitution, and seems to speak with effortless power. He resigns from the Senate as he is not *en rapport* with Wilson and Bryan. He may return to public life as he has charm as an orator and has learning and courage. He would not suffer if compared to Burke, Pitt, Fox, Webster, Clay, Benton, Ingersoll, Bryan, or Conkling. Many superb stallions are named "Joe Bailey" — an appraisal of the personal beauty, the Jovian presence, the lines of elegance of this man.

January 3, 1913. Senator Jeff Davis of Arkansas died last evening. Wife and I attended White House diplomatic reception given by President and Mrs. Taft. President Taft beamed cordially upon all and showed no disappointment that at recent elections he had carried but two states, viz., Utah and Vermont.

January 13, 1913. Senate voted on the various impeachment articles in re: Judge Robert W. Archbald. He is found guilty on several counts. Judge Archbald, Senator Lorimer, Eugene Schmitz, ex-mayor of San Francisco, and others demonstrate that now and then civic virtue demands a victim, seizes one, crushes and ruins him, and civic virtue then falls asleep.

January 16, 1913. Opulent Colonel E. A. Ayer, of Chicago, called. In 1882 Mr. Ayer built a sawmill at Flagstaff, Arizona. As a private soldier he marched through Arizona fifty years ago.

January 18, 1913. Whilst at the Capitol I was seized with agonizing pain in my stomach, tried to walk to my apartments at the Farragut, but was unable to do so.

January 27, 1913. Returned today from memorial services held at Ann Arbor, Michigan, in honor of memory of Representative Wedemeyer who jumped from a steamer on January 2, last, a few miles out of the harbor of Colon. Met my brother, Charles, at Ann Arbor. He is a lawyer in Detroit.

February 6, 1913. Received frantic telegrams from Prescott advising that troops at Whipple Barracks, Prescott, were about to be sent away, whereupon I protested to Secretary of War Stimson against the transfer.

February 12, 1913. The Senators marched to the House of Representatives and there, agreeably to the Constitution, the electoral votes were counted, the result ascertained and announced in legal but slouch form. My friend, Attorney E. E. Ellinwood of Bisbee, is here and we discussed the mutations of politics. He and I were associated years ago in many law cases. He was U.S. District Attorney for Arizona under the second Cleveland administration and proved to be a lawyer of large ability.

February 23, 1913. Lunched with Senator Newlands of Nevada at his home at Woodley Lane. In his youth Senator Newlands had a mass of independent red hair which the burdens of office have thinned away. He dresses à la Ward McAllister.

March 4, 1913. Inauguration. In the Senate, the hum of the galleries, the flashings of the costumes of the diplomatic folk, the eagerness of those so soon to come into power and the reticence of those soon to surrender position — all had a place in the picture. The various distinguished visitors were announced by the Sergeant-at-Arms and finally the outgoing and incoming Presidents entered amidst hush and then much applause. Vice-President Marshall and the new senators were inducted into office.

After the ceremonies in the Senate Chamber, the senators marched to the exercises outside. The Chief Justice of the United States, White, administered the oath to Woodrow Wilson, and a mighty shout from the assembled thousand went up. Not since the inauguration of Andrew Jackson in 1829 has there been such fervor amongst the Democrats. Many policemen and plain-clothes officials were required to keep the crowd from smothering the new President. Mrs. Ashurst viewed the parade from a window on Pennsylvania Avenue, but I employed the time in my office going through my mail and writing in this journal.

William H. Taft smilingly saw his successful opponent inducted into office amidst the shouting multitude, which four years before braved a violent snowstorm to shout for Taft. The ambition of T. R. destroyed Taft's chances for re-election. T. R.'s administration was never dull, while Taft's furnished no sensations despite the many problems with which Taft grappled. Economic changes came during Taft's administration, but he disdained the politician's art of capitalizing them. Of all political defects that hamper a President, to be prosaic is the most deadly. Witness old John Adams, John Quincy Adams, Tyler, Fillmore, Buchanan, Hayes, and Benjamin Harrison. A feature of our American system is a jealousy toward eminence or personal ascendence. In our politics and office-holding the leader has his day and then makes way for another leader, who in his turn is rejected. A republic "ping pongs" great offices from one man to another with nonchalant indifference to merit, talent, or experience.

In a republic the people are the source of authority, hence Wilson will have his day and make way for another, and so on ad infinitum. Individuals are grateful, the public never. Gratitude is a jewel, a noble attribute that becomes a prince, but a republic must not toy with so occult a gem.

March 5, 1913. Democratic senators in conference canvassing the candidates for sergeant-at-arms and secretary of the

Senate. Senator Mark Smith and I called upon Mr. McReynolds, the new Attorney-General.

March 8, 1913. Senator Mark Smith and I called upon the new Secretary of State, William Jennings Bryan, and there found place-seekers by the score, clamoring for admission.

Senator John Worth Kern of Indiana chosen Democratic floor-leader. He is experienced in politics and is stocked with "apt" stories. His dolorous appearance, his whiskers, and his gold-rimmed spectacles contribute to a saturnine make-up, yet wit, wisdom, and satire gush from him.

April 7, 1913. The Sixty-third Congress convened in special session. I believed when elected to the Senate, I would have time and opportunity to study, to explore histories and philosophies for truths that make nations great and peoples free, but alas! all my time since the elections has been consumed by applicants for political jobs.

During last January, February, and March, delegation after delegation of place-hunters came all the long way from Arizona looking for some "appointment." My weakness is that I have not cultivated the habit of saying *NO*.

When the second session of the Sixty-third Congress adjourned, President Taft gave a recess appointment to Judge Richard E. Sloan, as District Judge for Arizona, and he served until March 4, 1913, but the Democratic senators filibustered in Executive Session during December 1912 and January and February 1913, and thus defeated the confirmation of Judge Sloan.

The stock-growers are urging a tariff on imported meats, hides, wool, pelts, cattle, and sheep. I stated my views as to our party's promises in the 1912 campaign, whereupon, Senator Stone of Missouri, as is his custom, scolded me severely for "speaking prematurely."

April 8, 1913. President Wilson delivered his message to Congress, in person. The Senate marched to the House en body, and the senators were charmed with presidential rhetoric. This is the first time since November 22, 1800, that a President has personally delivered his message to Congress. The method is agreeable to the Constitution. Senator Lodge, Massachusetts, and

Senator Williams, Mississippi, criticised the President for "a speech from throne;" Senator Shafroth, Colorado, defended.

April 17, 1913. James Hamilton Lewis, the new senator from Illinois, presented himself today. He has radiant yellow whiskers, a cunning wig, and gorgeous diction.

April 19, 1913. Attended meeting of Committee on Woman Suffrage and heard Mrs. A. J. George of Brookline, Massachusetts, speak in opposition to Woman Suffrage. She is the most nearly perfect female orator I have heard for years.

April 21, 1913. Introduced bill to curb gambling on the stock market and it is about as popular as an alarm clock in a boys' dormitory.

April 25, 1913. Received the following letter from the President:

April 24, 1913
Washington, D.C.

My dear Senator:

My attention is so engrossed from day to day and I am so hurried from one thing to another that I actually do not know oftentimes what is going on outside of my own office. I have just learned, for example, through the current number of *Collier's Weekly* of the stand you took towards those of your constituents who urged you to oppose the Democratic policy with regard to the tariff. May I not express my warm admiration of the course you have taken? It is not only in the highest degree manly, but is most wise and public spirited.

Cordially and sincerely yours,
Woodrow Wilson.

May 16, 1913. Senate received the tariff bill from the House and some Republican senators made long speeches against it. The Democrats have a task of enormous dimensions before them. They are trying to reduce the cost of living to the city dwellers and not lower the farmers' price for his produce. Even in ancient times man tried to reduce the cost of living by laws. The law may indeed prevent combinations, forestalling, regrating, etc., but the remedies that I perceive are to increase production of the food supplies, and to aid the farmer in practical ways: good roads, rural credits, and cooperative marketing. To live within one's income, one must eliminate joy-rides and gambling.

June 13, 1913. On behalf of the Committee on Woman Suffrage, and at request of Senator Thomas of Colorado, the chairman, I reported favorably the joint resolution proposing to amend the Constitution, so that no person shall be denied the right to vote by reason of sex.

July 18, 1913. Senator Bristow of Kansas became enraged at me in the Senate and charged that I have used my telegraph frank for my "personal-political business." I am to blame for angering him as I read to the Senate a statement reflecting on him, moreover, I was so disturbed over the question of who shall be appointed as District Judge in Arizona that I hesitated to grasp the nettle boldly and telegraphed a vast deal to ascertain views of various persons.

July 23, 1913. Addressed the Senate and made statement as to all telegrams sent by me; and I leave the matter with the Committee on Audit and Control to determine whether or not the messages are "public business." Senator Bristow is a member of committee which is to make the decision.

August 13, 1913. Attorney Phil B. Thornton of Fresno, California, an old Williams, Arizona chum of mine is here.

October 25, 1913. Senators Bacon, O'Gorman, Brady, Thomas, Martine, and I attend as a committee to represent the Senate at the ceremonies upon the restoration of Independence Hall, Philadelphia. The old hall is now restored to the appearance it assumed when Congress met there in 1776. Amongst other speakers at the exercises were President Wilson and Speaker Clark.

November 23, 1913. He who approaches needed reforms calmly, will be deemed as lacking in courage and will be met with ridicule. That explains why reformers studiously cultivate bad tempers.

November 28, 1913. Yesterday, my wife and I attended the Pan-American Thanksgiving celebration at St. Patrick's Cathedral. President Wilson, Secretary Bryan, and other Cabinet officers were present. Diplomats from the Latin-American states and Chief Justice White, Justice McKenna, many senators and representatives were present. The church was decorated with American flags. His Eminence, Cardinal Gibbons, was present, and the Rt. Rev. Charles W. Currier, Bishop of Matanzas, Cuba, preached the sermon in which he deplored war as the natural enemy of good order. He pointed out in eloquent phrase that war subverts the moral order by opening wide the door to all manner of vices.

December 2, 1913. Tariff and Federal Reserve Bank bills have consumed most of our attention. To the radical, "tariff tinkering" is but making mud-pies, whilst our reserve bank bill enrages him. Radicals who are quick to find fault seldom suggest a remedy for the ills of the body politic. Many senators believe that high tariffs are the only reform this country requires. Not a few senators display vanity. Nearly all able men are vain or are impatient, rather, toward mediocrity. Vanity and jealousy are allied to self-defense.

Mankind is a braggart and so ingrained in man's nature is love of praise and adulation, that he believes God requires constant praise.

December 31, 1913. We allow days to slip into months and months to slide into eternity and never realize that we are well and happy. It is only when we are ill or unhappy that we realize that we are in the world.

January 1, 1914. For the first time in some years, there is no New Year's reception at the White House. The President and his family have gone to Pass Christian, Mississippi. Wilson's omission of the Inaugural Ball was forgiven, but his failure to greet official and social Washington on New Year's Day is hotly resented.

January 8, 1914. Mrs. Ashurst and I returned from New York where we visited Mr. Hearst and his family and had dinner and theatre with them and luncheon with Mr. and Mrs. Lewis Nixon.

January 15, 1914. If some of the members of Congress do not possess the courage of their own convictions, they at least have the courage of W. W.'s convictions and the unhappy part is, if Wilson should lose his strength with the people, members of Congress would at once become "independent."

January 21, 1914. Spoke in Senate in support of the Woman Suffrage amendment to the federal Constitution.

January 27, 1914. The Senate today confirmed the nomination of Mr. Thomas A. Flynn of Flagstaff, to be U.S. District Attorney for Arizona. He is fearless, incorruptible, and able. He never solicited this office. Why do not other office-seekers make themselves so useful that they may not be overlooked? It is a good and winning way.

February 4, 1914. Senate considered the right of Mr. Frank P. Glass of Alabama to a seat in the body, on appointment from the Governor. Mark Smith and I voted to seat him but partisanship denied him a seat. When I reflect that I have criticized some of the judges for yielding to prejudices and whims that constantly beset an official, I am ashamed, for when the courts are placed into juxtaposition with a partisan Senate, we perceive how courageous many judges are.

February 14, 1914. Senate in executive session considered the nomination of one Swindlehurst for postmaster in a Montana city, and I presided. While Senator Myers of Montana was speaking for Swindlehurst, Assistant Sergeant-at-Arms O'Toole informed me that Senator Bacon had just died.

February 17, 1914. Funeral services of Senator Bacon held in Senate Chamber. He presided with ability over the Archbald impeachment proceedings. Senator Clarke of Arkansas defeated Senator Bacon in March 1913 for President Pro Tem; this defeat broke Bacon's heart and he never recovered from the blow.

February 18, 1914. Visited Senator Stone of Missouri at his apartments at Continental Hotel where he is ill. He told me that I am to succeed him as chairman of the Senate Committee on Indian Affairs, and that he will succeed Senator Bacon as chairman of Foreign Relations. As chairman of Indian Affairs, I shall sit upon a volcano, and an eruption may come at any moment.

March 4, 1914. My wife and I and about thirty other senators and their ladies dined with Secretary of State and Mrs. Bryan, who have rented the old John A. Logan mansion. No wine was served, but W. J. B. was forgiven for lack of alcoholic beverage, as he gave each gentleman a cigar, one in a box marked "the pipe of peace." This is the first official dinner I ever attended where no wine was served.

March 5, 1914. President Wilson addressed the two houses of Congress in joint session and urged that the Act of 1912, Freedom from Tolls for American Coastwise Ships Passing Through the Panama Canal, be repealed.

In 1912, every Democrat in the Senate (who voted on the Panama Canal bill) voted for free transit and this free transit was pledged in the Democratic (Baltimore) National Platform. Governor Wilson, as a candidate for President on that platform spoke, at least once, in favor of "free transit." In 1912 we denounced the Republicans for their failure to keep platform pledges. Yet here is President Wilson urging that *we* now break *our* pledge. He declares apropos another question that nothing he says or does *today* shall bind him *tomorrow.* W. J. Bryan in 1909 said of men who broke their political promises: "They are embezzlers of political power, hence worse than embezzlers of money."

March 18, 1914. Spoke at the Friendly Sons of St. Patrick banquet at Philadelphia, last evening.

I have spoken for Woman Suffrage for years and voted for it while in the Arizona Legislature, but it is difficult to escape the conclusion that the matter of determining qualifications of voters in each state should remain as the function of and right of each state to determine for itself.

March 19, 1914. Senate voted on the Woman Suffrage Constitutional amendment: Ayes thirty-five, nays thirty-four, not the required two-thirds.

March 31, 1914. Went to the House to hear Speaker Champ Clark's speech opposing repeal of free transit for American ships through the Panama Canal. Mr. Clark's speech was the utterance of a brave, sincere man, but it did not aid the cause of free transit. The Republicans are in a state of felicity; they hope the bitterness amongst the Democrats upon this Canal tolls question will be the entering wedge that will split the Democratic party.

The President has been accused of "backing and filling" and of violating campaign pledges but the general public is not and cannot be in possession of all the facts. Washington and Lincoln were accused of "backing and filling." The condition of our foreign affairs is now fluid and unstable, hence the President must adopt fluidity and plasticity. He cannot be rigid whilst world problems are as protean and transient as the architecture of the clouds. He must be free to deal with the situation as it arises from day to day. Although I cannot vote for the Repealer, I shall not join the anvil-chorus now condemning Wilson for his "change of front" on the tolls question.

April 6, 1914. Senator McCumber delivered a "set" speech on the tolls. His opening sentence dogmatized as follows: "Will we hide behind the American flag while we burglarize the American treasury for the benefit of the coastwise shipping interests?"

April 20, 1914. General Victoriano Huerta claiming to be President of Mexico has refused to salute the American flag. Washington is tiptoe with excitement and Congress is ready to "stand by" President Wilson's Mexican "policy."

April 21, 1914. House sent to Senate the resolution justifying the President in using our army and navy in requiring General Huerta of Mexico to salute the American flag.

April 23, 1914. Speeches in the Senate were horripilating yesterday, and in the parlous situation we find ourselves, some senators and representatives are getting ready to "go to the front," provided they go as Brigadiers. Senator "Ham" Lewis of Illinois presided during the night session. He always acquits himself well.

May 16, 1914. President Wilson spoke at unveiling of Barry Monument and coined a phrase "hyphenated-American."

May 23, 1914. "If thou have a son, I would advise, lest his fair prospects you may perchance spoil, if you would have him in the state to rise, instead of Grotius, let him study Hoyle. If he shows a pretty turn of tricks indulge the bent, and a stacked pack may make a President."

The opponents of Wilson's administration are quoting the above and a hundred other couplets, anent Wilson's "tolls repealer."

May 25, 1914. Senate adjourns out of respect to memory of the late Senator Bradley of Kentucky.

May 31, 1914. Some days ago President W. W. and Speaker Clark were invited to deliver addresses at Arlington Cemetery on Memorial Day (May 30), and whilst W. W. pleaded press of business, Speaker Clark accepted the invitation. This led to criticism of W. W. and much praise of Clark. Last Thursday evening, W. W. reconsidered the matter and accepted the invitation; hence when W. W. arose to speak yesterday at Arlington he was formally cheered, but when Speaker Clark arose the assembled thousands cheered him lustily, and W. W.'s entourage was much vexed.

June 12, 1914. The Senate last night passed the tolls repeal. During the debate, it appeared that Senator Vardaman of Mississippi, and Senator West of Georgia would come to blows, and whilst they were angrily advancing toward each other, I stepped between them and held them apart.

Sir William Tyrrell, confidential secretary to Sir Edward Gray, Great Britain's Secretary of State for Foreign Affairs, recently spent some weeks in Washington and promised that the British government would aid President Wilson in eliminating General Huerta, de facto, President of Mexico, and would follow Wilson's lead in Mexican matters, if Wilson would secure repeal of freedom from tolls for American coastwise ships passing through the Panama Canal.

June 16, 1914. Many letters anent my vote against tolls repeal. During the 1912 campaign I made speeches and pointed to the Baltimore platform which promised free transit for American coastwise ships.

July 26, 1914. News comes that there may be war in Europe; Servia has refused to agree to Austrian demands. Europe sold heavily in the security markets yesterday; British and French bonds fell whilst Paris bid frantically for gold.

July 27, 1914. Russia issued warning against any invasion of Servia whilst Great Britain, France, and Italy made swift moves to avert war. Press says that the assassination of Archduke Francis Ferdinand, the heir apparent to the throne of Austria-Hungary, and his morganatic wife, at Sarajevo about a month ago, is the cause of the mobilization.

Twelve million dollars in gold started today from New York to London at rates which indicate the fear of the shippers that it may be seized on its way. Prices of securities crashed all over the world today and American wheat rose seventeen cents a bushel.

July 28, 1914. Austrian troops cross the Servian border despite threats from Russia. Sir Edward Grey in the House of Commons said that the failure to bring a peaceful settlement would "lead to the greatest catastrophe which could befall Europe, the consequence of which would be incalculable."

July 29, 1914. Austria declared war on Servia yesterday after rejecting efforts of mediation. The haste with which Austria rejected mediation indicates her *impatience* toward Great Britain, France, and Italy for their efforts toward mediation. The Vienna government evidentally does not desire a diplomatic settlement but may crush Servia, notwithstanding the growls of the Russia bear. Newspapers announce that the Triple Alliance and Triple Entente will fight.

July 30, 1914. Bourses and stock exchanges in Vienna, Budapest, Brussels, Antwerp, Berlin, Montreal, Quebec, and Rome are closed. The Paris bourses and stock exchanges are gorged with huge masses of Balkan State loans.

July 31, 1914. Information reached the Senate that all stock exchanges in England, France, and Germany have closed and that there are no more specie payments in those countries.

August 1, 1914. Official and diplomatic Washington excited over the news that on yesterday all London exchanges closed, being unable to withstand the torrent of liquidation. All American exchanges are closed.

How strange the mutations of mankind! The surface was serene one week ago, now Europe is on the "deadly circuit" and most of her states are "writhing in the toils of war." At this juncture I am reminded of the speech of ex-Governor Frank S. Black of New York in the Republican National Convention placing T. R. in nomination at Chicago in 1904.

One week ago no one could have dreamed what was coming, and even when the dispatches from Vienna were censored, we scarcely noticed it, but now a silence has fallen upon the world; ten millions of men are marching to battle. Embittered nations are maneuvering and are ready to strike.

August 2, 1914. The German Kaiser declared war on Russia last evening. President Wilson and Secretary of State Bryan conferred last night as to relief of Americans marooned in Europe. The general debacle has made it impossible for travelers to secure cash upon their letters of credit and foreign drafts. The wisest are caught off their guard. The only premonitory symptoms were those furnished by the stock exchanges. These stock exchanges with a precision that neither guesses nor thinks, but which merely perceives, told us startling things during the latter days of July, but no one could interpret their signals. I had believed that great wars were over, but it now looks as if the most colossal of all wars is about to begin. Secret-diplomacy, race-hatreds, land-hunger, ancient grudges, and Prussian Militarism are amongst the predisposing causes of this war, but these predisposing causes are cloaked under such euphonious phrases as "manifest destiny," "legitimate aspirations," and "historic missions."

My mother and my sister Maude have been visiting with us for the past few days but the general debacle in Europe has monopolized these pages.

August 5, 1914. The prices of copper and cotton fall to zero; we are without ships to carry our commerce to foreign markets. Fear paralyzes the Washington diplomats and politicians. Senator Nelson, the Viking from Minnesota, says that "while Europe is mobilizing its armies, we are mobilizing our credits."

August 6, 1914. German forces repulsed with loss meeting the Belgic forces at Leige. Aeroplanes and dirigibles play an important part in the battle.

Senator Kern announced to the Senate Mrs. Wilson's death, and the Senate adjourned out of respect to her memory.

August 10, 1914. Attended funeral services of the late Mrs. Wilson at the White House.

August 12, 1914. Mother and my sister Maude left this evening for California.

The Senate in executive session discussed the Bryan (Breathing Spell) Peace Treaties. If Austria had but allowed Servia a breathing spell? If Russia had not interfered with Austria?

On July 23 Austria served a forty-eight hour ultimatum upon Servia; on July 24 Austria refused to grant Servia further time, and on July 25 Servia yielded all points except the one which would have permitted Austria to interfere with the internal affairs of Servia. On July 26 Austria dismissed the Servian Minister, and the Austrian army moved. On July 27 Austria denounced the Servian reply and Great Britain urged mediation. Kaiser Wilhelm II arrived in Berlin and called a Council of Ministers.

On July 28 mediation failed, Austria moved toward Servia, whilst Russia protested against aggression toward Servia. On July 29 Germany warned Russia to make no attempt to save Servia, and Germany sent her forces to the Russian frontier. On July 31 Germany was placed under martial law and demanded to know England's attitude toward France. On August 1, Germany declared war on Russia, whilst on August 2, German forces invaded Luxemburg. Belgium appealed to England to save her from the German invasion.

August 13, 1914. Senate ratifies the Bryan peace treaties. No one, except Bryan, believes that his treaties will preserve the peace.

August 14, 1914. Nature is never so cunning as when dealing with her animal kingdom, hence she devised a powerful law to perpetuate the species; may it not be, therefore, that she now deems it necessary to exterminate some of her creatures, by fire, sword, and famine? Malthusian doctrine?

The war may collapse as suddenly as it began or it may be the initial war of a series of wars. We are admonished to be neutral. Is neutrality possible in a world-wide break-up?

Washington, September 1, 1914. Kipling's poem, "For all we have and are," appears here today.

September 24, 1914. Gratified to receive the following letter:

September 23, 1914

Hon. Henry F. Ashurst,
United States Senator

Sir:

The Financial Clerk informs me that . . . your telegrams, and especially those telegrams to which Senator Bristow of Kansas objected in July 1913, have been audited and decided by the committee to be official business and not private or personal business.

> Very respectfully yours,
> Charles P. Higgins,
> Sergeant-at-Arms,
> U.S. Senate.

September 29, 1914. The test of sanity in political campaigns is graciousness under responsibility. To remain serene after doing something one's constituents applaud or condemn, is an accomplishment of sanity; it soothes envy and begets good-will.

October 2, 1914. Mrs. Eva E. Marshall of Flagstaff, my school teacher of thirty-one years ago, is in the Senate Gallery as I write this entry. Mrs. Marshall, a descendant of the Schuyler family of New York, went to Arizona in early days. She taught school in a ten-foot by twenty-foot log house at Flagstaff, and doubtless her memory reaches across the gulf of ravening years to that day when my father, with his ranch-wagon, took my sister, my brother, Billie, and myself to her school. My parents were wholly uneducated. My father was of English ancestry and had mental strength; my mother was of French-Dutch ancestry, of courage and first-rate intellect.

They employed tutors to come to the ranch to teach. Our first tutor was Mr. Harry Fulton, a cultured man from Baltimore; our next tutor was an erudite Irishman named Joseph H. Terry who, at the ranch, went insane during a recitation hour and years later, died in an asylum. Our third tutor was an Englishman named Waukemphast who wore burnsides and a salt and pepper suit, but my father objected to his cockney accent, discharged him, and moved the family from the Ashurst Ranch to Flagstaff when the public school was established there in 1883.

October 10, 1914. Following letter from Secretary Lane:

> Washington
> Oct. 9th, 1914

My dear Senator:

I hasten to send you my sincere congratulations on your very able presentation of the achievements of our party. It made the reading of the Record today particularly interesting. And I want particularly to congratulate you on your peroration as to the nature of a nation.

> Cordially yours,
> Franklin K. Lane

Williams, November 16, 1914. Dr. and Mrs. E. B. Perrin entertained Mrs. Ashurst at their home whilst my friends tendered me a banquet at the Fray Marcos Hotel here this evening. Attorney George W. Glowner, toastmaster. Attorney X. N. Steeves said during his speech: "This is neither the time nor the place to speak of Senator Ashurst's many shortcomings, numerous though they be."

Washington, December 7, 1914. Congress convenes. Every senator who was a candidate for re-election and who was nominated, was re-elected Senator. Penrose of Pennsylvania says that his re-election was brought about by an uprising of the common people in his favor. Penrose weighs the goodly part of a ton, is a scholar and master of satire.

December 13, 1914. My wife and I lunched with Hon. Hannis and Mrs. Taylor, and met Hon. Hilary A. Herbert, sometime Secretary of the Navy under President Cleveland.

December 15, 1914. Returned from funeral of Hon. Sereno E. Payne held in Auburn, New York, yesterday. Senators Gallinger, Jones, Martine, and myself represented the Senate. I saw in Auburn the home of William H. Seward who served as Secretary of State under Presidents Lincoln and Johnson.

January 9, 1915. I spoke at the memorial exercises in the Senate in honor of the memory of Senator Johnston of Alabama and quoted from the speech Senator Johnston delivered in defense of Senator Lorimer in 1912.

January 27, 1915. Senator Fletcher is advocating administration's bill proposing to purchase German ships which took refuge in our harbors when Great War broke out. These ships are not interned and are free to depart. Democratic Senators are urging the purchase of these ships, whilst the Republican Senators in opposing the bill, argue that it would be a breach of American neutrality to pay Germany (thirty-five millions of dollars) for ships which Germany cannot use, and which ships if purchased by the U.S. would take the character of public vessels, the stoppage of which for carrying contraband might be an act of war.

February 1, 1915. Senator Clark of Arkansas with six other Democratic senators bolted the administration's bill proposing to purchase the German ships. The bolt defeats this bill and bitter words rang through the Senate.

February 8, 1915. For the first time in many years all senators (ninety-six), were present today and answered to their names. This indicates the intensity of the fight over the bill to purchase the German ships.

February 22, 1915. There are now two great powers not yet involved in the European war, viz., the United States and Italy; the latter although a member of the Triple Alliance (Central Powers), is showing signs of entering the war against her former allies.

March 4, 1915. Senators LaFollette, Gronna, and Lane killed the Indian Appropriation bill. Senator Stephenson (LaFollette's colleague) is a rugged, be-whiskered, opulent old lumber- and timberman.

Senate adjourned amidst ill-feeling and profanity, but relaxed its bad humor long enough to permit Senator Simmons to eulogize Senator Perkins of California who retires after twenty-three years of service.

Prescott, May 1, 1915. On March eleventh last, my wife and I left Washington, leaving John Renoe there. We stopped at Salt Lake City twenty-four hours; arrived San Francisco on March sixteenth, remained there ten days visiting the Panama Pacific International Exposition, attending conventions, balls, celebrations, and banquets. On March seventeenth, former Vice-President Fairbanks and I spoke at the banquet of the Knights of St. Patrick at the St. Francis Hotel.

The color, charm, beauty, and romance of this Exposition will never leave me. I addressed, at San Francisco, the annual convention of the American National Livestock Association and on April 15, my wife and I attended the dedication of the overflowing of the waters of the reservoir at Roosevelt Dam.

Nogales, May 9, 1915. Returned from a motor trip into Old Mexico and learned by dispatches from New York that amongst those lost on the "Lusitania" were A. C. Bilike of Tombstone, Arizona, and Elbert Hubbard and wife of East Aurora, New York.

Prescott, May 21, 1915. On the tenth day of this month, President W. W. delivered a speech in Philadelphia in which he uttered the cabalistic words: *"There is such a thing as a man being too proud to fight,"* and now waves of sarcasm and ridicule cover him.

He had in mind the noble line in Lord Byron's "Lament of Tasso" — "Too proud to be vindictive," but being tired and weary, W. W. misquoted the line.

Washington, D.C., June 8, 1915. To Department of Commerce with Senator Hoke Smith, then called on Secretary of Navy Daniels and found him worried. I then called at the State Department to see Secretary W. J. B. During my interview with

W. J. B., he let no word fall to indicate that he would within the hour resign his portfolio.

June 11, 1915. Bryan's letter to the American people explaining his resignation is published; it is of intense evangelism and eloquent theology. New York papers say that he has played "false" to his country and President Wilson.

June 12, 1915. W. J. B. issues an epistle to the "German-Americans."

June 20, 1915. My wife, John Renoe, Governor Hunt of Arizona, and I and about forty other Arizonians attended the launching of the S S "Arizona" at the Brooklyn Navy Yard yesterday.

At his request I gave the only manuscript of my address to Mr. Dwight B. Heard, Editor of the Arizona *Republican,* who said he "desired to publish it." Whilst at the Waldorf-Astoria Hotel in the evening, I received a 'phone from New York *American* that the Los Angeles *Examiner* wanted my speech. I searched for Mr. Heard but could not find him, so I entered a telephone booth and 'phoned the speech, consisting of eleven-hundred words, sentence by sentence, to a stenographer in the *American* office. The stenographer transcribed the same and it was then telegraphed to Los Angeles.

July 3, 1915. To the Senate reception room to survey the damage caused by a bomb exploded there last night by a crank.

September 15, 1915. Returned to Washington today from a seven weeks' tour on the Chautauqua through Indiana, Ohio, Pennsylvania, and Michigan, for the Coit-Albert Chautauqua Company of Cleveland. My wife and I left Washington on July 25, and went to Chicago, whence on July 25, she took train for Arizona. I received sixty dollars per speech, check every Friday. The Chautauqua Company paid my traveling expenses. During my tour I visited many cemeteries, saw the tomb of President William Henry Harrison at North Bend, Ohio. At Bethel, Ohio, I saw the grave of Senator Morris, born 1776, died 1844. John Greenleaf Whittier wrote his epitaph. Morris delivered the first abolition speech in Congress. I saw near Antioch, Ohio, the supposed birthplace of Tecumseh.

The Chautauqua, whose original purpose was to study the scriptures, was founded in 1874 by Rev. John H. Vincent, a Methodist clergyman who, on the banks of Lake Chautauqua, in New York State, arranged its first meeting.

The Chautauqua movement was organized with a sense of righteouosness that would today be called "The Uplift" and, in its early days, its energies were reverently called "The Work."

As its popularity grew it was expanded to include secular subjects and "pure, wholesome entertainment."

Leaders of other sects were later invited to participate and Lake Chautauqua became an interdenominational center of culture for many persons who had been denied a college training.

Among the thousands of individuals who attended the Chautauqua courses on the lake were some who carried the "plan" back to their home communities, and Chautauquas sprang up all over the country.

About the year 1904, the Chautauqua tent appeared, and today, especially in the small towns of the middle-west, as summer approaches, the advance agents of the Chautauqua, with banners, placards, and handbills, arrive in the respective communities that are on the Chautauqua circuit and announce the date of its opening.

On the appointed day, tents (some as large as circus tents) are set up, and young men (generally college boys on vacation) serve as ushers, propertymen, electricians, and cashiers and not less than thirty millions of persons during the Chautauqua season gather under the various tents.

Nowadays all the Chautauqua entertainers (whether bell-ringers, yodlers, elocutionists, travelers, jugglers, explorers, musicians, lecturers, clergymen, magicians, scientists, politicians, whistlers, divas, teachers, harpists, cornetters, or what not) are referred to as "The Talent" and everything done or said from the stage of the tent is called "The Message."

The widest variety of entertainers our country has ever known now appear in the various Chautauqua tents each season, and many of the "reforms" that lately have blessed or tortured the American people made their first and widest appeal from the stage of the Chautauqua.

The Chautauqua talent, now and for some years past, has comprised some far-famed persons.

Admissions to the tents are usually fifty cents for an afternoon and seventy-five cents for an evening.

Washington, October 14, 1915. The war in Europe has been unfolding its panorama for fourteen months, and today the world realizes the magnitude of the struggle. We now perceive that Great Britain's "Sea Power" kept her from starving.

> *It was sea power that saved Rome from Greece.*
> *It was sea power that saved Greece from Persia.*

It was sea power that gave to the Phoenecians the command of the ancient maritime world. Sea power built up the far-flung commercial empire of Carthage. Sea power made Athens ruler of vast territories, and it was sea power that made the Rome of antiquity mistress of the civilized world. Rome could not have subsisted without her sea power, because nearly all her wheat came overseas.

When Spain had great sea power she dominated Christendom; and Spain's decline began when storms and British seamanship wrecked her great armada.

The sea power of the American colonies, with the sea power of France, won the American Revolution, and the naval blockade defeated the Confederacy.

Washington, October 15, 1915. Learning that a plan was on foot to "ditch" Vice-President Marshall, I called on W. W. and told him that Mr. Marshall should be renominated for Vice-President and that President Wilson should say that Wilson wished it. W. W. "countered" on me by saying, "I have a very high regard for Vice-President Marshall and I wish you would tell him so." This was not an answer to my question, so I asked him again if I could say that President Wilson was for Mr. Marshall's renomination, and thereupon he gurgled out "Why! Yes!" and I wired the Vice-President who was in Scottsdale, Arizona.

October 23, 1915. Following letter from Vice-President Marshall yesterday:

Scottsdale, Arizona
Oct. 17, 1915

Dear Senator Ashurst:

I thank you for your telegram and kind letter, as much as for their contents. It pays a man for the little humiliations of life, to have such staunch friends as you and others are.

You saw of course, that I said I did not believe it. Whenever it is shown that I would be a burden to the President I would voluntarily withdraw, but I do not think I deserve to be kicked by men who lost their states while we carried Indiana.

Mrs. M. joins me in all good wishes to Mrs. Ashurst and yourself.

Again thanking you, I am
Faithfully yours,
Thomas R. Marshall

November 7, 1915. My wife and I dined with Mr. and Mrs. Thomas Pickford at the old Lord Baltimore mansion where Clay, Webster, and others dined, and wrote speeches.

November 28, 1915. Dispatches from the war zone say that reports from Mesopotamia indicate that a British expedition is near Bagdad. Bagdad is the ancient metropolis of the Moslem world and is a sordid slum of a city with a few tawdry mosques that serve to recall the power and magnificence of the caliphate of the days of Haroun Al Raschid, but it is potentially one of those gateways which from time to time adventurous armies strive to take. The country surrounding Bagdad is a land of solitude and mystery, and some say it was the cradle of the human race.

December 6, 1915. The Sixty-Fourth Congress convened. Much interest manifested in two of the new senators, viz., Warren Harding of Ohio and young Jim Wadsworth of New York. Mrs. Wadsworth is the daughter of the late John Hay.

December 31, 1915. The British defeat at Gallipoli is the most discouraging event since the World War began, and the prestige of the British Empire is damaged.

*The incredible has become
the commonplace.*

January 1, 1916. The New Year opens with the prospects of
the Democratic party below par. A whispering campaign is carried on against President Wilson. He has cleansed the Augean
stables and is the only Democrat with even a conjectural chance
of election to the Presidency this autumn. Therefore, to bring
suspicion and distrust upon him, falsehoods are circulated against
him. His marriage within seventeen months after the death of
the first Mrs. Wilson has set loose tongues to wagging.

We are now faced with a demand for military and naval
preparedness. To some members of Congress it is an issue they
cannot "size up." Old political signs are not pointing the way,
as once they did. Some members of Congress hesitate to vote
against an *adequate* navy, fearing that public opinion may later
defeat them, should the United States enter the war, and they
hesitate to vote *for* an adequate navy, fearing that the pacifists
may defeat them for re-election.

January 3, 1916. Mr. Nick Stark, my friend of bygone days,
is at the Belasco Theatre, playing in *Omar the Tentmaker* and
we talked of our exploits of twenty years ago at Flagstaff, Williams, and Phoenix.

January 5, 1916. Mr. George H. Kelly, Mayor Adamson, Mr.
Pirtle, and Mr. James S. Douglas are here to secure a cantonment
for Douglas, Arizona.

January 9, 1916. Luncheon at St. Patrick's Rectory, in honor
of Cardinal Gibbons. Present Chief Justice White and about
forty other distinguished men.

January 10, 1916. Land-hunger, selfishness, race-hatreds, bigotry, envy, intolerance, and revenge — ugly host of evil things

which constantly assail mankind — are ever plotting and launching their schemes. The immunities of free men, human-rights, and progress are protected by intelligently directed *force*. Since the dawn of civilization, those human beings who desired to lead peaceful and orderly lives have employed two methods to protect themselves against anti-social persons and to influence conduct and behaviour: one method is authority backed by *force* exercised by the police or the army; the other method is by the spoken word, that is to say, by example and by arguing, reasoning, persuading, preaching. The greatest teachers of religion — Christ, Buddha, Confucius, Lao Tse, and Zoroaster — rejected force and violence and believed that the power of the spoken "word of truth" was the proper method of controlling the anti-social and finding the "way of life."

January 23, 1916. It is more difficult to be good in middle life than in youth. Temptations in middle life are not more alluring than in youth, but middle life is the time of waning enthusiasm.

January 27, 1916. Senator Kenyon in Senate presented a petition signed by one million citizens opposing the exportation of arms and ammunition to the warring powers in Europe.

The petition was addressed to the President and to the Congress and it declared that the sale of arms and war munitions was not only of doubtful legality, but was morally wrong; it called attention to the orders of President Taft and President Wilson laying an embargo upon the exportation of arms to Mexico and it concluded by quoting W. W.'s proclamation at the inception of the European war anent our neutrality as follows: "We must be neutral in fact as well as in name, and we must put a curb on every transaction which might give a preference to one party in the struggle over another."

Senator Kenyon in presenting the petition said: "The signers are from every state in the union. They are not pro-British nor pro-German but they are pro-Americans, pro-humanity and pro-Christianity."

Senator Clapp was next up and said that "sooner or later an awakened conscience of our Nation would sweep aside the sophistries which have been invoked to permit us to send one ship laden with food and clothing for the widows and orphans and another ship loaded with instrumentalities to make more widows and orphans."

Senator Hitchcock was next up and supported the petition. He whispered to me that he felt short of breath and said, "I suppose I am getting old."

President Pro Tempore Clark and Senator Martine of New Jersey then spoke in support of the petition.

February 2, 1916. The Senate, after long debate on the bill which proposes a more autonomous government for the Philippines voted on the amendment thereto proposed by Senator Clarke of Arkansas, which amendment promises independence to the Philippines and directs the President to withdraw American sovereignty over the Philippines within the next four years. The vote on the Clarke amendment was a tie, forty-one to forty-one, and the amendment was carried by the casting of the vote of Vice-President Marshall.

February 14, 1916. President Wilson has English manners, I mean Herbert Henry Asquith manners; the manners of a courteous, detached, quiet scholar. He gives off the impression of a belief that those persons showing excitement or passion thereby exhibit weakness. His calmness is offensive to radicals; they detest suave imperturbability and suspect that good manners are a mask.

February 22, 1916. Senator Johnston of Maine read to the Senate today George Washington's farewell address.

Lloyd George says that no nation has ever reached the heights of the moral grandeur of France. He says that he sets her as England's constant model and that the French generals and soldiers show qualities of endurance, courage and military skill worthy of the highest deeds of Napoleon's army and that we are now too close to judge properly the immortal pages written by France in the books of history.

March 2, 1916. Senator Stone, Missouri, spoke opposing the concurrent resolution introduced by Senator Gore, warning American citizens that if they took passage upon an armed merchant ship it would be at their own risk. The President has written Senator Stone and Representative Pou that the adoption of such resolution would abridge the rights of citizens to travel upon the high seas, and the President's letter goes on to say: "The honor and self-respect of the Nation is (sic) involved . . . To forbid our people to exercise their rights for fear we might be called upon to vindicate them would be a deep humiliation indeed."

The President has told Senator Kern, Senate majority leader, that this resolution is embarrassing our foreign affairs.

Senator Stone, Senator Lodge, and Senator Williams supported the President's position. Senator Gore, in his speech, intimated that W. W. recently asserted that: "A state of war with Germany might not of *itself* or of *necessity* be an evil, and that the United States by entering the war now might be able to bring it to a conclusion by midsummer and thus render a great service to civilization."

Senator Stone denied that the President had made such statement.

I received the following letter from W. J. B.:

My dear Senator:

I believe we ought to keep our citizens off of belligerent ships. Officers may disobey instruction — they have to decide in a moment of excitement and may forfeit lives of all on board by resisting or trying to escape.

The facts may be disputed and we have to take sides with one country or against the others on facts. There is no reason why a few should be allowed to imperil the country.

Yours truly,
W. J. Bryan

March 3, 1916. Senator Gore's resolution warning citizens not to travel on armed merchant-ships came up today. Senator James moved to lay the resolution upon the table. The motion to lay on the table was not debatable. Parliamentary law granted Senator Gore the right to "perfect" his resolution, and he moved to strike out that part of his resolution which warned citizens not to travel upon armed ships and inserted the following in lieu thereof:

> The sinking by a German submarine, without notice or warning, of an armed merchant vessel of her public enemy, resulting in the death of a citizen of the United States, would constitute, a just and sufficient cause of war between the United States and the German Empire.

Upon roll call, the "perfected" Gore resolution was laid on the table.

By thus changing the text of his resolution, Senator Gore brought criticism upon himself from those senators supporting his original resolution.

April 5, 1916. Vice-President handed me a telegram that the famous Attorney Reese M. Ling of Arizona had just died.

April 26, 1916. Attended a dinner in honor of Cardinal Gibbons, given by former Speaker "Uncle Joe" Cannon. Amongst those present were Chief Justice White, Justices McKenna, Van Davanter, and Hughes, Speaker Champ Clark, Secretary of Interior Lane, a dozen senators, and two dozen representatives. After dinner "Uncle Joe" called Justice Hughes aside, and conversed with him, whereupon Senator O'Gorman said: "The leadership in the Republican party is now falling from the shoulders of 'Uncle Joe' Cannon and is settling upon Mr. Justice Hughes."

May 1, 1916. The House of Representatives today struck from the Philippine bill the Clarke amendment which promised independence and which directed the President to withdraw American sovereignty over the Philippines within the next four years. Thirty Democratic representatives bolted the Clarke amendment.

May 24, 1916. Senate Committee on the Judiciary reported favorable the nomination of Mr. Louis D. Brandeis to be Associate Justice of the Supreme Court of the United States. His confirmation has been resisted for months.

Augusta, Maine, June 19, 1916. Here with committee to attend the funeral of Senator Burleigh. After the funeral services, I went to see the old home of James G. Blaine who pursued the *ignis fatuus* of the presidency with a fervor that never abated. Blaine believed in signs, omens, signals, dreams, and portents. His house today looked gloomy and the door-plate marked "J. G. Blaine" was rusted. Rank weeds were growing in the yard, and this large vacant house with its gaping windows seemed the eerie abode of some troubled spirit. After Blaine's defeat for the presidency in 1884, he paced the floor of his parlor in this house for hours, with head bent in dejection.

June 28, 1916. Whilst speaking in the Senate today and sharply pressed by Senators Hardwick of Georgia, and Bryan of Florida, the Vice-President suddenly bellowed out, "How long is the Senator from Arizona going to talk?"

Washington, November 24, 1916. Since my last entry in this book, I have been re-elected to the Senate by 8612 majority. My Republican opponent was Judge Joseph H. Kibbey of Phoenix. Wife and I visited my mother in Los Angeles and then went to Flagstaff to the funeral services of Dr. Percival Lowell, a famous astronomer, who for the past twenty-three years, in his observatory at Flagstaff, has studied the planet Mars.

Until sunrise of November 8, it was believed that Woodrow Wilson had been defeated and that Charles Evans Hughes had been elected President. Mr. Hughes retired to bed on election night, November 7, believing that he had been elected. The press was of opinion that President Wilson had been defeated as Mr. Hughes had carried New York, New Jersey, Pennsylvania, Indiana, and Illinois. Early in the morning of November 8, the returns disclosed that all the western states but Oregon and South Dakota had voted for Wilson, except California which was in doubt. Thus, in order to win, Wilson must carry either

Minnesota or California; but Minnesota, by less than four hundred majority, sent her twelve electoral votes into the Hughes column. The nation waited during November 8, 9, and 10 the counting of California's votes, and on November 10 it was ascertained that the thirteen Wilson electors were chosen in California by about four-thousand majority. Not counting California, the Electoral Colleges would have stood: Hughes 252 electoral votes; Wilson 264 electoral votes — or two short of a majority. Adding California's thirteen electoral votes to the Wilson column brought the following result: Hughes 254, Wilson 277.

Senator Walsh, Montana, who was in charge of the Democratic headquarters in Chicago, telegraphed me on November 9 that should California finally fall into the Hughes column, the Minnesota returns would be contested and that the contest would be based upon the alleged illegality of the Saint Louis County (Minnesota) returns.

December 1, 1916. Senator Vardaman and I are members of the Democratic Executive Committee which is to tender a banquet to W. J. B. at Hotel Lafayette on the sixth instant. W. J. B. requested that a large portrait of himself covered by a curtain be placed behind the speaker's table and that when he arose to speak at the banquet, the curtain should be drawn aside and bring the painting to the view of the guests, but I replied that it would be incongruous to bring a picture into competition with the original. W. J. B. and Senator Vardaman urged that I go tomorrow with them to invite President Wilson to attend the banquet. With misgivings and doubt, I consented to go.

December 2, 1916. Senator Vardaman, Mr. Pickford, and myself of the committee of the Bryan banquet called on W. W. at the White House.

I told the President of the proposed banquet to Colonel Bryan in recognition of the services rendered by Bryan in stumping the western states in the recent presidential campaign, and

I added that a special feature of the banquet would be a suitable reference to California which was the pivotal state. Wilson said:

> I shall be glad to send a letter which may be read at the banquet but you surely must perceive that were I to attend, my presence would draw attention from the character whom you seek to honor and the fact that I am the President would have a tendency to throw him into the shade. At whatsoever function the President is present, under our system he is the first figure and must precede all others and this might prove embarrassing at some juncture of the banquet.

I saw the force of this statement and told him he was correct. Senator Vardaman's face grew dark and he indicated that my reply to W. W. did not suit him.

We were preparing to leave, when W. W. said:

> Another reason for my not attending the banquet is that I have no sympathy with all this talk that California should be specially honored because the returns from that state were in favor of the Democratic party. I owe no especial thanks to California for casting its vote for me and certainly no gratitude is due to any person or to any state for performing a duty. California but did her duty and I am not inclined to engage in fulsome expressions of gratitude.

This from W. W. infuriated Senator Vardaman and I was taken aback but said: "Good Morning, Mr. President. Send us the letter."

December 7, 1916. The banquet in honor of W. J. B. came off last evening: four hundred Democrats present.

Senators Vardaman and Hollis each promised me that in their respective speeches, they would eulogize W. J. B.'s "Breathing Spell" Peace Treaties of 1914, but their omission to do so drove Bryan to the exigency of eulogizing his treaties himself. Bryan told me he believes that his "Breathing Spell" Peace Treaties will honor his name one thousand years hence.

December 15, 1916. Mrs. Ashurst and I attended a dinner at the New Willard given by the Vice-President and Mrs. Marshall, in honor of President and Mrs. Wilson. Those present were the President and Mrs. Wilson, Senator and Mrs. Swanson, Senator and Mrs. Pomerene, Senator and Mrs. Hitchcock, Senator and Mrs. Reed, my wife and self, Senator and Mrs. Saulsbury, Senator and Mrs. Shiels, Senator and Mrs. Pittman, Senator and Mrs. Shafroth, Senator Phelan and Mrs. T. F. Walsh of Colorado. W. W. talked much and announced that he could not shake hands with Senator Henry Cabot Lodge.

January 4, 1917. Habit is a powerful master and only "habit" keeps me writing in this book.

It was the habit of many pioneers in early days of the West to keep a diary and to record one's movements, a description of storms, phenomena, data as to location of springs, trails, roads, and grasses and game. Moreover, fifty years ago books, papers, and magazines were scarce and mails infrequent in Arizona, hence, the diary was resorted to as a diversion. My father lost his life in the Grand Canyon and when the searching party, on February 20, 1901, reached his camp I found his diary and ascertained from it that the last entry was made on the eighteenth of the preceding January; I suspected that the lapse of so many days without an entry therein betokened disaster, for he was punctual as to his diary when camping. Discovering his body some hours later we found that he had been dead over a month.

Is the diary the waste basket of literature? Is is not rather as lawyers say, a part of the *res gestae?* It is a letter written to oneself, and whilst the diarist is drawing pictures of others, he is also drawing pictures of himself.

History is sometimes defective in making estimates of the characters and motives of men. The historian toils amidst musty tomes and bulky files of papers to find facts from which to draw conclusions and interpretations, but the diarist sees and hears the living man and records the events as they happen. Unfortunately, some diarists and autobiographers lack impersonal consciences or are so hemmed in by fear, pride, vanity, or conventionality that they set up sentinels of caution, orthodoxy, and prudence and refine away or whittle down the color and vitality of events and personages.

January 22, 1917. President Wilson today addressed the Senate regarding peace for Europe but his suggestions of "Peace without Victory" seemed nebulous. Various motives are ascribed to him. Is he using the Senate as a forum from which to speak to all chancelleries? Does he feel safe when only he may talk and nobody else's voice may be heard? Does the President seek company where only he be armed and his the only shot that may be fired? Has he made a stump speech from the "throne" to forestall public opinion? Is he the President of humanity or the President of the United States? Is he really some wise, farseeing man whose vision is clearer than his fellows? These are the questions asked today.

January 26, 1917. The *Washington Post* today says President's speech to the Senate on Monday the twenty-second was copied from a letter sent by Dom Pedro, Emperor of Brazil, to President Lincoln.

January 31, 1917. The German government has just handed to our Ambassador, Mr. Gerard, and to the representatives of the other neutral powers, a note stating amongst other things that the Imperial German Government will hereafter maintain a "dead line" around the British Isles, France, and Italy, and also around the Mediterranean, and that Germany had from three hundred to five hundred U *(Untersee)* Boats ready to sink any ship entering this zone, or passing this "dead line." If Germany should carry out this announced policy and sink ships flying the American flag, war between the United States and Germany would ensue.

February 1, 1917. The decision of the Imperial German Government to enforce, through the unrestricted use of the submarine, the peace it invited through diplomatic negotiations, has aroused a great sensation in Washington. Officials of our government were unprepared for this note from Germany, which Count Von Bernstorff, the German Ambassador, delivered to Secretary of State Lansing yesterday. The delivery of this fateful document was accompanied by dramatic settings. Strict rule of diplomatic deportment in presenting the note to our Secretary of State was observed by Count Von Bernstorff.

February 3, 1917. Everyone seemed to have foreboding of evil days soon to come. The German Ambassador, Count Von Bernstorff, has been told to ask for his passports. The senators led by Vice-President Marshall marched to the House and the President addressed the joint session.

William Jennings Bryan telephoned that he wanted to see me at the LaFayette Hotel. I found him excited; he said he would flood Congress with telegrams against war except in case of *actual* invasion. I studied this emotional man — this man so eloquent in utterance — and let him talk peace and acquiescence; then asked him: Does Americanism mean peace at any price?

February 7, 1917. For the past week my time has been consumed by the Indian bill. The American Indian is a mystic, a child of nature, a hunter, fisherman, and stockman. Senate adopted Senator Stone's resolution approving the President's action in dismissing the German Ambassador, Count Von Bernstorff. Senators Vardaman, Kirby, LaFollette, Works, and Gronna voted NO.

February 14, 1917. Electoral count today. Vice-President Marshall, in the presence of the two Houses of Congress, opened the certificates, and the electoral votes of the recent election were counted.

President Wilson and Vice-President Marshall were declared to be elected to be their own successors, respectively. For a time, after last election, it appeared as if a contest might confront this "count" of the electoral vote, but today the "electoral count" was so dwindled in importance that we had to urge senators to attend.

February 18, 1917. Eulogies in Senate in honor of the memory of three deceased senators. A noble eulogy of James P. Clarke of Arkansas, deceased, was delivered by Senator Robinson of Arkansas. Mr. Clarke was three times U.S. Senator from Arkansas. He was our Harry Hotspur of debate; he never forgot an injury, and he hunted fights with the zest of the huntsman. He used neither tobacco nor liquor; he ate sparingly and talked incessantly. In March 1913, he was chosen President Pro Tempore and he protected the right of every senator regardless of party. Clarke in 1913 defeated Senator Bacon for President Pro Tempore. I voted for Clarke in 1913, but in December 1915, Mark Smith and I voted against Clarke's re-election for President Pro Tempore and it was remarkable to see his hot scorn of some of those who voted against him. It required fortitude to withstand his blistering sarcasm.

February 19, 1917. I presided over the Senate all afternoon and evening and was required to sign warrants for the arrest of absent senators. I rode home at midnight with Senator Penrose of Pennsylvania who said he "would drive rapidly so that no one will know with whom" he was riding; it would do him "no good in Pennsylvania" to be seen in my "company."

February 24, 1917. Ill feeling pervaded the Senate all day. Senator John Sharp Williams precipitated a debate over foreign affairs. Senator Lodge delivered a philippic against the Wilson administration, whereupon Senator James Hamilton Lewis (whom we fondly call "Jim Ham") replied to Senator Lodge.

February 26, 1917. Early at the Capitol, it was announced that the President would address the two Houses in joint session today, but the announcement created no interest as we have had so many cries of "wolf" when no wolf came, that members are now blasé. The senators trouped over to the House, and the burden of the President's message was that the end of the present Congress is at hand and that the new Congress cannot be quickly assembled. He asked that Congress authorize him to supply American merchant ships with defensive arms. Senators, however, took up the flood control bill and within ten minutes forgot that the President had been on Capitol Hill. In the breaking up of a Congress, members rush about, plead, and threaten in attempts to pass their measures. "The Law of Talons" is then the supreme law. Every weapon in the parliamentary armory is called into requisition; meals are missed, no one sleeps, collars are wilted, hair disheveled. Our constituents bombard us with their frantic letters and telegrams. All eyes are red-lidded, all nerves frayed, and much profane swearing.

Washington now has a holiday appearance with its bunting and triumphal arches. W. W. will soon again ride up Pennsylvania Avenue to succeed himself. How strange the legerdemain of doom and the turn of the wheel of fortune! Chance and fate are magicians that play mighty parts in the destinies of public men. Had Mr. Hughes remained out of California during the 1916 campaign he would have succeeded President Wilson. Had James Gillespie Blaine not gone to New York City during the closing days of the 1884 campaign, he would thus have escaped the Jay Gould dinner, would have avoided Dr. Burchard's fatal R. R. R. alliteration, and would have been elected President. Hughes in 1916, and Blaine in 1884, were secure within their own fortifications. Had they remained at home and silently awaited the election day, they would have been victorious, but amateurs advised them or nemesis followed them.

Outside their own walls, Blaine and Hughes could not tread the tangled paths; they lost the clue and lost the elections. Lincoln made but one speech in the campaign of 1860.

February 27, 1917. Senator Vardaman directed my attention to Mr. Edwin Markham sitting in the gallery and said, "There sits the greatest living poet." And I replied that I had not heard of the death of Mr. Rudyard Kipling.

February 28, 1917. Rumors fly wildly; one rumor is that there shall be no more "notes" from our State Department to the Imperial German Government and that the President regards the sinking of the "Laconia" on the twenty-sixth instant as an "overt act" and would arm American merchant ships with defensive arms.

March 1, 1917. Mexico and Japan have been asked by Germany to attack the United States if the United States enters the war. Count Von Bernstorff is pictured as a leading figure in the plot. The sinking of the "Laconia" by a German U Boat with three American lives lost may be considered by W. W. as the "overt act" without which he says he will not urge a declaration of war. When the excitement of these days is forgotten, the impartial historian will say that W. W. valiantly strove to avert war.

March 2, 1917. Senate passed Naval Appropriation bill whereupon the bill authorizing the President to supply American merchant ships with defensive arms, was considered. The House returned the Naval Appropriation bill to the Senate alleging that in "tacking" thereon a "rider" providing for a bond issue, the Senate had trenched upon the privileges of the House and had thus violated Clause One, Section Seven, of Article One of the Constitution of the United States. The Senate promptly eliminated the objectionable rider from the bill.

March 3, 1917. Senator Fall of New Mexico spoke three hours for the bill authorizing the President to arm merchant ships. Senator Stone of Missouri (Chairman of the Foreign Relations Committee) spoke five hours against the bill. Administration senators were furious toward Mr. Stone for his refusal to support the President upon this measure.

March 4, 1917. At 4:00 this A.M. Senator Robinson read to the Senate a manifesto, as follows:

Washington, D.C., March 3, 1917.

The undersigned United States senators favor the passage of the bill to authorize the President of the United States to arm American merchant vessels and to protect American citizens in their peaceful pursuits upon the sea. A similar bill has already passed the House of Representatives by a vote of 403 to 13. Under the rules of the Senate, allowing debate without limit, it now appears to be impossible to obtain a vote prior to noon, March 4, 1917, when this session of Congress expires. We desire this statement entered in the *Record* to establish the fact that the Senate favors this legislation, and would pass it if a vote could be had:

F. M. Simmons, Henry Cabot Lodge, William E. Borah, G. M. Hitchcock, George Sutherland, Hoke Smith, George

T. Oliver, John W. Kern, J. W. Wadsworth, Jr., Thomas
Sterling, James H. Brady, William P. Dillingham, L. B. Colt,
Frand B. Brandegee, Clarence D. Clark, P. J. McCumber,
Morris Sheppard, Atlee Pomerene, Willard Saulsbury, C. E.
Townsend, Bert M. Fernald, Albert B. Fall, John K. Shields,
George P. McLean, Joe T. Robinson, Duncan U. Fletcher,
Reed Smoot, Ollie M. James, Claude A. Swanson, Thomas
S. Martin, N. P. Bryan, Thomas W. Hardwick, E. D. Smith,
Charles Curtis, Knute Nelson, W. G. Harding, T. B. Catron,
John Sharp Williams, J. Hamilton Lewis, T. J. Walsh, J. S.
W. Beckham, H. L. Meyers, Paul O. Husting, Henry F.
Hollis, James D. Phelan, Miles Poindexter, O. W. Under-
wood, John F. Shafroth, F. E. Warren, Carrol S. Page, W. L.
Jones, James E. Martine, Charles S. Thomas, George E.
Chamberlain, Lawrence Y. Sherman, William Alden Smith,
W. E. Chilton, John H. Bankhead, Henry F. Ashurst, Lee
S. Overman, Ed S. Johnson, Blair Lee, William Hughes,
John W. Weeks, James A. Reed, John Walter Smith, Luke
Lea, Key Pittman, Robert F. Broussard, James E. Watson,
H. A. du Pont, Robert L. Owen, Francis G. Newlands, Wil-
liam H. Thompson, Joseph E. Randsdell.

Senator Lippitt is out of the city. Senators detained from
the Senate on account of illness include Nathan Goff,
Jacob H. Gallinger.

The following senators have not had an opportunity to
sign this agreement: Mr. Gore, Mr. Tillman, Mr. Smith of
Arizona, Mr. Stone, Mr. Johnson of Maine, Mr. Culberson.

This manifesto made no mention of the senators who refused
to sign the same. As the names of the senators who had signed it
were read by the Secretary, hoots, boos, hisses, and cat-calls
came from the filibusters. At 8 o'clock this morning, I strolled
to the barbershop maintained by the Senate and which has been
operated by olive-skinned John Hickman since September 1, 1865.

March 5, 1917. At 11:45 A.M. the President Pro Tempore
Saulsbury assumed the Senate chair; the Speaker of the House,
the members and members-elect of the House were announced;
then came the diplomats of foreign powers, the Supreme Court,

and then the President. The gold lace, the braid, and decorations of military and naval officers flashed. My name was called first of those senators to be sworn in and as Mark Smith had not returned from Florida, Senator Tillman escorted me to the Vice-President's rostrum. The inaugural parade was not as long as the one in 1913. Twelve senators, by filibuster, prevented a vote on the armed neutrality bill.

March 9, 1917. Senate yesterday by seventy-six ayes, to three noes, passed a modified cloture rule.

Waves of public opinion surge angrily against the Senate filibusterers who defeated the armed neutrality bill. Not since the nineteen senators voted "not guilty" at the impeachment of President Andrew Johnson in 1868, has such scorching criticism been made of senators. The nineteen senators, who in President Johnson's impeachment voted "not guilty," were later declared by calm judgment to have voted wisely. Uninformed, ignorant public opinion may be tyrannical. Are the filibusterers condemned by an *informed* or by an ignorant public opinion?

March 19, 1917. German U boats sank three American ships since last Saturday.

Newspapers are demanding war with Germany, and resentment is furious against senators who defeated the armed neutrality bill.

March 20, 1917. Events follow one another so closely that the revolution in Russia is almost overlooked. Ten days ago, Nicholas the Second, Czar of all Russia, owned in his name 70 per cent of the land area of Russia. His personal income as Czar was $43 million per year and no law in Russia could diminish or divert any sum of money the Czar named for himself. In addition to this income, he also derived about ten million dollars annually from his private estates and mines.

These sums which the Czar received, went for the support of his family, his court, and numerous grand dukes and duchesses. The Czar has been overthrown; his flags and ensigns have been torn from the public buildings and the revolutionary flag hoisted instead. The officers and men of Russian army and navy have received the news of the Czar's dethronement with enthusiasm and the Russian ambassadors, envoys, and consuls remote from Russia have cabled assurances of loyalty to the revolutionary government. Millions of tons of wheat secreted by czarist monopolists and forestallers have been released in Russia. Meanwhile, the former Czar, Nicholas Romanoff, with his family, is enroute to some obscure village, with a limited expense fund, and will spend the remainder of his life in retirement.

Nicholas the Second is dull, apathetic, barren of intellectual power, and destitute of that vigor and vision so necessary to a ruler. He is calm, or indifferent rather, to catastrophic events because he does not comprehend them.

He is neither cunning nor cruel; he is a superstitious dolt dominated by the self-willed Czarina, a nervous woman who was in turn dominated by a shrewd fakir — a colossal fraud named Gregory Rasputin.

March 23, 1917. The incredible has become the commonplace. From inability to respond to each new amazement, the human mind now accepts multitudinous world-staggering events as matters of course. One day's news of these times will fill volumes for future investigators, historians, and poets. We are too near these stupendous destinies to catch their meaning. We see certain facts but do not know how to interpret them. We hear the reverberations of these happenings but we *see* only the outlines, and suddenly there comes another outline more portentous, more gigantic.

March 26, 1917. The pacifists are denouncing W. W. for defending "American rights," and the militarists are abusing him because he does not send "an army overseas to join the Allies."

March 29, 1917. Attended midshipmen graduation at Annapolis. Visited the Naval Academy's chapel and went to the crypt to see the sarcophagus containing the body of John Paul Jones.

April 2, 1917. Capitol building gorged with the morbid and excited. A pacifist and his wife assaulted Senator Lodge, but Mr. Ward Davis, an Arizonian, who happened to be near, beat them off. Hiram Johnson of California was sworn in as a senator. In the House, Miss Jeannette Rankin, from Montana, was applauded when her name was called. Honorable Champ Clark was re-elected Speaker. When the House was organized, the senators went to the House to hear the President's message. Those senators who filibustered the armed neutrality bill to death and whom W. W. had denounced as a "little group of willful men," were grave. Appeals to Germany as our ancient friend had failed. I was not surprised when the President urged Congress to declare war against the Imperial German Government. Near the end of his message, the President looked up from his manuscript and said: "It is a fearful thing to lead this great peaceful people into war."

Senate reconvened and Senator Martin introduced a resolution declaring that the U.S. accepted the State of War thrust upon it by the Imperial German Government.

Of all the phenomena now obtruding themselves, none is more inexplicable than the fervor with which this nation is demanding war.

If all those citizens who within the past thirty days have signed petitions, letters, and telegrams urging Congress to declare war against the Imperial German Government, shall enlist as warriors, we shall have a large army.

For years I have believed that large numbers of people were (varying in degree according to environment, locality, and habit) within that penumbra or zone between sanity and mental derangement. Our artificial life, our craving for stimulants. sensations, and joyrides, our fanaticism, bigotry, race-hatreds, and inveterate dancing, are not causes, they are effects.

The debate in the Senate on war resolution was prosaic. Senator LaFollette delivered a legalistic argument against the resolution. When the roll was called there were eighty-two ayes, six noes and eight absent. Those voting "no" were: Gronna, LaFollette, Lane, Norris, Stone, and Vardaman. Senator John Sharp Williams in a protracted speech said that Senator La-Follette was *"unable to distinguish between a prize court and a torpedo,"* meaning that England takes American ships into the prize court, whilst Germany torpedoes them.

April 6, 1917. The war declaration resolution passed the House today.

April 15, 1917. By unanimous vote the House passed bill authorizing issuance of bonds amounting to several billions of dollars. There are eras when the world spins so leisurely along its course, that for decades it seems to be at a "standstill;" then there comes the swirling time when it rushes along at such a pace that it covers the path of centuries in a year, and we are living in such a dizzy swirl now.

April 19, 1917. Whilst I was presiding, during a speech by Senator Borah, Mr. T. J. Mahoney, an attorney from Nebraska, dropped dead in the Senate gallery.

2

Wilson and the War

...for Nature has not equipped you to seek aggrandizement and secure empire, but you are clever at thwarting another's designs and wresting from him his gains, quick to confound the plots of the ambitious and to vindicate the freedom of all mankind.

Demosthenes

The free nations had to choose between
being overridden and becoming soldiers...

April 24, 1917. No one in history ever made a greater mistake than the German Kaiser and his war lords. Germany had a "place in the sun" and was enjoying the freedom of the seas. Her flag was found in every port; there was no discrimination against Germany in the tariff laws of "protection nations."

In the application of science to industry, in the management of cities, in social service and in the struggle against poverty, and in that battle, which brings durable values, the battle of man against nature, Germany had a place. In the eloquent words of another:

> The German language possessed such rich treasures of literature and such scientific and historical knowledge, that men of other tongues must needs study German. In music, that high expression of human emotion, she was making conquests.

The stupidity of German war lords interrupted German progress and brought blood and ashes.

April 26, 1917. Last evening I attended a reception tendered at the Pan American Building by Secretary of State Lansing to the Right Honourable Arthur James Balfour, His Britannic Majesty's Principal Secretary of State, for Foreign Affairs, and party composed of Lord Cunliffe, Governor of the Bank of England, and about thirty other persons high in civil, military and naval life in England, who are here to discuss plans for cooperation of the forces at war against Germany.

April 30, 1917. Senate Judiciary Committee considered the bill to use the German ships now interned in our ports. Senator

Walsh of Montana says that we should in a Prize Court condemn these German ships.

Wife and I attended a reception at the Pan American Building tendered by Secretary of State and Mrs. Lansing to Monsieur Viviani, Marshal Joffre, and Vice-Admiral Cocheprot of the French Commission.

May 1, 1917. Marshal Joffre, Vice-Premier Rene Viviani, M. Jusserand, Ambassador of France, and other members of the French Commission visited the Senate today. Senators Lodge and Hitchcock escorted the distinguished guests to the Vice-President's rostrum. Galleries crowded. Representatives of other foreign powers present in full regalia. Marshal Joffre wore scarlet breeches. M. Viviani addressed the Senate in French. His numerous gestures were graceful and his voice toneful. Then came loud cries for Marshal Joffre, whereupon the Marshal arose and shouted in English, "I do not speak English;" and then waving his cap he shouted in French, "Vivient les États Unis."

May 5, 1917. Espionage bill is up in the Senate. I am opposed to laws requiring publications to be "visaed" in advance of publication.

May 8, 1917. Mr. Balfour and his suite visited the Senate today. The Vice-President delivered an address of welcome. Mr. Balfour seemed weary and he spoke twenty minutes with little animation, using the word "unconscious" for the word "unconscionable."

May 10, 1917. I spoke on the espionage bill yesterday, arguing that "freedom of the press" as that phrase is used in the first amendment to our federal Constitution, means that publishers and others shall not be subject to pains or penalties for omitting to procure an official "OK" or sanction *before* publishing.

May 11, 1917. Ex-Senator Elihu Root, he of the superb intellect, will head the American Special Mission to Russia and told me that he fears that Russia will make a separate peace with the Teutonic allies.

May 19, 1917. President Wilson announced that General Pershing (Senator Warren's son-in-law) will command the American Expeditionary troops that go to France.

W. W. says the sending of the divisions to France will be "undramatic," and he declines to send T. R. to the front. The country will resent this refusal of a command to T. R. This is the first mistake, and I hope it may not prove to be the initial blunder of a series of blunders. In war, blunders do not come as single spies, but as battalions.

May 20, 1917. Visited the Naval Hospital but received no comfort. Surgeon says malady malignant, and requiring operation. I walked away from the hospital applying the only anodyne: philosophy.

May 21, 1917. It is now time to write something of the Congress which declared war against Germany. When this Congress convened in extraordinary session, the Democrats of the House, numbering about 212, induced a sufficient number of representatives, not members of either the Democratic or the Republican party to vote with the Democrats; thus Hon. Champ Clark of Missouri was re-elected Speaker, and the various committee chairmanships of the House went to the Democrats.

The Speaker, Mr. Champ Clark, is a scholarly, ruggedly-handsome, rigidly-honest man. He believes that he would have been inaugurated as President on March 4, 1913, had not W. J. B. "betrayed him" at the Baltimore Convention.

Claude Kitchen of North Carolina, the Démocratic leader, is brave and industrious. James R. Mann of Illinois, the Republican leader, is technical, crochety, and stubborn and is a close student of the measures that are "up" in the House.

Augustus P. Gardner of Massachusetts, Republican, son-in-law of Senator Lodge, is crisp and peppery in debate. He and F. H. Gillette of Massachusetts refused to vote for Mr. Mann for Speaker, alleging that Mr. Mann was pro-German. Uncle Joe Cannon of Illinois is the patriarch of the House and is now entering upon his twenty-second term. He is a "game cock" and philosopher. Henry D. Flood of Virginia is Chairman of the House Committee on Foreign Relations and measures up to his responsibilities.

The membership of the House is about 70 per cent political lawyers. It will continue to do what W. W. desires, but if the average member could secure applause "back home" by inveighing against W. W. he would do so. The House contains upward of five score members who are qualified for any place and embody the noblest ideals of our Republic. The Democrats of the Sixty-Fifth Congress were elected upon "peace" platforms. So here is a House made up largely of political lawyers, unused to dealing with world problems, and upon them are imposed tasks that would puzzle experienced men. Many members of this Congress, when elected, believed that at the next (1918) election they could secure re-election, by exhibiting a "record" of pacifist votes and an inventory of public buildings secured for their district. Now "pork" (public buildings) is engulfed in the demand for money with which to carry on the war. To the credit of American manhood, many new members have met their high duties as competently as the seasoned members.

Two-thirds of the present Senate are lawyers. On the roll call upon the war resolution Senators Gronna, LaFollette, Lane, Norris, Stone and Vardaman, voted "no" whilst Bankhead, Goff, Gore, Hollis, Newlands, Smith of Arizona, Thomas, and Tillman were unavoidably absent. All the others, eighty-two in number, voted for the war resolution.

Willard Saulsbury of Delaware is President Pro Tempore. He is not fluent in *speech* but is not irresolute. He resembles a cultured Englishman who loves creature-comfort. His father and uncle were senators from Delaware.

Senator Thomas S. Martin of Virginia, the Democratic leader, is without vanity or hobbies. Charles P. Higgins of Missouri is the Sergeant-at-Arms; James M. Baker of South Carolina is the Secretary; Senator Jacob H. Gallinger, a physician, who entered the Senate in 1891, is Republican leader; Senator Lodge came in 1893; Warren, Martin, Nelson and Tillman came in 1895; McCumber and Culberson came in 1899. No less than thirty-eight senators are now in their second term, and most of those are in the first years of their second term. More than thirty are only in their first term. Therefore, the present Senate has not acquired the "senatorial habit," and many raw recruits must aid in solving vital problems. We hear much about the "good old days" of the Senate, but this present Senate is as

able as the Senate of '61 to '65. That Senate contained no statesman of wider experience than Philander C. Knox and Hoke
Smith. It contained no senator who knew more of naval affairs
than does John W. Weeks. It contained no surer master in controversy than James A. Reed. It contained no such maker of
epigrams as Thomas P. Gore, who although blind, has luminous
"insight" into events.

Senator Hiram W. Johnson as Governor of California not
only brandished the knife of economy in government, but applied it with skill and courage. Furnifold M. Simmons and
Oscar W. Underwood ably advocate the "competitive" tariff
theory, whilst Boies Penrose and Reed Smoot ably advocate the
"protective" tariff theory. Simmons is bold and diligent; Underwood is master of himself and his subject. Penrose is aggresive
and resourceful. Smoot is a hard worker. James Hamilton Lewis
would be conspicuous in any assembly speaking the English
language. It is a delight to hear Brandegee speak. Lawrence Y.
Sherman is a "Josh Billings." Charles S. Thomas is learned.
Phelan is a litterateur and patron of art. Newlands is a statesman
and dreamer. Hitchcock is scholarly and speaks with toneful
distinctness.

John Sharp Williams is a Cyrano de Bergerac in debate.
Nelson is a Viking. Ollie James is a physical and mental giant.

The new Republican senators: Harding and Wadsworth
(neither of them is a lawyer) are Presidential "possibilities."

William Joel Stone is a *rara avis.* He is good at strategem
and can also charge and assault, and of all senators, Mr. Stone is
the most valuable to his party. His almost invisible chinlet ex-
plodes the absurd fiction that stubborn men have large chins.

Albert Bacon Fall is tenacious. His curly locks on the back
of his head dispose themselves with classic disarrangement and
in debate he points a long finger, as if to pierce the body of his
opponent, the while he is piercing with sharp sentences the
speech of his opponent. He has no bonhomie and his face is
marked by lines of harshness; his speeches are tart and rasping
and his demeanor is sour.

Marcus Aurelius Smith of Arizona served sixteen years in the House of Representatives as a Delegate from the Territory of Arizona and is one of the authentic scholars of the Senate.

Robert M. LaFollette of Wisconsin will loom large in history, but his ill health now interferes with his labors. His honesty, ability, and courage are beyond dispute.

Henry Cabot Lodge of Massachussets is our most distinguished senator and of all the senators he has the widest knowledge of foreign relations. He is slim and slightly under medium height. He walks slowly, and his snugly-fitting sack coat of English design is buttoned-up. His gray hair is curly, and he wears whiskers. His white face is corrugated and puckered with brittle ridges. He reads without glasses and smokes cigarettes. While listening to the debates or sitting through ceremonial functions, he places one knee directly on top of the other, constantly sways the suspended leg, whilst he arches and tilts his eyebrows, giving off traces of querulous impatience. He has physical courage. His contributions to literature are high-grade.

Amidst all the shining names that crowd the columns of our history, we have produced but few public men who had so much nobility of heart and brain as William E. Borah. His eyes are penetrating but not unkind; they are lights that flash far.

In making up this judgment I am guided by the debates that have come down in the Congressional Record and by the newspapers of '61 to '65. I have obtained much information from Mr. E. V. Murphy and Mr. T. F. Shuey who were official reporters in the Senate over fifty-five years ago, and are still official reporters of the Senate, in the harness daily. I am further fortified in these views by many conversations with Mr. C. N. Richards who is now and for more than fifty-four years has been "storekeeper" for the Senate. I have also obtained much information as to the '61 - '65 senators from John Hickman, colored, who is now and has been the manager of the Senate Barber Shop since 1865.

June 5, 1917. Arrived in Washington from the funeral of Senator Lane. I left here on May 25, with Senators Chamberlain,

King Kendrick, Thompson, Gronna, and Morris and ten representatives and we reached Portland, Oregon on May 29. Funeral of the dead senator was held on that day.

June 18, 1917. When the Great War broke out it was conventional in America to say: "They do not know why they are fighting." Our government felt no official obligation to protest the invasion of Belgium. Senator Lodge, who was in England when the war broke out, stated that we should be "not only neutral, but rigidly neutral."

Our Secretary of State, Mr. Lansing, lately sent a note to China. Japan is offended because the note to China was *not* sent through the Japanese Foreign Office.

June 21, 1917. W. J. B. is here and says that the war may make some military or naval hero, rather than himself, the Democratic nominee in 1920.

June 22, 1917. In presenting to the Senate, delegates, and commissioners from Belgium the Vice-President's speech, "Belgium will rise again," was long applauded.

July 3, 1917. The food bill, as it came to the Senate from the House, carries bone-dry prohibition. Senators doubt the wisdom of attempting in war times so radical a change in American habits.

July 10, 1917. Senator Chamberlain in charge of the food bill, yesterday presented motion signed by the required number of senators, moving that debate on food preservation bill be closed. This is first attempt to enforce cloture rule, adopted last March after the filibuster on the armed neutrality bill.

Many persons perceive in Washington a vantage ground for promoting their fortune, fame, or fanaticisms. All hotels, apartment houses, and flats are filled with lobbyists "seeking something." Contractors are looking for contracts. Steel, iron, copper, wool, oil, cotton, leather, sugar, and lumber have lynx-eyed friends swarming in the hotel lobbies. Army and Navy officers who have been for years on the retired list are "pulling" to be placed on the "active" list. Prohibitionists, suffragettes, long-haired men, short-haired women, fake-doctors, shysters, fortune-tellers, crystal-gazers, and palm-readers, are here by the thousands, trying to have their pet hobby galvanized into law.

July 16, 1917. On Friday the thirteenth instant, whilst walking along G Street, the iron frame of an awning weighing one hundred pounds fell twenty feet and struck me. I was taken to my office by Attorney Frank J. Hogan, but could not work owing to pain, so returned to my apartments in the automobile of the Sergeant-at-Arms.

July 19, 1917. Hundreds of persons are here seeking offices and privileges. I introduced the Arizonians to department heads, bureau chiefs, et al, but it is impossible to secure for them a tithe of the favors, perquisites, appointments, promotions, transfers, grants, bounties and tickets they desire. I have crippled my usefulness, by acting as a "state" senator instead of United States senator.

July 26, 1917. Russia is now *hors de combat* and may aid the Teutonic Allies. Mr. Kerensky is attempting to get Russia into the fight again for the Entente Allies. Congress realizes that England is starving, that France is bleeding to death and that *we* must defeat Germany, if she is to be defeated.

Statesmen should know that in war Americans demand blue-fire, hip-hip-hoorays, sky rockets, color, drama, and pomp and that the leader or the cause that does not furnish these will fail. An error was made in refusing to let T. R. go to France. The people do not believe that this is *their* war. There is enthusiasm here in Washington and in the Atlantic seaboard cities there is some emotion, but it was foolish to assert that in the hinterland there is a "noble rage" supporting the war.

August 27, 1917. Read of the death of Mr. Eugene Semmes Ives of Arizona. In 1911 Eugene Semmes Ives, Brady O'Neill, Reese M. Ling, H. L. Pickett, A. F. Parsons, Marcus A. Smith, and myself were candidates for United States senator. All are now dead except Mark Smith and myself, and Mark feels that he is gliding toward the eternal gulf. The campaign of 1911 lasted months, and during that period we spoke five or six times per day.

Mr. Ives came from a distinguished family and was superbly educated. He was sometime a member of the New York State Senate and was twice president of the Arizona Senate.

His conversation was exquisite. His oratory whilst fervid was a pure and strong eloquence. He wasted no word and uttered no redundant phrase. He was subtle and ingenious; his learning was vast, his industry prodigious. He was loyal to his friends and fearless toward his enemies.

Of more than medium height, his bearing indicated self-confidence; whilst his charm of manner, his dignity of posture, the graceful curves of his nostrils, and his eyebrows were alluring. Had he been elected as United States senator, he would immediately have taken, not only high, but the highest place in the Senate.

August 28, 1917. Governor Stewart of Montana told me of labor troubles there. I knew Mr. Stewart in Arizona, in 1893. I was then a turnkey in the County Jail under Sheriff "Sandy" Donahue, and Mr. Stewart was employed in the Harvey Hotel at Williams.

August 30, 1917. Disasters tread upon each others heels. Russia has collapsed. Von Hindenburg, German Commander, says he can take Petrograd at discretion but sees no military advantage in doing so as he prefers to use his force in taking Odessa and the surrounding grain country.

September 11, 1917. A large cage-like wooden structure has been suspended from the balcony in the rotunda of the Capitol, and in it Mr. Charles Dyer Whipple, an artist, is working on a proposed continuation of the Brumidi-Costaggini frieze which now ends abruptly with the group representing the discovery of gold in California. It has been a mooted question for the past forty years as to what should be placed into the vacant space in the frieze. Mr. Whipple says he will fill the vacant space with the following episodes, viz., the invention of the locomotive and the application of steam to transportation; the development of the modern battleship and aeroplane, whilst the grand episode is to be the opening of the Panama Canal.

September 13, 1917. Maine has rejected Woman Suffrage but I predict that Women Suffrage will finally obtain. Most people do not realize the source of their discontent; some therefore plunge into excitable work, travel, or espouse a cause. Give a suffragette an ideal husband and she will cease to be a suffragette, is not literally true, but the statement illustrates the fact that the contented person ceases to be a reformer. The happy person is not heard from. The smug and comfortable are satisfied with things as they are.

September 17, 1917. Memorial addresses were delivered in the Senate yesterday in honor of the memory of Senator Lane, deceased.

Senators Norris, LaFollette, Vardaman, and Gronna were speakers and are now accused of resorting to a memorial exercise as the medium of a reply to the criticisms they encountered when they filibustered against the armed neutrality bill. Well, what of it? The Memorial address is frequently resorted to when men desire to speak where they may not be replied to.

September 18, 1917. Wife and I are reconditioning the house we are purchasing at 1602 K. Street.

September 29, 1917. Washington is now a boom city; it is rushing, shouting, building and hurrying. Owners of lots are letting contracts here for the construction of more hotels and theatres, although wages and the price of material have "sky-rocketed" within the past thirty days. In the olden days of the West, we had "boom towns," such as Virginia City, Gold Hill, Placerville, Carson City, Leadville, Tonapah, Goldfield, Brodie, Rawhide, Tombstone, Cripple Creek, Dawson et al, but Washington is our first "boom city."

October 6, 1917. Senator LaFollette spoke two hours in his own defense. He quoted from Webster, Clay, Sumner, Corwin, and from a speech by Lincoln in the House of Representatives to support his contention that citizens may criticise the conduct of the war. Senators Kellogg, Robinson, and Fall replied to LaFollette.

It would be idle to say that this war appeals to the citizen. This is partly because the scene of action is far away and may not be visualized; then again, Roosevelt, who rouses the "Ta Ra Ra Boom De Ay" spirit, has been kept in the background; moreover, there has developed as yet no naval nor military hero, and I "know my United States" too well to fail to observe that during a war Americans expect sensation, music, banners, shouting, etc. A war without the trappings, the caparisoned steeds, the orators, the bugles, bulletins, extras, goodbyes, were like the play of Hamlet with the Prince of Denmark left out. To date nothing has happened that appeals to sensation-loving people; hence, to many persons the war seems a "failure."

October 14, 1917. John J. Pershing has been made a Lieutenant General, so that he may sit with those of like rank.

Many men now in obscurity may answer a call to fame before the war closes. Destiny casts for no favorite when she throws the dice. Every great activity of peace or of war discloses men who lost popularity through some trick of fate, some caprice of change, some error of judgment, or some unavoidable disaster.

November 29, 1917. My wife and I have returned to Washington. We left here October 21 and on my way to the West I spoke at St. Louis, Kansas City, Denver, Salt Lake City, and San Francisco. On November 7 with Congressional Party, I reached Honolulu. A small boat met our party and informed us that Mr. John Purroy Mitchell, mayor of New York City, had been defeated for re-election and that New York State had voted for Woman Suffrage.

Reaching our hotel, the Moana, at Waikiki, we learned of the illness of Liliuokalani (Mrs. John O. Dominis) last Queen of the Islands. Before sunup, November 11, my bellboy informed me of Liliuokalani's death. I attired myself in conventional black and drove to Washington Place, the Queen's residence, to extend the sympathy and condolences of the Congressional party, which had the evening before sailed for another island. On Monday evening, November 12, the body of the Queen was removed from Washington Place to Kawaiahao Church amidst the wailings and weird lamentations that arose from the native Hawaiians who lined the streets. Pomp and native splendor were exhibited and tributes of respect were paid to the memory of the dead ruler who during a troubled career was queenly in bearing, in training, and in education. At midnight, I went to the church where the body lay in state. About the bier were the Kahili bearers, who constantly waved the Kahilis — a long plumed staff of state, the insignia of Hawaiian royalty. Her hands were bejeweled and upon her head was the crown with some diamonds four carats in weight. The crown had lain for years in a safety deposit vault pledged for debt. Releases, bonds, stipulations, and lawyers were required to bring the crown once more to the head of royalty. The body was covered with an ivory-hued brocaded silk garment and rested upon a pall of yellow plush. The tabu-stick was there, but the royal feather-cloak of ancient Hawaii did not drape the body as the authorities of the Bishop Museum could not, under the law, permit its removal from its steel case in the museum. The ancient rites for royal dead continued throughout the night and following day.

With the death of Liliuokalani, the last ruling monarch of Hawaii passed. The old Hawaii of halcyon days and romantic memory was gone — the Queen was dead — there was no successor.

December 3, 1917. Congress convened. Senator LaFollette announced the death of his colleague, Senator Paul G. Husting, who last October, whilst duck hunting in Wisconsin, was accidentally shot.

December 7, 1917. Senate passed resolution declaring war against the Austro-Hungarian Empire. With the exception of Senator Lodge's arraignment of the Turkish Empire, the proceedings were prosaic. The vote was unanimous. The House soon passed the resolution, and it was signed before nightfall.

December 11, 1917. A prominent Mexican, close friend of President Carranza, told me today that Carranza is in desperate need of money and wishes fifty million dollars gold. I am arranging conferences and will propose that the United States buy Baja — Lower California. I have elaborate maps and data respecting the same. The acquisition of the peninsula ought to be within the domain of diplomatic resources of our present-day statesmen.

January 8, 1918. President Wilson addressed Congress in joint session and his proposed "peace terms" reveal that, in his opinion, concessions must be made by Germany, which would, if Germany accedes thereto, shatter her dream of *Mittel Europa.* These terms demand that Germany and her allies shall relinquish 210,000 square miles of conquered territory inhabited by forty millions of people.

W. W.'s speeches do not appear to be addressed to his countrymen as directly as they are to Central Powers. The able George Creel, Chairman of the Committee on Public Information, has advised Wilson to declare America's anti-imperialistic attitude. These declarations are to be sent into Germany via Holland and Russia to strike vitally at enemy morale.

January 21, 1918. The President today denounced as *untrue* a statement in Senator Chamberlain's speech in New York City on last Saturday wherein the Senator said: *"Our military organization has fallen down completely and has stopped functioning."* W. W. goes on to say that Secretary of War Baker is one of the most efficient men in America.

January 22, 1918. Called upon W. W. and found him in a fighting mood. His jaw was set. His eyes shot fire. He is angry at Senator Chamberlain. He told me that when he entered the White House, in March 1913, he had a high opinion of General Leonard Wood and retained Wood as Chief of Staff but that he no longer had confidence in him.

I told Wilson that T. R. was embittered against him (Wilson) to the point of desperation and that he ought to send T. R. to France. He replied that although he was constantly importuned to send T. R. abroad, he would not do so.

January 25, 1918. Senator Chamberlain, in the Senate, in a lawyer-like speech replied to W. W.

Yesterday at the Press Club, Colonel Theodore Roosevelt (T.R.) came in. This was the first time I ever saw him. He was introduced by the president of the club and in his speech he hammered W. W. and the War Department. I sat within ten feet of him during his one hour's speech. He snapped out words rather than pronounced them.

February 1, 1918. John Lawrence Sullivan, the pugilist, died today. He was the hardest hitter, the most savage fighter of all the "champions." A few days ago he sent me his photograph.

February 6, 1918. Washington is a bewildering farrago; it is filled with men of disordered dreams and wild fancies; men with theories of war and economy; reformers of public and private morals; leaders of "uplift" movements; speculators; embryonic philosophers; versifiers, paragraphers, cranks, crystal-gazers, inventors, grafters, thieves, liars, stock-jugglers, profiteers, unfinanced financiers, opaque editors, briefless lawyers, and decapitalized capitalists, and most of these persons put in their time searching for hotel accommodations and trying to induce somebody to listen to them.

February 8, 1918. Senator Thomas, Colorado, speaks at length, as usual. He says that Wilson is being "bushwhacked."

February 9, 1918. The Bolsheviki in Russia are now rulers and have possession of those places and things which make a de facto government. I had tea today with a Russian named Romanoff who told me that no government, save the Bolsheviki, could be set up in any part of Russia.

February 11, 1918. The President today delivered another "address" to the Senate; he stated that the pre-peace period had been reached and indicated elasticity of his terms heretofore stated.

February 12, 1918. Demobilization of all the Russian armies has been ordered. Announcement was received from Brest-Litovak that Russia has declared the war to be at an end, so far as Russia is concerned. The Russian premier or foreign minister, Leon Trotsky (a few years ago a reporter on a New York newspaper, at a salary of twenty dollars per week) has announced that further discussions will be held with Germany and Austria, looking toward the establishment of business relations with Russia's late antagonists. Russia has signed a treaty of amity and peace with the Ukrainian Republic, a new state which agrees to furnish foodstuffs and manufactures to Germany and Austria which latter governments have ceded to the new Ukrainian Republic a strip of Russian Poland behind the Teutonic lines, about 125 miles long and from thirty to sixty miles wide.

February 13, 1918. Senator Ollie M. James of Kentucky, ruggedly eloquent, spoke two hours in the Senate today in the old time "sledge hammer" fashion. His giant arms swung as flails as he mauled Senator Chamberlain.

February 25, 1918. I am at last learning to say "NO," the one word which, if I had learned to say twenty years ago, might have made me an opulent and probably useful man. My failures, defects, and collapses have come because I could not or would not say "NO."

February 26, 1918. Russia has accepted Germany's peace terms. Russia by these terms gives to Germany 381,000 square miles of land and 50 million persons. The U. S. special missions to Russia are now annulled; credits and aid, military and financial, are now stopped. The depots of American supplies at Archangel and Vladivostock are now under the control of the British and Japanese vessels.

March 20, 1918. T. R. who has been ill for past month has resumed his articles for the papers and says that we are making a mistake by "coddling" Russia.

March 22, 1918. All senators went to the Ellipse to see a French aviator who did spirals, twists, and somersaults. The Lamp of Aladdin and the Purse of Fortunatus are prosaic today, and the wildest hyperbole of twenty years ago is commonplace now.

March 30, 1918. President Wilson cabled congratulations to General Ferdinand Foch, who is to be the Generalissimo and is to command the Allied and the American forces; and the President also cabled General Pershing to report to General Foch.

April 10, 1918. On a streetcar Senator Stone of Missouri was stricken with paralysis, and at the time I saw him lying on a couch in Senator Cummins' office, whither he was carried, he was unconscious.

April 14, 1918. Senator William Joel Stone of Missouri, aged seventy, died today. On the tenth instant, I saw him lying on a couch in the Senate Office Building and never expected to see him alive again. He wore an overcoat, rusted and faded, which probably cost twenty dollars. He had been in the public service over thirty-five years, and died a poor man. With many opportunities to acquire wealth, he disdained opulence and was economical in habits of life.

April 17, 1918. Following letter from W. W.:

16 April 1918.

My dear Senator:

That was a brilliant, and, so far as it concerned me, an exceedingly generous speech which you delivered in the Senate the other day and I cannot deny myself the pleasure of sending you this line of admiration and sincere personal appreciation.

Cordially and sincerely yours,

Woodrow Wilson.

April 28, 1918. Senator Chamberlain, Chairman, Senate Military Affairs Committee, introduced a bill which provided that persons charged with violating espionage laws shall be tried by a military tribunal. Such law is not necessary; all courts are open and are functioning. The President "killed" the bill with one denunciatory blast. Here the President stood forth as the champion of liberty under the law.

April 26, 1918. My stepson, John Renoe, is going into the army as a private, and my secretary, Mr. Maurice McKelligan, whom I brought here in March 1912, resigns and Mr. Maurice H. Lanman succeeds him.

Speaker Champ Clark announced that he would not accept the Senate seat tendered him by the governor of Missouri to succeed the late Senator Stone.

May 18, 1918. Anti-administration senators demanded an investigation into the collapse of our aircraft program. The President has named ex-Justice Charles Evans Hughes to probe this collapse and Mr. Hughes' appointment is a guarantee that the probe will be thorough.

May 27, 1918. The President sent a message urging that Congress remain in session and enact revenue laws so that expense of the war may not fall entirely upon purchasers of government bonds.

June 5, 1918. News today of the death of former Vice-President Charles Warren Fairbanks. The traditions of the Senate hold him in high esteem. In the winter of 1906, I was in Washington protesting against joining of Arizona and New Mexico as one state. I was here again in the winter of 1908, and on both occasions he gave me a seat in the Vice-President's gallery. How he could have obtained the nickname of the "human icicle" I do not know. I have spoken with him at banquets, have ridden with him, and found him to be genial. Probably his six feet eight inches in height, his trellis-like whiskers and his long cylindrical Prince Albert coat, which covered stomach and stern with equal impartiality, gave him an appearance of austerity.

June 11, 1918. Secret understandings amongst rulers in Europe have led to wars, but there are questions of national policy which must be discussed in "executive" session. To do otherwise would mean that our country could not take counsel of itself. Senator Borah is leading the fight to eliminate all secret sessions of the Senate. In debate he is magnetic and plausible. He does not follow a pattern of correctness, and is scornful of conventionalities in a debate as was James G. Blaine and as is W. J. B.

June 13, 1918. I am to speak in Wilmington, Delaware, tomorrow, and whilst turning over in my mind some points for my speech I realized that romance has faded from war. When World War broke out and General Von Kluck's legions crossed the Belgic Border, the Belgians walked the via dolorosa that led to duty, death, and glory, yet few individual strokes were exhibited.

"La Belle France," with a bravery beyond the range of eulogy, was the next to meet the impact of the German; General Foch sent his message: "My right is crushed; my left is broken; but I shall attack with my center." Yet there were but few flashes of personal valor.

The British Navy melted into the mists of the North Sea; lighthouses were darkened which, along the English, Irish, and Scottish coasts for decades, had pierced the dark with fingers of light and had guided storm-tossed ships to harbor.

There was an assembling of food, guns, machinery, money, ships, and millions of men, but glamorous war was gone. The tank, a solid iron rhinoceros with hellfire in its horn, chugged along with a heavy scorn of danger, but the tank lacked the romance of the crusader on the palfrey! Opportunity for personal exploits seemed meagre, until there dashed forth what Lloyd George called the "Cavalry of the Clouds," and aviators rode to dizzying altitudes with eye that never winked and wing that never tired. The highway of the eagle became the highway of warriors of the sky, entering a tournament as did the knights of bygone days who tilted with Ivanhoe. The nervous and temperamental airplane became the epic of the war.

June 14, 1918. Spoke at Wilmington, then returned to Washington where news was received of victory of the Allies, in which American soldiers fought valorously.

July 3, 1918. Senator Benjamin Ryan Tillman (Cyclops) of South Carolina died today. President T. R.'s detectives pried into Tillman's mail and produced documents indicating that Tillman considered acquiring a tract of government land in Oregon. Although he was not guilty, the hubbub that followed almost broke Tillman's heart, and he fell unconscious on the Capitol steps and could not walk for a year. When he could hobble about, he began a regimen of diet, sleep, and exercise, so that when I came to the Senate in 1912, he could walk a mile.

In March 1913, Tillman urged me to take up the fight he began in 1896 for a government factory for making armor plate and ordnance. I agreed to attempt the task the old gladiator had begun. Tillman was a stormy speaker; he would quote the classics, and his black basilisk would flash fire the while his lips would let out oaths and imprecations, yet, amidst it all, was much fustian.

July 8, 1918. Spent several hours interviewing James W. Jones, a negro, now carried on the Senate Rolls as a messenger. Jones is ninety years old; was the servant and coachman of Jefferson Davis, President of the Confederate States and was present when Mr. Davis was captured by Union troopers in 1865. The old negro Jones, whose mind is clear, denounces the tradition that his master, Mr. Davis (whose personal courage was never questioned) was resorting to a disguise. Jones with circumstantiality of detail told me that Mr. Davis was sitting in a tent with Mrs. Davis when the Union troopers drew near; that the morning was cold and rainy. that Mr. Davis started out of the tent wearing a raglan, and as he went out of the tent, Mrs. Davis threw a shawl with a wide red border over him. Jones says that the shawl fell over Mr. Davis' hat as well as his shoulders and bent down the brim of his hat so as to present him in the appearance of wearing a bonnet. Nonagenarian Jones denounces what he calls "the liars that circulated the stories that Mr. Davis would dress up like a woman." Jones went on to say: "Mr. Davis was a gentleman, Sir. A brave man, Sir."

War Department officials today showed me the raglan and shawl Mr. Davis wore on that morning and although it was over fifty-three years since Jones last saw them, his description of the garments was correct.

There is a legend that the Great Seal of the Confederacy had been intrusted to Jones' keeping and that when the Confederacy was going the way of all earthly things — to dust — Jones was instructed to hide the seal where mortal eyes could view it no more. Jones says that he was *not* charged with hiding any seal but that there were two Great Seals, one of which Jones says was made in England and was brought home by William L. Yancey, that *"it would not work and was of no value."* Jones says that he was ordered to destroy one of the parts thereof, which he says he did.

July 19, 1918. Washington is gay over the news of the successful drive the Americans and French made yesterday against the Germans. T. R. at the New York Republican State Convention charged "inefficiency" in the War Department, but the cables telling of the success that within the past twenty-four hours has come to American arms, answered T. R.'s speech.

September 13, 1918. Friends called at our residence in evening. We were about to sit down to refreshments when a lady announced that there were thirteen of us at the table and that this was Friday, the thirteenth. Dismay came to the countenances of six of the party and I could not induce two of the guests (a Washington lady and gentleman from Chicago) to sit at the table, so terrified were they of this cabalistic number. Neither science, experience, nor philosophy will take away from some persons their delusions or their cherished superstition. I wish I were superstitious; it would act as a balance, a restraint and guide, or a guard rather. I regret that I am not a believer in omens, dreams, portents, etc. In my first senatorial campaign I wore a black opal, and friends besought me to leave it off, saying that "Victory could not come to anyone wearing an opal." I clung to my opal. I might not have worn a diamond, as it looked too flashy for a "tribune of the people." By the same token a "tribune of the people" should be neither fat nor funny. He should never appear to be comfortable.

September 24, 1918. M. Jules J. Jusserand, the Ambassador of France, on behalf of the French Republic, presented to the Senate two large vases from the National Manufacture of Sèvres. The Ambassador in his speech, paraphrasing Pascal, said: "Justice without force is powerless, and force without justice is tyranny, and therefore the French Commission last year to the United States headed by M. Viviani and Marshal Joffre represented Justice and Force."

Senator Mark Smith, an authentic scholar, declared that Vice-President Marshall's speech of acceptance was one of the great speeches of the Senate.

September 27, 1918. War Department advises that my nephew, Albert Pitts of Arizona, was killed in action on August 29, last.

A caller from Arizona today waxed hot because I could not quickly tell him how he could borrow "one million dollars" from the government.

Received telegram advising that Mother's sister (my aunt Lydia Boland) had died yesterday at Red Bluff, California.

October 7, 1918. President Wilson received a dispatch from Prince Maximilian, the new German chancellor, requesting the President to restore peace.

October 11, 1918. Deaths from influenza here now claim five persons per hour. Nurses and physicians are working without sleep or refreshment, trying to control the epidemic. All theatres, schools, and churches are closed and public meetings of every sort are prohibited.

October 12, 1918. Germany sent a reply to President Wilson's inquiries. This "note" or reply did not use the word "Imperial" in referring to the German government as had heretofore been used. This "note" associated Austria-Hungary, but not Turkey, with the German government, which gave the inference that Turkey was no longer Germany's ally, as Germany has always heretofore mentioned her allies in the dispatches.

Displeasure was obvious in officialdom against the President for corresponding with Germany.

October 14, 1918. When the Senate convened, the galleries were empty (no visitors allowed because of influenza); the sun shone but the day was cold.

Senators charged that President Wilson had softened toward Germany and that (by opening correspondence with the German government) he was resuming "note writing." Senators were mystified as the President had not taken any of them into his confidence. Many feared that the President's "altruism" would lead him to a reply to Germany that would lack directness. We knew that an ambiguous reply would chill the ardor of the people and depress the Liberty Loan. The strain was enormous; the rumors were that the President's mind was not made up so I resolved upon my own course; I called an automobile and went to the Executive offices of the White House where the President's secretary, Mr. Tumulty, read me a three-page letter he had just sent to W. W. urging that a firm reply be sent to the German note. Tumulty's letter was eloquent and embraced a coherent plan for future peace. I then dispatched a note to W. W. saying that I was in the Executive offices and desired an interview with him. He received me graciously; we exchanged salutations; whereupon the following dialogue took place:

Sen. HFA. "Mr. President, you might as well know in advance that I am going to say plain and unpleasant things. The time for plain talk is here."

Pres. Wilson. "Why! my dear fellow, sit down and tell me what is the matter."

Sen. HFA. "Mr. President, the Senate, the press, and the people are nervous, they expect and desire that you demand an 'unconditional surrender' of the German armies. Please give assurances that your reply to the German note will be one that will meet America's expectations? If your reply should fail to come up to the American spirit, you are destroyed. It is now widely feared, indeed charged in the Senate, that by your 'notes' to the German government you are signing away with the pen much of the advantage that our valorous soldiers won with the sword."

Pres. Wilson. "So far as my being destroyed is concerned, I am willing if I can serve the country to go into a cellar and read poetry the remainder of my life. I am thinking now only of putting the U.S. into a position of strength and justice. I am now playing for one-hundred years hence; I laid down my terms to Germany in my Fourteen Points speech to Congress on January eighth last, and in my Fourth of July speech and my speech of September 27. When Germany fully meets our terms we are through. Can it be that the people do not remember my Fourteen Points and my speeches of July Fourth and September 27?"

Sen. HFA. "No, Mr. President, they do not remember the details of those speeches."

Pres. Wilson. "Well, I remember."

Sen. HFA. "Mr. President, it is feared everywhere that an armistice would permit Germany to gain some advantage by diplomacy that she could not obtain militarily."

Pres. Wilson. "I am not making armistices; they must be left to the Commanders in the field."

Sen. HFA. "Do you intend to demand that Alsace and Lorraine shall be restored to France?"

Pres. Wilson. "Read my speech of January 8th, 1918, wherein I said: 'the wrong done to France by Prussia in the year 1871 in the matters of Alsace and Lorraine must be righted.' Now what was that wrong? It was the taking of Alsace-Lorraine."

Sen. HFA. "The Allies should demand of Germany a ship for every ship sunk by the German submarine."

Pres. Wilson. "Such matters can be left safely to the Peace Treaty."

Sen. HFA. "Mr. President, you should as a symbol, require the German Commander actually to deliver his sword to General Foch, Haig, or Pershing in Berlin."

Pres. Wilson. "Why?"

Sen. HFA. "Because symbols, next to habit, most powerfully influence human beings."

He then asked me to speak in the Senate and say that the country need have no fear as to what he would do. I started to leave, and told him I was "somewhat" cheered. He said, "Why are you only 'somewhat' cheered?" and I told him that his failure to demand unconditional surrender would give him leisure in which to read poetry, and that he would read it in a cellar to escape the cyclone of the people's wrath, and then I walked out.

October 22, 1918. Last evening the President received another note from Germany. The note seemed an attempt to soften the blows that our soldiers are delivering to the enemy upon the battlefield. The note was condemned in the diplomatic and official circles because of its apparent attempt to deny responsibility for the outrages in Belgium and the sinking of the "Lusitania."

October 25, 1918. Today the President addressed a letter to "his fellow countrymen" urging the election of a Democratic Congress. He stated in substance that were the Democratic Congress repudiated, it would be misunderstood across the water and that our enemies and friends as well would misconstrue it as a repudiation of war.

November 1, 1918. Roosevelt and Taft (the only living ex-Presidents) yesterday issued a joint statement opposing President Wilson's election letter. This is the first time that ex-Presidents have thus attacked an occupant of the White House. The Republican leaders demand an unconditional surrender of German armies; they dislike Wilson's replies to the German notes; they dislike Secretary of War Baker; they want a bipartisan Cabinet; they resent the implications in Wilson's letter asking for the return of a Democratic Congress, and they want Wilson to send T. R. and General Leonard Wood to France.

Meanwhile, President Wilson is by cable advising Colonel House, his personal emissary at Versailles, as to the position Colonel House should take on the various proposals advanced at the coming conference.

November 3, 1918. Strange it is, that one so fameless as Colonel House should play a leading part in the peace conference in Europe which will dispose of thrones and crowns, estates, titles, and dynasties, as boys arrange their marbles for a game of "keeps." There sits in Washington in gloomy neglect a man whose disappointment is as deep as plummet can sound into human emotions — William Jennings Bryan.

Bryan believes that his many years of crusading installed Wilson into the White House and that his (Bryan's) leadership for disarmament and peace, his oratory and his foreign travels should have seated him at the peace conference.

When Bryan was Secretary of State he telephoned me to send him some quotations on "Opportunity," whereupon I dictated to him over the telepehone the lines of Senator John J. Ingalls' sonnet, "Opportunity," but Bryan said it was too pessimistic for his speeches. I then dictated to him the lines of Walter Malone's poem on "Opportunity" which he much approved.

Had Bryan as Secretary of State recognized and improved his opportunity by diligently studying treaties, consular reports, laws and traditions, and *then kept silent,* signing his name when and where his chief bade him, he would have been the War Premier and would have sat at this peace conference.

Bryan has the orator's artistry, eloquence, poetry, and animal passion but the orator is evanescent. The spontaneity, repartee, rhetoric, and flashing eye, and the physical beauty soon evaporate. Bryan's fame will be as that of Patrick Henry, Fisher Ames, James Otis, Sergeant S. Prentiss, Webster, Clay, Wendell Phillips, Ingersoll, Roscoe Conkling, James G. Blaine, and Joseph W. Bailey.

November 4, 1918. The indigation of Wilson's critics mounts high anent his sending Colonel House as envoy to Versailles; these critics declare that Colonel House is inadequate to meet such a responsibility.

Who is this Colonel House who enjoys the confidence of the President, Whence did he come, what has he accomplished and whither is he headed?

During the years 1914, 1915, and 1916, Colonel House went to European capitals to bring back first-hand information for the President. In September 1917, the President appointed him to assemble data needed at the peace conference.

November 5, 1918. Churches, schools, and theatres are opened after being shut for past thirty days. Diplomatic circles here are again active and there is joy over the surrender of Austria. Coming out of the theatre, I procured an "extra" announcing Republican victory at the elections today.

November 6, 1918. Morning papers announce that Democrats have lost both Senate and House. I went to the Senate, and the few Democrats assembled there were cheerless. Each dispatch brought tidings of political disaster. Americans desired from Germany an "unconditional surrender" and whilst expecting to be thrilled by a demand for such surrender, they were called to analyze, rather, a diplomatic maneuver. Two opinions sprang up: One that Wilson had blundered and the other that he had not, therefore he faced the elections with a sharp division of sentiment as to his leadership.

November 11, 1918. Senate Sergeant-at-Arms 'phoned me the President would address the two Houses in joint session this day.

The Senators led by the Vice-President went to the House. At one P.M. President Wilson appeared and shook hands with Vice-President Marshall and with Speaker Clark. The galleries were filled and many celebrities occupied seats. The faces of Lansing, Secretary of State, McAdoo of Treasury, Baker of War, and Daniels of Navy, beamed, whilst Lane, Secretary of Interior, sat an unreadable sphinx. The Chief Justice of the United States accompanied by the Associate Judges sat in a semicircle around the rostrum where the President stood. Hon. Charles Evans Hughes, former Governor of New York, former Associate Justice of the Supreme Court and lately Republican nominee for President, led the applause. Senator LaFollette who usually remains quiet joined in the applause. This dauntless little giant from Wisconsin, this man of keen intellect and phenomenal industry, has borne with much fortitude the insults and the lampoons which his attitude toward the war brought him.

The President used but few words by way of preface, and at once read the terms of the Armistice, signed by Germany; he had read but a few sentences, when out rolled the statement that Alsace-Lorraine must be evacuated. The pent-up emotions of his auditors whose nerves were at high tension, then broke loose. Tumultuous shouts seemed to rive the stained-glass roof; the portraits of Washington and LaFayette to the right and left respectively of the President, seemed to smile benignantly.

The President read the message (which took thirty minutes) without rhetorical effort, dramatic pose, or note of triumph. "The war thus comes to an end," was the only sentence he emphasized.

After the joint session, my wife and I entertained the Ambassador of France and Madame Jusserand at lunch at the Senate Restaurant, and the brilliant diplomat wept from joy.

November 18, 1918. The President today issued the Thanksgiving Proclamation in part as follows. "God has in his good pleasure given us peace. It must not come as a mere cessation of arms, a relief from the strain and tragedy of war. It has come as a great triumph of Right."

November 19, 1918. The signing of the armistice terminates the World War — a war which in some way touched every individual in every civilized nation. Millions of men have died from battle-wounds or disease; cities have been destroyed, and provinces plundered. Emperors were slain or deposed. Great dynasties (Hapsburg, Hohenzollern, and Romanoff) woven through centuries into Europe's history, were extirpated. Hideous injuries have been sustained and inflicted by millions of men. Oceans have engulfed unnumbered others. Men have perished in snowdrifts and starved in storms. War taxes have crushed and for decades to come will continue to crush industry. In millions of homes, women will wait in vain for men who will never return. The free nations had to choose between being overridden or becoming soldiers.

V   November, 1918 – December, 1919

...the splendid fervor and the noble rage
of America's participation in the War
have burned out.

November 23, 1918. Congress adjourned last Thursday. Senators Sherman, Illinois, and Watson, Indiana, denounced W. W. for his proposed plan of addressing the peace conference at Versailles, and Senator Reed, Missouri, said the League of Nations "was a spider's web into which the American fly is invited."

Secretary of the Treasury McAdoo has resigned. The presidential nomination was for a time within Mr. McAdoo's orbit, but now he perceives in the recent elections the return of the Republican party.

The nation opposes the President's proposed trip abroad. W. W.'s friends know that in cool locution and that in reaching elevated heights of moral leadership, he is matchless, but they believe that when the peace conferees gather at Versailles, he will be required to match wits with shrewd traders.

W. W.'s friends know that, whilst he could hold his own in discussing the philosophy of human freedom, he has neither shrewdness in "bargaining," nor the intuition telepathically to read other men's thoughts. Many persons assert that he will be an interloper at the peace conference; that his domination of Congress for the past six years has given him a taste of power, and that he is now anxious to extend it to wider fields.

His friends argue that there is much land to distribute, many obligations to discharge, that some of the Allies are not free from selfish designs; hence, Wilson should go to see that the results of the peace conference shall be reached by justice.

November 26, 1918. Last night the Ambassador of France and Madame Jusserand held a reception at the French Embassy

[89]

to celebrate the entrance of the French and American troops into Alsace-Lorraine. The Embassy was aglow with lights and Old Glory mingled with the tri-colors amidst pine branches representing the pines of Alsace. The President and Mrs. Wilson were present; Chief Justice White was there. Secretaries Lansing, Baker, Daniels, Lane, Houston, and Redfield of the Cabinet were there. The diplomatic folk were in full regalia. No members of the House present. Senator and Mrs. Saulsbury, Senator Lodge, Senator and Mrs. Pomerene, Senator and Mrs. McCumber, Senator Thomas, Colorado, Senator and Mrs. Hitchcock, Nebraska, and I and wife were present.

November 27, 1918. Ex-Presidents Roosevelt and Taft today have articles in the newspapers opposing the President's trip to Europe.

There is talk that when W. W. reaches foreign soil a resolution will be passed in Congress declaring the Presidency vacant by reason of the President's inability to perform his duties.

November 29, 1918. Lawyers assert that whilst the Constitution does not specifically prohibit the President from going to foreign countries, unwritten law does. The parents of Mrs. Vice-President Marshall reside at Scottsdale, Arizona, and it was the intention of the Vice-President and Mrs. Marshall to leave for Arizona tomorrow, but W. W. called upon the Vice-President at his hotel last night and urged him to remain in Washington. This indicates that W. W. is looking toward having his successor in Washington should misfortune happen.

November 30, 1918. W. W. today announced that he will head the delegation at the peace conference. The other members of the delegation are Secretary of State Robert Lansing, Colonel E. M. House, Hon. Henry White, former Ambassador to Italy, and General Tasker H. Bliss.

December 1, 1918. Two months ago W. W. was the foremost character in the world. He had reached a high pinnacle of human distinction. Today I doubt if he has twenty friends in Congress.

By a series of moves (amongst which were his failure to demand of Germany an "unconditional surrender," his many notes to the German government, his election letter to the public last October, his refusal to appoint any senator to attend the peace conference, his appointment of himself as a delegate) he has aroused the country to flaming anger. He will address the two houses of Congress in joint session tomorrow. Some senators declare they will question from the floor.

December 2, 1918. Vast crowds assembled in the corridors attempting to secure admission to hear W. W. address the joint session. The disgruntled senators trooped over to the House. When the President appeared the applause was meagre; his message was long, and surely he must have felt the chilliness of his reception. Two or three times his friends attempted to incubate an ovation for him, but it was impossible. Talk of questioning him from the floor of the House evaporated when he appeared.

December 3, 1918. I called upon W. W. After greetings the following conversation occurred:

Pres. Wilson. "What are those . . . on the hill doing today?"

Sen. HFA. "Mr. President, the House of Representatives would impeach you and the Senate convict you if they had the courage. Their lack of nerve is all that saves your removal from office; Congress opposes your going to Europe."

Pres. Wilson (with percussion on each word). "Congress has a brain-storm but as soon as I am on the high seas they will recover."

The mercury of the President's manners fell and I detected in him such frigidity and symptoms of uncivility that in ordinary circumstances I would have delayed asking him to reverse the action of one of his Cabinet ministers, but I refused to be taken aback and presented my item for his attention.

December 10, 1918. Another precedent was set today by the Wilson regime in that Vice-President Marshall presided informally over the Cabinet meeting.

December 13, 1918. President Wilson landed in France and for the first time an American President is in Europe.

January 7, 1919. Spoke in support of my resolution to purchase Lower California. Spoke in part, as follows: "The peninsula of Lower California is nearly 800 miles long, its greatest width is about 150 miles. It is the vermiform appendix to Mexico. It is the Achilles heel to the United States."

January 8, 1919. Congressional party of forty senators and one hundred representatives attended funeral of Theodore Roosevelt at Oyster Bay. Captain Archie Roosevelt, his face pale, his frame shrunken, was one of the ushers in the church.

Chancel of the church was banked with flowers. Above the entrance to the church was the American Flag. Bishop Talmage read the beautiful Episcopal funeral service and at the Lord's Prayer, the congregation joined. At the graveside in Young's Memorial Cemetery, ex-President Taft stood apart near the tufts of grass visible amid the snow, and tears ran down his cheeks.

In his lifetime Colonel Roosevelt, like all public characters, was charged with inconsistency. His ambition was to advance the firmness and efficiency of our nation. He played a majestic part and never played the part of idler or slacker.

February 15, 1919. Papers filled with accounts of the constitution of the League of Nations as reported at the peace conference in Versailles.

February 21, 1919. Senator Borah attacked the proposed entry of the United States into the League of Nations as an abandonment of our traditional foreign policy and a step toward internationalization.

February 22, 1919. Senator Reed attacked American entry into the League of Nations. Senate galleries filled, and hundreds clamored for seats. He concluded with a brilliant peroration.

February 24, 1919. President Wilson landed in Boston and spoke in defense of the League of Nations.

March 4, 1919. Last evening a "round robin" was presented by Senator Lodge, signed by thirty-seven senators and senators-elect, announcing their opposition to the Versailles Treaty.

Wife and I in New York City this evening. At Metropolitan Opera House we heard President Wilson and ex-President Taft speak in support of the League Covenant. Governor Smith presided.

March 11, 1919. Landed at Port-au-Prince, capital of Haiti. This island on its western end comprises the Republic of Haiti where the natives speak French; the eastern end of the island comprises the Dominican Republic where the natives speak Spanish. Haiti's great statesman, soldier and martyr-patriot was Toussaint L'Ouverture whose life and elevated character were the subject of Wendell Phillips' famous rhapsody.

Los Angeles, California, May 6, 1919. Spent yesterday conferring with Colonel Emelio Kosterlitzky who was born in Poland. Colonel Kosterlitzky was, for about thirty years, commander of the Mexican Rurales (Mexican mounted police) and during that time his energy and personal courage aided in sustaining President Porfirio Diaz. The Colonel said that General Carranza "is a failure" and that a group of men will soon bring General Obregón forward as a candidate for the presidency of Mexico, upon a platform of law and order. The Colonel went on to say that the peninsula of Lower California was a "white elephant" to Mexico.

Flagstaff, Arizona, May 10, 1919. My nephew, Harvey Pitts, and I motored to the "Old Ashurst Ranch" whither I had not been for twenty-six years. The log cabin in which I was taught to read and write was a ruin. The fences, corrals, dairy-house, and chickenhouse had vanished. In the cabin was the same fireplace before which the family had huddled in winter and on whose hearth of large, flat stones, my brother Thomas and my brother Andrew were born and on which my sister Margaret had died.

The spring was bubbling from the cliff as of yore, but its waters did not seem so cool as in the long ago when my mother kept butter and milk, in crocks, in its clear stream. I trod the few acres where once my parents grew garden vegetables. The same huge malpais boulders were sitting as grimly by the trails in the canyon as in the days when they formed our skyline from the cabin door. There were the crevices where my father hid our supplies when the Indians came on the warpath. I entered the cave wherein my mother concealed her children as the savages passed by on the day when even hope seemed to have fled. The old cookstove was standing in the cabin. This stove, purchased in San Francisco, came by sea-going vessel around the peninsula of Lower California to the mouth of the Colorado River, thence up the Colorado River by small steamer to Ehrenberg, thence in *1878,* it was freighted to Prescott by bull team and finally to our ranch by my father's team of horses. The stove cost $105, the transportation charges, by steamers and bull team, aggregated $100 additional, and it then required three months for a consignment of goods to reach the interior of Arizona from San Francisco. Before we got the stove, all meals were cooked with primitive utensils by my mother, at a campfire or at a firepelace. My mother made many garments for the household, she cured the meats, worked in the garden, made candles, soap, and rag rugs, straw hats, and moccasins, and nursed wounded men and sick children.

The taciturnity of the pioneer derives from the solitude of the forest and the desert. When the pioneer looked at the sky, it was not to figure out the fantastic things that formed and floated above him in the transient architecture of the clouds, but to prognosticate rain or shine. When the pioneer looked at the moon, it was not so much to contemplate its beauty, as to foretell whether it would be a "wet" moon or a "dry" moon. When the pioneer examined the ground, it was to find the tracks of his missing pack animals or to stalk game wherewith to eat. When the pioneer's eye swept the horizon of the desert or the prairie, it was to descry whither and why the wild life had fled and to guard against the Indians who snaked through the grass or desert sands to kill.

My father was a frontiersman, an explorer, hunter, and mineralogist — always hoping for a new El Dorado. He was skillful in circumventing the dangers incident to border life. He approached the magician in fertility of devices. During his prosperous days in the early 1880's, it was his habit to bury his surplus money, and when payments were to be made for cattle or sheep delivered to his ranch, he would walk to a nearby willow patch or rockpile and unearth the gold required for the payment.

Thus there grew up around him a legend or myth, which he seemed to encourage, that there was much gold buried at his ranch. When his financial independence took wings through the double misfortune of his lending money without security and a deadly decline in the price of cattle, the myth of his buried gold survived.

When his death was announced, although it was midwinter and two feet of snow lay on the ground, many unauthorized and unrecorded individuals went from Flagstaff to his ranch, twenty-five miles distant, to dig for buried treasure. Whether or not any money was unearthed, I do not know, but this ranch was soon pitted with potholes and excavations, evidencing how stubbornly was fixed the myth that "On Old Man Asher's Ranch Gold Was Burried." [sic]

May 19, 1919. The Sixty-Sixth Congress convened in extra session. Representative Gillette of Massachusetts (Republican) was chosen Speaker of the House. *This* Senate has forty-nine Republicans and forty-seven Democrats. Some of the insurgent Republicans disrelished Senators Penrose, Pennsylvania, and Warren, Wyoming, for important committee chairmanships, but the insurgents had to swallow this pill or permit the Democrats to organize the Senate.

If even *one* insurgent voted with the Democrats a tie would result, viz. 48-48; the Democratic Vice-President, Marshall, would have the "casting" vote and would thus have given control of the Senate to the Democrats. Therefore, last December the Republican leaders began courting Senator LaFollette who was then under charges because of some speech he made in Minnesota in September 1917, and on the sixteenth of last January, the LaFollette "case" was laid before the Senate; a rollcall was had, and LaFollette was "cleared." I voted to "acquit" him as he was not guilty of any wrong in delivering the speech which formed the basis of the accusation against him.

Amongst the new senators today was the handsome ex-Governor David I. Walsh of Massachusetts. Other notables were Medill McCormick of Illinois, ex-Governor Arthur Capper of Kansas and Pat Harrison of Mississippi.

May 20, 1919. The President's Message to Congress, cabled from Paris, recommended returning the railroads to their owners and contained a hint of a protective tariff for some American "infant industries."

May 23, 1919. Senator Lodge, the Republican Leader, is trying to heal the old breach between Republican "stand patters" and the Republican "progressives," both of which factions dislike Wilson's foreign policies.

May 28, 1919. I spoke on the Rush-Bagot — Great Lakes — Treaty of 1817 of the Monroe administration as an example of international neighborliness and practical method of "armament reduction." This treaty has saved hundreds of millions of dollars to the people of the two countries (Canada and the United States) and has probably saved many human lives.

May 29, 1919. President Wilson still in Europe. I do not perceive how he can obtain ratification of his League Treaty when there are forty-nine Republicans in the Senate and forty-eight of them, or all but Senator McCumber of North Dakota, are opposed to the League whilst Senators Reed and Gore, Democrats, will also vote against it.

June 20, 1919. Senator Sherman, Illinois, spoke three hours denouncing the Covenant of the League. In reply I said in part, as follows:

We are now required to assist in the liquidation of the war. In taking part in the war we gave reasons so noble that we made a high place for America, and we are now in that posture which confronts many a man where he must either lower the tone of his preaching or live a nobler life.

The practical question which confronts us is, shall the allied powers . . . patch up a mere temporary armed truce, or shall international justice and moral courage be employed to prevent unnecessary wars?

Is the world to drop back into its former attitude of *laissez faire* and let matters drift haphazardly along? Must those nations that wish to live orderly, useful, and noble lives be forever imperiled and harassed by a sword of Damocles suspended over them?

New York, July 4, 1919. The Tammany Hall reception committee escorted Senator Pat Harrison and me from our quarters at Hotel Savoy to the Wigwam of the Society of Tammany or Columbian Order where Senator Harrison and I delivered the "Long Speeches" and Governor Alfred E. Smith read the Declaration of Independence. Eight hundred Tammany Braves present. Grand Sachem John R. Vooris, ninety years old, clear-eyed, lithe as an archer, presided. Present also was Tammany's chief, the silent Charles F. Murphy, a reservoir of mental and physical strength.

Washington, July 9, 1919. President Wilson reached here last evening. Some journals of high repute and many men of character believe that Wilson has cast America into the European mill where she may be ground to pulp. It was useless to attempt to describe the maledictions now heaped upon him in the Senate, in the press, and in the pulpit. Wilson's adherents assert that his achievements at the peace conference transcend those of any other statesman of whom history speaks; his opponents declare that he has cast America into the European maelstrom.

President Wilson announced that he will address the Senate tomorrow in defense of "The Covenant for a League of Nations."

When Wilson sailed for France he knew but little of how men "double on their tracks;" but he saw that the world was in flux and likely to precipitate almost anything. It may be when some future Ironquill writes of affairs critical now amongst the nations but which affairs we cannot at this time interpret, that W. W's achievements at Versailles will shine luminously.

Collier's has an editorial this week entitled "The Magician" in which the foremost living American orators are discussed. *Collier's* says not one may be compared to W. W. The editorial says *inter alia* that W. W. "has the 'bel canto' but always in perfect control," that "he is as certain of his cadences as a good singer and apparently as indifferent to them," that "he is always at ease and that he beguiles the intellect and soothes the senses of his hearers," that "to say his power of statement is marvelous is to give him the faintest praise."

July 10, 1919. Of the forty-seven Democrats in the Senate, at least thirty-seven are supporting the League of Nations and believe that the League will aid in sterilizing the seeds of future wars.

Wilson's opponents say the American people gave him no commission to go to Versailles but that he himself hit upon the

League of Nations plan and carried it into effect without a mandate from the people, that he nonchalantly took the jewel of American isolation to Europe, and that his impudence was so colossal as to be overpowering, especially when his act is glossed over by the sentimentality of "trying to prevent another world war."

July 11, 1919. When Abraham Lincoln delivered his oration at Gettysburg in 1863 (which oration nobody discovered to be "immortal" until Lincoln had been dead some years) he turned to his friend, Mr. Ward H. Lamon, and said, "Lamon, that speech won't scour." Scour was then a folklore word analogous to our slang "make good." President Wilson's speech to the Senate yesterday may in the long future be highly regarded, but it did not "scour" today. Everyone in the Senate was on tiptoe of expectation. The President's opponents as well as his supporters expected a masterpiece. Here was the President just home from Europe where he had met and had matched wits with cunning men. Here were the League supporters hungry for arguments in support of the League, whilst supporter and opponent alike, expected explanations of obscure portions of the Covenant; for example: Why was Shantung Peninsula awarded to Japan when it is the Chinese Holy Land? What about the safeguarding of the Monroe Doctrine? What does Article Ten mean? Why are Poland and Czechoslavakia set up as independent states and Ireland's seven-hundred years of struggle for independence unrecognized? How may the U.S. withdraw from the League? What mandatories do we assume? These and many other vital questions were ignored.

I was petrified with surprise. The League opponents were in state of felicity; they winked, thrust tongue against cheek, and whispered that Wilson had failed to "make good." Wilson's speech was as if the head of a great corporation, after committing his company to enormous undertakings, when called upon to render a statement as to the meanings and extent of the obligations he had incurred, should arise before the board of directors and tonefully read Longfellow's "Psalm of Life." Wilson was called upon to render an accounting of the most momentous cause ever entrusted to an individual. His audience wanted raw meat, he fed them cold turnips. Completing his speech, the President laid the bulky Versailles Treaty upon the Vice-President's rostrum and walked from the Senate Chamber oblivious of the failure of his address.

There was a contraction of the back of his neck and a transparency of his ears, infallible indicia of a man whose vitality is gone.

The moral elevation of his address may not be doubted, and he may have had a wise purpose in refusing to furnish a popular speech.

The portion of the press supporting the League Covenant avers that he acted wisely in leaving details to be explained to the Senate Committee on Foreign Relations. A copy of the Treaty of Peace with Germany, ordered printed yesterday, was today as "Document No. 49" placed upon each Senator's desk.

July 15, 1919. The President and Mrs. Wilson attended a reception at the French Embassy last night, given by the French Ambassador and Mme. Jusserand in honor of Bastille Day (The French "Fourth of July"). This is the second time that W. W. and his lady have thus honored Ambassador and Mme. Jusserand, the other occasion being last November, to celebrate the entrance of French troops into Alsace-Lorraine. The guests assembled in the reception rooms of the Embassy and were welcomed by the exquisite Jusserand and his wife. Daniels, Burleson, Lane, and Redfield of the Cabinet were there; Burleson wore white clothes in contrast to the dress suits and flashing military and naval uniforms. In the dining room a buffet dinner was served. Soon W. W. came in escorting Mme. Jusserand and the Ambassador escorting Mrs. Wilson.

Mr. Jusserand, in speaking, recalled how gloomy the outlook was one year ago and how changed now. W. W. responded but observed the proprieties by not making a better speech than did his host. Representatives of the foreign powers which declared war upon Germany were present. Senator Lodge left before W. W. came in. The other Senators were Overman, Pomerene and Lady, Warren and Lady, Newberry and Lady, Ashurst and Lady. Speaker Gillette and Representative Flood, Nicholas Longworth and John J. Rogers were present.

July 17, 1919. W. W., perceiving that by his refusal to take Senators into his confidence ratification of the Versailles Treaty is imperiled, is now asking senators to come singly, to come by twos and by threes, and he personally urges them to support the Treaty. W. W. has at last taken steps — belated steps — toward mollifying the Senate.

Considering the possibilities of the World War for bringing characters to the front it would seem that few figures of immortal exploits have appeared. General Pershing is one American whose fame the War enhanced.

In England, David Lloyd George is now the outstanding figure. Sir John Jellicoe, Kitchener, Northcliffe, and Haig will be remembered. The fame of General Jan C. Smuts of South Africa has been enhanced.

In France, Clemenceau, Foch, and Joffre will live. The Balkans give Venizelos to history.

Albert, King of the Belgians, has added a dignity to kingly power. Cardinal Mercier goes into history as a hero.

Irresolute Nicholas Romanoff will be forgotten. Kerensky speeches were evanescent. Russia presents Trotsky and Lenin.

August 8, 1919. There is a nervous collapse amongst millions of persons. For five years past, civilization has lived upon its nerves; now comes depression; the world is a maddened, runaway orb.

Many men once of sound mind now have obsessions; arteries so long engorged with blood have lost their power to contract at night, and sleep is impossible. Another phenomenon is that wild "shopping" such as buying diamonds, silks, furs, automobiles, bric-a-brac, and bijouterie at prices four- or five-hundred per cent higher than the normal price.

August 11, 1919. While Senator Mark Smith, Representative Hayden, Judge O'Connor, and Mayor Feidler of Nogales and I were "cooling our heels" in Secretary Baker's ante-chamber (where we were detained two hours), Mark Smith fumed and fretted at being required to wait, but I found interest in the sparkling ex-Governor Richard Yates, representative-at-large from

Illinois, whose father was in the Senate at the time of the impeachment trial of President Andrew Johnson. Mr. Yates told me that his father looked upon "Andy" Johnson to be a traitor, not only to party but to country; that thirty-five senators who voted for President Johnson's conviction were moved by a fierce fanaticism and believed Johnson was frittering away the victory won by Union arms. He adverted to the widespread belief that W. W. is now losing the advantages won by American soldiers. Thus history repeats itself; nations or people "en masse" learn but little, if anything, from the past.

August 12, 1919. Senate galleries filled to hear Senator Lodge oppose the Versailles Treaty, but Senate recessed two hours to see the parade of the marines.

When Senate reassembled, Senator Lodge read a scholarly essay opposing the treaty. His reading occupied one and one-half hours and whilst he was in good voice, he was not impassioned, but when he sat down, the galleries broke into tumultuous applause in which the marines joined by pounding their tin hats on the gallery seats. The Vice-President's rebuke to the galleries was feeble. When order was resumed, Senator John Sharp Williams began an arraignment of Senator Lodge, and when he accused Lodge of "making a show of himself," the galleries broke into a storm of hisses and cat calls which angered Williams and caused him to refer to Lodge in harsher terms, whereupon the galleries hissed again. The Treaty opponents frequently choke with rage (simulated or real I know not) when they attempt to discuss it.

August 20, 1919. W. W. had the Foreign Relations Committee to luncheon yesterday, and all but Senator Fall were present. After luncheon the interrogatories were resumed. President Wilson might have saved his Treaty had he taken with him to Versailles men of tested statesmanship. The people, the press, and the Senate distrust Colonel House's capacity. An injustice is done to Colonel House in placing a low estimate upon his attainments, but he is too secretive, furtive, cloistered, and mysterious to win favor with the Senate or the country. It is by some asserted in extenuation that Colonel House is President Wilson's "Man Behind the Throne," just as Mark Hanna was reputed to

be President McKinley's "Man Behind the Throne," but Mr.
Hanna was known in the business and political world; he daily
met scores of his fellow-citizens; he was a senator, he addressed
audiences, he dined and traded with people, and he lived a flesh
and blood existence. He avowed his purposes and the people
knew what Mr. Hanna desired. Colonel House is a man of
mystery, and such men do not earn the confidence of a Republic
be they ever so deep philosophers and unselfish friends of truth.

August 23, 1919. The Committee on Foreign Relations today
struck from the Versailles Treaty the provision transferring
Shantung Peninsula to Japan, which peninsula was promised to
Japan by England and France to obtain Japanese aid when
England and France were hard-pressed by the Teutonic powers
early in the World War.

Opulent with ironies as are all human affairs, I recall no
impishness more perverse than the circumstance that a powerful
influence now injecting lethal potions into the Treaty is furnished by Point Number 3 of W. W.'s Fourteen Points, viz.,
"The removal, so far as possible, of all economic barriers and
the establishment of an equality of trade conditions among all
the nations consenting to the peace and associating themselves
for its maintenance." Many persons fear that this "point" may
be an approach to free trade among the League members and
fear that Article 231 of the Treaty, laying the entire war-guilt
upon Germany and her allies, will be a source of resentment in
the days that are to come.

August 25, 1919. The Department of Justice is making efforts
to reduce the cost of living by *prosecutions.* The real remedy,
to wit, "rigid economy," is within reach of all persons, but
Americans do not like such a remedy. Many persons who complain of "low" salaries are expensively clothed, have choice seats
in theatres and are whizzing along the road in high power automobiles scattering the farmer's poultry.

August 26, 1919. Senator McCumber, Eagle of the Dakotas,
Republican of Foreign Relations Committee, denounced the
Committee for adding to the Versailles Treaty an amendment
proposing to transfer to China certain leasehold rights now held
by Japan in Shantung and Kiochow Bay. Senator McCumber

asserted that such action was a "poisoned blade" thrust out by Senators Lodge, Borah, Brandegee, Fall, Johnson of California, Moses, New, Harding, and Knox.

August 27, 1919. Reuben's observation to Cynthia: "That everyone is crazy but thee and me, and at times thee is a little queer," is now apt. Sanity is a relative thing. During the past five years the pressure has been more than the normal human being could withstand, hence an abnormal mind akin to madness pervades. Everybody is uneasy; the philosopher is rare. Pessimists are multiplying; the optimist is looked upon as a cheerful idiot. The poor are crushed by the high prices they must pay for sustenance, and the wealthy are frantic as they perceive their increments and income depleted by taxes and other demands. The nerves of the world are frayed.

The world may now be compared to a rudderless ship without sail or steam, drifting upon an unknown sea, and sent by vagrant winds toward a whirlpool that must soon overwhelm every life on board. Yet the comparison is not apt, for the persons on board that helpless ship would settle down to a calmness and would implore peace in a world to come (in which most persons believe when in danger) whilst our runaway orb is chattering, drinking, swearing, feasting, racing, and acting as one huge — I was about to write — asylum. More men are now walking in that wide penumbra between the shadow of insanity and the light of reason than future generations will believe could so walk at one and the same time. The present condition is the natural reaction to the Great War. The earth is peopled by "human" beings after all.

Soon after the Senate convened today, Senator Fall commenced a defense of the Committee on Foreign Relations in amending the Versailles Treaty. He had not proceeded far when Senator Knute Nelson, the Viking from Minnesota, resented Fall's suggestion that he (Nelson) was in his "second childhood." Senator Fall continued and soon ran afoul of Senator McCumber. There was much loud talk and clenching of fists.

August 29, 1919. Senator Knox (Secretary of State under Taft) urged that the Versailles Treaty be rejected. He said it is so severe as to be impossible of fulfillment by Germany.

August 30, 1919. Some eminent American citizens of Irish ancestry are now addressing the Senate Foreign Relations Committee in opposition to the Versailles Treaty. The refusal to set up an Irish State as was done at Versailles respecting Czechoslovakia and Poland insulted the pride of many Irish Americans whose skills in politics and whose eloquence are valuable to a political party.

These Irishmen, alas, are *lost* to the Democratic party at the coming elections. At 3:00 P.M. this day, the ten Republican members of the Senate Foreign Relations Committee are listening to the speeches of orators of Irish ancestry who are opposing the Treaty, whilst only one Democratic member of the committee is present, and the Republican members of the committee punctuate the proceedings, from time to time, by calling the roll of the committee to make manifest that the Democratic members are absent.

September 1, 1919. President Wilson soon leaves Washington for a "swing around the circle" speaking for the Treaty. The trip can do him no *harm* politically for he has reached the lowest ebb of popularity ever reached by a President, save when President Washington urged the ratification of the Jay Treaty with England, when President John Tyler quarreled with the Whigs, and when President Andrew Johnson announced that the Reconstruction was an executive, not a legislative, function.

September 4, 1919. Senator Lodge, chairman of Foreign Relations Committee, reported the Treaty to the Senate with four reservations, in substance as follows.

1. United States reserves the unconditional right to withdraw from the League.

2. United States is not bound by Article X and accepts no mandates except by joint resolution of Congress.

3. All internal affairs of the United States are removed from the League's consideration.

4. Monroe Doctrine is declared outside the League's jurisdiction.

All the Republican members of the committee voted for these reservations; even Senator McCumber, Republican, upon whom the champions of the Treaty relied, voted for the reservations. Senator Shields, Democrat of the committee, voted with the Republican members.

September 5, 1919. Mr. David Lawrence of W. W.'s entourage, says in today's *Washington Star* that Ohio, a state which clung to W. W. in the 1916 elections, has turned a deaf ear to him.

Some journals say that W. W. is egotistical; if such be true, it is well for him. An egotist never knows when he is snubbed or defeated.

September 11, 1919. In writing his report on the Versailles Treaty, Senator Lodge, chairman of the Foreign Relations Committee proves that he is master of speech. Lodgesque enough, the report contains some sarcasm for which its author is noted. I believe that he learned this "quirk" from Hon. John Hay.

September 12, 1919. Senator Hitchcock, Pennsylvania, on yesterday reported from the Senate Foreign Relations Committee the views of the minority on the Treaty. His report fully measures up to the high standard of literature set by Senator Lodge.

Opposition to the Treaty is increasing here and unless checked (how, I do not know) the heat of popular resentment will consume the Treaty, root and branch.

A President who essays a speaking trip is assured of audience, but W. W. has made no converts to the Treaty.

Eminent persons returning from Europe say that the U.S. is the only government attempting utilitarianism in good faith; hence, they say we shall sit into the international game with the "cards marked and stacked against us." The Treaty opponents argue that instead of freeing small nations, the Treaty is welding an iron ring around the small nations. Scores of speakers of the various political parties are crusading night and day against the Versailles Treaty. Senator Johnson of California and Senators Poindexter, Borah, and Reed are "hot on the trail" following President Wilson.

These speakers and other Treaty opponents assert that the Treaty confirms Japan's exploitation of the Chinese province of Shantung and has dictated a "settlement" in Thrace whereby Bulgaria (Germany's ally) is rewarded at the expense of Greece, a member of the alliance of democratic nations. These Treaty opponents declare that the Treaty transfers Fiume, with its Italian population, to alien rule in order to provide a seaport for Yugoslavia; that it assents to the plundering of China to gain Japan's adherence to the League of Nations; that it winks at the dismemberment of Hellenic territory to placate Bulgaria, and that China is wronged in the Shantung settlement, whilst the beneficiary is Japan.

September 17, 1919. The First Division of Regulars, led in person by General John J. Pershing, marched up Pennsylvania Avenue. At the head of the column was a stalwart fighting unit, viz., a composite regiment assembled from the infantry brigades of six divisions. At 1:00 P.M. the march started by swinging into line at the east front of the Capitol; at 1:25 P.M. General Pershing passed under the Arc de Triomphe and three minutes later he passed the White House reviewing stand where he saluted Vice-President Marshall representing W. W., who was in San Francisco pleading for his Treaty. In the White House reviewing stand with the Vice-President were General March, the Chief of Staff, Admiral Benson, the President's Cabinet, and representatives of various allied and associated powers.

September 18, 1919. Received following telegram:

San Francisco, Cal., September 18, 1919

Hon. Henry F. Ashurst
United States Senate
Washington, D.C.

I know I can count upon you and do not credit the report that you are not supporting the League in your usual whole-hearted and forward looking way.

Woodrow Wilson

To which I replied.

Washington, D.C., September 18, 1919

To the President of the United States
San Francisco, California

You have borne many trials and crosses in your noble contests to serve our country and to keep her in the paths of beneficent achievement, peace and righteousness and I should regret to add to your already heavy burdens, but it would be uncandid were I to fail to tell you that I am disturbed over some of the provisions of the League Covenant.

Cordially,

Ashurst

September 22, 1919. Senator Reed spoke four hours today. He inveighed eloquently against the Treaty, and his words were whips of scorpions. When he concluded the gallery occupants cheered until they were exhausted

September 24, 1919. Cardinal Mercier, of Belgium, reached Washington yesterday. The failure to subdue this man was the first defeat the Germans sustained in the War when he said to Von Bissing: "We render unto Caesar those things that are Caesar's, for we pay you the homage due to strength, but we keep closed to your encroachments the domain of conscience, the last refuge of the oppressed."

September 25, 1919. Today I telegraphed W. W. as follows:

Washington, D.C., September 25, 1919

To the President of the United States
Pueblo, Colorado

Although I have had, as you know, doubts and misgivings as to some parts of the League Covenant, I am nevertheless convinced that Germany would obtain a material advantage and would come out of the war practically a victor were the Treaty amended or were any reservations adopted.

To my mind, it is this Treaty or no treaty, and I for one am not willing to assume the frightful responsibility of precipitating chaos upon the world by some hazardous amendment or reservation. I have studied this tremendous question from every angle and am sure that at this juncture I can render my country, indeed the entire civilized world — a great service by voting for the Treaty without amendments or reservations.

Cordially,
Ashurst

I gave a copy of my telegram to Senator Hitchcock who in turn gave same to the press.

September 26, 1919. Received the following telegrams:

The Honorable Henry F. Ashurst
U.S. Senate
Washington, D.C.

May I not express my admiration of your statesmanship attitude toward the Treaty and sense of gratitude with which I have read your message?

Woodrow Wilson

To Senator Henry F. Ashurst
Washington, D.C.

Congratulations on message to President. History will praise your support of Treaty without reservations.

W. J. Bryan

At 1:00 this P.M. I was informed that President Wilson had abandoned his speaking trip by reason of illness. His strength is as a cornsilk, not as an iron band.

October 2, 1919. The Senate began voting upon the amendments of Senator Fall to the Treaty, which strike from the Treaty those parts granting the U.S. authority to participate in the various International Commissions set up by the Treaty. All amendments defeated.

Tonight the President is seriously ill; he arrived here last Sunday and walked from the train to his automobile.

October 3, 1919. Morning papers say that the President has taken a turn for the worse. Dr. F. X. Dercum, neurologist, of Philadelphia and Dr. Sterling Ruffin of this city are called into consultation.

W. W. had expected to preside at the first meeting of the League of Nations, but the certainty that the Treaty will not be ratified by the Senate, except with reservations tantamount to amendments, destroys his opportunity to preside at the League's first meeting.

W. W. correctly interpreted American sentiment when he declined the suggestion that the German ex-Kaiser be brought to the United States for trial. What court, what jury would have tried him? When Napoleon Bonaparte, after Waterloo, took refuge on board a British man-of-war, and sought to reside in England, there was a disposition on the part of the reigning House to lend ear to Bonaparte's request, whereupon Lord Liverpool wrote to Lord Castlereagh in part as follows: "You know enough of the feelings of the people of this country not to doubt that he (Bonaparte) would become an object of curiosity immediately and of compassion in a few months."

After the Allied victory at Waterloo, when the allies were at a loss to know what to do with Bonaparte, they suggested that he be tried in the United States.

The German ex-Kaiser now claims sanctuary in Holland and says that sanctuary is as old as the human race, and that pagans and savages, not to mention civilized man, have observed it.

Senator Ball of Delaware, a physician, told me that the strain upon W. W. during the past two years had broken his strength and that W. W. was seriously ill.

The federal Constitution, so far as it related to "inability" of the President, has never functioned, but there are two instances when there was an approach to action under the "inability" clause; the first was when President Garfield languished from July 2 to September 19, 1881, during which period he was unable to transact business; but Congress was not in session and the Supreme Court would not decide a moot question. A few days before President Garfield's death, the Cabinet had decided to ask Vice-President Arthur to act *ad interim*. The second instance was when President Wilson was in Europe, some attorneys contended that he was "unable" to attend to the duties of the office.

The Constitution is not clear as to when or how or by whom "inability" or "disability" is to be ascertained.

There is no authorization for a medical survey or physical examination. It would seem that the "inability" or "disability" should be so definitely known as to cause a court to take judicial notice thereof, before the Vice-President could be installed "ad interim."

October 16, 1919. Senate rejected the Shantung Amendments to the Peace Treaty; Ayes, thirty-five, Nays fifty-five; three Democrats voted with the Republicans and fourteen Republicans voted with the Democrats.

This roll call indicates that while no textual amendments will be adopted, drastic reservations will be embodied in the Resolution of Ratification.

October 21, 1919. At the Senate I was informed that Senator Hitchcock, Democrat leading the fight for Treaty ratification, had gone to the White House to inform Dr. Grayson, who in turn is to tell W. W. that the Treaty cannot be ratified without vital reservations. A good move, but it comes too late. Such information should have been conveyed to W. W. sixty days ago.

Leading Democratic senators counted noses today and found forty-nine Republicans and six Democrats for reservations whilst the Democrats have but forty-one votes to oppose the fifty-five, so the Democratic senators are now "framing reservations" but the Republicans will defeat every Democratic proposal. They will then vote for their own reservations and go to the elections pointing to the fact that the Republican senators "Americanized the Treaty."

October 27, 1919. Shouts of welcome are floating through my window from the cheering thousands assembled upon the Capitol grounds to greet the King and Queen of the Belgians, whose train has just reached Union Station. It was intended that their Majesties should be quartered at the White House, but the illness of the President made this impossible; hence they will occupy the home of Hon. Breckinridge Long, Assistant Secretary of State.

October 28, 1919. The King and Queen of the Belgians visited the Senate. The King towered some inches above the heads of the Senators who escorted him into the Chamber. President Pro Tempore Cummins introduced the King who read in English a graceful response. The King's son, Duke of Brabant, heir-apparent to the Belgic throne, sat to the right of his father, and his boyish face gave off a bored expression. Queen Elizabeth was seated in the President's gallery. She was gowned in white, wore a wine-colored cloak of velvet and her countenance was grave.

October 29, 1919. Vice-President and Mrs. Marshall entertained the King and Queen of the Belgians at a dinner-party last evening at the home of Mrs. Thomas F. Walsh, on Massachusetts Avenue. The company was strictly official such as would have been invited to the White House had President and Mrs. Wilson entertained their Majesties.

October 30, 1919. On Tuesday last I noted in this Diary that when the King of the Belgians was welcomed in the Senate, his son, the Duke of Brabant, appeared "bored," and apparently I was not mistaken. His Highness was asked today, "What do you think of our American girls?" Whereupon the handsome boy of seventeen years replied, "I have not met any."

Poor fellow, forced by royal etiquette to shake hands with senators, governors, and mayors; to be gallant to dowagers; to salute generals and converse with cabinet ministers, his lot is cruel, for while he may inherit a throne he is robbed of that most beautiful of kingdoms — the kingdom of youth.

November 1, 1919. Senator Fall asked Senator Hitchcock, Democratic Leader, to fix a time when all debate on the Versailles Treaty and on all amendments and reservations thereto, should cease and a final vote be had. Hitchcock requested that Fall's proposal be reduced to writing. The Pro-Leaguers are now in the situation where they may be deprived of opportunity to vote upon their own Resolution of Ratification. Each side is maneuvering to have a direct vote upon its *own* particular Resolution of Ratification. There is a rocky road ahead for the Pro-Leaguers as the Anti-Leaguers will adopt at least fourteen reservations; whereupon Senator Lodge, Republican Leader, will offer a Resolution of Ratification embracing these fourteen reservations which, from the Pro-League viewpoint, eviscerate the Treaty. The Resolution of Ratification to carry must receive a two-thirds vote, but at least thirty Democrats will vote against the Lodge Resolution of Ratification. It is Senator Hitchcock's plan, immediately upon the defeat of the Lodge Resolution of Ratification, to introduce another Resolution of Ratification with reservations of such character as will, so he hopes, secure the votes of the "mild reservationists," viz., Capper, Colt, Kellogg, Lenroot, McCumber, McNary, Nelson, and Sterling; whereupon a question will arise to be decided by the presiding officer, namely: After the Treaty has been defeated, as it will be by the failure of the Lodge Resolution of Ratification to secure a two-thirds vote, may another and different Resolution of Ratification be introduced or must a motion first be made to reconsider the Treaty?

November 5, 1919. Senator Lodge presented a request for unanimous consent to vote finally upon the Treaty within ten days, to which Senator Hitchcock objected; whereupon Senator Hitchcock presented a request for unanimous consent to limit all debate upon the Treaty and all amendments and reservations to fifteen minutes for each senator but fixing no hour for final vote. To this request Senator Lodge objected.

November 7, 1919. Convinced that it is not possible to "amend" the Treaty, the Senate today centered its attention upon the "reservations," fourteen in number, proposed by Senator Lodge and approved by the Foreign Relations Committee.

To the outsider it would appear that the so-called "Mild Reservationists," viz., Capper, Colt, Kellogg, Lenroot, McCumber, McNary, Nelson, and Sterling, caused the delay in reaching an agreement to adhere to the fourteen reservations; whereas in fact the difficulty in reaching any agreement was caused by the La Follette, Borah, Johnson of California, Brandegee, Poindexter,

Fall, Norris, Knox, France, Moses, Sherman, and McCormick, irreconcilable group, which group for a time refused to be reconciled to anything save a flat rejection of the Treaty. Therefore, with diligence, Senators Lodge, the Republican Leader, and Watson, the Republican Whip, finally induced the irreconcilable group to stand with the Lodge Reservationists.

Thus Lodge Reservation Number One was today adopted; Senator McCumber, Republican, voting No, and Reed, Gore, and Walsh of Masasachusetts, Democrats, voting Aye.

Pro-League Democratic senators caucused last night. I was amazed that some of the Democratic senators still believed that the Treaty might be ratified without reservation. The Republican factions in the Senate are united on this issue.

November 12, 1919. His Royal Highness, The Prince of Wales, arrived yesterday and was met at the Union Station by Vice-President Marshall and General Pershing.

November 13, 1919. Vice-President Marshall tendered a reception to the Prince of Wales last night at the Library of Congress. Diplomatic and official Washington in full regalia, and the Prince was the cynosure of all eyes.

The corridors of the Congressional Library with its incised brass inlays, red French marble and white Italian marble, yellow mosaics, stairway figures, mural decorations, and splashes of lights made a pageant transcending a king's dream.

His Royal Highness smilingly greeted each person. The Vice-President stood at the left of the Prince (Mrs. Marshall was absent from illness) and in the receiving line were Viscount Gray, Ambassador of Great Britain to the United States, and Secretary of State and Mrs. Lansing.

The Prince wore full dress and extended his left hand. The right hand was swollen as a result of handshaking at previous receptions.

In the Senate yesterday, Senator Lodge presented a motion signed by more than the required number of senators, that debate on the Treaty be closed; which motion was presented under the "cloture" rule adopted by the Senate at its special session in March 1917.

November 15, 1919. Many senators demanded to have their reservations and amendments to the Treaty read before the cloture vote would shut them off. The Vice-President read the cloture provision, being a part of Rule XXII, and then he began to read his opinion that should the Lodge Resolution of Ratification lack the necessary two-thirds vote, he, the Vice-President, would hold that other and further resolutions of ratification would be in order; Senator La Follette made the point of order that the Vice-President was out of order, inasmuch as the cloture must be decided without debate. The Vice-President overruled the point of order. La Follette appealed from the decision of the chair. Appeal was laid upon the table; whereupon the Vice-President finished reading his opinion.

Thus the so-called "cloture" rule began to function. Just as all new machinery has some rough edges that must be worn off, the cloture rule did not work at first without friction but within one hour the rule was working smoothly, and before adjournment, the Senate adopted several of the Lodge Reservations.

November 18, 1919. Senate sat twelve hours adopting more reservations. At adjournment the pending question was the Lodge Resolution of Ratitfication with the various reservations that have been stapled to it.

November 19, 1919. Breakfasted early and went direct to the Capitol, to attend the caucus called by Democratic Leader Hitchcock upon the Lodge Resolution of Ratification. The breeze from my motor car stirred the dead leaves strewn about, and I knew that President Wilson's Treaty would soon be as dead as those leaves.

Every Democratic senator who favored the Treaty was present at the caucus except Senator Culberson of Texas, who for months has been ill. Senator Underwood moved that the Democratic senators vote against the Lodge Resolution of Ratification. Democratic Leader Hitchcock then drew from his breast pocket and read the following letter from President Wilson:

The White House
Washington, 18 November 1919

My dear Senator:

You were good enough to bring me word that the Democratic Senators supporting the Treaty expected to hold a conference before the final vote on the Lodge Resolution of Ratification and that they would be glad to receive a word of counsel from me.

I should hesitate to offer it in any detail, but I assume that the Senators only desire my judgment upon the all-important question of the final vote on the resolution containing the many reservations by Senator Lodge. On that I can not hesitate, for in my opinion, the resolution in that form does not provide for ratification but, rather, for the nullification of the Treaty. I sincerely hope that the friends and supporters of the Treaty will vote against the Lodge Resolution of Ratification.

I understand that the door will probably then be open for a genuine resolution of ratification.

I trust that all true friends of the Treaty will refuse to support the Lodge Resolution.

Cordially and sincerely yours,
Woodrow Wilson

To Hon. G. M. Hitchcock
United States Senate

Examining the letter I perceived that it was not signed by President Wilson but that the words "Woodrow Wilson" were affixed thereto by a rubber stamp facsimile in purple ink.

At noon the Senate convened, and within ten minutes newspapers containing W. W.'s letter to the caucus were brought into the Senate Chamber. Senator Lodge read the letter into the *Congressional Record*. The Democratic Senators were astounded that the letter had been given publicity; it enraged the "Mild Reservationists" and two or three of them let off oaths in an undertone.

Roll call on the Lodge Resolution of Ratification. Result: Ayes, 39; Noes, 55; Absent, 1; Vacancy from Va., 1.

On this vote all the senators who attended today's Democratic caucus voted against the Lodge Resolution of Ratification. Senator Reed, Missouri, moved to reconsider the vote; his motion carried. The administration senators sought an adjournment but were defeated, whereupon the Vice-President held that the motion to reconsider which had just been carried, placed the Treaty before the Senate in a posture where it was subject to amendment, and where further reservations could be offered. Senator Lodge appealed from the decision and the chair was overruled; the Pro-Leaguers voting to sustain, and the Anti-Leaguers voting to overrule the chair, and within ten minutes the Chair was overruled two more times by the same "line-up." In vain the Pro-League senators attempted adjournment; in vain they proposed motions to recommit, and tried to effect compromises with the "Mild Reservationists," but the time for compromises had gone. The Pro-Leaguers had sinned away their day of grace by failing to compromise last August. After parliamentary maneuvering another vote was taken on the Lodge Resolution of Ratification and three Democrats, to wit, Myers, Owen, and Pomerene voted with the Lodge Reservationists, but all other Pro-League Democrats stood against the Lodge Resolution of Ratification. Senator Underwood then asked unanimous consent for a vote upon the ratification of the Treaty *as it came from the President's hands*. A roll call was had without debate and the naked Treaty without reservations received thirty-eight votes. Thus the Versailles Treaty which has been ratified by the principal allied and associated powers, mustered but thirty-eight votes in the Senate.

November 25, 1919. Received letter from William Jennings Bryan today as follows:

Hot Springs, Arkansas
November 23, 1919

My dear Senator:

As to the Treaty there must be a compromise. This question must be gotten out of the way. Our chances do not look bright next year for Democrats, but they will be worse if we try to ignore domestic questions and make the fight against the reservations — some of them good. The most objectionable thing is the preamble. I hope that can be changed so that *acquiescence* will be sufficient without formal acceptance. But even the preamble is better than defeat to the treaty. If the nations refuse we will be in no worse position as a nation and in better position as a party, because rejection of reservations would justify our fight against them and they might accept — I think they would. But the treaty must be ratified. See Senator McCumber.

Yours,
Bryan

December 2, 1919. Assistant Secretary of the Senate, Mr. Rose, had not read four sentences from the President's annual message when I became convinced that W. W. wrote it, for there were the Wilsonian elegancies with which he constructed his sentences.

December 5, 1919. Senate Committee on Foreign Relations directed two of its members to "consult" the President anent Mexico, but really to determine the truth or falsity of the rumor that President 'Wilson is "incapable" of performing the duties of his office. Senator Fall, Republican, and Senator Hitchcock, Democrat, were designated by the Committee to perform this "duty;" they telephoned the White House that Monday the eighth instant, would be agreeable to them but the White House replied that 2:30 P.M. *this day* would be satisfactory. Thus this afternoon there proceeded to the White House a Senate sub-committee, upon a mission not paralleled in our national history, viz., a sub-committee to inquire into the "disability" of the Chief Executive.

The "committee" found the President sitting in a wheeled chair; he shook hands with his right hand. In discussing Mexico, W. W. recalled Mr. Dooley's joke that "Mexico was contagious to us."

The "committee" remained with the President forty-five minutes and both senators returned to Senate declaring the President fully capable of transacting the public business.

December 8, 1919. The Republican National Committee will meet here on the tenth instant, and the Democratic National Committee meets here within a fortnight.

The League of Nations may be good for the U.S.; it may be bad. That question is arguable, but that it is fatal to the Democratic party in the coming elections is *not* debatable.

Mr. Frank H. Simonds, overseas writer, is here and says that America has retreated; that one year ago America was altruistic; that one year ago the United States was a cornucopia; a nurse binding up the wounds of bruised men; an almoner feeding starving peoples, but that a reaction has come in the U.S. where, as Simonds says, materialism now has full sway, and "Let America stay within her own walls" is now the keynote. The splendid fervor and the noble rage of America's participation in the War have burned out. A reaction has set in and every person in Washington (except W. W.) is aware of it.

New York, December 28, 1919. Whilst walking up Fifth Avenue, I was seized with a painful cramp in my left foot and limping along, I heard a voice sing out: "What's the matter, Senator?" Looking about I descried Mr. J. G. Darden, an old-time Arizonian. I here record the circumstance of meeting him *solely* because he is the only man I know who believes that the Democrats will elect their presidential nominee in 1920.

VI

January, 1920–February, 1921

*…Wilson's cabinet was
an incongruous mosaic.*

January 1, 1920. In the energies of the year just closed, we made no progress toward liquidating the World War.

The League Covenant failed in a popular sense as truly as it failed in a parliamentary sense in the Senate. The cabalistic phrase "League of Nations" was suspected — feared. One of the defects of the Versailles Treaty is that it carves up nations contrary to "self-determination;" the allied and associated powers have grasped too many colonies, and some nations have been denied admission into the League.

Freedom from the menace of future wars argued for a League; religion and idealism approved a League. The raw materials existed for a moral and materialistic appeal for a League of Nations, but the materials were only tolerably employed. The stage was set, an expectant audience waited for actors who never appeared, the disappointed audience clamored around the box-office for a time and then went away.

"A crime wave," the backwash of war, is sweeping the land.

The attitude of many persons toward life is now cynical. Motor cars, amusements, rich foods, luxuries, ease, and comfort are sought by many citizens who say that religious teachings are remote and too austere for people seeking "success" and pleasure.

Orators, editors, and statesmen during the Great War promised that victory would bring a freer and easier life and that persons crushed by poverty would be released into repose and plenty. Such promises cannot be fulfilled, and the disillusionment has promoted communism and syndicalism.

[119]

January 4, 1920. For the past week, upward of twenty senators have been drafting compromises on the Versailles Treaty.

At the Jackson Day Banquet to be held here on January 8, it is expected that W. W. will send a letter anent the coming campaign and that W. J. Bryan will speak. Like the genii out of the fishermen's urn has come a popular demand for W. J. B. I do not laugh as I write this entry, as I have a split lip. Bryan has features of strength not possessed by any other politician. For W. J. B. could, at the 1920 presidential election, secure the Drys and he is esteemed by clergymen, teachers, and farmers; moreover, he is not offensive to the Irishmen whose eloquence and whose genius for command contribute much to Democratic victories, but the nation is sick and tired of reformers.

January 5, 1920. Those who come to Washington usually try to take something *out* of the government, whilst very few persons come here to try to *put something into* the government.

Senator Lodge told me it is impossible to ratify the Versailles Treaty unless the Lodge Reservations are adopted.

January 7, 1920. 'Phoned Dr. Grayson at the White House; told him to caution the President *against* sending to the Jackson Day Banquet a demand for the ratification of the Versailles Treaty *without reservation;* and that if the President sent such letter to the banqueters it would drive the wedge still further between the factions in the Senate. Doctor Grayson replied: "The President is *not* going to send such a letter to the banqueters."

January 8, 1920. If the interest shown in the Jackson Day Banquet to be held tonight be symptomatic of the coming campaign, it will have no dull moments, as the banqueters now number two thousand, and two hotels (the New Willard and the Washington) are scarcely commodious enough to entertain them. The speakers will "orate" at both hotels, that is, as soon as they finish a speech at one banquet hall they will proceed to the other hotel and repeat.

W. J. B. came to town early yesterday morning, bubbling and healthy.

At 4:00 P.M. Dr. Grayson 'phoned me that W. W. requested *him* to assure *me* that I "need have no misgivings" as W. W. would *not* in his letter to be read to the banqueters tonight, demand that the Peace Treaty be ratified *without* reservation.

January 9, 1920. Set out in a "box" on the front page of morning papers in heavy type is an extract from W. W.'s letter sent to the banqueters in which he says:

We cannot rewrite this Treaty. We must take it without changes which alter its meaning, or leave it.

If there is any doubt as to what the people of the country think on this vital matter, the clear and single way out is to submit it for determination at the next election to the voters of the nation, to give the next election the form of a great and solemn referendum, a referendum as to the part the United States is to play in completing the settlement of the war.

Thus W. W. makes the Versailles Treaty the issue in the campaign. This gives the campaign of 1920 an unusual feature, to wit, we know now in advance what will be the result.

January 11, 1920. It is now time to appraise the Jackson Day Banquet. The various Democrats seeking presidential nomination were present, either in person or by proxy. Vice-President Marshall was invited to speak but declined. Mr. McAdoo wired felicitations from Texas whither he had gone on business.

W. J. B. was the guest of distinction. What does W. J. B. mean to do? Is he seeking a fourth nomination? He was the guest who was suspected — feared and hated.

W. J. B. had the advantage of carrying no excess baggage, i.e., he was without the impediment of office (state or federal) and he could say what he pleased.

He was *the* speaker who was allocated; he presented a plan for treaty ratification that appealed to those senators who know the fatality of the Versailles Treaty as a campaign issue.

W. J. B. tauntingly stated his attitude on the issues and challenged the various candidates to proclaim their own views. He let fall no equivocal nor enigmatic sentence. He declared for government ownership of interstate railroads. He was not lionized at the banquet. He knew that he was looked upon as a suspicious character but his boldness, his eloquence, and his agility in digging himself from under an avalanche of ballots and smilingly reappearing, whilst his opponents are celebrating his political demise, caused him to be treated with simulated enthusiasm.

January 16, 1920. Representatives of Great Britain, France, Italy, Greece, Belgium, Spain, Japan, and Brazil, members of the Council on the League of Nations, met in the French foreign office today. Mr. Leon Bourgeois of France was elected president of the Council and Sir Eric Drummond of Great Britain was confirmed as secretary. Mr. Bourgeois said: "The task of presiding at this meeting and inaugurating this great international institution should have fallen to President Wilson."

January 23, 1920. The demand of the Allies upon Holland to deliver the former Kaiser to the Allies, for trial upon a charge of violating the sanctity of treaties, has been refused and the Dutch Minister at Paris states that Holland is not a party to the Versailles Treaty and that Holland will follow her long-established rule of refuge to ex-rulers who seek sanctuary.

February 2, 1920. Senator Lodge gave notice that on Monday the ninth instant, he would ask unanimous consent to reconsider the Versailles Treaty with reservation.

Mr. Carter Glass, appointed last November by the Governor of Virginia to succeed the late Senator Martin, left the Treasury portfolio and took oath as a senator today.

February 7, 1920. Democratic senators caucused. Senator Hitchcock read a letter from W. W. dated January 26, stating that he wanted the Treaty ratified without amendment or reservation, but that he would not object to "Interprétative Reservaions." Senator Carter Glass, Virginia, who left the Wilson Cabinet one week ago, announced that W. W. would refuse to exchange ratifications with the signatory powers, if the Lodge Reservations were adopted.

Senator Glass then went on to say that W. W. charged that Lord Gray while here had conspired with Senator Lodge; and that he, W. W. was going to make the Treaty the issue in the coming campaign. Senator Walsh of Montana inquired how W. W. would make the Treaty an issue. Senator Glass replied that the President possessed sufficient leadership to bring the question before the people.

Senator Pomerene spoke next and said he was disappointed at the attitude assumed by W. W.

Senator John Sharp Williams then lauded W. W.'s attitude and denounced the suggestion that we should enter the League upon different terms than the other signatories.

February 9, 1920. Senator Lodge asked unanimous consent to suspend the rules and consider the Versailles Treaty to which Senator Norris objected, whereupon Lodge moved to suspend the rules. Yeas were sixty-three and Nays were nine.

Lodge then moved to reconsider and Senator Norris made point of order upon ground that another reconsideration could not be had, as the subject was reconsidered on November 19 last. The Vice-President overruled point of order, Norris appealed and chair was sustained. Yeas were sixty-two and Nays were ten.

Thus the Versailles Treaty was brought from the Senate archives where it had slumbered since November 19, 1919, and was recommitted to the Committee on Foreign Relations.

February 21, 1920. The Versailles Treaty up. Lodge Reservation Number One was agreed to.

Eight Democrats, viz., Ashurst, Chamberlain, Fletcher, Gore, Henderson, Myers, Nugent, and Trammell voted *for* the Reservation.

February 27, 1920. President Wilson's threat to take no further part in European affairs, unless the Adriatic controversy shall be settled on the basis agreed to by the U.S., was made public today, and the diplomatic *notes* between our government and Great Britain and France on Adriatic affairs are published.

Diplomats here are aghast at some of the phrases W. W. employed in opposing Italian claims; for he goes on to assert that Italy's demands are "unjust," "inexpedient," and "importunate;" that Italy proposes a "forcible seizure of coveted territory," that her ambitions are "improper" and that the U.S. will take no part in assisting Italy to "maintain injustice."

Thus we have a taste of American participation in European political affairs.

The premiers of Great Britain and France respectively are now in a posture which would embarrass the most skilful diplomat, that is to say: when disaster darkened the banner of the Allies and repulse after repulse was their portion, they negotiated in April 1915, the secret treaty of London, wherein Italy was promised concessions on the Adriatic, if she would enter the war. Acting upon this promise, Italy entered the war.

Prior thereto, to wit, March 1915, the premiers of Britain and France negotiated a treaty with Russia granting Constantinople to Russia, and they also executed the secret treaty dividing the German islands of the Pacific between Japan and Great Britain. Thus when David Lloyd George took his seat at the Peace Conference at Versailles in January 1919, his breast-pockets were bulging with these secret treaties, but the *Washington Post* asserts that these treaties were not secret; that our Secretary of State (Robert Lansing) knew of their existence at least one year before Mr. Lloyd George presented them to the Peace Conference, and the *Post* asserts the failure of Secretary Lansing to call them to President Wilson's attention was a "stupendous blunder."

March 6, 1920. Received a letter from W. J. B. written at Miami, Florida, anent the Peace Treaty:

My dear Senator:

At least 49 Senators ought to be willing to agree to support ratification with such reservations as a majority will agree upon. If you could get 49 members to sign such an agreement, it would end the fight and get the treaty out of the way. As a Democrat, you know that it would be fatal to us to go into the campaign, and make a fight over the little differences that exist between the two sets of reservations. The reservations, readopted Saturday by more than two-thirds, is the saving clause in the whole thing. If we can withdraw in two years, that fact lessens the importance of any concession made because we can come out of the League if we find it dangerous to stay in.

Very truly yours,

W. J. Bryan

March 9, 1920. There was made public yesterday a letter to Senator Hitchcock from W. W. wherein he denounced reservations to the Treaty and "demanded" that Article Ten of the League Covenant be adopted as written at Versailles.

March 11, 1920. I arose in Senate and "let off" *inter alia,* the following: "As a friend of the President, I declare to the President: 'If you want to kill your own child because the Senate straightened out its crooked limbs, you must take the responsibility and accept the verdict of history'."

March 19, 1920. Senator Walsh of Montana urged the Democratic senators to vote for the Lodge Resolution of Ratification. Roll call on the Lodge Resolution of Ratification with the following result: for ratification, forty-nine, against ratifiction, thirty-five.

When the President Pro Tempore announced that the Lodge Resolution of Ratification had failed, Senator Lodge moved that President Wilson be so advised and that the Treaty be returned to him. Motion carried: yeas, forty-seven, nays, thirty-seven.

Thus some Democratic senators joined the "Irreconcilables" and for the second time rejected the Treaty.

The Republican leaders then searched for Mr. Sanderson, Secretary of the Senate, to send the Treaty to the White House forthwith, but, to their disgust, Mr. Sanderson had gone home. He was soon brought back to the Senate by the savage words shouted to him over the telephone.

April 9, 1920. The House passed the Peace Resolution (the first of its kind in the history of Congress) and it embraces five important points, to wit:

It declares the war at an end.

It repeals all the war powers of the President.

It stipulates that unless Germany accepts the terms of the resolution within forty-five days, the President must effect a complete embargo against her.

It provides a penalty for violation of the resolution.

It declares that the United States reserves all rights and advantages received under the armistice, and it ratifies seizure of German properties by the United States.

May 5, 1920. The so-called Peace Resolution, which passed the House on the ninth ultimo, has been favorably reported. Senator Knox spoke two hours in support of the Resolution. The Senate gave but desultory consideration to the Resolution, as it is known that the President will veto the same and that it cannot be passed over his veto.

May 15, 1920. The Senate adopted the H. J. Resolution proposing to terminate the state of war which Congress declared on April 6, 1917.

For adoption of the H.J. Resolution

Republicans	40	
Democrats	3	(Reed, Shields and Walsh of Massachusetts)
Total	43	
Against adoption		
Republicans	1	(Nelson)
Democrats	37	
Total	38	

May 19, 1920. General Carranza, de facto President of Mexico, has been driven from the City of Mexico. Just before his flight he said to his Cabinet Ministers: "We are lost, good bye, Gentlemen."

May 22, 1920. Senator Fall told me that General Carranza was slain yesterday. Whether the General was betrayed by his own soldiers and was a victim of "Ley Fuga," which seven years ago slew President Madero and Vice-President Suarez, is unknown. General Alvaro Obregón, leader of the forces which overthrew the Carranza regime, is aghast at the tragic death of Carranza and has announced that those guards "who failed to protect Carranza should have died defending him, and that thereby they would have been honored by public opinion, would be at rest with their consciences, and would have escaped the shame of cowardliness."

May 24, 1920. Message came from the White House, and our assistant secretary, Mr. Rose, had read only a few sentences when we ascertained that W. W. was urging Congress to grant him the power to accept a mandate to protect Armenia.

The Senate was "slim" when Mr. Rose began reading, but soon messengers were calling for senators as it was apparent that W. W. was following the hint in the Resolution reported favorably by Senator Harding from the Committee on Foreign Relations on May 11, and which passed the Senate on May 13, wherein the President was requested to dispatch a warship to Batum with a force of Marines "with instructions to such Marines to disembark and to protect American lives and property at the Fort of Batum and along the line of the railroad leading to Baku."

When the Senate passed the Resolution it did not perceive the "opening" the Resolution gave to W. W., and inasmuch as Senator Harding, Republican, had urged its passage, the Republican leaders did not realize its implications.

The Resolution spoke of the suffering of the Armenians and congratulated them upon the recognition of the independence of the Republic of Armenia by the United States Government. Since the Resolution was adopted, the Bolsheviki have taken Baku and Batum. The President took this Resolution as a "hint" that the Senate favored an American mandate over Armenia, but nothing was farther from the Senate's intention and it is now embarrassed by its own Resolution which was but a gesture.

Nothing is more certain than that Congress will *not* grant W. W. the power to accept a mandate for Armenia. In thrusting forward the Armenian mandate question, W. W. lays emphasis upon the character of the Armenian population and thus he touches a chord which will find a response from the well-meaning citizen who does not perceive that to accept the Armenian mandate is practically to enter the League of Nations.

It may now well be imagined how eloquently W. W.'s friends will picture bleeding and bereaved Armenia, beset by the Ottoman Turk on the south and by the Bolsheviki on the north, calling upon us for help and mercy. Alas! Armenia will call upon us in vain; so mobilized is public sentiment against the Versailles Treaty that not even an interstice may be found into which the thinnest wedge may be inserted to divide those voters who are grimly waiting for "their day of vengeance;" the day when they may reject "internationalism."

May 25, 1920. I plumped into W. J. B. at LaFayette Hotel, who said he opposed the Armenian mandate not only because of the expense thereof, but also upon the ground that when a republic accepts mandates, it assumes the character of a despot.

W. J. B. says he will be a member of the Committee on Platform and Resolutions at the coming Democratic National Convention at San Francisco and that he will see to it that there is *no* endorsement of the League of Nations.

May 26, 1920. The veto of the Peace Resolution was received by the House, and if W. W. be suffering, as his critics assert, from muscular paralysis, this message evinces that at least his capacity for luminous expression is not impaired.

By his veto of the Peace Resolution the rigidity of Wilson's foreign policy is exemplified. The President demands that our foreign relations shall fit into a bed of procrustean fixity whose dimensions he prescribes. Likewise the Senate has a procrustean couch of its own into whose narrow confines our foreign relations must be made to fit, hence, our foreign affairs do not rest well.

Those persons following the President and those following Senator Lodge, fail to perceive that these parlous times call for statesmen who can yield on non-essentials.

August 1, 1920. Mrs. Ashurst and I are quartered at Hotel La Salle, Chicago, and I have just returned from Dixon, Illinois, where I delivered an address and visited the Nachusa Tavern which in bygone days housed Lincoln, General Grant, Stephen A. Douglas, Horace Greeley, and Bayard Taylor.

Winnemucca, Nevada, August 5, 1920. My mother met us here and we are all quartered at the Overland Hotel. During the day we motored to a point near the head of Water Canyon about seven miles from Winnemucca, and my mother identified the spot where the tent stood in which I was born. The canyon (called Cross Canyon when I was born there) is not unattractive; bushes with red berries peeping out amongst the greenery are abundant, but when one leaves the canyon, a dreary prospect of desert sand is presented.

Flagstaff, Arizona, August 19, 1920. My wife and I found the streets cluttered with tourists arranging for their departure by autos to the Hopi (Moqui) Snake Dance. Scores of autos were threading their way through the streets. Interspersed in the throng were many celebrities. Here was Mary Roberts Rinehart, the authoress; here was Carter Harrison, sometime mayor of Chicago and there stood Mr. Swinnerton, the artist. Amongst my callers were J. J. (Sandy) Donahue and L. S. (Tom) Drum. Mr. Donahue was sheriff of this county in 1893 and 1894, Mr. Drum was the under-sheriff and I was the turnkey at the county jail here.

August 22, 1920. At noon we reached Leupp Indian Agency on the Little Colorado River, where one hundred autos were preparing to ford the stream. I was surprised to find no bridge here. Two years ago I secured appropriation to construct a bridge at this point.

Oraibi Village, Arizona, August 23, 1920. This village, Oraibi, is one of the Hopi pueblos of the ancient Province of Tusayan and was discovered in 1540 by a force of men under Pedro de Tovar accompanied by Fray Juan de Padilla sent hither by Francisco Vasquez Coronado. Every Hopi house is a museum of the environment.

The Hopi pigments and dyes are numerous and every Hopi Indian seems to know the places whence these materials may be obtained.

The region where the Hopis live is famous for its natural colors, which are displayed in the Painted Desert. Their villages are perched upon high mesas that may be reached only by ascending the trails difficult to climb. The Hopis possess an artistic sense, as exhibited by their pottery and basketry. They are industrious, docile, frugal, hospitable, and are faithful in their marital relations.

August 24, 1920. Snake Dance at Hotaville today. During the dance, which is a prayer for rain, various sorts of live snakes (including rattlesnakes) are carried by the dancers who march and countermarch on the Plaza. The snakes are then released unharmed about a mile from the Plaza. The dancers return to the Kiva where the snake priests drink copiously of an emetic made from herbs, and then the liquid is regurgitated. This is called the purification. The dancers' bodies are washed, and then the dancers feast upon corn, melons, and bread. The Hopi snake dance is a religious affair, and visitors are requested to refrain from laughter and loud talk during the ceremony.

Nogales, Arizona, October 10, 1920. Escorted by local celebrities, I called upon General Alvaro Obregón, president-elect of Mexico and then proceeded across the International Line to Nogales, Mexico, to a sumptuous luncheon attended by American citizens and by Mexican citizens. Cocktails were served but General Obregón drank *not* a drop of liquor. General Obregón, speaking in Spanish, said, amongst other things, that when he became president, he would confound the diplomats by telling the truth. The General has a large head, heavy moustache, red cheeks, and is of Irish descent. His right arm was shot away years ago.

October 11, 1920. Governor Cox, Democratic presidential nominee, faces defeat. The issue in this campaign is Woodrow Wilson, and the reaction against Wilson is strong.

In every presidential campaign for the past twenty-four years, either Bryan, Roosevelt, or Wilson was to the front. These are the only men within a generation who have attracted voters from one party to another, hence after so many years of political "stars," the present candidates appear prosaic.

Prescott, Arizona, October 27, 1920. The morning *Journal Miner,* opposition organ, says *inter alia:*

ASHURST AT PINNACLE

The League of Nations, an imperfect document, but insurance of the coming of the Brotherhood of Man; the election of Mark Smith, the due appreciation of Theodore Roosevelt and Woodrow Wilson — these were the things that United States Senator Henry F. Ashurst pleaded for last night. He had a refined and tempered eloquence.

Taking as his theme the general proposition that the world must accept the doctrine of brotherhood and reject the theory of Cain that no man is his brother's keeper, the Senator rose to new heights of oratory in his masterly handling of the League. . . .

He described President Wilson as a man broken in health and spirit by his mammoth fight in behalf of his ideals. Gone was the thunder, the philippic, but present in Senator Ashurst's disquisition was a new dignity, a new argumentative resource, a clearer appeal to sentiment and to reason. . . .

A new mind has taken control of the world as a reaction and backwash from the war, the Senator began. He pictured the condition as unstable, touchy, dangerous, and eloquently pleaded for the return of Mark Smith to the Senate.

He then launched into a truly masterful eulogy of the President. No sweeter words ever were uttered about a modern American than the Senator had for President Wilson.

Of all the speaking during the present campaign no better oratory has been offered to Prescott. Because there was nothing especially rancorous, the audience was able to sit tight and drink in the golden words without distraction by the rousing of their emotions.

Chicago, November 5, 1920. I learned here that Governor Cox had carried eleven states and Senator Harding thirty-seven. New York State has given the Harding electors over a million majority. In the electoral colleges, Harding will have 404 votes, Cox 127.

The Republicans have displaced Democratic senators in the following states: Kentucky, Oklahoma, South Dakota, California, Maryland, Oregon, Nevada, Idaho, Arizona, and Colorado; and the Republicans also retained the forty-nine seats in the Senate they held when Congress adjourned last June. Thus the Senate of the Sixty-seventh Congress will be: Republicans, fifty-nine, Democrats, thirty-seven, or a total of ninety-six.

America's entry into the World War was not repudiated by the elections of last Tuesday, but the administration which conducted our operation during our participation therein, has been overwhelmed. Any administration conducting so colossal an enterprise would have met the same fate. The nation is tired of ideals, altruism, and high endeavors. Champ Clark has been defeated for re-election to the House. Clark's noble face, his honesty, courage, and his faithful service to his country availed him nothing in the day of the people's wrath, when they were determined to rid themselves of the old and to usher in the new.

Never was the reserve vote brought out so fully as in this election. The composite voter in this election may be visualized as a person schooled by high prudence to curb his emotions, who grimly waited for the day when he could "turn out Wilson and his works."

New York City, February 13, 1921. Quartered at Hotel Astor whither I came yesterday, agreeable to invitation extended me by Senator Calder and Representative Hamilton Fish, Jr. of New York, to address the Dutchess County Society at its banquet here last evening.

As Mr. Brady escorted me to the banquet hall, he whispered: "We expect you to deliver a witty speech filled with *bonhomie*." Although ill and hardly able to stand, I drove ahead, and spoke forty minutes and no one suspected how ill I was.

At my right was Mr. Franklin D. Roosevelt, Assistant Secretary of Navy, candidate for Vice-President on the ill-starred Cox ticket. During my speech, I said that "Cox and Roosevelt had in the late campaign kept their own self-respect, something that votes could neither give nor take away."

February 25, 1921. It is now time to write of the Wilson Cabinet. During Wilson's administration, the following gentlemen were Secretary of State: Williams Jennings Bryan, Robert Lansing, and Bainbridge Colby.

The distinction of Mr. Bryan as an orator is beyond the range of eulogy. He is clean-lipped and chivalrous. He has enormous energy and a Gargantuan appetite. The routine of the office of Secretary of State irked him.

Mr. Lansing felt comfortable only when following oft-trodden paths; he was cautious which probably makes him a safer war-time premier than would have been some ambitious and daring man.

Of Mr. Colby's talents it would be difficult to speak extravagantly. He is of superb intellect, is a close observer of men and events, and is full of imagination and reflection. Mr. Colby has pungency of speech and a golden voice. Language when used by him becomes a fabric in which are mingled silken threads of romance, corks of practicality, and edged ribbons of steel. He was once a Republican and in 1912 was one of the founders of the Progressive party.

The following gentlemen were Lords of the Treasury: William Gibbs McAdoo, Carter Glass, and David Franklin Houston.

Mr. McAdoo is industrious, fertile, and ingenious. His self-reliance, executive ability, and experience make him a useful public official. He is a sound lawyer and has a flair for history. His energy as Secretary of Treasury and as Director General of Railroads during the World War eclipsed that of any other man of his day.

Mr. Glass, now senator from Virginia, is a scholarly newspaper publisher of red hair and fiery temper. Whilst he was a member of the House of Representatives, he and Senator Owen, in 1913, exhibited statesmanship of a high order in the formulation of the Federal Reserve Bank Act. His writings are a combination of Junius and Jefferson.

Mr. Houston is courageous and able. He has a well-groomed body, but not an "outdoor mind." He has had no practical experience with the world and its people. He does not make friends with Congress nor with the public.

The following gentlemen were Secretary of War: Lindly H. Garrison and Newton Diehl Baker.

Mr. Garrison was a trained lawyer and a fearless, capable administrator.

It would take many words adequately to portray Mr. Baker. That his capacity for administration is large may not be denied. His work as Secretary of War was surpassing great. In describing the tasks he performed, language easily runs into superlatives. Amidst criticisms that would blister the paint on a chair, this man of small stature never flinched; no anvil was ever less malleable than he, under the reiterated blows of public opinion. I recall no one who ever vanquished him in dialectics.

The following gentlemen were Attorney General: James C. McReynolds, Thomas W. Gregory, and A. Mitchell Palmer.

Under these three gentlemen, the Department of Justice maintained a high standard of efficiency. Mr. McReynolds became a Justice of the Supreme Court of the United States.

Mr. Gregory was from Texas and prior to his appointment, he was the attorney for Colonel E. M. House. He left the Department of Justice to resume private practice.

Mr. Palmer was born in Pennsylvania in 1872. He was elected to the Sixty-First, Sixty-Second, and Sixty-Third congresses. He measured up to a high standard of statesmanship, but was defeated for the Senate in 1914 by Senator Penrose. During the War he was alien property custodian.

Mr. Albert S. Burleson held the office of Postmaster General during W. W.'s administration. He possessed the capacity to impress his ideas upon others and the tact to carry his bold projects into successful execution.

Mr. Josephus Daniels was Secretary of the Navy during W. W.'s eight years. Like Secretary of War Baker, Mr. Daniels never flinched under the hottest fire, and while he had not the fertility to parry the keen thrusts of his critics, he possessed the fortitude to endure them. His conduct of our naval operations during the Great War was to his credit.

The following gentlemen were Secretary of the Interior: Franklin K. Lane and John Barton Payne.

Mr. Lane's talents and merits were great. His brain, like a sponge, absorbed everything that came his way, and his annual reports of the energies of his department read like editorials. He was humane and generous and had vision and learning.

John Barton Payne earned a fortune in law practice in Chicago, and not an unclean penny ever came to his hand. I have seen Mr. Payne go full tilt at many capable men and have never seen him unhorsed. He reaches decisions with startling celerity. For boldly crushing stinging nettles, he excelled all the Wilson appointees. Mr. Payne illustrates his arguments with anecdotes but there is no malice in his jests. Even when his barbed arrow pierces the recipient, he emulates the pearl-maker who drops a grain of sand into the gaping oyster and thus leaves the germ of a jewel in the wound.

The following gentlemen were Secretary of Agriculture: David Franklin Houston and Edwin T. Meredith. Mr. Meredith is the editor of a farm journal in Iowa.

The following were Secretary of Commerce: William C. Redfield and Joshua W. Alexander.

Mr. Redfield is a New York business man engaged in the manufacture of engines and heating, ventilating and cooling apparatus.

Mr. Alexander is from Gallatin, Missouri, and came to the Cabinet from the House of Representatives where he served many years.

William B. Wilson of Pennsylvania was Secretary of Labor during the W. W. administration. He was born in Scotland and came to the U. S. in 1872. He once worked in the coal mines of Pennsylvania.

Wilson's Cabinet was an incongruous mosaic, incapable of cohesion, but they were each and all free from mercenary motives and they approached every task with a desire to serve their country. All of them wore eyeglasses but the political vision of some of them was beyond the aid of optical adjuncts.

3

The Post-War World

*Wisdom in diplomatic negotiations
is more to be desired than bravery in battle...*

Cicero

*...gun powder has given way
to talcum powder...*

March 4, 1921. Warren G. Harding inaugurated. I went to the Senate where, at intervals, were announced and admitted in their order the following dignitaries:

The members of the House, led by their Speaker and with them was Miss Robertson, the new representative from Oklahoma, wearing a corsage bouquet of violets but with no hat over her white hair; the retiring Cabinet; the ambassadors, ministers, and chargé d'affaires of foreign countries, whose jewels and decorations flashed amidst the gold-braid, embroidery, and purple of their costumes; then amidst cheers came John J. Pershing, the General of the Army; Admiral Coontz, Chief of Naval Operations; General LaJeune, Commandant of the Marine Corps; and General Peyton C. March, Chief of Staff. At this time the Senate clocks pointed to 11:55 A.M.

"Will Woodrow Wilson be here?" was the whispered question now asked by all. "The Chief Justice and the Associate Justices of the United States," cried the Sergeant-at-Arms and in walked the judges in black silken robes; Chief Justice White greeted M. Jusserand; the Ambassador of France, whose red sash of the Legion of Honor flashed a deeper red when the black robe of the Chief Justice was pressed against it.

The galleries hummed with undertone conversations and were hued with the millinery of beautiful women; the Vice-President-elect was announced and into the Chamber there walked Mr. Coolidge, a medium-sized man of auburn hair who was escorted to Vice-President Marshall's right. "The President-elect," cried the Sergeant-at-Arms, and now we knew that Wilson would not come into the Senate Chamber. Then, escorted by the inaugural committee, Mr. Harding walked into the Chamber where for five years he had taken a decent but not high place in legislation. His face was ruddy, his eyes clear, his clothing was of finest material and fitted superbly.

The incoming Cabinet were seated among the senators; near me sat Mr. Hughes, soon to be Secretary of State. At my right sat Mr. Hoover, soon to be Secretary of Commerce.

Vice-President Marshall administered the oath of office to Mr. Coolidge and in delivering his valedictory, Vice-President Marshall was much applauded when he said:

> While the old order endures let representatives represent the old ideals: Let it be understood that they are not mere bellboys subject to calls for legislative cracked ice every time the victims of a debauch of greed, gambling or improvidence feel the fever of frenzied need.

The Senate of the Sixty-Sixth Congress then adjourned *sine die.*

Mr. Marshall left the rostrum. Mr. Coolidge, the new Vice-President, called the Senate to order and the Chaplain offered prayer. The proclamation of President Wilson convening the Senate of the Sixty-Seventh Congress in extra session was read whereupon Vice-President Coolidge with nasal eloquence delivered his address.

Among the new senators were Samuel M. Shortridge, the California orator, and Thomas E. Watson, the Georgia storm petrel, whose publication *The Jeffersonian* during the World War was denied the use of the mails for opposing the Draft.

Mr. Watson has written a *Life of Napoleon* and other books. He looks like the harmless zealot of some occult society, is in poor health and weighs about one hundred twenty pounds.

The senators then proceeded to the east front of the Capitol where Mr. Harding took the oath of office and delivered his inaugural address. Concluding his address, Mr. Harding now President, entered the Senate Chamber and set a precedent by announcing in person the nomination of his Cabinet which was immediately confirmed.

Meanwhile President Wilson's motorcar had reached the Capitol at 11:00 A.M., where the wheelchair of Senator Penrose was tendered to him, which he declined, and went direct to the President's room where he signed a number of bills and greeted callers, amongst whom were General Pershing, Admiral Coontz, Mr. Harding, Mr. Coolidge, and a few senators, but *did not* enter the Senate Chamber.

When Senator Lodge entered the President's room to announce that the Senate of the Sixty-Sixth Congress was ready to adjourn, President Wilson said: "Tell them I have no further communications to make. I thank you for your courtesy."

On this day, official responsibility took leave of a dying leader — Wilson — a leader who fought for his ideals with gameness and the charm of a poet. Thus passed into history the administration of Woodrow Wilson, an epoch crowded with complex domestic problems; grave international emergencies, the surmounting of which ran to the foundations of our national existence; training and transporting vast armies; providing and deploying an immense navy; and raising revenue aggregating billions of dollars.

In these tasks Wilson was moved by a zeal as warm as ever inspired the breast or nerved the arm of patriot warrior.

The temptation to obtain some trifling benefit for constituents who may vote today although it sacrifices the Nation's future interests has been the Circean spell that has deflected the purpose and weakened the fibre of not a few statesmen, but such temptation never diverted Woodrow Wilson.

Never in any other administration was there a commingling of so much success and so much failure as marked the Wilson administration. A fierce division in the Republican party on domestic issues sent Wilson into the White House, and a still fiercer division in his own party, on international issues, restored the Republicans to power. Even under the pressure of catastrophic events Wilson would not negotiate compromises; he could see but one side; he could not "give and take." He strove valiantly to exterminate the Moloch of War. He did not consider *what was* or *was not* expedient, and he reckoned not the cost to his party, to his health or to his fame, but pressed forward to his duty as he saw it. Today he is bereft of popularity, but when the waves of malice and revenge now beating furiously about him shall have spent their force, and when the evil passions of these times shall have expired, far-shining will be his fame.

March 5, 1921. Funeral services for former Speaker Champ Clark held in House of Representatives. Senator Reed and Representative Mann eulogized the dead statesman. Whilst sitting at my desk in the Senate Chamber (the Senate having adjourned), in walked Mr. W. R. Hearst accompanied by Senator Reed. I extended my hand, and all exchanged salutations.

To protect polite amenities from partisan rancor has ever been my rule, and I do not permit political warfare to disfigure the social graces that give zest to life. I once suggested to President Wilson that he extend to Mr. Hearst such civilities as a President could accord to a citizen and publisher, but I learned from Secretary of Interior, Mr. Lane, that W.W. disrelished my proposal.

March 12, 1921. Sailed from Norfolk on steamer "Christobal" bound for Panama Canal. Senator McKinley of Illinois and forty-seven representatives on board.

March 19, 1921. Ships transited through the canal usually discharge their passengers who then cross the Isthmus on the railroad, but our party remained on the "Christobal" during the transit. At Gatun Locks, Representative Hayden met us, he and Mrs. Hayden having come hither from New York on another ship.

Visited St. Joseph's Church, saw the gold altar which was hidden during the raids of the buccaneer Morgan in Old Panama City and later was carried to the present Panama City.

March 24, 1921. Left Panama City for Colón on the Atlantic side. In Colon is the freight house built in 1855, where were stored commodities awaiting transhipment to California during the "days of Forty-nine."

March 25, 1921. Senator McKinley and Representatives Hicks of New York, Denison of Illinois, and Connolly of Texas and Mr. Henry M. Pindell, editor from Peoria, Illinois, and myself and wife, were served a tropical luncheon at the American Consulate by Consul and Mrs. Dreher.

The word "Panama" means place of many fishes, but place of many adventures would not be amiss. Ever since the day when Cortez in poetry and Balboa in history crossed this neck of land, it has been the theatre of cruel tyrannies, brave exploits, and daring business ventures.

The raiders and buccaneers, merchants, conquistadores and commanders of caravels who came here in olden days are now asleep but mankind dare not here relax his vigilance in resisting nature's aggressions else the jungle would soon take his houses and machinery into its strangling embrace.

Nations were for centuries charmed with the possibility of severing the Isthmus, and their eyes visioned that the Hand which gave the seas and formed the land left it possible to dig a canal. American labor and American money have transformed this Canal Zone from a pest-hole into a zone of health and beauty. Workmen have hewed down the jungle, severed the mountain, and ships are now transited through the canal with the same ease that an elevator ascends to the top of a skyscraper.

Kingston, Jamaica, March 28, 1921. Quartered at the Myrtle Bank Hotel. The American Consul, Mr. Charles J. Latham, arranged for our party to land without passports.

April 2, 1921. Left the "Christobal" in Norfolk. Amongst the representatives in our party was William E. Mason from Illinois, once a senator from that state. He is seventy-one years old and corpulent, but sings and dances.

My wife and Senator McKinley and I went to Richmond, Virginia and visited St. John's Church where in 1775, Patrick Henry thrilled his countrymen with his oratory in the "Convention of Delegates from the several Counties and Corporations of Virginia."

April 11, 1921. The Sixty-Seventh Congress convened. William Bourke Cockran, the New York orator, born in County Sligo, Ireland in 1854, is again a member of the House.

April 12, 1921. President Harding following precedent set by President Wilson, addressed joint session of Congress in person. Speaker Gillett presided, and Vice-President Coolidge sat at the Speaker's right. Mr. Harding was pale and Senator Mc-Lean of Connecticut whispered to me that he feared the new President was in ill health. His voice was strong, his face ghastly. The only feature of his address approaching an ovation was when he looked up from his manuscript and said: "In the existing League of Nations, world-governing with its super-powers, this Republic will have no part."

Senate considered treaty negotiated by Secretary of State Bryan in April 1914, between the United States and the Republic of Colombia, which proposes to pay to Colombia twenty-five million dollars to settle the differences between the U. S. and Colombia arising out of events on the Isthmus of Panama in 1903. This treaty was reported to the Senate favorably from the Foreign Relations Committee in 1914 by Senator Stone, then the chairman. On March 14, 1917, Senator Knox spoke, urging ratification of a treaty with Colombia to settle the differences between the two countries, and on the same date, Senators Lodge, Mc-Cumber, Borah, Brandegee, and Fall submitted the views of a minority of the committee *opposing* ratification and their minority report was *inter alia,* as follows: "We cannot afford to purchase cordial relations with any country. We cannot afford to answer a blackmail demand. Once respond to such a demand and we shall be held up for every fancied wrong by other countries."

Senator Lodge today spoke supporting ratification of this same treaty. He read from the message which President Harding, on March ninth, last, sent to the Senate as follows: "The early and favorable consideration of this treaty would be very helpful at the present time in promoting our friendly relationships."

Treaty opponents argued that Senator Lodge and former Senator Fall, now Secretary of Interior, opposed this same treaty in 1917. Senator Lodge then read two letters addressed to himself by Secretary Fall; one letter asserted that Theodore Roosevelt had changed his attitude respecting the Colombia treaty, and the other letter went on to say that the British government had assumed control of the oil exploiting corporations of Great Britain and that the U.S. is in peril of being shut off from oil supply in the future unless it deals with Colombia.

April 19, 1921. Wife and I called on Mr. Pickford but found him entertaining W. J. Bryan. This Mr. Thomas H. Pickford, born in Toronto, Canada, has through his ability in fiscal affairs, earned a fortune. Although Irish, he resembles the stocky, florid English Lord of the Manor, and in his hotel, the LaFayette (at 16th and Eye Streets) diplomats, senators and representatives are not infrequently gathered around the table.

In the Democratic National Convention in Baltimore in 1912, he was one of the managers for Speaker Champ Clark, and had Mr. Clark taken Mr. Pickford's advice Mr. Clark might have been nominated. It would *not* have been a difficult task even for tyros in diplomacy to have won W. J. B. over to the Clark cause and Pickford urged that overtures be made to Bryan, but the Clark leaders evinced hostility toward Bryan, and when the Clark forces bolted in large numbers against Bryan for temporary chairman, Bryan began a series of savage thrusts toward Clark, which were deadly to Mr. Clark's chances.

Mr. Pickford tried while W. J. B. was Secretary of State to bring a reconciliation between Bryan and Clark but in vain, for Mr. Clark said, "It was not in the power of Bryan, or any other man, to repair the wrong."

Although all personal and political intercourse between Bryan and Clark was forever terminated by this breach in Baltimore, they each visited Mr. Pickford. Gray days have now come to Bryan. His lectures are not in demand. His wife has been ill for a year. Politicians whom he has traveled many miles to aid are now indifferent to him. But Mr. Pickford is his constant friend, not only *generous* but just toward him; this *justness* Mr. Pickford manifested by telling Bryan that his conduct toward Clark in the Baltimore Convention was unfair; and this generosity he exhibits by furnishing W. J. B. with meals and lodging without charge at the Hotel LaFayette when Bryan comes to Washington.

April 20, 1921. Opponents of the treaty to pay Colombia argued that to ratify this treaty would put a blight upon the memory of Colonel Roosevelt. Senator Borah introduced amendment:

> That neither said payment nor anything contained in this treaty shall be taken or regarded as an admission that the secession of Panama in November 1903, was in any way aided or abetted by the United States of America, its agents, or representatives, or that said government in any way violated its obligations to Colombia.

Amendment defeated. Yeas—thirty-nine; Nays—forty-nine.

When Senator Lodge voted for this amendment, derisive shouts arose. Senator Pomerene sent Senator Lodge a note advising him that Senator Borah would demand another roll call on this amendment and Pomerene warned Lodge that if Lodge again voted for such amendment, the Democrats would reject the treaty. This drove Senator Lodge and others to vote *against the amendment* a few moments later and the Democrats shouted "inconsistent" when Senator Lodge, the Republican Leader, changed front. Treaty ratified. Yeas—sixty-nine; Nays—nineteen.

April 25, 1921. Senator LaFollette spoke, urging that the independence of Ireland be recognized by the Washington government. He reviewed the history of the United States from the day on which Thomas Jefferson as Secretary of State formulated our American policy. LaFollette asserted that the present government of the Republic of Ireland was the *de jure* as well as the *de facto* government and he declared that Ireland had never yielded sovereignty to Great Britain.

April 30, 1921. Joint resolution by Senator Knox repealing World War resolution passed Senate. Senator Hitchcock argued that the Knox resolution was usurpation of President's prerogatives.

Senator Heflin charged that by this resolution, the U.S. was abandoning her Allies and "was making a separate peace with Germany."

Senator Heflin wears even in summer a double-breasted white waistcoat, gray trousers, a black broadcloth coat of ample skirts, a shock of iron-gray hair, and a pince-nez of heavy tortoise shell frame.

May 2, 1921. U.S. Supreme Court reversed the conviction of Senator Newberry, decided that Congress has no power to enact laws anent the primaries, and that the evidence does *not* disclose that Mr. Newberry had knowledge of any unlawful expenditures.

May 7, 1921. Yesterday Secretary of State Hughes sent to the British Ambassador a note advising that the U.S. had accepted the invitation of the Allies to resume our participation in the efforts of the Allied powers now trying to avert chaos in Europe.

The State Department said that the Allied Supreme Council and the Conference of Ambassadors at Paris were not created by the League Covenant, and that while the Reparation Commission was set up under authority of the Versailles Treaty, it was not a League body.

Upon this subject Republican Senators divided themselves into two groups; viz., those who asserted that the U.S. was not entering "entangling alliances;" and the "Irreconcilables" who said that W. W. tried to enter European affairs by the "front door," Harding was trying to enter by the "back door."

May 11, 1921. Senate adopted the Emergency Tariff Bill. The bill carries a high duty upon dye-stuffs and related chemicals. Senator King upbraided those Democratic senators who voted for such tariff.

President Wilson while in Paris in May 1919, sent a wireless message to Congress urging high tariff duty on dye-stuffs.

May 12, 1921. Mrs. Ashurst and I attended a reception at the Pan-American Union Building tendered to President and Mrs. Harding by the ambassadors, ministers, and chargé d'affaires of the twenty-one republics of the western hemisphere.

This Pan-American Union Building costing one million, one hundred thousand dollars (pre-war figures) has an international significance. Mr. Andrew Carnegie contributed eight hundred and fifty thousand dollars toward its construction and the U.S. and the other western hemisphere republics contributed the remainder.

The Pan-American Union was founded by the twenty-one republics to foster commerce, amity, and peace.

May 15, 1921. "Supper" with Senator and Mrs. Medill Mc-Cormick, of Illinois. Ex-Senator Theodore E. Burton of Ohio, now a representative from Ohio, shot the following question at me:

> Q. By Mr. Burton: "If President Harding should send the Versailles Treaty to the Senate, how many of the irreconcilables would vote to ratify?"
>
> A. By Senator Ashurst: "Not one."

It is now charged that ours is a nation without manners. Our graceful elegance, indeed, passed away about twenty years ago when we gave up chirographic correspondence. Ours is a hurried age; no time for thoroughness. In order to be gracious and polite, one must be unhurried.

May 17, 1921. At Senate Restaurant, I passed the table where sat ex-Senator Chauncey M. Depew and Mrs. Depew. He arose, embraced me, and congratulated me on my "able speech at the Convention," whereupon I said "What speech, Senator Depew?" and he replied, "Why at the Republican National Convention, where you placed Harding in nomination last June." I said: "Alas, Senator Depew, you believe that I am Senator Willis of Ohio, but I am Senator Ashurst of Arizona, and please do not let my friend Willis know that he resembles me, it would promote vanity."

June 14, 1921. Attended the graduation exercises at Georgetown University where Maurice H. Lanman and William A. Dyke, both of my office, and my stepson, John R. Renoe, were graduated and received degrees.

June 18, 1921. President Harding relies quite as much upon Secretary Fall in Mexican affairs as he does upon Secretary of States Hughes.

W. W. was accused of "wiggling and wabbling" upon the Mexican problem. Some persons who inveighed against Wilson's "bungling" of the Mexican question are now advisers of President Harding, and they find refuge in adopting the laissez faire attitude toward Mexico which W. W. followed.

Commercial depression is raging in the U.S. Speculators who during the World War won millions of dollars in wheat, cotton, iron, oil, leather, wool, and rubber, are now, as Vice-President Marshall said in his farewell address to the Senate, calling for "legislative cracked ice" to slake their gambling fevers.

The farmers' crops of 1920, whether tobacco, wheat, corn, cotton, or whatnot, brought only one-third the cost of production. Cattle and sheep, hides, pelts, and wool do not bring one-half the cost of production, yet the phenomenon of high prices of food and clothing still obtains.

Thousands of persons who one year ago possessed independent means are today penniless.

It is futile to allocate the blame and expose the causes of a panic. Men in the "crowd" do not learn from experience. The panics of 1810, of 1837, of 1873, of 1893, and of 1907 (as well as this one) — each brought ruin, and each panic was largely the result of the violations of natural laws and "first principles."

During the past seven years, enormous business expansions have taken place, which caused imprudent grants of credits by banks.

Moreover we have as individuals, as cities, as counties, as states, and as a nation, lived far beyond our means and the virus of winning a living by *gambling,* instead of *earning* a living by *working,* has infected the nation.

During this reckless foray upon safe business methods and upon tested laws of political economy, our circulating medium has inflated from thirty-four to fifty-seven dollars per capita, which diminishes the purchasing power of the dollar.

June 30, 1921. President Harding today nominated ex-President William Howard Taft to be Chief Justice of the U.S.

The doors were at once closed, reporters excluded, and the smokers lit their cigars. Senator Borah was first up and said that Mr. Taft had not tried a lawsuit in thirty years; that he was repudiated in the elections of 1912, carrying but two states aggregating eight electoral votes, and that we were coming to strange times when the Republican party lays its hand upon the U.S.

Supreme Bench and takes a Judge (Hughes) and makes a politician out of him, and then reaches its hand into politics, takes an
ex-President and makes a Chief Justice out of him.

Senator Knox said: "If the Senate intended to do the handsome thing it should be done in a handsome manner."

Senator Underwood, Democratic Leader, said that he would
vote for the confirmation of Mr. Taft whose talents and merits
he considered great.

Senator Pomerene, Democrat of Ohio, said that he had
known Mr. Taft for a lifetime and had a high opinion of Taft's
character and his talents as a lawyer and a statesman.

Senator Smith, Democrat of South Carolina, said that President Taft's action in declining to appoint negro officials in the
South had endeared him to southern hearts.

Senator Overman, Democrat of North Carolina, who years
ago was an orator but who now talks too rapidly, eulogized Taft.

I was next up and suggested that a good President might
make a poor judge and a poor President might be a good judge;
that a President should be Cossack and Chesterfield combined.

Senator Johnson of California said he had been a political
antagonist of Mr. Taft and had assisted in bringing about Taft's
defeat for re-election in 1912; that he would like to appear mag-
nanimous and vote for Taft, but that he could not do so as duty
should be placed above "handsome" action.

Senator Ed. Broussard, Louisiana (brother of Senator Rob-
ert Broussard, deceased) said that when Mr. Taft was Governor
General of the Philippine Islands, he (Broussard) served under
Mr. Taft and that he regarded him as a just and able man.

No senator spoke over five minutes. Upon a roll call the
yeas were sixty and the nays four; the nay votes being cast by
Borah, Johnson, LaFollette, and Watson of Georgia. Thus the
Senate for the first time in its history confirmed a former President for a judicial office.

July 8, 1921. Telegrams from cotton growers in Arizona,
excoriating the Arizona delegation because the tariff bill just
reported to the House places raw cotton on the free list.

July 12, 1921. President Harding entered the Senate and spoke from manuscript in opposition to the Adjusted Compensation (Bonus) Bill. He stated that (whilst no expense should be spared in hospitalizing the sick and wounded soldiers) to grant a cash bonus from the Treasury for able-bodied soldiers was unwise and was a burden which the national Treasury could not stand.

July 13, 1921. No more annoying question can come before Congress than a general revision of the tariff. During the pendency of a tariff bill, Washington becomes a bewildering farrago where are gathered representatives of the manufacturers who demand that "raw materials" shall be on the free list, but also demand a high tariff duty on the manufactured goods; and here also are the representatives of the farm, field, forest, mines, and ranch, who demand a *high* tariff on the "raw materials" but who demand a low tariff on the factory products.

They are all "free traders" after they get their own interests protected by a "high tariff wall," which shuts out competition on that which they produce.

July 19, 1921. Luncheon at Senate Restaurant with Mr. Guarmo Villalobos, President Obregón's personal friend. Mr. Villalobos, on behalf of President Obregón, invited me to visit Mexico City within the next few months at the expense of the Mexican government, which invitation I declined.

The Mexican government has purchased for its embassy and chancellery here, at a cost of one million dollars, the palace on Sixteenth Street built by Mrs. Franklin MacVeagh, whose husband was Secretary of the Treasury during the Taft administration.

July 28, 1921. Senator Norris, after a three-hour speech, collapsed this afternoon and was given medical aid by Senator Ball, Delaware, who is a physician.

Viscount Northcliffe's feud with the Lloyd George regime was transferred to Washington today. His lordship, proprietor of the London *Times,* arrived here this morning and has been denied the hospitality of the British Embassy. Not only was his invitation to stay at the Embassy while in Washington abruptly withdrawn, but a dinner in his honor which was to have been given at the Embassy tonight was cancelled.

Viscount Northcliffe intrigued with Mr. Lloyd George in 1916 to hasten the fall of the Asquith ministry, and now he and Lloyd George are at dagger points. Mr. Lloyd George dealt Northcliffe a heavy blow in his recent speech in Parliament denouncing Northcliffe for quoting the King. Unless Northcliffe can clear himself he will be ostracized in Great Britain. To the British, their King is their symbol; to quote the King, discuss his personality, or place His Majesty in a compromising attitude, is unforgivable.

August 8, 1921. Senate considered bill to prevent use of beer and other malt liquors for medicinal purposes. Senator Stanley's amendment, making it a misdemeanor to search the premises or property of any person without search warrant, agreed to viva voce.

In enforcing the Prohibition law some officers, without search warrants, have entered homes and apartments, have broken open pantries, closets and trunks, ransacked cellars, and have searched automobiles and traveling bags.

The Anti-Saloon League's members are numerous, many of them are respectable in character and its purpose is to extirpate intoxicating liquor from the U.S. Its lobbyists are shrewd and audacious. Senators and representatives are furnished with bulletins giving directions as to how they should vote, and not a few "dry" speeches delivered in Congress are written by the Anti-Saloon League.

August 11, 1921. Formal invitations to a disarmament parley to be held in Washington, on November the eleventh next, were issued today by Secretary of State Hughes.

Identical forms of the invitations were sent to Great Britain, France, Italy, and Japan, whilst a modified form thereof was sent to China.

August 17, 1921. Whilst Senator Lodge and I were conversing, Senator Reed approached us and said that when the conference report on the anti-beer bill is considered, he will pay his respects to the Prohibition advocate, Representative Volstead. Senator Reed went on to say that Mr. Volstead's "countenance resembled Old Torquemada," and that he intended to say so in his speech. Senator Lodge told him not to pronounce it Tor-que-may-da but Tor-que-mäh-da.

I adjured Senator Reed not to speak offensively of Mr. Volstead, as such reference to a House member would be a breach of that comity between the two Houses which must be preserved in a bicameral legislative body.

August 18, 1921. I spoke anent the Fourth and Fifth Amendments to the Constitution. When I concluded, Senator Reed said:

> Until the other day I never had the pleasure of seeing the distinguished author of the Volstead Act. I do not know what his ancestry may be, but I do know that I have gazed upon pictures of the celebrated conspirators of the past, the countenances of those who have led in fanatical crusades, the burners of witches, the executioners who applied the torch of persecution, and I saw them all again when I looked at the author of this bill.

August 22, 1921. Mr. Charles E. W. Smith, broker, of New York City, called. He was a client of mine in Williams, Arizona, twenty years ago and spent one hundred thousand dollars searching for platinum in Cataract Canyon, Arizona.

One bleak morning in March 1901, whilst he and I were crossing the Hudson River on the ferry, I urged him to abandon any further squandering of his resources and impoverishment of his family in such a doubtful venture, whereupon he turned pale and had I not supported him he would have fallen. Recovering, he inveighed against me for my lack of faith in his platinum enterprise, and I replied, "Spend your money in that venture and your inevitable end will be poverty." My prediction was mournfully verified later.

August 27, 1921. Mr. Peter A. Drury, president of the Merchants Bank and Trust Company, and my wife and myself, with

Mr. Stephen O'Mara, Lord Mayor of Limerick, Ireland, and his wife, motored to the Drury's summer home at Bluemont, in the Blue Ridge Mountains.

September 7, 1921. When the guns of the World War fell silent, claims against the federal government aggregating billions of dollars were filed, and claim agents and oleaginous lobbyists flocked hither to prosecute these claims. Officialdom here, accustomed during wartimes to entering improvidently into "contracts" and approving claims for huge sums of money upon vouchers neither sufficient nor conclusive, continued this practice until lately.

September 9, 1921. On New York Central train, I lunched with ex-Senator Elihu Root, one of the President's delegates to the coming Disarmament Conference. Alighting from the train at Herkimer, New York, I motored to Richfield Springs to address the banquet of the New York Coal Dealers. I was taken aback when one of the guests said: "I wish he would ditch that manuscript," whereupon I said: "Ladies and Gentlemen; A set speech at a banquet is generally a failure." Tearing the manuscript into fragments I said: "I shall now talk to you without setting up sentinels of reserve."

October 3, 1921. Former Vice-President Marshall in town. I placed my office and my assistant secretary, Mr. Dyke, at his disposal.

October 6, 1921. Mrs. Ashurst and I gave a dinner to former Vice-President and Mrs. Marshall. Our other guests were Senator and Mrs. Reed, Senator Pomerene, Senator Kenyon and Senator Walsh, and Mr. and Mrs. Pickford.

October 8, 1921. Attended meetings of agricultural "bloc." Ten Republican senators and ten Democratic senators comprise this "bloc." The responsible Republican leaders are sour toward this "bloc."

October 12, 1921. Senator Philander C. Knox of Pennsylvania dropped dead this evening at his residence within a half-block of our house. Mrs. Ashurst went at once to the Knox residence to offer assistance. Mr. Knox was Attorney General in Cabinet of President McKinley and President Roosevelt; he came to Senate in 1904, resigned from Senate to become Secretary of State under President Taft; again elected to Senate in 1916.

It was largely through efforts of Mr. Knox as Mr. Taft's Secretary of State that free transit for U.S. coastwise ships through the Panama Canal was enacted into law in 1912.

Mr. Knox was of small stature, he had a commander's nose, a cherub's smile, and being always starched up to his full dignity, he was an impressive figure.

He was chairman of Committee on Senate Rules, and at meetings of his Committee he served a sumptuous luncheon to his fellow committeemen. He smoked many strong cigars each day. He was man-of-affairs, statesman, and lawyer. Sitting in his Senate seat his feet would not touch the floor, but in the chancellery, in the courtroom, and in the Senate when he stood up to speak, no man could drive him off those same, prim, neat little feet.

October 13, 1921. I addressed the unemployment conference, presided over by Secretary of Commerce Herbert Hoover.

October 14, 1921. Senator Cummins, President Pro Tem is scornful of the agricultural "bloc." Senators Myers and King tell me they expect soon to denounce "blocs" and say they regard "parliamentary blocs" but "little short of treason."

Visiting Arizonians say that Governor Campbell has captured the hearts and votes of my constituents. What shall I do when out of office? Votes fall from public men as autumnal leaves fall from a tree. I shall write no silly twaddle about the ingratitude of constituencies; the voter has the right to displace his servants at any time.

October 18, 1921. Senate considered German peace treaty. Senator Shortridge said that had Washington, Jackson, or Roosevelt been President in 1914, Germany would *never* have invaded Belgium, and I observed that Colonel Roosevelt said for publication in 1914, "The overrunning of Belgium by Germany was no affair of the U.S."

Senator LaFollette spoke one hour and denounced W. W. The German treaty ratified by yeas, sixty-six — nays, twenty.

Senator Glass of Virginia whose influence elected Senator Underwood to be Democratic Minority Leader, criticised Mr. Underwood for supporting this treaty.

October 19, 1921. Assistant Secretary of Treasury Colonel Edward Clifford, in charge of Public Health, excoriated me for twenty minutes and charged that I was the dupe and the tool of boards of trade, Kiwanis and Rotary Clubs, chambers of commerce, merchants, and contractors of Arizona, who desired that federal funds should pour into that state further to stimulate their trade and business.

October 21, 1921. Telegrams and letters *still* come urging further expenditures of federal moneys in Arizona.

Agricultural bloc met and declared unanimously for *reduction* in freight rates; one Senator moved to propose decrease in wages of railroad employees, whereupon the "bloc" became panic stricken and adjourned.

October 22, 1921. If a lady in Nilrebo or Pinhook should fail in courtesy toward another lady, the consequence would not influence national policies or defeat legislation. If, however, a lady in official Washington should fail in courtesy toward another lady in official Washington, grave consequences could flow therefrom. A curt reply, a barbed joke, a supercilious snub, a failure to call or to return a call could bring the downfall of a Cabinet member, the defeat of a senator, the rejection of a nomination.

Amongst the many charms and attributes of woman, which are the glory of her sex, her skills and finesse in preventing *faux pas,* smoothing out rough places, bridging over enmities between statesmen, and adding zest and grace to life in national capitals, are extremely valuable. Mrs. Harding has asked the senatorial ladies to receive with her at the White House this afternoon. This plan will enable the senatorial ladies to receive the Cabinet ladies. It is a fatiguing task for Cabinet ladies each year to call upon all the senatorial ladies. Not a few ladies in official circles undermine their health and reduce themselves to poverty in attempting to observe all social duties.

October 24, 1921. Washington has "dressed up" during the past week. Hotels and apartment houses have been renovated and are decorated with the flags of the various delegations to the Disarmament Conference.

At Union Station yesterday thousands greeted Admiral Beatty of the Jutland naval battle, General LaJacques, leader of the Belgic armies, and General Vittorio Diaz, organizer of Italy's "elastic defense," and their entourages.

October 28, 1921. War belches many distresses upon a nation and one of these is heavy taxes. The captains of industry say that the federal government is their preferred but profligate partner, that if they succeed, the government takes in taxes most of their earnings; if they fail, the government says, "Your loss is no concern of mine."

Marshal Ferdinand Foch arrived tonight and was welcomed by cheering throngs.

October 29, 1921. Lord Macauley wrote of the superb palaces and porticoes of ancient Rome, before which rolled the ivory chariots of Marius and Caesar and before which had marched the captives, the shouting legions with their laurelled fasces and golden eagles, but said Macauley, when Petrarch was crowned, the "captives" won the hearts of admiring nations.

During the day, Marshal Foch passed the "superb palaces" of Washington, cheered by thousands whose hearts *he* had *captured.* He called at the French Embassy and then with Mr. Jusserand, French Ambassador to the U. S., he called on President Harding; then on Vice-President Coolidge. When he entered the Vice-President's room at the Senate, his eye fell upon Rembrandt Peale's portrait of General Washington and clapping his heels together he saluted. He then called upon Cabinet members, thence he went to the residence of former President Wilson, where the butler took his card but brought word that Mr. Wilson was too ill to receive visitors. The Marshal lunched with President Harding at the White House, then motored to Mount Vernon, and laid a wreath upon the tomb of General Washington. Foch is the greatest French soldier since Napoleon and possesses a nobility of nature never reached by Napoleon. From boyhood to Waterloo, Napoleon dreamed of an oriental empire. The throne of Constantinople or Hindustan was his earliest fancy; visions of pagodas, oriental splendor and absolutism were an incentive to Napoleon's Egyptian campaign.

Marshal Foch relies upon the power of truth and justice and has faith in righteousness and spirituality. He is called the Gray Man of Christ and amidst the thunder of the guns, he was often found at prayer, and his faith strengthened him like the Harp of David on the troubled breast of Israel's King.

Foch's One Hundred Days ended victoriously; Napoleon's One Hundred Days sent Napoleon to St. Helena and despair.

October 31, 1921. China is in the throes of civil war and presents a tragic figure at Washington. Her cry to the Disarmament Conference is "Save us from Japan."

Delegates from the government of Dr. Sun Yat Sen, who has set up a republic in South China, are here denouncing the Peking government as the creature of Japanese war lords.

November 1, 1921. For years, Mrs. Ashurst and I had planned to visit the principal capitals of Europe to get a glimpse of celebrities but the pressure of the public business prevented our sailing. We shall, however, soon see more celebrities here in Washington than we would see by visiting a dozen European capitals. Delegates soon to participate in, or solicit the attention of the Disarmament Conference arrive here daily.

November 2, 1921. I introduced amendment to tax bill proposing to appropriate $18 million to authorize the Director of the Veterans' Bureau to provide additional hospital facilities for disabled ex-servicemen.

Senator Penrose, in charge of tax bill, shouted that the Senator from Arizona, Mr. Ashurst, need not pretend that he had a monopoly on patriotism, and then the mordant humor and satire for which Penrose is famous flashed forth.

Senator Penrose was noted in college for scholarship and youthful exploits. He comes of a famous family, and more nearly typifies the public conception of "politician" than any other living character; he is sagacious and bold, and before he fell ill, he weighed near three hundred pounds.

His legs have swollen so that each one is now the size of an ordinary torso; his neck and face have shrunk terribly, and his ears have the transparency of tissue paper, but he sits daily in his Senate seat, piercing a casque now and then with a sword that "thrusteth sure," and ever and anon coining *bon mots*.

November 3, 1921. Motoring home tonight, I descried old John Hickman, colored, struggling through the snow. I took him to his lodgings. Hickman has known all senators who have served since September 1, 1865; on that date he took charge of and still has charge of the Senate Barber Shop. He is feeble and cannot live a twelvemonth.

November 5, 1921. Autumn frosts have turned the leaves hereabout to gold and to red and yellow; every bough is a jeweled arch, whilst daily through the streets there parade spangled and plumed delegations representing some foreign power.

The American delegates are: Secretary of State Charles E. Hughes; Senator Henry Cabot Lodge; Senator Oscar W. Underwood; and Mr. Elihu Root.

November 7, 1921. As this crisp blue autumn day faded, the French delegation to the Arms Parley arrived at Union Station. Squadrons of army automobiles and details of cavalry were drawn up, and *when* Aristide Briand, the present French Premier and René Viviani, sometime Premier, emerged from the depot at the head of their entourage, shouts of applause arose. Sabres flashed, officers snapped salutes and then came the "Marseillaise" sounding so wildly well.

November 9, 1921. The "Olympia," Admiral Dewey's old flagship, which brought the body of an "Unknown American Soldier" who fell in France, docked at the Navy Yard here. The bringing hither for burial in the National Cemetery at Arlington the body of an unknown American soldier is a tribute of this nation, combining mystery and symbol, to all Americans who died in the World War.

As is often the case, the weather today was in sympathy with this mystery and symbol. Rain had fallen all day and the leaves but recently so golden and red, lay in soggy, brown heaps; the streets and pavements were wet and the early lights made wavery paths in them. The casket, draped with the American flag, containing the body of the Unknown Soldier, was taken in a motorhearse accompanied by a mounted band with muffled drums to the rotunda of the Capitol, placed upon the same catafalque that had borne the coffins of Lincoln, Garfield, McKinley and Admiral Dewey, where surrounded by the pictured and sculptured story of America, beneath Brumidi's still unfinished frescoes with many guards of honor to keep the vigil, the body of the Unknown Soldier will rest until next Friday.

November 10, 1921. The skies were clear today and one hundred thousand persons with the silence of a phantom host, entered the rotunda and looked upon the casket containing the body of a soldier, namelessly immortal, unknown by name or rank.

November 11, 1921. Senate assembled at 8:00 A.M.

All senators, except Underwood, Poindexter, Swanson and Myers, wore top (high silk) hats. Such headgear went into eclipse here when the World War began, hence some of the top hats worn today were of a vintage of years ago. Many senators wore the long cylindrical Prince Albert coat.

The justices of the Supreme Court, the governors of States, the Cabinet members were placed ahead of the senators in the cortege.

We had marched but two hundred yards when convulsive shouts and muffled cries broke out — cries somewhat of sympathy and admiration but more of vengeance and rage — cries similar to those which welcome victims of injustice and denounce the tormentor when the victims escape from some oppressor. The shouts and cries were for W. W. who with Mrs. Wilson had just entered the procession in an open horse-drawn vehicle. As we proceeded along Pennsylvania Avenue, W. W. received ovations and applause. His face was pale; he lifted his hat with his right arm. He was too weak to go to Arlington and proceeded to his home in S. Street. Thousands of persons followed him thence and called for a speech. He appeared at the door and saluted them. Mrs. Ashurst, who rode in an automobile with W. J. B.

and the Pickfords, was caught for two hours in a traffic jam. The congestion of the autos was so severe that President Harding barely reached the amphitheater in time to be present for the "two minutes of silence." Some high officials and foreign dignitaries sat in their automobiles for hours unable to go forward or backward and thus missed the exercises; Secretary of State Hughes abandoned his automobile and proceeded on foot. Stalled automobiles, abandoned sightseeing cars, and motor trucks clogged the bridges and roads.

During the World War the discipline, self-immolation, and suffering awoke us to the nobility of service and it was expected that the nations thus purified by these cleansing flames would cling to high ideals, but soon after the Armistice, hands that, during the long dark night of War, had been upthrust in prayer, lowered to pick up worldly things. The purifying fires "winked out." Never before did nations descend so quickly from the peak of spirituality into the swamps of materialism.

Within six months after the Armistice was signed, cynicism and bigotry and a quest for sensations and frivolities seized us. This attitude received no rebuke from statesmen and but little rebuke from clergymen. This arrival in Washington of the body of the Unknown Soldier and its interment in Arlington Cemetery, no less than the pending Arms Parley, has rekindled this cleansing flame and has evoked altruistic and religious emotions. The spirituality of art, labor, and sacrifice, seems to breathe again.

November 12, 1921. Went to Arms Parley at D.A.R. Building where ticketholders threading their way through the throngs were eager to catch glimpses of top-hatted, gray-spatted, long-tail-coated dignitaries and uniformed delegates.

Entering the gallery reserved for the senators, I looked down into the hall upon the green-topped tables placed together in the form of a horseshoe, upon which ink, pens, pencils, and pads of paper were disposed.

Then entered the delegates from the various powers, and finally but five vacant chairs remained at the green-topped tables. Applause rang out; the American delegation was entering single file, Secretary of State Hughes leading, followed by Senator Lodge, Mr. Elihu Root, and Senator Underwood. There was now but *one* vacant chair at the table; it was a large high-backed chair between Mr. Hughes and Mr. Balfour.

Came loud applause; Mrs. Harding had just entered the box where sat Chief Justice Taft and Vice President Coolidge. Immediately President Harding entered and walked briskly to the vacant chair at the head of the table. The assemblage rose and Secretary of State Hughes said: "Prayer will now be offered by Reverend Abernathy of the Calvary Baptist Church of Washington."

After prayer, Mr. Hughes announced, "The President of the United States," whereupon President Harding spoke and said *inter alia* "I can speak officially only for the United States. Our hundred millions frankly want less of armament and none of war." The senators and representatives led the applause in the galleries, and W. J. B. led the applause in the press section. After Mr. Harding had left the chamber, Mr. Hughes announced that both French and English would be the official languages of the Conference, whereupon Mr. Camerlynch, interpreter of the League of Nations, translated Mr. Hughes' announcement into French.

Mr. Balfour was then up, and speaking in English, he complimented President Harding's speech, and went on to say that the character and capability of the American Secretary of State made it appropriate that Mr. Hughes should preside. Mr. Hughes then proposed a ten-year holiday in naval building and further proposed that the "capital ship-building" program, actual and projected, be abandoned and that the United States should scrap thirty ships, Great Britain should scrap nineteen ships and Japan should scrap seventeen ships, making a total of sixty-six fighting ships to be scrapped, with a total tonnage of 1,878,943 tons.

When Mr. Hughes said: "The United States is willing in the interest of immediate limitation of armament, to scrap all these ships" (certain described ships which the Secretary of State had named) the delegates, galleries, and the press were amazed.

Among the delegates were men astute in penetrating secrecy and in deducing the plans of opponents by dovetailing meagre shreds of information; at that table were men capable of divining what another person may do or say; yet, so carefully had Mr. Hughes guarded his speech that it carried a surprise.

When the American Secretary of State said: "It is proposed that Japan shall abandon her program of ships not yet laid down," the faces of the Orientals remained unreadable.

When Mr. Hughes proposed that Great Britain should scrap nineteen ships and abandon construction of others, Earl Beatty, Admiral of the English Fleet, lowered his chin, and Mr. Balfour and Ambassador Geddes scribbled notes of what was said.

The senators shouted loudly for Premier Briand of France, who arose and spoke in French.

November 14, 1921. Secretary of State Hughes, by laying before the conference his definite plan of armament reduction, not only illuminated a pathway that may be trodden by statesmen seeking to sterilize the seeds of future wars and to reduce taxation levied for upkeep of armaments, but he also pleaded his cause so concretely that criticism will fall upon any power refusing to give him a definite reply.

This evening Mrs. Ashurst and I attended reception given by Secretary of States Hughes at the Pan-American Building to the foreign delegates attending the Arms Parley.

November 16, 1921. Mrs. Ashurst and I, with many senators, went to Georgetown University where a sword of honor was presented to Marshal Ferdinand Foch and the degree of Doctor of Canon and Civil Law was conferred upon him by the University.

November 22, 1921. Mrs. Ashurst and I attended reception at British Embassy. In the receiving line were Sir Auckland Geddes, the Rt. Hon. A. J. Balfour, the Rt. Hon. Lord Lee of Fareham and Lady Lee. Motley throng. Present were men wearing fezzes; men wearing headpieces resembling the mitre; men with rainbow-shaped noses; tall, silent men with long straight noses that bulbed at the end; tawny men with dark silken whiskers sprayed over their chests; men with bulging pouches under their eyes and men with huge moustachios. It was like a crowded caravanserai in the Hedjas, and it had the flavor of London, Shanghai, Trebizond, Damascus, and Samarakand.

November 23, 1921. Senator Reed telegraphed Senator Curtis, Republican whip, withdrawing the language he used last August in his Senate speech denouncing Representative Volstead.

November 27, 1921. Each delegation to the arms parley (save the Belgic and the Portuguese) is accompanied by military and naval officers and by advisors, bursars, economists, experts, historians, and interpreters. The delegates and their suite complain that the receptions, levees, dinners, and ceremonial functions here (which they may not decline) consume so much time that important work of the Parley is neglected.

This Conference on Limitation of Armament was convened to sterilize the seeds of future wars, and at least in Washington, gunpowder has given way to talcum powder; Mars is here surrendering to Venus and Mercury.

Social climbers and tuft-hunters are bombarding the foreign visitors with hospitality.

Senator La Follette has denounced the secret meetings of the delegates and Senator Borah says that President Harding's plan to organize an association of nations, is an attempt to enter the League of Nations.

November 29, 1921. A demand has arisen for copies of the speech I delivered in the Senate in May 1919, on the Rush-Bagot Treaty between Canada and U.S.

This Rush-Bagot treaty, convention, or arrangement (for each of these terms has been applied to it) reduced the naval armament of each signatory power upon the Great Lakes to four vessels not exceeding one hundred tons burden for each vessel and each vessel to carry not to exceed one eighteen pound cannon; it provides that all other armed vessels shall forthwith dismantle, and no other vessel shall thereafter be built or armed on the Lakes.

Never before had so important a document been compressed into so small a compass as this treaty.

December 6, 1921. Agreement was signed at London by which Ireland is to become a "Free State" in the community of nations making up the British Empire and shall possess the same status, rights, and powers possessed by the Dominion of Canada, the Commonwealth of Australia, and the Union of South Africa. The Province of Ulster may remain out of the Irish "Free State" if she so elects.

December 10, 1921. During the plenary (open) session of the Arms Parley, Senator Lodge of American delegation presented the draft of a treaty, initialed but not signed, "between" the U.S., Great Britain, France, and Japan for the maintenance of their several rights in their *insular possessions* and *insular dominions* in the Pacific Ocean. Senator Reed denounced this Four Power Pact as "treacherous, treasonable, and damnable."

December 12, 1921. During debate in Senate on the Four Power Pact, the "Irreconcilables" said its ratification would place obligations upon the U.S., similar to those in the Versailles Treaty.

December 16, 1921. Governor Campbell thanked me for courtesies and said that my efforts here were appreciated. This projected me into felicity, but my "felicity" evaporated when at my office I read the angry telegrams demanding legislative "cracked-ice" to cool gambling fevers.

December 21, 1921. Senator Kenyon spoke against seating of Senator Newberry. Senator Spencer, who wrote report exculpating Mr. Newberry, sat near Kenyon but the sulphrous sentences and verbal bombs of Kenyon's speech drove the urbane Spencer from the Chamber.

During the first weeks of the Woodrow Wilson regime, place-hunters cluttered Washington. They cajoled and threatened senators and representatives. Many of these office seekers were worthy men and it was distressing to see them deplete their slender means and waste their time. The Republican journals referred to the "hungry horde upon Washington," and whilst the advance of the place-hunters upon Washington in 1913 was a painful scene, the presence here of a cynical gang of place-hunters who since last March have pestered and annoyed Republican senators and Cabinet members is disgraceful.

Colonel Forbes, Director of the Veterans' Bureau, tele-phoned me inquiring why amendment for further hospitalization of ex-soldiers proposed yesterday to the Russian Relief Bill gave the Treasury Department instead of himself authority to dis-burse the money. I told him that senators doubted the capacity and the probity of (himself) Colonel Forbes.

December 27, 1921. Mrs. Ashurst and I dined with Reverend Sam W. Small and his sister at Casa Selva, Rosslyn, Virginia. Doctor Small was sometimes secretary to Ben Hill, U.S. Senator from Georgia, and was also secretary to ex-President Andrew Johnson who was elected to the Senate in 1875.

December 29, 1921. It is feared that France is cool toward that proposal of Arms Parley to check construction of capital ships and their auxiliary craft. Great Britain, sitting in her sea-girt isolation, naturally desires to outlaw the submarine.

The fears of France may or may not be reasonable; but France has twice within the last fifty years seen the German spearhead upthrust itself from the gates of the Rhine.

January 1, 1922. Senator Boies Penrose of Pennsylvania died here last night. In constructing a temple, in cooking a din-ner, in winning a battle, or in leading a political party, someone must do the laborious, tedious, unlovely work; someone must touch the grime, endure the heat, bear the weight, and give and receive the blows. Such persons must be strong and vital and such a man was Boies Penrose. He had a good intellect and was, educated. He was cynical and was an enigma even to his con-stituents, but their faith in his capacity to serve Pennsylvania was unshakeable.

His aims were the success of ·the Republican party and the perpetuation of himself in power. He was a baron of the feudal system of our politics, and he held his political organization to-gether by finesse or by iron bands, as exigencies required. He deceived no man; he wore no phylactery.

Not a few statesmen (some of them eminent) who received his help in their hour of need, abandoned him in 1912 as rats leave a sinking ship, but he kept his craft afloat and was re-elected to the Senate in 1914. He reached his zenith in 1920 and not only re-elected himself but nominated Warren G. Harding for the presidency. No wife, no child, wiped the death-damp from his brow and five minutes before his death he said to his physician he was "comfortable." All fair fighters hope that in the undiscovered country, Boies Penrose is comfortable.

January 7, 1922. My wife and I dined with Mr. and Mrs. Peter A. Drury at their residence. Among the guests were Senator Welsh of Massachusetts, Representative W. Bourke Cockran, Admiral Wm. S. Benson, Dr. Hannis Taylor, Attorney Frank P. Walsh of Kansas City, Mr. John McCormack, the Irish tenor, and Mr. and Mrs. Stephen O'Meara, the latter of whom was my dinner partner. Mr. O'Meara is the Lord Mayor of Limerick.

At dinner Mr. O'Meara received a cablegram from Mr. de Valera, President of the "Irish Republic," directing O'Meara to sail for Ireland, and he left immediately.

January 9, 1922. Senator Newberry spoke in his own defense and denied knowledge of "illegal expenditures."

It was assumed that Mr. Newberry would be subjected to a grueling cross-examination, but the questions propounded to him were so destitute of point that a reaction in Newberry's favor was created.

January 14, 1922. Luncheon at Hotel LaFayette given by Phil-Hellenic Society in honor of Mr. Tennadius, sometime Minister from Greece to U.S.; Mr. Alex Vourous, here on behalf of Greece seeking recognition for King Constantine's government; and Mr. Papafrango, president of National Bank of Greece.

Messrs. Tennadius, Vourous, and Papafrango asked me why recognition had not been extended to King Constantine's government; I made no reply but Senator King of Utah, who himself speaks like a cultivated Greek, replied that the banishment of former Premier E. Venizelos and the restoration of King Constantine, the brother-in-law of the former German Kaiser, who opposed the Allies during the World War, was not palatable to America.

January 29, 1922. Made my way through deep snow to Knickerbocker Theatre whose roof caved in last night, at Eighteenth Street and Columbia Road; found First Church of Christ Scientist, on Euclid, transformed into a temporary morgue. On the concrete floor of the church basement were mangled dead bodies brought from the ruined theatre. Another part of the same church served as temporary hospital where physicians and nurses were treating the injured. Sailors, soldiers, and marines were removing the dead and injured from beneath the twisted iron beams and the tons of snow, steel, and concrete which fell upon the audience last evening. Around the proscenium arch of the stage which was not demolished, the gilded masques of comedy and the faces of tragedy grinned upon the ruins.

The senators and representatives from the Colorado River Basin met at the residence of Secretary of Commerce Hoover, to discuss problems of the Colorado River.

January 31, 1922. The President nominated Senator William S. Kenyon to be United States Circuit Judge.

Comments of senators were tart. Senator Borah: "And he told me he would never accept." Senator Glass: "Harding is blocking the agricultural bloc." Senator Harrison said that President Harding, by placing Senator Kenyon, chairman of the agricultural bloc on the federal bench, was trying to destroy the agricultural bloc; whereupon the President issued a categorical denial.

February 2, 1922. Ex-Governor Hunt of Arizona arrived here having completed his term as our minister to Siam. Long talk with M. Jusserand, ambassador to U.S. from France. He said he was discouraged. He charged that England had misrepresented France by trying to make France appear as militaristic, and that his twenty years of work *here* had come to naught.

February 6, 1922. The Armament Conference closed. Amidst the praise showered upon President Harding for calling the Arms Conference, it is remembered that the Conference was initiated by Senator Borah who in December 1920, introduced a resolution requesting the President to call a naval disarmament conference and that in May 1921, the Borah Resolution,

as an amendment to the Naval Supply Bill, passed the Senate
with Yeas, seventy-four and Nays, none, and on June 29, 1921,
the Borah amendment passed the House by a vote of Yeas,
three hundred and thirty-two and Nays, four.

February 10, 1922. President Harding in person submitted
to the Senate the treaties, seven in number, of the Arms Parley-
ites, as follows:

The covenant of limitation to naval armament between
our Republic, the British Empire, France, Italy, and Japan.

The treaty "between" the same powers in relation to the
use of submarines and noxious gases in warfare.

The treaty between the United States, the British Empire,
France, and Japan relating to their insular possessions and
their insular dominions in the Pacific.

A declaration accompanying the four-power treaty reserv-
ing American rights in mandated territory.

An agreement supplementary to the four-power treaty de-
fining the application of the term "insular possession and
insular dominions" as relating to Japan.

A treaty "between" the nine powers in the Conference
relating to principles and policies to be followed in matters
concerning China.

A treaty between the nine powers relating to Chinese
customs tariff.

VIII   February, 1922 – September, 1923

Europe should forget its past.

Pittsburgh, Pa., February 21, 1922. Am writing in my room in the William Penn Hotel and am *not* intimidated by the telephone. The babbling in Washington anent bonus, tariffs, four-power treaty, foreign debt, primaries, and appropriations is inaudible now.

February 22, 1922. Addressed Pennsylvania bankers at William Penn Hotel last night; sophisticated and critical audience numbering eleven hundred.

Senator Lenroot was to be the speaker and I was a substitute because of Lenroot's illness.

February 24, 1922. Senator Capper of Kansas was elected chairman of agricultural bloc. The agricultural bloc had a recruit today in the person of Senator Frank B. Kellogg of Minnesota who is up for re-election and believes that agriculture must have encouragement.

February 25, 1922. By the Versailles Treaty, Germany renounced to the principal allied powers, to wit, the United States, the British Empire, France, Italy, and Japan, all her rights *in* and *to* her overseas possessions. The League of Nations Covenant (part of the treaty) agrees that these ex-German overseas possessions shall be mandated by the Council of the League, and the Council has vested mandatory power *in Japan* over the ex-German islands lying north of the equator.

By treaty between U.S. and Japan, signed in Washington February 11, 1922, it is agreed that the U.S. and its nationals shall have free access to the Island of Yap.

The ratification of this treaty and the Quadruple Alliance (Four-Power) Treaty will be, say the "Irreconcilables," the initial step of a series of steps on the part of Japan looking toward dominating the Orient.

February 28, 1922. President Harding addressed both Houses and urged a subsidy of 10 per cent from customs duties to be paid to American owners of vessels flying American flag.

March 1, 1922. Senate ratified the treaty between U.S. and Japan regarding Island of Yap.

March 13, 1922. Senators Johnson of California, Borah, Reed, and Robinson thundered against Quadruple Alliance and argued that when Russia resumes her place among the first rate powers, she may try to recapture Karafuto (Saghalein) and fishery rights on the Russian Pacific Coast of which she has been stripped by Japan, and that Quadruple Alliance might draw the U.S. into the controversy.

March 26, 1922. The Washington *Star* of this date says that Mrs. Ashurst may be appointed as Minister to the Irish Free State.

That Mrs. Ashurst is qualified to be the consort of an American Minister to a foreign government or to act as such Minister herself, there can be no doubt. During her years here she has capably met the responsibilities that devolve upon those in high official circles in the national capitol. Her judgment of men and events is telepathic and is unerring in its accuracy; her executive ability is of a high order. Formed in the most symmetrical proportions of her sex, compactly built, graceful in carriage and elite of movement, there is discernible about her a certain imperiousness, authority, and distinction. With superb brows of brown and a wealth of dark auburn hair, with gowns of dignity, disdainful of jewelry, she attracts immediate attention in any assemblage by her natural charm and easy grace.

March 29, 1922. Limitation of Naval Armament Treaty ratified; Yeas, seventy-four; Nays, one. Under this treaty the U.S. agrees to make no further fortifications in Guam and the Philippine Islands.

Treaty relating to use of submarines and noxious gases, ratified — Yeas, seventy-four; Nays, none.

March 30, 1922. Office cluttered with callers who want something from the government.

Young Theodore Roosevelt, now Assistant Secretary of the Navy, once said: "We need men who will put something into the government instead of taking something out of the government."

Senate ratifies Nine Powers Treaty with China; Yeas, sixty-five; Nays, none.

April 3, 1922. Many Arizonians here to secure issuance of licenses to develop hydro-electric power on the Colorado River. Secretary of Interior Albert Fall told me that, at Cabinet meeting, it had been decided that no hydro-electric power licenses will be granted to private capital to generate electricity on Colorado River until Congress first decides whether Boulder Dam shall be constructed.

April 11, 1922. Senate in executive session determined that Senator Smoot and Representative Burton are eligible for membership on World Court Foreign Debt Commission.

Letter few days ago from Mr. Archibald Douglas of New York advising me that Mr. Henry Merwin Shrady, sculptor of the massive statues making up Grant Memorial here, was penniless and ill at St. Luke's Hospital, New York.

Mr. Douglas' letter said that he would soon be in Washington looking toward Mr. Shrady's relief. Mr. Douglas whilst in my office today received telegram that Mr. Shrady was dead.

April 18, 1922. Washington government gloomy today. Whilst the Allies at Geneva Conference were discussing methods of compelling Germany to pay indemnities, the representatives of Russia entered into a treaty of trade and amity with Germany, canceling all claims Russia has against Germany.

April 21, 1922. Senator King spoke opposing recognition of Obregón government; he said that U.S. has claims against Mexico amounting to hundreds of millions of dollars, for lives and property of American citizens destroyed in Mexico during past twelve years and that there should be no recognition of any government until these claims are adjusted.

April 27, 1922. Grant Memorial unveiled. Did any one remember the destitution of the sculptor, Mr. Shrady?

May 9, 1922. During War days, through the efforts of Mrs. Marshall, wife of Vice-President Marshall, an organization was formed known as the "Ladies of the Senate." A room in the Senate Office Building was set apart for these ladies and on Tuesdays they made garments for the Red Cross. The wife of the Vice-President is the presiding officer and Mrs. Coolidge has kept the organization alive.

May 12, 1922. Senator Spencer of Missouri says Senator Reed of Missouri has strong opposition to re-nomination.

Mr. Reed is of more than medium height, with large head crowned by much gray hair. He has a wide mouth with its corners turned down. Attired in a sacksuit of blue in winter and white or gray in summer, he is the ever ready and deadly duelist upon any field where words are weapons.

May 27, 1922. Senator Lodge commenced his remarks on a parliamentary question with the sentence: "This discussion is one upon which I can restrain my feelings, etc., etc." A few minutes later he approached Senator Fred Hale, Republican, Maine, waved his clenched fists in Senator Hale's face and denounced him. I was not astonished as I knew of Senator Lodge's gameness, but it was surprising to see Lodge white from rage so soon after his boast that he could "restrain his feelings."

Philadelphia, June 1, 1922. I addressed graduating class of Pennsylvania Museum and School of Industrial Art, an institution founded here in 1876, and which grew out of the inspiration furnished by the Centennial held in this city during that year.

June 12, 1922. Brotherhood of Locomotive Firemen and Enginemen at their annual convention indorsed me for re-election.

June 14, 1922. Senator McCumber in charge of the tariff bill denounced Republican journals opposing high rates in pending tariff bill. He exhibited to the Senate razors, crockery, straw-hats, etc., made in Germany and sold here at 300 to 600 per cent above cost of manufacture.

Senator McCumber has ability and Scotch grit. His defeat for re-nomination is certain, but he goes down crimsoning the flood that engulfs him. In debate he exhibited a large cuckoo clock, made in Germany at a cost of one dollar and selling here at twenty dollars; Senator John Sharp Williams, thinking to bedevil McCumber, tried to start the cuckoo clock to crowing but like most things John Sharp has attempted lately, he made a "frizzle" and down fell the clock with loud clatter.

Senator Williams, sour in spirit, refuses to stand for re-election.

It is a dreary life here for disappointed men; all Senator Williams' old companions, viz., Senators Stone, Bankhead, Shivley, and Mark Smith are gone from the Senate, and he longs for his farm in Mississippi, remote from the din and hum of this mad world.

July 12, 1922. Mr. George H. Maxwell called at my house to discuss Colorado River problems. The tedious debate of the day, and my dinner of onions, milk, lettuce, tomatoes, asparagus, and other soporific foods, coupled with the heat, brought upon me drowsiness deeper than poppy or mandragora could have produced. I dared not appear indifferent to Mr. Maxwell, expert irrigationist, so unbeknown to him, I took my pocket knife and scarified the calf of my leg until the blood ran. Every time drowsiness re-appeared, I scraped the raw flesh with the knife; this kept me awake and thus I listened for three hours to Mr. Maxwell.

July 29, 1922. Mrs. Ashurst remarked today that I was slouchy in dress. Whilst she was thus talking, the postman brought an Arizona newspaper which says that I do nothing but "dress up" and parade myself as the "best dressed man in Washington."

August 9, 1922. Senate placed the hides of cattle *upon* the *free list*. Agricultural bloc defeated; Senator Lodge victorious.

The manufacturers of boots and shoes demanded "free hides." Influential constituents notified Senator Lodge that he as the Republican Majority Leader was so powerful as to drive through the Senate the treaty paying Colombia for Panama Canal Zone, he should be able also to obtain that which so redoubtable a protectionist as James G. Blaine championed, viz., "free hides."

Tombstone, Arizona, October 16, 1922. This is the town where my former colleague, Senator Mark Smith, began his career.

The chairman of my meeting here was Mr. Ostora Gibson, the first boy I met on that September day in 1883 when my father took my sister Eva, my brother Billie, and myself to the log schoolhouse in Flagstaff.

Since that day Mr. Gibson and I have been friends. When I was trying to be a cowboy he was likewise trying, and when I was turnkey in the Flagstaff jail, he was clerk of the court. He is strong of heart, purpose, and brain; is a lawyer, and is a poet of no mean order.

October 20, 1922. In my room at Safford I was seized with violent pains in stomach.

Motored to Pima; here Dr. Dryden told me I was dangerously ill from ptomaine poisoning.

Globe, October 21, 1922. Foolishly, I attempted to come here from Safford, eighty-five miles per auto; every few miles my companions lifted me out of the car and laid me on the sand by the roadside till the paroxysm passed.

October 22, 1922. Spoke last night in Globe and at conclusion of speech was carried to my hotel. I am on a diet of boiled milk.

October 26, 1922. I acted wisely yesterday in denying myself to callers. Those persons who buzz around a candidate and sap his strength will be the last to forgive if, from exhaustion, his evening speech lacks vigor.

October 27, 1922. Speaking at Buckeye, I lost control of the audience.

The opposition has attacked Mr. Hunt, Democratic nominee for governor, charging that he encouraged communism and syndicalism. I alluded to fact that Senate had confirmed Mr. Hunt's nomination as Minister to Siam and that such charges were exploded by favorable Senate action. During my speech I turned to a large man who had been raucously guffawing and asked him if he thought President Harding as a senator had acted wisely in voting to confirm Mr. Hunt's nomination.

"Yes, indeed," replied the scornful one; "Harding conferred a favor on our country in voting to send Hunt out of it, and the farther away he sent Hunt, the better for the country."

Prescott, November 8, 1922. Published letter of thanks.

To the People of Arizona:

For the third time you have elected me to the United States Senate, an office of great dignity and great responsibility, and in this hour of victory, I am very humble and very grateful. All my energies of heart and brain, modest enough, will be employed to guard and promote the safety, prosperity, and the honor of the people of our state and nation.

Henry F. Ashurst

The *Evening Courier* says that ex-Senator Albert J. Beveridge, Republican of Indiana, is defeated for U.S. Senate. Mr. Beveridge's defeat destroys his lifetime ambition to reach the Presidency. He helped to split the Republican party in 1912.

A political landslide means that, in their minds or in their bodies or in both, the voters are uncomfortable and strike at the tallest heads, and those are apt to be the heads in office.

November 10, 1922. I am elected by about eighteen-thousand majority.

Received beautiful letter from my late opponent Colonel McClintock.

Washington, November 30, 1922. Thomas Francis Bayard is new senator from Delaware. His father, Thomas Francis Bayard; his grandfather, James Asheton Bayard; his great-uncle, Richard Henry Bayard; his great-grandfather, James Asheton Bayard, and his great-great-grandfather, Richard Bassett, were U.S. senators from Delaware.

Defeated Republican senators are trouble-worn. Two years ago, having defeated Wilson and his works, they became "toploftical;" today they are dejected.

Moderation and restraint are the virtues of victory; patience and fortitude are the virtues of defeat.

December 6, 1922. The states of Arizona, California, Colorado, Nevada, New Mexico, Utah, and Wyoming having been, by act of Congress, authorized to enter into a compact apportioning waters of Colorado River, the commissioners from these states, with Honorable Herbert Hoover, Secretary of Commerce, presiding, met in Santa Fe, New Mexico, last November and signed a compact apportioning and dividing the waters of the Colorado River.

December 8, 1922. Heard the "Tiger" Georges Clemenceau speak at Memorial Continental Hall. He is old, sour, and bereft of hope. He is a philosophic pessimist, an ironic misanthrope, but has flashes of wit such as characterize his race. He wore, as usual, dark grey suede gloves, and even when he delved his hand into his pocket he did not remove his glove. He chided the U.S. for signing the Versailles Treaty (The League of Nations) and then "leaving France in the lurch" by failing to ratify the same. He says he has twice seen the Germans overrun France.

December 27, 1922. Senator Lodge opposed Senator Borah's amendment to Naval Bill proposing international conference to discuss the plight of civilization. Lodge says such conference would raise false hope and bring more disappointment.

December 28, 1922. President Harding sent letter to Senator Lodge opposing Borah's amendment proposing international conference and says the adoption of Borah's amendment would hamper the Executive in the diplomatic interplay now progressing.

December 29, 1922. Upon assurance from Senators Lodge and Watson that the Administration was sounding European chancellories as to an economic conference to be called by President Harding, Senator Borah withdrew his amendment to Naval Bill. Senator Johnson, in a speech bristling with sharp words, said Borah amendment was more likely to embroil the U.S. in European controversies than would the League of Nations.

January 6, 1923. France may seize Ruhr Valley; Senate passes resolution requesting President to withdraw American troops from Rhineland.

January 11, 1923. Senator Cameron, Republican, told me that he will not endorse ex-Governor Campbell, Republican, for Secretary of Interior.

The German Ambassador here handed Secretary of State Hughes Germany's protest against invasion of Ruhr Valley by French troops. Protest says that the invasion is oppressive and that the default in deliveries of coal and wood as per reparations was only technical.

January 19, 1923. President Harding entered the White House believing that T. R. rushed callers out and that President Wilson froze them out with curt words; therefore Mr. Harding resolved to be "urbane" toward callers.

President Harding is ill today; his strength worn away by callers who, learning of this "urbanity," overstay their welcome.

January 21, 1923. Mr. David Lloyd George, in an article in Mr. Hearst's *Times-Herald* says, anent the French invasion of the Ruhr: "When French troops marched on Essen they began a movement, the most far-reaching and probably most sinister in its consequences that has been witnessed for many centuries in Europe."

January 30, 1923. I spoke urging Constitutional amendment allowing the electors in the various states to vote directly upon amendments hereafter submitted.

February 14, 1923. Telegrams from some members of Arizona Legislature asking how a member should vote on ratification of Colorado River Compact. Replied that it was improper for a federal senator to indicate how members of a state legislature should vote and that members of a state legislature should remain free to vote as their judgment directed.

February 16, 1923. Senate passed bill funding the British debt. Senator Carter Glass of Virginia enthralled Senate and galleries by his eulogy of Great Britain's heroism during the World War. He said that but for Great Britain's navy, "thousands of American soldiers would have found a grave at the bottom of the Atlantic Ocean."

February 28, 1923. Introduced several Arizonians to Secretary of Commerce Herbert Hoover who presided at conference at Santa Fe, N. Mex., where Colorado River Compact was signed. Secretary Hoover said that no licenses for private power plants on Colorado River will be considered unless and until this Colorado River Compact is ratified by all the respective legislatures of the various states, signatory to the Compact.

March 1, 1923. Telegram from Governor Hunt asking me to vote *for* confirmation of Mr. Fred C. Jacobs, nominated for District Judge in Arizona.

March 3, 1923. Nomination of Mr. Jacobs for District Judge in Arizona was confirmed. Former Senator Mark Smith came into Democratic Cloak Room of Senate and urged some of the Democratic senators to vote against Mr. Jacobs' confirmation.

March 4, 1923. Amongst the fifteen senators retiring today are Senators Culberson of Texas and McCumber of North Dakota; each of whom has served twenty-four years. Culberson, skillful in tactics and finesse, was prevented by ill health from employing the political arts of which he is a master.

McCumber, the gritty Scot, was smothered beneath the chaff which fell upon him from the pitchforks of the agrarians of North Dakota.

March 9, 1923. Left Washington with Congressional party to inspect Boulder Canyon damsite on the Colorado River and to study Colorado River problems. We are accompanied by our ladies and are traveling in two Pullmans. Representative Phil B. Swing of California is in charge of the trip. Senator George W. Norris of Nebraska is the "star" of our party and is an able advocate of federal power plants to generate hydroelectric energy.

March 12, 1923. En route. Representative Hayden and I telegraphed to Governor Hunt of Arizona to be in Yuma on March 16, to welcome the Congressional party.

Las Vegas, Nevada. March 13, 1923. Many Arizonians here. Automobiles to Boulder Canyon, where the U.S. Reclamation Service is boring for bedrock. A gasoline launch, by making three trips, took all the party (our ladies excepted) to the damsite.

Some of my constituents were irritated because the arrangements to go to the damsite per the launch excluded them, and when we returned to Las Vegas, I spent some time urging my offended Arizona friends to attend the banquet tendered by the local Chamber of Commerce, which they did.

March 15, 1923. Reached El Centro and quartered at Hotel Barbara Worth, which derives its name from one of Mr. Harold Bell Wright's novels. The Colorado River some distance below Yuma now flows along and on the top of a deltaic cone (a hogback) and this hogback separates Imperial Valley from the head of the Gulf of California. It is a rampart of sand, higher than the Gulf of California and higher than Imperial Valley.

Imperial Valley and Salton Sea are below the level of the ocean, and the tendency of the Colorado River to leave this hogback and seek lowland requires no demonstration.

March 16, 1923. To Mexicali, where we were welcomed by Honorable José Lugo, governor of North District of Lower California.

At Andrade, California, we were met by Governor Hunt and about one hundred citizens of Yuma.

March 17, 1923. Inspected levees and examined Laguna Diversion Dam above Yuma.

Party not a little irritated last night by the long speech made by Colonel Fly at Yuma. Many speeches. I made the shortest and said: "If the Southwest does not become the master of the Colorado River, it will become its victim."

Governor Hunt and I, following our custom, refrained from reference to politics and we did not give to each other any opinion as to the Colorado River Compact.

Mr. Frank E. Weymouth, chief engineer of the U.S. Reclamation Service, declared that the construction of a storage reservoir on the Colorado River and the All-American Canal were necessary to save Imperial Valley from destruction. He opposes issuance of licenses for private power plants on Colorado River.

San Diego, March 20, 1923. Bay trip, as guests of Admiral Welles; inspection of coast defenses and Naval Training Station at San Diego Bay. During this trip I have limited my speeches to five minutes. Mr. Anturo del Toro with us today. He says Mexico will not sell Lower California. Motored to Tia Juana, Lower California. Amusements and gambling going full blast. Painted harridan and pale-lipped gambler, race track tout, and flashily-dressed sportsmen mingled in the throng.

Los Angeles. March 22, 1923. Quartered at Alexandria Hotel. Delegation from the Young Men's Democratic Club invited me to deliver political speech, which invitation I declined, owing to the auspices under which I am here. Scores of Arizonians waiting for us.

Near Long Beach, on Signal Hill, we saw 750 wells and ninety-five of them are producing oil. One well took fire recently and threatened the entire field whereupon ten Trojan workmen were employed at one-hundred dollars per hour; asbestos clothing was put upon them, and after ten fiery hours of Gehenna, these brave salamanders capped the well, put out the flames, drew their pay, and returned to their homes. Before going to work, each man drew his will and said his farewells, but they won the fight and saved the field.

Los Angeles. March 25, 1923. Party dissolved today; some start for Grand Canyon, some for Europe, some for Alaska, and some for home.

From Flagstaff I find criticism of myself and Representative Hayden for "allowing the Congressional junket" to go to the Colorado River per Nevada instead of Arizona.

March 30, 1923. To Azusa, where I spent the day with Mother. She told me of the days in 1876 she spent on a ranch near what is now Williams, Arizona, where her nearest neighbors were the Pittmans, an excellent family, fourteen miles away, but that she had not seen any of that family for over forty-six years. She had no sooner finished her statement than an auto stopped at her door containing callers, one of them, to her great surprise proved to be Mr. Sidney Pittman, of the family we had just discussed, and who resides near.

Globe, Arizona. April 6, 1923. At the Globe Luncheon Club, I said: "A destiny we could not escape would require the U.S.

to participate in settling grave questions by the rule of reason and justice as announced by an International Court."

Phoenix, April 8, 1923. Sandy Donahue of Flagstaff gave me newspapers from northern Arizona from which it is obvious that much "soreness" exists there because Representative Hayden and I did not *compel* the Congressional party to visit that region.

April 10, 1923. Attended reunion of Arizona pioneers at Riverside Park, Phoenix, where were assembled over one thousand men and women who trekked into Arizona before the railroads came. Representative Hayden, Governor Hunt, Colonel McClintock, State Historian George Kelly, Mr. John Orme, Mayor Whitney, and former Governor Richard Sloan, and I spoke. This is the first public function in which Mr. Sloan and I have jointly participated since our difference in 1912 over the district judgeship.

Judge Sloan, in his speech, went on to say that neither the migration of the Scandinavians nor those of the Spanish Conquistadores were comparable to the exploits of the American pioneers, who conquered, first the forest, then the plain, then the desert, and built states as they migrated.

Amongst my callers was "Sandy" Donahue, once healthy and prosperous; but his strength has oozed away and he is now penniless. Vast sums of money have slipped through his fingers, for large was his bounty before his money took wings. He requested a loan of twenty-five dollars which I was glad to grant, for I cannot forget that he called me from cowboy life, thirty years ago, where I was eating sourdough bread, drinking rank coffee, and riding hard under the winter stars for pitiably small wages, to my first real "job," viz., turnkey in the county jail, at sixty dollars per month, then a princely salary.

Prescott, April 13, 1923. My brother William (teaching school at Cherry) is in Prescott tonight. I showed him on Montezuma Street the building which was Dan Hatz' Hotel, where in 1879, in Prescott's early days, our family once put up.

April 22, 1923. Met Mr. J. M. (Roxie) Duncan, who thirty-seven years ago was camped near the Ashurst Ranch as a cowboy for the Aztec Cattle Co. Whilst shoeing a horse, a piece of the shoe nail flew into his eye and destroyed it. My father took him to Flagstaff for treatment. "Roxie" never resumed cowboy life but became a bartender and when the light of the saloons went out, he worked as a janitor.

Phoenix, May 7, 1923. Wife left Phoenix per Santa Fe train for Washington, and I left per Southern Pacific train for California.

May 10, 1923. Mother and I passed through Stockton, Calif., where twenty-eight years ago I learned to write shorthand. I could recognize nothing but the depot and it looks the same as it did the morning I arrived there to begin my study of pothooks and curlicues.

At Sacramento visited Sutter Fort, the greatest of the old trading posts of the West. It contains a collection of the reliques of the days of "forty-nine." Saw a "prairie schooner" of oak, hickory, and iron, which traversed the deserts and negotiated the mountain passes, bringing hither during the gold rush not only entire families, but supplies for the Jasons and Argonauts. As we passed through Tehama, California, Mother pointed out to me a brick building where she attended school sixty years ago.

May 11, 1923, Salem, Oregon. Brother Edward and I stopped at hotel whilst the ladies remained at Edward's house. Edward will graduate next month from the Willamette University and will receive license to practice law. With zeal and self-denial he has pursued his studies under many handicaps.

May 14, 1923. Mother and I at Seattle.

Leaving Mother in the hotel, I went to Big Lake to see my brother Andrew.

May 17, 1923, Billings, Montana. Ex-Senator Myers took me to Hotel Grand, where we discussed his prospects. Senator Myers during the last year of his term was anxious to leave the Senate and resume law practices, but he now perceives that it is difficult to resume the place he held at the bar when he went to the Senate.

Washington, May 23, 1923. I saw Senator Borah, who says that if Idaho Republicans do not nominate him, the Democrats will.

May 25, 1923. Mr. Appleton P. C. Griffin of Library of Congress, told me that ex-Senator Beveridge who wrote *Life of John Marshall* is now writing *Life of Abraham Lincoln.*

Mr. Griffin said that Mr. Beveridge was unable to secure access to certain Lincoln data inasmuch as the surviving son, Mr. Robert T. Lincoln, had sealed up memoranda of his father and placed them into a vault in the Congressional Library, directing that same shall not be opened until Robert T. Lincoln shall have been dead twenty-one years.

May 26, 1923. Called on President Harding who soon leaves for Alaska. I warned him to conserve his strength. He said the labor of assembling material for his speeches on this trip would be immense but could not be avoided; that he could not employ the same speech on all occasions, but must have a different one for each function.

July 2, 1923. My wife and I reached Tilbury Docks on the Thames, London, today. Quartered at Imperial Hotel, Russell Square. To Prince of Wales Theatre in Coventry Street and saw an Anglo-American Comedy *So This Is London.*

July 3, 1923. Called at the American Embassy; the Ambassador, Honorable George Harvey, was in Washington, but Mr. Post Wheeler, the chargé d'affaires, extended civilities.

Thence to the lobby of the House of Commons; I sent cards to the Honorable Thomas P. O'Connor, dean of the House of Commons, called "Tay Pay." Mr. O'Connor showed us a golden snuffbox which the members of the House gave him in honor of his forty-third consecutive year as a member.

Mrs. Ashurst was placed into the Speaker's Private Gallery, whilst I was inducted into the Distinguished Stranger's Gallery. Animated debate was in progress on the question of repealing that part of the Land Transfers Act requiring the sending to the Land Valuation Department full particulars as to transfers of realty. As I entered, former Premier, Mr. David Lloyd George, was concluding his speech in opposition to the repeal. Mr. Austen Chamberlain broke from his own party lines to oppose the repeal and he counseled his party associates not to screen misdeeds regarding property transfers. Adverting to his objection to testing the consistency of members, he said: "I hope we shall rid, and quickly, of any idea that consistency in these matters is a virtue."

Former Premier, Mr. Herbert Henry Asquith, was next up and also opposed the repeal. Thus two ex-Prime Ministers (Asquith and Lloyd George) joined forces on this question. The Land Valuation Act was passed whilst Mr. Asquith was Prime Minister. Mr. Asquith is a Yorkshire Englishman of dignity of presence, of trenchant dialect, and strength of language. He clings to his old habit of pressing his clenched hands against his breast whilst speaking. There is about him a scholarship, an authority, and distinction. In his speech he paraphrased Grattan and said: "I have watched by the cradle and am now following the hearse of this law." As an orator Mr. Asquith possesses the majestic style of bygone days. I must ride my pen on the curb-bit when writing of this favorite of mine. Before the World War broke out, he brought as Prime Minister many reforms, then denounced as "radical," e.g., Workmen's Compensation Act, Insurance Acts, Taxation Act, and modernizing the House of Lords. Whilst he will not reach the fame of Chatham, Disraeli, and Gladstone, he superbly served his day and generation.

Sir W. Joynson-Hicks, nicknamed "Jix," was next up and supported the repeal. Although "Jix," was shelled by heavy artillery like Asquith, Lloyd George, Austen Chamberlain, and Ramsey MacDonald, he gave a good account of himself. Mr. J. Ramsay MacDonald (Labor), the leader of His Majesty's Opposition in the House of Commons, was the next up and his speech brought out cries of "Hear," "Hear." At a late hour, Prime Minister Baldwin arose, and in closing the debate he assured Members that the *Land Valuation Department* would go on functioning and that *only the taxes and fees* incident to registration of transfers would be repealed. The majority in favor the repeal was seventy-three, a victory for the Prime Minister.

At adjournment came cries of "Who goes home?" This cry comes down from those troublous times, centuries ago, when the members went home in squads to defend themselves against robbers.

The word "Hear" shouted in England by auditors, is a part of the phrase, "Hear him" — originally employed to silence disturbers and remind them of their duty of listening to the discussion — and is now and long has been a cry of admiration and acquiescence, although sometimes used derisively.

July 4, 1923. Londoners make a gala day of the Fourth of July, or "Independence Day," as they call it. Went to National Gallery in front of which is a statue of George Washington, a replica of the Statue by Houdon, the originals of which are in Richmond, Virginia and in the rotunda of the American Capitol.

In this gallery are the works of artists who have vindicated the pencil by showing its power of delineating human emotion.

Thence to the Royal United Service Institution, in a building which was once the banqueting hall of Whitehall Palace and is the only remaining mark of the old palace.

In this museum is Cromwell's watch, about the size and shape of a large tomato. Here is Lord Nelson's spyglass which he put to his *blind* eye, so that a signal to retreat would be invisible.

Mrs. Ashurst and I went to a reception tendered by Chargé d'Affaires and Mrs. Post Wheeler of the American Embassy. Mr. Gordon Selfridge, once of Chicago but now a London merchant, loaned to our Embassy for this reception, his residence, the Lansdowne House in Berkeley Square. Three thousand Americans present.

July 5, 1923. To Westminster Abbey — the British national sanctuary.

Westminster Abbey is an epic poem of the English-speaking race set in stone. It bears the impress of England through the shifting prisms and shadows of tumultuous centuries. Here are gathered memorials linked by memory's chain to generations long vanished.

Here sleeps the dust of Kings and Queens; here are monuments of remembrance; whilst here and there rise preposterous monuments which are no criterion by which to judge the career of those intended to be commemorated.

There was once the custom of carrying in the funeral procession of the dead King or Queen a waxen effigy of the sovereign clad in the royal apparel of the deceased. In a chamber of the Royal Chapel are waxen effigies not only of some of the deceased sovereigns but of other persons such as the Earl of Chatham, General Monk, and Lord Nelson.

The coronation chair, which was made for Edward the First, is in this abbey and beneath its seat is the Stone of Destiny.

The Chapter House of Westminster Abbey is an octagonal building with a slender central pillar. This building was completed in the middle of the thirteenth centutry and the House of Commons was born in this room nearly seven centuries ago, for here Parliament first assembled when Simon de Montfort laid the foundations of constitutional government. It now contains some seals and ancient charters that belong to the Record Office.

This room has seen the age-long struggle of the English people for liberty.

A few steps away is the Chapel of the Pyx. The word "Pyx" has no ecclesiastical significance as it refers only to the huge chests, (still there) in which the standards of references for testing the coin of the realm were kept.

July 7, 1923. To Westminster Palace, where I was introduced to Brigadier General John Sanctuary Nicholson, member of the House of Commons representing Westminster Abbey constituency. General Nicholson is a historian and antiquarian and on Saturdays he escorts visitors through Westminster Palace, giving a sketch of the origin of Parliament.

The Palace of Westminster, where the two Houses of Parliament and their committees assemble, derives its name from the fact that it was, in early times, the seat of Kings. The only remaining part of the old Westminster Palace is Westminster Hall. This structure (Westminster Hall) was built by William the Second (Rufus the Red) as a place to feast his barons and was known for generations as "Rufus' Roaring Hall." Carpenters were today finishing their ten-year task of saving its roof from the ravages of the death-watch beetle, which insect has tunneled lineally along the great oaken timbers of the roof. This roof was built during the reign of Richard II and is "an unrivalled masterpiece of medieval carpentry." Carved angels are still floating on stiff wings at the end of the hammer-beams. In this hall were tried: Sir Thomas More, Anne Boleyn, Protector Somerset, Northumberland, Norfolk, Warwick, Arundel, Guido Faux, Strafford of the Policy of Thorough, King Charles I, The Seven Bishops, Warren Hastings, and other suspected of *lese majesty.*

After the Restoration, Charles II caused Oliver Cromwell's body to be exhumed from Westminster Abbey, first to be hanged, then decapitated. Cromwell's head, after severance from the body, was taken to Westminster *Hall* and stuck upon one of the long iron spikes, on the Hall's roof, which were reserved for the display of the heads of traitors. Cromwell's skull remained there for twenty years, until one stormy night, when the spike, eaten through by rust, broke off, the skull fell into the street and was carried away by an unrecorded individual.

July 8, 1923. Motored to Hampton Court, a palace begun by Cardinal Woolsey, thence to the Island of Runnymede in the Thames, where King John in 1215 signed Magna Charta. About this tiny island, clusters the birth of some principles vitalized by the American Declaration of Independence. Thence we went to Windsor Castle, the favorite seat of most of England's rulers and here sleeps the dust of that much-married monarch, King Henry VIII.

July 9, 1923. Spent the day at the High Court of Justice. An interesting case came on in the Court of Criminal Appeal of the King's Bench Division in the Lord Chief Justices Court, as follows:

Edward Fitzgerald, Duke of Leinster, had been convicted in the Recorder's Court of purchasing an automobile on credit without disclosing to the vendor that he, the Duke, was an undischarged bankrupt. The recorder remanded the Duke into custody for two weeks within which time the Recorder will determine what punishment, if any, will be inflicted.

The Duke, through Barrister Mr. Comyns-Carr, applied for bail, which was denied by the Lord Chief Justice's Court with a celerity which caused the barrister to flush to a deeper scarlet than that of the gowns which the Justices wore.

Visited the "Temple" within which, for the past eight-hundred years, generations of statesmen, politicians, philosophers, poets, authors, novelists, historians, lawyers, and judges have lived, studied, and toiled.

Before our Revolutionary War, many of the men sent out to the American colonies to hold judicial position as well as a number of the lawyers born in the American colonies had been students at the Temple.

Noblemen placed their sons into the Temple's Inns not only to have them learn the law and live by its practice but also to learn to sing and to dance.

In the Temple church are effigies on the coffin lid of Crusaders, in purbeck marble, with their legs crossed at appropriate places to indicate whether they went to one, two, or three crusades and here is the organ selected by Lord Chief Justice Jeffries just before he set out for the Bloody Assizes. Nearby is the building where Oliver Goldsmith lived the last nine years of his life, and nearby is his grave.

In the hall of the Middle Temple is the platform made of heavy oaken planks taken from the "Golden Hind" in which ship Sir Francis Drake sailed on his voyage around the world, and in this hall, Shakespeare played in his *Twelfth Night.* In the middle of the Temple hall below the dais is a serving table also made from the timbers of Drake's "Golden Hind."

I walked to the top of St. Paul's Cathedral, built by Sir Christopher Wren, of whom it is said, "When he died, architecture in England fell asleep."

We attended a musicale given by Chargé d'Affaires and Mrs. Post-Wheeler at Chelsea Embankment where we met Viscountess Astor, of Virginia birth. Her husband, Waldorf Astor, was made a Viscount in 1917, and she is entitled therefore to sit in the Peeresses' Gallery of the House of Lords and is also entitled to a seat in that particular Gallery of the House of Lords designated for Members of the House of Commons.

Lady Astor is disturbed by the French occupation of the Ruhr, and went on to say that if civilization permitted another World War to take place, civilization would not survive and did not *deserve* to survive.

We also met Mr. Hamlin Garland and his wife and daughter. Mr. Garland is a famous American writer; he has a dignified mien and a large head covered with longish iron-grey hair. Honorable Andrew W. Mellon, our Secretary of the Treasury, and a score of other prominent Americans were present.

Mrs. Post-Wheeler said it was now time to go to the buffet-supper room and that I must lead the procession thereto with the Ambassador's daughter, Mrs. Thompson, as my partner.

July 10, 1923. To the British Museum. Read some of Lord Macaulay's manuscripts and read the letter of George Washington dated April 22, 1793 addressed to Lord Buchan, advising His Lordship that "It is the sincere wish of united America to have nothing to do with the political intrigues or squabbles of European nations."

Upon invitation of Lord Huntly, I again visited the House of Lords. Viscount Grey of Falloden asked the government whether their Lordships might on next Thursday expect a statement on the Ruhr, and the Marquis of Salisbury said a statement would be made on that day. Viscount Grey then moved the second reading of the Wild Birds' Protection Bill and spoke fifteen minutes in its support.

I *stood* in the appropriate gallery and Lord Huntly explained that the two Houses of Parliament are not as generous in providing seats for visitors as are the two Houses of the American Congress.

July 11, 1923. Visited the Tower of London built by William the Conqueror. It is a series of towers and in it are kept the crown jewels and a collection of armor and ancient weapons. It is a storehouse where are recalled memories of mistakes and bygone blunders.

During the American Revolution, Henry Laurene of South Carolina, sometime President of the Continental Congress, whilst on his voyage to Holland, there to serve as our Minister, was captured by a British vessel, kept a prisoner in the Tower of London for fifteen months until exchanged for Lord Cornwallis.

Attended court at Old Bailey, criminal court of London county. A man named Alexander Mason was on trial charged by an indictment found by a grand jury with the murder of a taxicab driver.

There was no *voir dire* examination of the jurors. Their names were drawn in open court from a list of the qualified voters. The jury was selected in seven minutes and each juryman was sworn separately. Two women were drawn but were peremptorily challenged and dismissed.

Defective indictments are at once amended upon order of the court.

Jurors take copious notes during the trial and writing materials are provided for this purpose.

The attorney general usually designates the prosecuting officer and such prosecutor may or may not be a King's counsel, but likely it is one who has "taken silk."

The witnesses stand during their examination. Leading and direct questions, such as are not permitted in American courts, seem to be welcome.

No time limit is placed upon the arguments to the jury.

The trial judge comments upon the evidence before the jurymen retire to deliberate, and this is called a "summing up."

Dublin, Ireland, July 12, 1923. Quartered at the Shelbourne Hotel, Dublin. This hotel facing St. Stephen's Green was the town house of the Lansdowne family. In this hotel, the Constitution of the Irish Free State was formulated.

July 13, 1923. We visited St. Patrick's Cathedral built A.D. 1190 by John Comyn, Archbishop of Dublin, on the site of the ancient Celtic Church of St. Patrick. In this church are buried Dean Swift and Stella. Thence to the Cathedral of the Holy Trinity (Christ Church), built by Strongbow and the Anglo-Normans.

Thence to Glasnevin Cemetery where sleep Daniel O'Connell, Charles S. Parnell, Michael Collins, Harry Boland, and Arthur Griffith. Statues fill the niches of the public buildings and adorn parks of this city.

July 14, 1923. Called on American Consul and thence to University of Dublin (Trinity College), incorporated by Charter of Elizabeth and opened for students in 1593. This university has one hundred teachers and about a thousand students, many of whom live the communal life such as is lived by students at Oxford and Cambridge. Here is the beautiful Book of Kells and other relics of the early Christian church. The University of Dublin receives a copy of every book published in the United Kingdom. Protestants, Catholics, and Jews alike are admitted as students. In front of the college are statues of Oliver Goldsmith and Edmund Burke.

Visited the Castle of Dublin rebuilt A.D. 1700. All of the woodwork of the interior of its Chapel Royal is of carved Irish oak. Thence visited the Bank of Ireland occupying a building which was until 1800 the Irish Parliament House.

Ireland's soil is fertile; its climate genial and its position for trade advantageous. The talent of the Irish for public affairs, their driving force, and their genius for administration and command will keep the Free State on an even keel. The Irish Free State has its own flag, prints its own postage stamps, and will mint its own coin.

The landscape of Ireland is frequently hidden in mist and rain, but when the sun shines there is richness of coloring and the hills glow with green and purple.

July 15, 1923. We drove through Phoenix Park founded by Lord Chesterfield whilst he was Lord Lieutenant of Ireland. Lord Chesterfield is remembered in Ireland affectionately but his fame is world-wide through his book, *Letters to his Son;* a book cynical yet sincere, a book that would instruct Machiavelli in the art of deceit, and yet withal, this book was never intended for publication.

July 16, 1923. The American Consul, Mr. Hathaway, furnished us with letters of introduction to Mr. Desmond Fitzgerald, Minister for External Affairs of the Saorstat Eireann (Irish Free State), who escorted us to the building where was in session the Dail Eireann (Chamber of Deputies) or popular branch of the Oireachtas (Irish Parliament). The Seanad Eireann (Irish Senate) was not in session. The Dail was holding its session in a theater of the National Museum of Science and Art of the Royal Dublin Society. One fundamental question to which the Oireachtas is addressing itself is land-ownership. This troublesome question of agrarian grievances had its origin at the time of the invasion of Ireland by Strongbow.

We met the Sergeant-at-Arms of the Dail, Mr. Byrne. His cravat-pin was a large gold nugget such as those found around Prescott, Arizona. I said to him, "Mr. Sergeant-at-Arms, you have been in Arizona or Alaska and have worked in the gold mines." He replied: "Yes, but I have returned to my native land."

Kilkenny, Ireland, July 17, 1923. Visited St. Canice's Church built in the twelfth century. Hard by stands a cylindrical tower of stone one hundred feet high, built *some* say in the third century by sun worshippers and *some* say in the ninth century as a point of defense against marauding Danes. Saw the house where my wife was born. For centuries the Ormond family has been puissant and opulent in Ireland, and Ormond Castle is almost in the center of this town.

London, July 20, 1923. In theory, the will of Parliament in England is omnipotent. The House of Lords under the 1910 veto law may not reject a bill sent to it by the House of Commons more than twice in the same consecutive session.

The power of tradition, in England, especially in her Foreign Office and her Treasury, is great. It is difficult to imagine a Prime Minister giving effect to a policy opposed by the Foreign Office staff and the Diplomatic Corps. These officials could not be ousted without breaking down the elaborate system of British diplomacy established throughout the centuries. The Treasury is almost a law unto itself and in its hands are concentrated the vast details of financial administration.

There are two contrasting sides of the Englishman, Irishman, Scotsman, and Welshman, for they have at *one* and the same *time* a realism which produces practicality and self-control, whilst the other trait, mysticism, gives them a tendency to moralize and to trust to the Law of Compensation.

The Englishman has a self-sufficiency — an insularity, and in a formal way with staccato voice says "Thank you;" he is not interested in the political and religious quarrels of the past, but is attached to his form of government. To him, the King is a symbol of the strength, order, and progress of the British Empire. He believes in the firmness and efficiency of authority. He serves on the jury and votes "Not Guilty" or "Guilty" without regard to consequences to himself. He takes vacations and looks out for his creature-comfort. The aged Englishman looks with mingled pride and envy upon the American nation and regards it as a runaway youth who has amounted to considerable. The younger Englishmen are proud that America speaks the English language and that we have drawn our laws and customs so largely from England. Both the young and old, however, seem to believe that we are a money-grabbing, hurrying people, devoted to the gods of speed, majority, success, bulk, and height, rather than to the gods of quality, repose, and durability.

There are seventy-thousand joint stock companies in England that hold meetings each month. These joint stock companies rather than the newspapers, in the final test, control public opinion.

Paris, July 21, 1923. From Folkstone we crossed the Channel of Boulogne, France. I had a tin box containing forty cigars, which cost me in Los Angeles five cents each. When the French Customs officer saw them, he let out a sibilant "Ah—ha—a—a" and charged me one dollar twenty cents duty on my cigars.

We are quartered at the Hotel Silvia at the Rue Gaudot-de-Mauroy, just behind the Boulevard de Capucines.

July 24, 1923. Visited Rue de Rivoli, Tuileries Gardens, Palais de la Legion d'Honneur, Quai d'Orsay, Avenue des

Champs-Élysées, Arc de Triomphe de l'Etoile (Tomb of the Unknown Soldier), Monument to Victor Hugo, Palais du Trocadero,
Champ de Mars, Pantheon de la Guerre (National Panorama),
les Invalides and Tomb of Napoleon. Colonel Robert G. Ingersoll once referred to "that sarcophagus of *black* Egyptian marble"
but the sarcophagus is hewn out of a solid block of *red* Finland
marble.

July 25, 1923. Visited the Opera House (National Theatre)
and the Louvre Museum wherein we saw *Venus of Milo,* a
masterpiece of ancient statuary dating back to the fourth century B.C.

Called on Lieutenant Colonel Bunau-Varilla whom we met
in 1921, in Washington at Arms Parley. He is an authority on
the Panama Canal and was a friend of de Lesseps. Colonel
Bunau-Varilla lost a leg at Verdun. He says Georges Clemenceau
was a war premier of first magnitude but that at the Peace Conference in Versailles he yielded too much to Lloyd George.

July 26, 1923. Visited the Palace of Versailles. At this Palace
the French kings held the most fashionable court of modern
times. Saw the Galerie des Glaces (Hall of Mirrors) where the
Emperor, William the First, was proclaimed German Emperor
in 1871, and where the delegates of Germany signed the Peace
Treaty on June 28, 1919.

At noontime the visitors to Versailles proceed to nearby
restaurants and drink champagne to the shade of King Louis
XIV. But it is not only in the cafes near Versailles that the
American visitor to Paris encounters the battalions of Bacchus.

Thence to the palace gardens and those of the Grand Trianon, also the Petit Trianon and the rustic hamlet where Marie
Antoinette sought rest from the tedium of state ceremony by
doing the work of a dairymaid. Visited the Chateau of Mal-
maison (the residence of Napolean and Josephine) which has
been restored to the appearance it had at the time of the fallen
Emperor's last visit thereto before his departure for St. Helena.

July 27, 1923. To the Pantheon, devoted by the Constituent
Assembly to the memory of great men; thence to the Sainte-
Chapelle built in the thirteenth centutry to preserve reliques

brought to Paris from the Crusades. It contains two chapels; the Chapelle Basse and the Chapelle Haute. Near the fourth window on the right in the Chapelle Haute is a recess which Louis XI built to enable him to hear Mass without being seen.

The ceiling of the Chapelle Basse is of deepest blue, but the principal ornamentation of the Chapelle is fifteen stained-glass windows each of which is a dazzling jewel. All are of thirteenth-century workmanship.

Thence to Notre-Dame, a cathedral begun in A.D. 1163, and 300 years in building. Here is a rose window forty feet in diameter. All its windows are of thirteenth-century work.

July 28, 1923. Colonel Bunau-Varilla with a Cadillac car and a Roumanian chauffeur took us to Belleau and its tragic Wood. Thence to Chateau Thierry. It owes its name to the Chateau, built in the fifth century to serve as a prison for the King Thierry II.

Thence to Rheims, the centre of the champagne trade, and here is the hull of the cathedral, the construction of which was begun in the year 400 A.D. and which cathedral has seen the consecration of nearly every French King, from Clovis. In front of this cathedral is an equestrienne statue of Joan of Arc (concealed during the War), a replica of the statue on Meridian Hill at Washington.

Thence we went to Fismes, a town mentioned by Caesar. My nephew, Albert Pitts, took part in a battle here in 1918 and was later killed at Juvigny a few miles away. Visited the battlefield where he was slain.

July 30, 1923. The English, Scotch, and Welsh have a certain seriousness of aspect, and preoccupation of faculty. Life, with them (whilst not as complex as it is for us in the United States) is a heavy task.

All insular people bear weighty burdens. A nation sitting in seagirt isolation (England) needs must closely watch its highways of commerce, the seas. The English and Scotch and Welsh are slow to rebound and gather new strength. The Irish and French bounce like a rubber ball or float like a cork.

In France, life seems joyous; the beggar and the flower-girl; the opulent merchant-prince and the man with a tinkling tambourine; the grand dames and the girls struggling against penury, each and all have a graceful mien. Mars or Venus, with equal quickness, stirs French blood. The Parisian finds rapture in a pulseless statue in the park; he believes no one is "cultured" who is ignorant of the history of Paris. He loves the sunshine which is poured over France from the inverted goblet of the skies. The French are fountains of vivacity. They have curiosity, emotion, and enthusiasm and they have filled Paris with statues and paintings.

In England, the people are inclined to travel in ruts worn deep by their customs and traditions.

With them life is discipline, self-regulation, and self-restraint.

The orderly sequence of events, doing today what they did yesterday, does not appear monotonous to the English.

With the average Parisian there are bypaths leading him temporarily from the dull day into pleasant pastures of harmless relaxation.

This is not to imply that the people of England lack manly and vigorous sports, for they are indeed game sportsmen. Neither is it to imply that the Parisian's existence is a mere flitting from joy to joy, but I *do* say that the Parisian restores his exhausted strength and takes new hold on life after he has patronized any device, abstract or concrete, that amazes or delights.

He can banish trouble for a week by hearing one neatly turned bon mot and he beams after hearing a pungent epigram.

July 31, 1923. The courier furnished by Messrs. Cook and Son took us to Quai d'Orsay station. At noon we started for the dining car but the train conductor made us to understand that as we had no dining car *tickets* we could not secure dining seats for at least two hours. An Englishman (owner of the largest cucumber farm in England) acted as our interpreter. I handed the conductor forty francs, telling him to hold them before his eyes and he would perceive two empty seats in the dining car. We were seated immediately. At nightfall, at Pau, found a café near the depot and secured roast mutton and tea. Never was better beverage brewed than that pot of tea we drank at Pau.

At twenty-four of the clock (midnight) we reached Lourdes. One-thousand feet above the town, was a gleaming cross fifty feet high, made of many incandescents, on the summit of the Grand Jer Mountain.

In the afternoon we ascended the Grand Jer by the funiculaire or cable railway and from the top of the Jer we saw many peaks of the Pyrenees.

In Lourdes are many Basque peasants with faces seemingly carved out of dark oak; with long thin lips, half-ironical and half-cordial; here, oxen with sheepskin head-coverings and caparisoned with white blankets like the sacrificial oxen of olden times, are driven slowly along the roads.

These Pyrenees Mountains are ramparts behind which are customs, manners, and dialects that have changed but little during the past one-thousand years.

Night comes like a great blue bell slowly capping the town, and here, as in Arizona, the western sky, reluctant to be robbed of its evening colors, clings long to its wedges of flaming gold and its tapestry.

Lourdes, August 1, 1923. Flinging open the shutters this morning, I was charmed by a medley of mountainside farms and picturesque nature above the town. There were the Pyrenees Mountains and on their verdant slopes were white farmhouses with red-tiled roofs. Below our window there rushed the Gave de Pau, a clear stream fed by the dew and rain and snow of the Pyrenees Mountains.

Attended services in the gleaming white basilica. Its interior is relieved by soft lights and graceful arches.

At four o'clock P.M. the procession started in which all the pilgrims in Lourdes take part. The procession leaves the Grotto, follows the pathways of the Esplanade and is led by the ecclesiastical dignitaries.

At the evening procession each pilgrim carried a lighted candle and hymns were sung by the various pilgrims in their respective language. The care of the sick persons who visit Lourdes — numbering scores of thousands annually — their conveyance from the railroad station to the Grotto, and their immersion in the baths, is confided to two pious associations named "Hospitality." The Grotto consists of three clefts of unequal size in a rock named "Massabille" which signifies "old rock." The statue in the niche represents the Apparition and is made of Carrara marble.

August 2, 1923. Secured an English-language paper which said that President Harding had been stricken with ptomaine poisoning on his Alaskan trip and that pneumonia had set in.

August 3, 1923. Secured an English-language paper, printed at Paris yesterday morning, and learned that President Harding was recovering.

Went to Castel-Fort, standing in centre of the town, built on a rock one-hundred thirty-six feet high. Roman, Vandal, and Visigoth successively occupied this fort. The Sacracens when defeated by Charles Martel retreated toward the Pyrenees, and some of them took refuge within the walls of this fort.

August 4, 1923. My wife went shopping. I went to newsstand and secured yesterday morning's Paris edition of *New York Herald,* printed in English. The headlines anent President Harding's condition read as follows:

"President's Physicians Declare Danger Passed"
"Doctors Show Optimism — Dr. Sawyer Says
Recovery is Matter of Time."

I walked on to the post office nine blocks distant and thence aimlessly returned to the same newsstand, but no sooner had I re-entered the newsstand than I saw in *La Petite Gironde,* a newspaper published in Bordeaux this morning, the headlines:

"Le President Harding Est Mort"
"Au moment on il était retabli il succombe
à une attaque d' apoplexie."

The text of the article printed in French, said that President Harding had died in San Francisco on the second of August.

August 5, 1923. Paris edition of *New York Herald*, did not arrive today but I secured a copy of the *Daily Mail*, an English language newspaper printed in Paris under date of August 4, and alas! the dispatches of yesterday announcing President Harding's death are true.

Berlin, Germany. August 10, 1923. Quartered at Hotel Esplanade. We have too much luggage. The fact that one pays porters and baggage-men to place one's luggage into trains or into one's room or into one's taxi is not sufficient, as luggage requires constant personal attention.

We would not have brought so much luggage but are to attend formal functions at the Interparliamentary Union at Copenhagen where I am to serve as one of the American delegates.

The merchants follow the dollar and the pound sterling hourly and may increase their prices at any time, whereas the working-man and those on stated sums may at best secure an adjustment of wages only week by week.

Germany's peasants and businessmen might in time restore this debilitated nation and pay her obligations, but Germany is exploited by money-sharks and by revengists. A money-shark cannot plan durable reforms, and a revengist cannot guide a people to peace and justice. Europe should *forget* its past; the United States should *remember* Europe's past but my sojourn in Germany is too brief to form conclusions.

August 11, 1923. At Warnemunde, where we left Germany, the luggage and the person of all passengers, male and female, were strictly searched as Germany allows no money other than German marks (or such money as the traveller actually had when he entered Germany) to be taken out. My *laissez passer* spared my wife and self from search. Our compartment car was then shunted upon a Danish steamer and we crossed an arm of the Baltic Sea to Gjedsen, Denmark, where our train was again made up. Reaching Copenhagen we registered at Hotel D' Angleterre.

August 12, 1923. Attended services at the Lutheran Marble Church. It has a richly ornamented copper-sheeted dome.

August 13, 1923. We called upon the American Minister, Honorable John D. Prince.

I walked to the top of the Lutheran Marble Church and obtained a superb view of Copenhagen.

Mrs. Ashurst, Mr. Arthur Deerin Call, Secretary of the American Group of the Interparliamentary Union, and I went to a musical comedy at Scala Theater as guests of Senator McKinley. None of our party understood a word that was uttered, but we hugely enjoyed the evening, as music and female loveliness speak a universal language.

August 14, 1923. Copenhagen in the Danish means "Merchant's Harbor." Since early in the twelfth century it has been the trading-center of the Baltic countries. For over thirty years past Copenhagen has been a free port.

The Town Hall at Raadhuspladsen is a large structure and is a leading specimen of modern Danish architecture.

The Domhuset — Courts of Justice — is built in Greco-Roman style, and in the vestibule there is a statue of Absalon, founder of Copenhagen.

Thorvaldsen's Museum is rich in reliquaries of ancient and modern Scandinavian culture; it is built in the shape of an Etruscan tomb, and Thorvaldsen is buried there amidst the glories he gave to Denmark.

August 15, 1923. The delegates to the Twenty-first Conference of the Interparliamentary Union assembled in Christiansborgs (Parliament Palace where the Danish Parliament meets) and were called to order by Baron Theodore Adelsward of Sweden, the Permanent President of the Interparliamentary Union, who then called Mr. L. Moltesen of Denmark to the chair, as the country extending the hospitality to the delegates also furnishes the presiding officer.

Minister and Mrs. Prince tendered the American group a luncheon at their residence.

In the evening all delegates attended a reception at the City Hall tendered by the Municipality of Copenhagen. The Burgomaster delivered a speech of welcome and the delegates then sat to a buffet supper to which the strictest gourmet would have given hearty approval and indeed would have despaired of achieving any further delight in the aesthetics of eating. Although champagnes of all flowers were served, the American group, observing the prohibition policy of their own country, declined liquor.

August 16, 1923. The American group was conducted to the King's Palace by American Minister, Mr. Prince, where *all* delegates of the Interparliamentary Union shook hands with the Danish King, Christian VII, and his Queen. The Queen is convalescing from illness but the tall King was vital and strong.

August 17, 1923. Debate over the resolution as to what expression, if any, this conference should make over war-debts and reparations. The American group unanimously declined (so far as the United States is concerned) any expression as to reparations. Ex-Senator Theodore Burton said the United States entered the World War with a debt of one billion of dollars and came out with a debt of twenty-four billions of dollars; this money, he said, which we spent or loaned to Europe, came not from an overflowing treasury, but from the American people. He said that reparations and debts must not be considered together as America desires no reparations but *expects* repayment of moneys loaned. Representative Montague of Virginia announced that with reparations, America had nothing to do.

Senator Robinson was next up and said that American group had no power to bind the American government or to contradict or direct its policy. Senator Fernand Merlin of France then said that debts and reparations were bound up together and that he was sorry to hear the American delegates say that debts and reparations are separate.

Herr Paul Lobe, President of the German Reichstag, was next up and said that Germany *had* paid all that it was possible for her to pay.

Senator Swanson of the American group said that the American position was that reparations and debts would not be commingled.

The Parliamentarians of the American group were: Senator William B. McKinley of Illinois, president of the American

Group; Senator Claude A. Swanson of Virginia; Senator Henry F. Ashurst of Arizona; Senator Joe T. Robinson of Arkansas: Senator Thomas Sterling of South Dakota; Senator John W. Harreld of Oklahoma; Representative Theodore E. Burton of Ohio; Representative Andrew J. Montague of Virginia; Representative John E. Raker of California and Representative Carl R. Chindblom of Illinois, whilst the Non-Parliamentary American delegates were: Hon. George T. Buckingham of Chicago; Mr. Henry I. Green of Urbana, Illinois; and Mr. Leo Pasbolsky of Washington, D.C.

The tactful direction of Senator McKinley, president of the American group, and the experience of Mr. Call, its secretary, aided the American Group in their labors whilst the American Minister, Dr. John D. Prince and Mrs. Prince, and the American Consul-General, Mr. Marion Letcher and Mrs. Letcher, extended courtesies.

English and French were the official languages at this Conference. Delegates were present from the following countries: United States, Austria, Belgium, Bulgaria, Czecho-Slovakia, Denmark, Dutch East Indies, Esthonia, Finland, France, Great Britain, Germany, Hungary, Holland, Ireland, Italy, Iceland, Japan, Lithuania, Latvia, Norway, Poland, Rumania, Spain, Sweden, and Switzerland.

In the evening, all delegates and their ladies were banqueted at the Palace Theater by the Danish Group of the Interparliamentary Union. Mrs. Ashurst was escorted to table by a Spaniard, whilst my partner was a Miss Madison, whose father was a delegate from Yorkshire, England. Had Lucullus come to this banquet he must needs have marveled at its dignity. The American delegates took an attitude complimentary to the law of their own country and declined all alcoholic liquors.

Many of the delegates believe the Covenant of the League of Nations to be the hope of the world, whilst others believe it will be a fertile source of wars. A delegate from Holland characterized the League as a "Sleeping Beauty."

The Interparliamentary Union is but a "quasi-official" body. Its discussion and findings are not official and its delegates, called

Parliamentarians, relieved of official restraint, seemed to speak with more freedom for that reason.

The most distinguished delegate is Count Albert Apponyi, sometimes Premier and at present Speaker of the Hungarian House of Representatives. The Count, who is now seventy-five years of age, is six feet, six inches tall. At the outbreak of the World War he possessed estates, houses and lands, and lived in dignified luxury, but during the war all his property turned to ashes and he now needs must practice strict economy to have even the bare necessaries of life.

August 20, 1923. Left Copenhagen per steam-cars and we travelled on passes given us by the Danish government. At noon we passed Odense where was born Hans Andersen, who spun for children some of the tenderest fairy tales ever told. At Esbjerg we boarded a fifteen-hundred ton steamer bound for Harwich, England.

August 21, 1923. Sixty miles out of Harwich we met a ship such as is rarely seen nowadays. She had neither steam nor wireless, and all the canvas on her three masts was spread. She was bound for the Baltic Sea and "time" is no object to those on board, for she depends solely upon the wind.

London, August 22, 1923. Quartered at Savoy Hotel. Met Representative Upshaw of Georgia who has been speaking here for prohibition. Called upon American Consul General Skinner and here met Mrs. Louise Eckly MacNichol, now clerk in the Consulate here and who years ago was a stenographer in my law office in Prescott, Arizona.

At an Elk's memorial service in Prescott I delivered an address of which I thought so little that I threw the notes away, but without my knowledge Mrs. MacNichol fished the notes out of the wastebasket, pieced them together, and to my surprise the speech appeared in the next morning's paper.

August 23, 1923. Visited Waterloo Place and, although surfeited with statuary, I saw some superb statues here. Amongst others is one of Field Marshal John Fox Burgoyne. On its base is an inscription from Coriolanus: "How youngly he began to serve his country; how long continued."

Thence to the Bank of England, called "The Old Lady of Thread Needle Street." Thence to Cheapside and to the old church of Saint Mary-le-Bow built by Wren. One born within the sound of its bells is called a Cockney.

Washington, September 7, 1923. My trip to Europe was brief, but it convinced me that Europe's salvation depends upon itself. If Europe is to be saved she must reduce her armaments and must practice forgiveness and the Golden Rule. Fortunately these healing medicines are within her own easy grasp. If Europe shall stubbornly refuse these simple and safe amelioratives, she will receive a stroke of apocalyptic retribution.

Some Americans, whilst in Europe, repress their approval of America's institutions and achievements, hoping thereby to be "dubbed" cosmopolite. These "tuft-hunting" folk, criticising their fellow-countrymen at all times, forget that a nation is nourished, not a little, by generous appreciation from its own citizens. Obviously, Americans in foreign lands need not transmute themselves into braggarts, blowing the incense of flattery upon their countrymen, but they should retain a modest pride in America's noble contributions to civilization.

Suspicion and distrust
pervade Washington...

September 24, 1923. Governor Hunt and other Arizonians, at hearings before Federal Power Commission, opposed Colorado River Compact.

Attorney Cleon T. Knapp of Arizona ably argued for issuance of licenses for hydroelectric plants on Colorado River.

September 26, 1923. Colonel Fly of Yuma, at hearings before Federal Power Commission, denounced Governor Hunt for opposing the Colorado River Compact.

September 28, 1923. Saw ex-Senator Mark Smith who will use crutches the remainder of his life, as the calculous deposit in his hip has disabled him. He wistfully said that but few — probably but a dozen — of his cronies of his early days in Arizona are now alive.

Introduced Mr. James Girand to President Coolidge. The President said he believed that my silence on ratification of Colorado River Compact was due to my desire not to embarrass Governor Hunt.

Rochester, N.Y., October 11, 1923. Addressed the "Rochester Ad Club" and met Mr. George W. Glowner, who once practiced law in Arizona. He has inherited a farm near Auburn, New York, and will not return to the West.

October 18, 1923. With ex-Governor Tom Campbell of Arizona to War Department where the Governor recommended issuance of license to Mr. James Girand for hydroelectric power plant on Colorado River. Secretary of War Weeks said that Mr. Girand might be *entitled* to such license, but that the issuance thereof would militate against construction of government dam at Boulder Canyon by absorbing the market for hydroelectric energy.

October 22, 1923. General John F. O'Ryan, counsel for the Senate Committee to investigate the Veterans' Bureau, was making charges of malversation of public funds against Colonel Charles Forbes when a man with disheveled hair, loose lips, troubled eyes, and trembling hands arose before the Committee and shouted that he had come to defend himself. This agonized man was Colonel Forbes, former Director of the Bureau.

In another room of the same building the Senate Committee on Public Lands began investigating leasing of Teapot Oil Dome in Wyoming to Mr. Harry Sinclair by Albert B. Fall, whilst Mr. Fall was Secretary of the Interior.

Mr. Fall was present and had no troubled eye, no trembling hand but was belligerent and truculent.

October 24, 1923. Evidence before the Committee investigating Veterans' Bureau shows that the present Director, General Frank T. Hines, has brought order out of chaos during the few months he has had charge of that Bureau.

October 25, 1923. Mr. David Lloyd George is here as the guest of the Washington government. The only criticism heard of him is that whilst here as a guest of America, he has criticised France.

November 2, 1923. Heard per radio the farewell speech of Mr. David Lloyd George delivered in New York. This is the second time I have heard a speech broadcast over the radio.

November 12, 1923. Went to the Hotel Curtis, Minneapolis, but the reception committee told me that I would be quartered at the Minneapolis Club. Reporters asked about World Court, prohibition, Ku Klux Klan, and the agricultural bloc. They asked: Can Germany recover? Will Lloyd George again become English Premier? And will Coolidge be re-nominated?

Whilst Senator Shipstead and I and Captain Mellon, marshal of the Armistice Day parade, were reviewing the parade, an elderly man accosted me. He proved to be Rev. N. F. Norton, a Methodist minister, whom I had not seen since he left Flagstaff thirty-two years ago.

Spoke at Knights of Columbus banquet at Leamington Hotel.

To St. Paul and spoke before the School of Social Studies at the Athletic Club.

November 27, 1923. Spoke at banquet of the Chamber of Commerce at Colonial Hotel at York, Pennsylvania. In this city the Continental Congress convened from September 1777 to June 1778.

Parkersburg, West Virginia, December 2, 1923. Spoke at Camden Theatre under auspices of Elks. Thence to uninhabited Blennerhasset Island in Ohio River.

On this island Colonel Aaron Burr left his beautiful daughter (Theodosia Burr Alston) in company with Mrs. Blennerhassett whilst he assembled the batteaux and the supplies for his ill-starred expedition.

December 5, 1923. Senator Reed of Missouri asked appointment to the Senate Foreign Relations Committee, but the Democratic Steering Committee refused because of his opposition to the World Court.

Magnanimity and noblesse oblige should have induced the Steering Committee to give Senator Reed this appointment.

December 7, 1923. President Coolidge read his message to Joint Session yesterday. Farmer-Labor Senators from Minnesota (Johnson and Shipstead) denounced the message.

January 16, 1924. Those persons who come from Arizona seeking legislation, I call "parliamentary solicitors;" those from other states I call "lobbyists." A "pork barrel" bill is one that carries no appropriations for *my* state.

I wrote in this Diary on October 22 last, when the Senate Committee on Public Lands began to investigate leasing of Tea Pot Oil Dome to Harry Sinclair by Secretary of Interior Albert B. Fall, that *"Mr. Fall was present and had no troubled eye, no trembling hand, etc."* Alas, since I made that entry, evidence before the committee has been adduced carrying serious implications against Mr. Fall, who has sent a letter to the committee stating that he is too ill to "undergo the ordeal of an examination." Late in the year 1920 Mr. Fall was reported as arrear in his taxes. After leasing Tea Pot Oil Dome, he spent, so it is charged, nearly one hundred thousand dollars in acquiring additional lands in New Mexico; three thousand dollars for Hereford bulls and eight thousand dollars for back taxes. The ultimate facts are: the oil lands have been leased and Mr. Fall is unwilling or unable to explain his suddenly-acquired wealth.

January 24, 1924. Mr. Edward L. Doheny, oil magnate, appeared before the Senate Committee and testified that in November 1921, he loaned one hundred thousand dollars in cash to his old-time personal friend, Mr. Albert B. Fall. Mr. Doheny denied that the leases to himself of Naval Oil Reserve Number One, by Secretary Fall, was influenced by this loan.

Some weeks ago when Mr. Fall was before the committee he said:

I never approached E. L. Doheny or any one connected with him or any of his corporations, nor have I ever received from either of said parties (Doheny or Sinclair) one cent on account of any oil lease, or upon any other account whatsoever.

January 25, 1924. Mr. J. W. Zevely (attorney for Mr. Sinclair) testified before the committee that after Mr. Fall resigned as Secretary of Interior, Mr. Sinclair loaned Mr. Fall about $25,000 and paid Fall's expenses to Russia where Mr. Fall and Sinclair's attorney went to explore oil possibilities. Alas! Alas! A tide of evidence surges against Albert B. Fall.

Mr. Fall is broken in health and is abandoned by his fair weather friends.

January 27, 1924. Wiley Emmet Jones, sometime Attorney General of Arizona, is dead; crushed by juggernaut, viz., automobile. In taking my final leave of this brilliant man it is my hope that he is now telling his wondrous stories and coining his shining phrases in a grand company.

Wiley Jones loved music, sunlight, laughter, eloquence, birds of beautiful plumage and birds of sweet song. May he have them today!

January 28, 1924. Senator Walsh of Montana spoke three hours, urging President Coolidge to institute proceedings to cancel the oil leases to Doheny and Sinclair.

Ex-Secretary Fall is now ill and helpless. Every way he turns he is assailed by a new anguish. His career teaches us to walk humbly.

January 29, 1924. Galleries crowded all day. The exposé in the oil leases to Doheny and Sinclair overshadows all other questions before Congress.

Secretary of the Navy, Denby, says the oil leases were unknown to him. He signed the leases, and the Republican leaders are demanding that he defend them or resign.

January 30, 1924. Senator Norris of Nebraska laid responsibility for the oil leases at President Harding's door. Others spoke but all was anticlimax after the terrible speech of Senator Norris.

February 1, 1924. At Commodore Hotel I addressed the stock exchange firms in New York City. Mr. Seynour Cromwell, President of New York Stock Exchange, presided; nine hundred members present, but the shadow of ex-President Wilson's illness was upon the audience.

February 2, 1924. Ex-Secretary Fall appeared before Senate committee and declined to testify declaring that his answers might tend to incriminate him.

February 3, 1924. Woodrow Wilson died at 11:15 this A.M.

When on last Friday he said, "I am ready," he spoke with Christian obedience and philosophy. He had enlightened many young men; he had enriched literature and had taught a nation how to be honest in diplomacy; he had led America through the World War and had striven to banish war hereafter. He had risen to superlative heights of fame, and descended with dignity. Such a man is always ready.

February 4, 1924. Senator Robinson, Democratic leader, announced the death of ex-President Wilson and delivered an eulogy rich with glowing praise.

February 6, 1924. After services at the Wilson home on Ess Street, the cortege proceeded through lanes of mourners to Mount Saint Albans where this bleak afternoon ex-President

Wilson's body was entombed in the sepulchre in the Bethlehem Chapel of the Cathedral of SS. Peter and Paul.

In the Cathedral Chapel were heard the sweet voices of the boy choristers, the measured cadence of Bishop Freeman's recital of the stately Episcopal burial ritual and on the organ Chopin's "Funeral March," whilst gleamed meanwhile a tri-cornered lamp, symbolizing the Trinity.

February 8, 1924. Senator Walsh of Montana spoke two hours supporting Senator Robinson's resolution requesting the President to remove Secretary of Navy, Edwin Denby.

Senator Walsh was born in Wisconsin in 1859, was principal of several high schools, and went to Montana to practice law. For years he endured a piratically large black mustache that sprayed itself over his cravat and concealed his mouth and chin, but lately he has worn it closely clipped. He is under medium height and is slim, spare, and frail.

He is as soft-spoken at a seminary graduate; is a teetotaler and non-smoker; is spiritual and seems to glide through political and legal circles, rarely to touch earth and never to touch things earthy. His carriage is easy and graceful. He has power of analysis and has knowledge of literature, law, and history.

February 11, 1924. Senators Johnson of California, and La Follette spoke supporting Robinson resolution urging President to request resignation of Secretary of Navy Denby.

Senator Johnson went on to say that the "rascals should all be swept out of power."

Senator La Follette read his speech, and an invisible wire of prudence seemed to hold him and prevent diffusiveness or over-emphasis. He wore a cutaway coat and gray trousers and spoke like the leader of a party conscious of responsibility.

He said Mr. Denby as Secretary of the Navy held our fleets, arsenals, docks and naval oil reserves "in trust" for the nation and that Mr. Denby had permitted the oil reserves to pass into private hands.

Feberuary 13, 1924. Senator Ralston of Indiana, who looks like Grover Cleveland, spoke on problems of government. With firm voice he read from small typewritten sheets held with his left hand and gestured with his right hand.

February 27, 1924. Secretary of State Hughes addressed both Houses of Congress upon the life, character, and public services of the late President Harding.

President Coolidge and his Cabinet, the Justices of the Supreme Court and the Representatives of foreign governments were present.

Secretary Hughes recited the code of ethics Mr. Harding enforced in his own newspaper in part as follows:

Remember there are two sides to every question. Get them both.

Be truthful. Get the facts.

Mistakes are inevitable, but strive for accuracy. I would rather have one story exactly right than a hundred half-wrong.

At Hotel LaFayette and met Colonel Bryan who reeled off a half-dozen witty stories and then adverted to politics.

February 28, 1924. Spoke in Senate urging that a time limit be placed upon all proposed Constitutional amendments hereafter submitted so that a conglomerate mass of proposed amendments floating about "in nubilous," will not be handed down to posterity.

March 1, 1924. Senator Fess denounced the appointment of so many investigating committees as "making a sluice-way of the Senate." Senator Wheeler's resolution to investigate the Attorney General's office was adopted. Senate elected Senator Brookhart for chairman of this committee and elected Senator Jones of Washington, Senator Moses, Senator Wheeler, and myself as members thereof.

March 12, 1924. Committee to investigate Attorney General's office began to take testimony.

Counsel for Attorney General Daugherty, viz., ex-Senator Chamberlain and ex-Representative Paul Howland asked that the investigation proceed along the lines of the trial of a criminal case.

U.S. Circuit Judge Kenyon told me that President Coolidge had offered him the Navy portfolio; that he had declined the same but told President he would accept appointment of Attorney General.

Kenyon told President that Attorney General Daugherty was too heavy a load for any administration to carry.

March 22, 1924. Mr. H. S. Schaife, employed to aid the Daugherty Investigation Committee, advised me that Colonel Kosterlitzky now in the U.S. Secret Service had told the Department of Justice that I had attempted to promote the acquisition of Lower California.

I saw Colonel Kosterlitzky for a two-hour interview in Los Angeles, California, in May 1919.

March 23, 1924. Confidence in political parties rises and falls quickly. In the summer of 1918, President Wilson's popularity was world-wide. By a series of events (I chronicled them in this book long ago) his party met defeat in the elections of 1918.

Early in 1923, it was taken for granted that President Harding would be renominated, but defeated. The Republicans then were searching for some other person than Mr. Coolidge for Vice-Presidential nominee.

The death of President Harding and the sportsmanship of the American people which said "give President Coolidge a chance," raised Republican spirits. Mr. Coolidge grew in strength and by Christmas of 1923, the Democratic hopes were low when suddenly came the oil scandals.

Scenes shift so rapidly and events evolute so frequently, that the vanquished may be restored.

March 24, 1924. Mr. Schaife brought Mr. W. A. Wiseman of San Antonio, Texas to my office who told me that Colonel Kosterlitzky had furnished to the Secret Service within the past week, a full report of my conversation with the Colonel in May 1919.

March 27, 1924. Colonel Kosterlitzky called, but I made no reference to his statement to the Department of Justice anent myself. Whilst the Daugherty Investigation Committee was taking testimony, the committee was handed a note stating that Senator La Follette had pneumonia.

March 28, 1924. Attorney General Daugherty upon request of the President has resigned. Mr. Daugherty issued a statement implying that the President removed him because of "political expediency." Mr. Daugherty was confident that he could rely upon President Coolidge to sustain him, but is now disillusioned and has left Washington a gloomy man. He was born at Washington Court House, Ohio, was President Harding's close friend, and his efforts contributed not a little toward Mr. Harding's nomination.

April 1, 1924. Charges, denials, counter-charges, and denunciations fill the air. Suspicion and distrust pervade Washington.

Received letter from Mr. George H. Maxwell, promoter of the High Line Project of Colorado River, "denouncing" me for "permitting Mexico to steal the Colorado River from Arizona." Mr. Maxwell goes on to say that "Department of Justice is guilty of conniving at the stealing of this river."

Lobbyists here ply their vocation daily, but they spend no money, exhibit no feminine allurements, and dispense no alcoholic liquor; they rule by threats.

April 3, 1924. Senate passed Senator Cameron's bill authorizing Secretary of Interior to construct San Carlos Reservoir on Gila River, Arizona.

April 4, 1924. Letter from ex-Senator Charles A. Towne. What a tragedy that this learned man, now penniless and ill, should be vexed to rake together money for meagre subsistence. Fashioned by nature and education for orator and statesman, his earnings slip through his fingers, and the demon of impecuniosity has pursued him for a decade.

April 5, 1924. Senator Cameron is elated by the passage of his San Carlos Dam bill and regards his political fortunes as recouped. This bill will pass the House through efforts of Representative Hayden.

April 7, 1924. Old Tom Keller of Senate phoned me that ex-Senator Mark Smith was dead. Arriving at Mark's apartment at the Occidental Hotel I found my old friend cold and rigid. The coroner soon came and announced that Mark dropped dead about one o'clock this morning. Mark left word last night to be called at one this P.M., but when the boy called him, he had already answered the Messenger who beckons for all.

On Mark's table, written in his clear hand were several sheets of biographical sketch of his mother.

Princess Bibesco, daughter of Herbert Henry Asquith — wife of Prince Bibesco, the Rumanian Minister, thanked me for an article I recently wrote of the talents of her father.

April 8, 1924. Senator Burton K. Wheeler of Montana has been indicted by a federal grand jury in Montana, charged with accepting a fee for appearing before some department after his term as senator had commenced.

I gave out interview stating that I knew Mr. Wheeler when he was a struggling law student in University of Michigan and that I believed him to be an honest public official.

April 9, 1924. Senator Brookhart, the chairman of the Daugherty Committee hearings, announced that "this investigation would go forward with greater vigor than ever." Senator Wheeler stated in Senate that he had accepted no fee or compensation to appear before any department. Democratic Senators and many insurgent Republicans congratulated him.

Telegram from sister Maude (Mrs. West) at Azusa advising that my mother is ill.

April 10, 1924. A Senate committee was appointed to sift the charge that Attorney General had "framed" Senator Wheeler.

It is now time to write of Senator Burton K. Wheeler of Montana. He was born in Massachusetts in 1882 and was graduated from the public schools there. I met him when my brother Charles and I were in the University of Michigan. He began law practice in Montana; is of medium height and is slim and stoop-shouldered. He has a large head and his sunburnish hair is vanishing.

Soon after his induction into the Senate, he attacked the Republican Regulars, and Senator Lodge being importuned to make reply said "I decline to do so; that man is more ruthless than Jim Reed."

Am writing this in the Hotel Biltmore, New York City, where have just addressed the American Drug Manufacturers.

April 11, 1924. Sensations leap forth so swiftly that a brace of shorthand writers is required to record them. Last month the Senate authorized a special committee to investigate the Bureau of Internal Revenue. Secretary of the Treasury (Mellon) complained of this committee's special counsel and President Coolidge today sent to the Senate a message (one of the most censorious ever sent to the Senate by an executive) inveighing against this investigation.

April 12, 1924. Telegram from my brother William advising that my mother is very ill.

This is written on Pennsylvania train on my journey to Azusa, California.

I gave to Mr. John W. Crockett, Reading Clerk of Senate, manuscript of my speech to be read by him on April 15 at dedication of Arizona Stone in Washington Monument.

April 16, 1924. Each station into which my train draws fills me with alarm, fearful that I may receive telegram with dolorous news.

Reaching Azusa, I entered Mother's house and found her alive and cheerful.

My brother Edward and wife and son are here from Oregon; my brother Andrew is here from Big Lake, Washington State; my brother Billie is here from Arizona, and my sister Maude, worn by the long vigil, is here from Needles, California. Mother's house is bright and clean and has just been painted and has new wall paper.

April 17, 1924. Arose at 5:00 A.M. and soon the great cathedral of out-doors was filled with feathered songsters, singing songs that meant a thousand things.

'Phoned to Los Angeles for heart specialist who came and says mother will live some weeks.

Azusa, April 18, 1924. Mother's only living brother, Andrew J. Bogard, arrived from Goldfield, Nevada. He is seventy-eight years old, was a frontiersman, and saw life's seamy side in the early California settlements. He is gentle and soft-spoken. I have not seen him for twenty-nine years.

April 19, 1924. Mother much better this morning.

The old light returned to her eyes, and with that unfailing regard for other persons which was a rule of her life, she said to me: "Go back at once to the Senate; your duty is there. You must not shirk; therefore return to Washington."

My brother Charles will arrive from Detroit this evening.

April 22, 1924. To LaSalle Hotel, Chicago, where the clerk handed me a telegram. After seating myself I opened it and read the stabbing words:

Mother died 4:30 P.M. Sunday.

Billie

Thus end the actions and words but not the influence of a brilliant, dauntless woman who constantly gave her strength for those who needed help and mercy. No one doubts the existence of an Infinite Power and I am content that a Divine Healing will recompense her for the distress and misery she encountered in her seventy stormy years here.

April 30, 1924. Senate considered Veterans' Relief. I argued that tuberculous persons when too closely confined in hospitals, do not improve and that alimentation and digestion are prime factors in promoting recovery from tuberculosis.

May 1, 1924. Senator Cameron, Representative Hayden, and I went to White House where Senator Cameron declined to permit us to go with him in the President's Room.

Emerging from this conference with the President (which lasted twenty minutes) he said he had secured President Coolidge's approval "written" on the San Carlos Dam Bill, but he refused to allow us to see it and said that he could not have secured approval if we had been present.

May 8, 1924. Senators from the Pacific Coast are angry because Conference Report on the Immigration Bill carries a provision that Japanese nationals may enter the United States until March 1, 1925; also a provision requesting President to negotiate a treaty with Japan regarding admission of Japanese nationals.

May 11, 1924. Now in the Hotel Astor, New York, having just come from the banquet hall where I addressed the Independent Order of B'nai B'rith.

Rabbi Stephen S. Wise, orator-superb, learned and golden voiced, was the other speaker. The toastmaster was Mr. Leonard Obermeier and at my right was my friend, Honorable Henry Goldfogle, sometime representative in Congress.

May 13, 1924. Mrs. Ashurst and I lunched at Senate Restaurant with Princess Bibesco, daughter of Mr. Asquith.

May 14, 1924. Ex-Governor Campbell of Arizona is here. He was recently elected Republican National Committeeman triumphing over my colleague, Senator Cameron.

The special committee appointed to investigate Senator Wheeler's case, exonerates Senator Wheeler. The report was signed by Senator Borah, chairman, and by Senators McNary, Swanson, and Caraway, whilst Senator Sterling dissented.

May 15, 1924. Conference report on the immigration bill agreed to in both Houses. This is the most rigid exclusion bill ever passed and it repeals the "Gentleman's Agreement" with Japan.

President Coolidge vetoed the Soldiers Adjusted Insurance (Bonus) Bill; he objected to this bill not only because it would wreck his economy program but also upon principle.

May 17, 1924. House of Representatives today by three to one, overrode President's veto on the Soldiers' Bonus Bill.

May 19, 1924. Called at White House to present the University of Arizona polo team, but President had a cold and received no visitors.

Senate passed Soldiers' Bonus Bill over President's veto. Senator Greene of Vermont, who about three months ago was shot in the head by a stray bullet fired by a prohibition officer, entered the Senate during the rollcall and, prompted by his secretary and physician, voted to sustain the veto.

In executive session Senator Cummins pleaded with his fellow senators to confirm Mr. Harbach to be Postmaster at Des Moines, Iowa, the home town of Senator Cummins, but Senator Brookhart of same state demanded the rejection of this nominee, and Senator Cummins was overwhelmed by the combined vote of the Democrats and the insurgent Republicans.

May 20, 1924. Senator Borah spoke in defense of Senator Wheeler and asserted that the evidence fully exonerates him.

The tax reduction bill recently passed by Senate, contains a provision making income tax returns "public."

Opponents of publicity argue that personal incomes are amongst the ultimate intimacies of life and that to make income tax returns "public documents," would subject all persons to the mercy of the Paul Prys and Meddlesome Matties.

May 23, 1924. The Senate, adopted by fifty-six Yeas to five Nays the Borah Resolution exonerating Senator Wheeler. It was the opinion of some senators that the indictment of Wheeler had been secured to frustrate his investigation of the Department of Justice under Mr. Daugherty's regime.

May 26, 1924. The President issued a statement expressing regret over refusal of Congress to settle by treaty instead of by legislation the admission of Japanese nationals.

Boston, May 29, 1924. Quartered at Bellevue Hotel. Mr. Gleason L. Archer, founder of the Suffolk Law School, escorted me to State House where we called upon Governor Cox, then we called upon Mayor Curley. I delivered the commencement oration to the graduating class of the Suffolk Law School.

Washington, May 29, 1924. "Detective" Gaston B. Means testified before Daugherty Investigation Committee. Mr. Means seems ubiquitous; he was here, he was there. He blows and swallows at one and the same time. He weighs three hundred pounds, rolls his huge head from side to side and thrusts out his beefy tongue before replying to questions. Senator Wheeler is assailed for calling such a witness to testify, and Wheeler retorts that Attorney General Daugherty appointed Means to be an "under-cover" detective in the Department of Justice.

May 30, 1924. President Coolidge in his Memorial Day Address advocated entry of the United States into the World Court, created by the League of Nations Covenant, and I opine that Mr. Coolidge will be assailed for this speech.

June 1, 1924. Senator La Follette, whose popularity during the World War shrank to the vanishing point, now guides the insurgents in both Houses. Vital and ruddy, he attends the Senate sessions, having fully recovered from pneumonia.

June 7, 1924. To White House with Senator Cameron and Representative Hayden where President signed San Carlos Dam Bill. In every successful enterprise, there are unknown and unrewarded men whose ability and courage bring the victory. Such a one was present today in the person of Mr. Edgar B. Merritt, assistant commissioner of Indian Affairs, who long ago commenced his able advocacy of this project. Mr. Merritt begged me to request the Secretary of Interior, who was present, to christen this the "Coolidge Dam." Whereupon, I asked the President to withhold his pen while the Secretary of Interior made the announcement.

June 9, 1924. Governor Ritchie of Maryland, Senator Walsh of Massachusetts, Mr. Pickford, Representative Clancy and I dined with Captain Hewitt at Silver Spring, Maryland.

June 13, 1924. Motored from Phillipsburg, New Jersey to Bangor, Pennsylvania, where I spoke at Flag Day exercises under auspices of Elks.

June 15, 1924. Motored from Detroit to Jackson, Michigan, where under auspices of Holy Name Society, I addressed audience of ten thousand persons at Fair Grounds.

In the audience were my brother Charles and his wife Emma, who took me back to Detroit in their auto.

June 16, 1924. Motored to Ann Arbor where Charles and I were law students. Saw the house on Division Street where we boarded in bygone days.

New York, June 28, 1924. Visited Democratic National Convention. Honorable Homer Cummings of Connecticut reported the Platform. Former Secretary of War Baker, diminutive and pale, indifferent to phrase or grace, pleaded for plank for entry of the U.S. into League of Nations.

Convention rejected Mr. Baker's plank for League membership for the U.S. and then came debate upon plank offered by Mr. Pattangall of Maine, denouncing Ku Klux Klan.

Mr. Bainbridge Colby, sometime Secretary of State, led the fight to denounce the Klan. Mr. Colby looked the orator that he is. Lithe and handsome, his voice never broke; no sentence was crude. He denounced the Ku Klux Klan as cowardly and corrupt.

W. J. B. opposed the plank denouncing the Ku Klux. Galleries hissed and many delegates hooted him.

Twenty-eight years ago at the Democratic National Convention at Chicago, W. J. B. with raven locks and frame of oak, spoke eloquently and won a Presidential nomination. Tonight, sour, emotionally sere, barren of hope, no longer handsome, eyes like occult jewels, he seemed to be a crotchety, crabbed, played-out man.

After roll-call amidst bedlamic chaos, Chairman, Senator Walsh of Montana, declared the plank denouncing the Ku Klux rejected. Refusal to denounce Ku Klux Klan destroys all chance of Democratic success at this election.

Bluefield, West Virginia, July 16, 1924. Addressed West Virginia Bankers' Association here.

Flagstaff, Arizona, July 27, 1924. Long talk with Mr. William Roden who came here from Texas forty years ago driving two thousand head of cattle belonging to his father. When my parents were ranching, this Mr. Roden was a dashing "cow-hand." Selling his own cattle he went with me to attend a business college at Stockton, California, but after one day at the college, the romance of the thundering herd called him and he returned to the cattle range where he remained until a few years ago when a tangled lasso lamed his right arm and he quit the range forever.

August 11, 1924. At my Brother Billie's Ranch in Gila County, Arizona, one hundred miles from any railroad. This ranch has much cedar, juniper, and pine timber. He and his son, Thomas, have cleared and fenced eighty acres, dug two wells, built first-rate ranchhouses and corrals. Beans are the staple product of this homestead, but the market is too distant. Billie's son, Thomas, aged twenty-two, is one of the most wholesome of my numerous tribe. His skills in surveying, carpentry, and wheelwright are excellent and his life has been spent in the forest.

August 16, 1924. Visited Mormon Lake in Coconino County, now a famous fishing resort. The dairy operated by the Latter Day Saints here forty years ago has vanished. I stood upon the spot, where at the age of six years, I heard for the first time, religious services. The sermon was eloquent and was preached by Mr. Lott Smith, a Mormon patriarch. In those days Mormon Lake was fenced off into fields but the water is now thirty feet deep and covers thirty-six square miles.

Washington, September 8, 1924. At the request of the Phoenix Gazette I am here, with many railroad officials before Interstate Commerce Commission urging merger of El Paso & Southwestern Railroad with Southern Pacific Railroad, conditioned upon a main line railroad being constructed through Phoenix. Mr. Krutschnitt, president of the Southern Pacific Company announced that Southern Pacific would absorb the El Paso & Southwestern agreeably to such condition. I presented all the railroad officials to President Coolidge.

September 12, 1924. Luncheon at Wyomissing Club, Reading, Pennsylvania, as guest of Attorney Keppelman, grand marshal of the Parade. I then spoke in Baseball Park on rostrum erected in pitcher's box.

New York, September 23, 1924. Introduced Attorney Ellinwood of Arizona to Mr. Davis, the Democratic presidential nominee. In evening I spoke at Huntington, Long Island.

September 24, 1924. I attended an old fashioned barbecue and delivered a Democratic speech at Lake Compounce, Connecticut.

September 28, 1924. Left Chicago per Northern Pacific for Bozeman, Montana. Forty years ago, at Flagstaff, the task of reading Gibbon's *Decline and Fall of the Roman Empire* was set me by my parents, whereupon I read a few pages thereof — probably fifty.

Packing my luggage, I determine to resume the reading broken off so long ago; so today I read three hundred pages of Gibbon and the Antoninnes, and Commodus, Pertinax et al are in my mind tonight.

September 30, 1924. In my speech at Bozeman tonight I said that the nation expected Montana to re-elect Senator T. J. Walsh who conducted the Senate oil investigations.

Spokane, Washington, October 2, 1924. Called upon Mr. and Mrs. Harris Baldwin and dined with them at Hotel Davenport. Mr. Baldwin, superbly educated, came to Arizona about 1882 from Columbus, Mississippi and left Arizona many years ago. In his Arizona days he dressed fashionably, and with him speech was important. He did not slummock any word. Every sentence he uttered, whether on stagecoach, in camp, in court or in legislature was as a freshly-minted coin.

When I was turnkey in the county jail and attended terms of the court at Flagstaff, Mr. Baldwin was one of the leaders of the Arizona bar and to hear him try a case was a lesson in philology and syntax. I took him aback tonight by repeating to him many sentences and some short speeches I heard him deliver in days agone.

At dinner he said that he was, at one time, ambitious to serve in the United States Senate. I told him that had he been elected to that office he would have taken high rank as scholar, statesman, and lawyer but that I had, at the age of sixteen years — in the year 1890 — in Arizona — witnessed an episode foretelling that he might encounter difficulty in reaching the Senate, worthy and competent though he was.

He seemed amazed at my statement; the mercury of his courtly manners and the dignity of his demeanor fell. I asked him to bear with patience whilst I identified the episode. Then I said: "In Arizona, in the year 1890, you and Marcus A. Smith, delegate to Congress, James H. Wright, ex-Chief Justice of the Arizona Supreme Court, William Owen (Buckey) O'Neill, famous sheriff and soldier and I (to mention a small name amongst great names) were passengers on a thirty-six hour stagecoach ride from Phoenix to Prescott. The stagecoach left Phoenix at sunrise, and about sunset upon arriving at the supper-station, named Gillette, on the desert we found the station buildings, barn and fences covered with black, glistening bugs, probably of the Coleoptera type, with hard horny wings and these bugs soon embossed the stagecoach, horses, and harness. The station keeper seemed to pay no attention to this entomological avalanche which invaded his eating-house. During the meal Delegate Smith, Judge Wright, Sheriff O'Neill, and I employed one hand, unobtrusively, to shovel or spoon the bugs out of our plates and coffee cups the while eating such food as was set before us, making no other sign that we recognized the presence of the six-legged repulsives, but you declared that you could not eat "in such circumstances." I observed that the station keeper who served the meal gave you what was then called the "bad eye" as you left the table. Soon thereafter you were a candidate for Territorial Senate (Council) and although elected you received not *one* vote in Gillette. I concluded then that a politician who was squeamish about Coleoptera Beetles in a desert eating-house would hardly be elected to the Senate."

Twenty-two years later Mark Smith and I on the same day entered the Senate. That thirty-six hour stagecoach ride was an education for me. Messrs. Baldwin, Smith, and Wright were classic orators of the Bob Ingersoll — Billie Breckenridge type, and Sheriff O'Neill was a facile writer and charming talker. On that stagecoach those four men talked learnedly all day and when the sun went down, the stars, always effulgent in the desert night, seemed to pale before the brilliancy of their discussions which embraced scripture, art, science, law, literature, poetry, and what not. For example: a lengthy argument ensued amongst them as to whether Vergil in his *Aeneid* (written 2000 years ago) had plagiarized from Homer's *Illiad* (written 2800 years ago), and then came another discussion as to why Shakespeare had never in any of his works mentioned any contemporaneous event or any contemporaneous person.

During the journey I said almost nothing, but upon alighting from the stagecoach at Prescott I walked with pride for I felt that by their learned talk I was already graduated from Oxford, Harvard, or Yale.

Los Angeles, October 5, 1924. I was accosted by a taxicab driver who said: "You are Mr. Ashurst and you once prosecuted me for robbery." Looking closely I perceived he was Mr. "Blank" whom nearly twenty years ago, I prosecuted in Coconino County. He took me for a ride in his taxicab and says he now has a wife and is prospering. With my wishes for his success we parted.

Globe, Arizona, October 13, 1924. Received telegram that Senator Frank B. Brandegee of Connecticut committed suicide this morning in Washington by inhaling illuminating gas.

Brandegee was able and cynical, was a bachelor, and recently lost his fortune in real estate investments.

November 8, 1924. It is now time to write of the Coolidge landslide. When President Harding, in June 1923, started upon his ill-starred Alaskan trip, the Republican leaders believed he would be defeated for re-election. Republican leaders at that time agreed that Mr. Coolidge would be refused a re-nomination for Vice-President, but fate is a mighty magician.

A few hours after President Harding's death, Mr. Coolidge's father, as notary public, administered the presidential oath to his son Calvin at midnight by the flickering rays of an oil lamp in a Vermont farmhouse. The simplicity of this episode fired the public imagination.

Mr. Coolidge's message to Congress in December, his fight for tax reduction and his veto of the bill increasing pensions for soldiers of the Civil War and the Spanish-American War and his veto of the bonus for ex-servicemen of the World War brought him enormous popularity.

Mr. John W. Davis, the Democratic nominee, was of high character, requisite attainments, large experience, serene temper, and smooth diction, but was conservative and President Coolidge had captured the conservative vote long before Mr. Davis entered the field.

Senator La Follette's candidacy injured Mr. Davis' candicacy. The radicals voted for LaFollette. The Democratic constitutionalists, fearful that LaFollette's electoral vote might devolve the election upon the House of Representatives, abandoned Mr. Davis and united upon Mr. Coolidge.

November 10, 1924. Senator Henry Cabot Lodge died yesterday. Mr. Lodge gave forty years to his party but when in the last session of Congress he voted to override the veto of President Coolidge on the Soldier's Bonus Bill, a wave of calumny rolled over him. His forty years of service to his party and his scholarly speeches defending its principles availed him nothing when "party expediency" required that he should be occluded.

December 3, 1924. President's annual message recommended rigid economy in expenditures and a repeal of the publicity clause of the income tax law.

Mr. Coolidge is not a mere theoretical economizer. Whilst his message was being read he and Mrs. Coolidge were on their way to Chicago, travelling in the Pullman car with the same accommodations that may be obtained by any private citizen. Seldom, if ever, have the conditions and resources of the two major political parties been so disproportionate. The Republican National Committee aggressive, opulent, victorious, has a surplus in its treasury whilst the Democratic Committee has a deficit. The Republicans overnight may obtain sinews of war, whilst the Democratic Committee (unable to secure funds with which to pay rent for two rooms for National Headquarters) has moved into one small room. The facilities for Republican propaganda are ample, the facilities for Democratic propaganda are nil.

The Democratic forces are shattered. The McAdoo-Smith adherents threaten to renew their warfare for the 1928 elections. These conditions would seem to bode ill for the Democrats but in fact, no matter how sweeping the triumph of one party, a complete upset is always probable within four years. Nemesis, a menacing apparition, always stands in the offing.

North Adams, Massachusetts, December 7, 1924. Motored to Williams College, alma mater of President Garfield, and spoke at Elks Memorial Service in North Adams in the Berkshire Hills on the Old Mohawk Trail.

December 11, 1924. Biltmore Hotel, New York City. Addressed annual banquet of the Rubber Trade Association. One of the principal speakers, the Reverend Warren Giles, spoke an hour and poured forth a cascade of literary gems. After such a speech, my own was an anti-climax.

December 15, 1924. The two Houses met in joint session in the House of Representatives and paid official tribute to the memory of ex-President Woodrow Wilson. Military and naval officials were present. President Coolidge and his Cabinet were there. Also present the Supreme Court Justices and Chief Justice Taft, whom Wilson defeated for the Presidency in 1912; also present Secretary of State Hughes whom Wilson defeated in 1916. Occasionally Chief Justice Taft's countenance denoted acquiescence, and sometimes dissent, but Mr. Hughes' countenance registered a corrugated forehead and tightly compressed lips. Senator Cummins, President Pro Tempore of the Senate, presided.

The orator was Dr. Edwin E. Alderman, president of the University of Virginia, and he demonstrated the majesty and amplitude of our language. His free elocution and his scholarship almost made the audience forget the subject of the eulogy, so transfixed were they by the artistry of the speaker.

Dr. Alderman occupied eighty minutes and although his speech was written out on small sheets of paper, he seemed not to refer to manuscript.

Hughes' eulogy of Harding, Lodge's eulogy of Roosevelt and John Hay's eulogy of McKinley were worthy; Blaine's eulogy of Garfield was brilliant, whilst Dr. Alderman's eulogy of Wilson was noble and effulgent.

December 17, 1924. At Committee on irrigation. Senator Hiram Johnson urged his bill to build Boulder Canyon Dam in Colorado River and All-American Canal from the river to Imperial Valley.

A question was asked as to what amount of waters of the Colorado River the Republic of Mexico was entitled to receive. I observed that under *no* principle of International Law was Mexico entitled *as a matter of right* to any of the waters of the Colorado River; that there existed no treaty upon the subject, hence, any waters from the Colorado River reaching Mexico would go to that nation as an Act of Grace on the part of the Washington government.

Senator Norris, Republican, charged that President Coolidge was coercing senators into voting against government operation of the Muscle Shoals hydroelectric and fertilizer plant.

December 27, 1924. M. Jusserand, after twenty-two years service as the Ambassador of France to the Washington government, finished his diplomatic labors here. I attended a farewell reception given by Ambassador and Madame Jusserand last evening at the French Embassy.

December 29, 1924. Senator Bruce, Democrat of Maryland, declared the Democratic party deserved defeat last autumn because it had flirted with radicalism and had embraced paternalism.

January 2, 1925. Received check for $500 from *Saturday Evening Post* of Philadelphia for manuscript of my article on constitutional amendments.

January 19, 1925. Rochester, New York. Attended banquet of Chamber of Commerce and spoke on "Our National Sin — Extravagance."

Mr. George W. Glowner, once of Arizona but now residing here, was present.

Boston, January 21, 1925. Called upon Mayor Curley whose secretary, Mr. Wilcox, took me to Faneuil Hall and other buildings of colonial days.

Luncheon with the Mayor and in the evening spoke at banquet of St. Alphonsus Association.

4

Republican Era

*...but to secure gentle treatment
for the poor is not an easy thing,
since a ruling class is not always humane.*

Aristotle

X   February, 1925–December, 1927

He is inscrutable, calm, courteous,
and silent...

February 6, 1925. Healthy conservatism now characterizes the government. The Wilson struggle to elevate the "crowd" is absent. The Harding fraternizing is absent. Mr. Coolidge neither coddles politicians nor radiates camaradarie. He believes that if business prospers all else follows.

New York, February 12, 1925. Spoke at banquet of National Retail Dry Goods Association at ballroom of the Pennsylvania Hotel here. Eight hundred banqueters present.

Amongst the speakers were Reverend Charles E. Jefferson, pastor of Broadway Tabernacle, and Mr. Tom Terris, English movie actor, who bored the audience on Egyptology until Mr. Tilz of Philadelphia, the toastmaster, urged him to cease speaking, but Mr. Terris replied: "I cannot stop speaking now, for I have not yet described the sphinx." Whereupon I shouted to him, "The sphinx is a symbol of silence." Mr. Thomas Hardy, my representative, was rapturous over my address.

February 14, 1925. Mr. Asquith, who lost his seat in the Westminister Parliament in the recent English elections, has been translated to the House of Lords and is now the Earl of Oxford and Asquith.

Of the great Liberals in English politics, (Roseberry, Morley, Bryce, Campbell-Bannerman, and Asquith) who looked upon Mr. Gladstone not only as their political chief but as a moral leader as well, only Asquith is alive.

Richmond, Virginia, February 21, 1925. Spoke last evening at banquet at Hotel Jefferson in the lobby of which is a marble statue of Thomas Jefferson. This hotel was damaged by a fire years ago and in carrying out this statue the head was broken off, but the sculptor (Valentine) replaced the head so skillfully that the break is not noticed.

February 23, 1925. Agreeably to previous appointment, I read "Washington's Farewell Address." Upwards of sixty senators listened to the reading which occupied one hour.

March 4, 1925. Coolidge inaugurated. Senator Cummins, the Senate's President Pro Tempore, administered the official oath of Mr. Charles G. Dawes, the new Vice-President. After prayer, the new Vice-President commenced his address and soon launched into a diatribe against the Senate rules, especially the rule preventing previous question. His voice became shrill and his gestures gyratory and gymnastic. President Coolidge's face gave off a bored expression. Concluding his address, the Chief Clerk read the President's proclamation convening this special session of the Senate.

The names of Mr. Blease, Mr. Borah, Mr. Bratton, and Mr. Brookhart, senators-elect, were called and they advanced to the rostrum, took the oath, and signed the roster. The names of Mr. Capper, Mr. Couzens, Mr. Deneen, and Mr. DuPont were called and whilst they were advancing to the rostrum the Vice-President directed the Chief Clerk to "call the names of *all* the Senators who are to take the oath," whereupon the names of the other twenty-four senators-elect were called but they made their way with difficulty to the rostrum, owing to the cluttered aisles and crowded forum. The oath was administered to them en bloc but before they could sign the roster the Vice-President directed the Senate to "Proceed to the inauguration of the President on the east front of the Capitol." The departure of the Senate guests should have been as formal as their entry but confusion reigned. The feet of the President were trodden upon, the Justices of the Supreme Court were jostled; ambassadors straggled out, and the senators white from rage at the V.P. trooped to the east front of the Capitol.

President Coolidge's message was broadcast and amongst his paragraphs were:

I favor the policy of economy, not because I wish to save money, but because I wish to save people. Every dollar that we waste means that their life will be so much the more meager. . . .

We need not concern ourselves much about the rights of property if we will faithfully observe the rights of persons. Under our institutions their rights are supreme. It is not property but the right to hold property, both great and small, which our Constitution guarantees.

My wife and I then went to the residence of Governor and Mrs. Pinchot of Pennsylvania, where a buffet luncheon was served to several hundred guests.

March 5, 1925. Attended banquet complimentary to ex-Senator David I. Walsh. Senator Reed of Missouri spoke at length, and Senators Bayard, Dill, Sheppard, Kendrick and I spoke briefly. Rev. Father Dinand, president of Holy Cross College, Worcester, Massachusetts, delivered eloquent oration.

March 10, 1925. Senate considered nomination of Mr. Charles Beecher Warren of Michigan to be Attorney General. Senator Cummins, Chairman of Judiciary Committee, defended Mr. Warren.

On roll call on confirmation it was obvious before the last name was reached that the result would be a tie which would reject the nominee. Republican leaders frantically phoned Vice-President Dawes, who was at the Willard Hotel, to hurry to the Senate to cast the deciding vote.

Dashing out of his hotel the V.P., Dawes, sped to Capitol Hill but too late. During the recent campaign Mr. Dawes was hailed as a "Minute Man," hence he was subjected to not a little raillery today over the fact that he was not at his post on this vital vote.

March 17, 1925. At Wilkes-Barre, Pennsylvania. I was met by Detective O'Dea of Washington and Mr. McHugh, chief of police of Scranton, Pennsylvania.

Quartered at Hotel Casey, Scranton; spoke at banquet of Irish-American Society. Nine hundred guests present.

Atlantic City, March 19, 1925. Addressed the banquet of National American Wholesale Lumber Association. The humorous speaker was Mr. Charles Milton Newcomb of Cleveland, Ohio, who spoke on the "Philosophy of Laughter."

Washington, March 21, 1925. Are American politicians un-trustworthy? Have idealism and noblesse oblige no place in our politics? Is politics the science of selfishness? Constituencies are not free from blame for the cynicism of their public men. Con-stituencies too often look upon magnanimity and moderation as flabbiness. The politician will practice the virtue of moderation only upon the demand of the constituency.

March 22, 1925. How easy to exaggerate our own importance? Senator Thomas Sterling of South Dakota, after his defeat for re-nomination, was offered by President Coolidge a place on In-ternational Joint Commission, at several thousand dollars per year. Mr. Sterling declined this place but asked to be made Sec-retary of State or Attorney General to which the President de-clined to listen.

Mr. Sterling, later perceiving his error, offered to accept International Joint Commission only to discover that the Presi-dent had given that place to another.

Phoenix, April 27, 1925. Procured copy of *Saturday Evening Post* issued on April 25 and read my article "Making Amend-ments."

Called upon ex-Senator J. Ham Lewis of Illinois, here for a visit.

Each year here I observe the increasing decrepitude of the old frontiersmen who were leading figures in pioneer life when I was a boy. Very few of them are financially independent in their declining years.

May 8, 1925. Mr. Venia Powell called. He and I were desk-mates in the Flagstaff Public School over forty years ago. In youth he was athletic and as lithe as a panther, but his attempt to cultivate a tract of land without adequate water has bent his frame and stiffened his joints.

Prescott, May 13, 1925. Visited tubercular patients at Vet-erans Bureau Hospital. Tuberculosis is almost an imponderable. Sometimes it brings a melancholia which retards the all-impor-tant alimentation.

May 14, 1925. Gave to the Elks Lodge here my iron safe in my old law offices.

Prescott, May 18, 1925. I lunched today, here in Prescott, at the Palace Restaurant which in bygone days, twenty years ago, was the Palace Saloon, then operated by three expert sports: Messrs. Bob Brow, Ben Belcher, and Barney Smith. At that time, at a long mahogany bar defended by a footrail of shining brass, bartenders clad in snowy linen, graceful as Sir Roger de Coverly, served ale, porter, gin, rum, brandy, lager beer, and old whiskies.

In the cafe in the rear of the saloon were then served Lucullan viands. There Bacchus reigned, and champagnes of choicest flowers, which painted landscapes even in sterile brains, went roaring down thirsty throats. There Venus smiled and fleet-footed Mercury was often dazzled by the bales of crisp currency and the clink of golden coin at the gambling tables. The whirr of the roulette ball, the thud of the dice at the crap-games which were as clods falling upon the coffin-lid of fortune, and the rattle of ivory poker-chips were then to be heard above the dulcet notes of the wingless angels who warbled all night long in that house of joy and tears.

The back bar then gleamed like a ledge of jewels as its cut glass and silver and ebony were reflected by huge mirrors. There lawyer, tourist, "tenderfoot," merchant-prince, sportsman, savant, public-official, hard-rock-miner, cowboy, and remittance man mingled on equal terms. In that house, remorse sometimes fastened its fangs into men's souls, or fed itself upon the husks of their blighted hopes; there earnings were squandered — diced away in a night — there noble resolves were broken by those persons who entered into the domain of vice through the beautiful gate of temptation. Like enchanted fruit in the dwelling of a sorcerer, the objects of admiration lost their attraction and value as soon as grasped, and all that remained was regret for the time lost in their pursuit. The tear of sympathy welled quickly to the gambler's rayless eyes, and the hands of the proprietors of the Palace were horns of plenty, for not only were their hearts warm and their impulses generous, but the fixed principle of their code was that "jinx" and "hoodoo" kept away from him who *never* turned deaf ear to needy persons.

Now the great hall is tenantless save for the wraiths of frequenters of long ago. Spiders have festooned the back bar with cobwebs; dust now begrimes the tables where once the bets were laid. The gambler of that day has "cashed in" all his chips and has entered that vast realm where aces, kings, and queens alike are counted as deuces. The battalions of Bacchus are shattered, the singers are silent — their songs perished twenty years ago — and the restaurant is now conducted by a Chinaman named Dong.

Douglas, June 3, 1925. Amongst my callers was a Mr. Hohstadt who knew my mother at Tehama, California, when she was a little girl. To Bisbee to luncheon at Copper Queen Hotel with committee of businessmen.

June 4, 1925. Subcommittee on Public Lands (Senator Cameron and I) began hearings.

Cattle-raisers testified that the fees charged by government for grazing livestock on national forests are ruinously high, and Mr. Hoval Smith, eloquently argued for legislation encouraging prospectors searching for metals.

Tucson, June 5, 1925. Cattle-raisers testified that red tape of forestry bureau is strangling the cattle industry.

Luncheon at Old Pueblo Club; Senator Cameron spoke thirty minutes anent Colorado River problems. Dinner dance at Country Club where was assembled an audience of such persons as politicians seldom, if ever, meet, viz., "The Four Hundred." They preferred Terpsichore to speeches but I spoke to my satisfaction.

Tucson, June 6, 1925. Senator Cameron is receiving enormous publicity from his position as chairman of this sub-committee but the reports of my speech at Country Club last evening are soothing to my vanity.

Globe, June 8, 1925. Tom Ashurst, my nephew, here from his ranch one hundred miles in the forest.

Many cattlemen at hearings. Banquet at Dominion Hotel; critical audience. Senator Cameron's speech was much applauded.

Globe, June 9, 1925. It is now a habit on the Mexican border to slip, surreptitiously, a bottle of tequila (Mexican whiskey) into the luggage of politicians visiting border towns. Several politicians have lately suffered from such pranks, hence, whilst in Phoenix last week, I caused substantial locks to be placed on my bags and this served me well as an attempt was lately made to place whiskey into my luggage. Automobiles, persons and luggage are searched along the border without search warrant.

Phoenix, June 10, 1925. Governor Hunt at the committee hearings charged encroachments by federal authority upon state rights.

The speeches of Senator Cameron and Chief Forester Greeley and myself at Chamber of Commerce banquet tonight, to my regret, were controversial. Senator Cameron charged that National Forestry Bureau was oppressing livestock growers and Colonel Greeley hotly replied. Cameron was wildly applauded. My brother Billie was surprised at excellence of Cameron's address.

Prescott, June 12, 1925. Senatorial party attended Smoki snake dance at fair grounds. Citizens of Prescott have at much expense and labor reproduced here the Hopi snake dance. These citizens have done a service to the American people in perpetuation over the opposition of the Indian Bureau this snake dance, which is the most remarkable ceremonial rite indigenous to the western hemisphere.

Flagstaff, June 16, 1925. At hearings, Forester Greeley stated that moderate grazing of livestock on forest reduced the fire hazards thereon.

Citizens of Williams tendered committee banquet at Hotel Fray Marcos, and Senator Cameron made impassioned speech against "bureaucracy."

June 19, 1925. At St. Johns, committee heard ten witnesses. I was welcomed by Mr. Sol Barth who came to Arizona in 1860 and who for many years in Saint Johns wielded the influence of a feudal baron.

Springerville, June 20, 1925. Heard twelve witnesses. Senator Cameron and Governor Hunt spoke at barbecue. The burden of their song was "The federal government does not respect the reserved rights of the states."

Senator Cameron, with his usual acumen, has made not a little political headway out of this investigation. Representative

Hayden will be Senator Cameron's opponent for Senate next year, and Mr. Hayden's friends disrelish my accompanying Senator Cameron. What was I to do; sit in hotel lobbies and twiddle my thumbs while Senator Cameron is making gestures of saving the livestock industry? Governor Hunt gave Senator Cameron high praise for this investigation.

Near Petrified Forest, I overtook Governor Hunt, who travels slowly, and I rode many miles with him in his new Cadillac which purred over the desert like a wheeled palace. I should now be content with a duty performed but Cameron's enemies and Hayden's friends disapprove my attending these hearings with Cameron.

Washington, July 28, 1925. Reporter on New York World telephoned me that William Jennings Bryan had died at Dayton, Tennessee, where Colonel Bryan was counsel in the prosecution of Professor Scopes, charged with teaching, in a public school, that the human race "descended from a lower order of animals."

Between the time Bryan became a national figure thirty-five years ago, and this day, he served two terms in the House of Representatives, was defeated for United States senator, was nominated and defeated three times for President.

He dominated the Democratic National Convention at Baltimore in 1912 and destroyed the possibilities of Governor Harmon, Speaker Clark, and Senator Underwood as potential nominees.

He served twenty-seven months as Secretary of State in the Wilson Cabinet.

He toured Europe in 1903, and in 1905 he made a world tour. For twenty-two years he edited the *Commoner,* at Lincoln, Nebraska, and in the 12,775 days between his entry into public life and his death, he delivered over 10,000 speeches, and he traveled 350,000 miles in the *United States.* He rode in all sorts of equipages and endured many physical hardships.

With apostolic zeal he crusaded for the income tax, woman suffrage, prohibition, and direct election of senators. He assembled inarticulate thoughts and sent them forth on silver wings.

July 31, 1925. To New York Avenue Presbyterian Church to serve as honorary pall-bearer at the funeral of W. J. B.

Mrs. Bryan, crippled from arthritis, with orchids in her lap, was rolled into the church in a wheel chair accompanied by her son, her two daughters, and her brother-in-law, Mr. Charles W. Bryan.

The services were conducted by Reverend Joseph R. Sizoo, who said that years ago he had enrolled as a student in a midwestern college to prepare himself for a gainful profession, but upon hearing Mr. Bryan's lecture, "The Value of an Ideal," he was so impressed that he prepared himself rather for the ministry.

No military caisson bore Bryan's body. At the graveside Rev. Sizoo completed the rites of the church. Rev. George R. Stuart, evangelist, of Birmingham, Alabama, referred to Bryan as the "champion of the rights of the common people."

Behind his grave are rows of the World War dead; in front of his grave and across the Potomac River is the Lincoln Memorial; the marble shrine of the Tomb of the Unknown Soldier flashes through the green trees. The Washington Monument rises like a huge finger and in the distance may be descried the dome of the Capitol where as a representative in Congress Mr. Bryan began his public career, but The White House, to which thrice in vain he aspired, is invisible from the graveside.

Louisville, Kentucky, September 2, 1925. Addressed Board of Trade Luncheon at Hotel Kentucky, a new eighteen-story hostelry which opened today. I was first guest to register.

September 15, 1925. Right Reverend James E. Freeman, Bishop of Washington, and I spoke at Shoreham Hotel before Costello Post, American Legion.

September 17, 1925. Yesterday I called upon President Coolidge and asked him to set aside, for aviation purposes, two sections of land, near Tucson, Arizona. Letter, today, from White House advising that the President will set aside the land.

Los Angeles, California, October 23, 1925. Quartered at Hotel Biltmore. Sixty callers have come to my rooms thus far this day, and a queue of callers is awaiting admittance; most of them desire to talk Boulder Dam. Amongst my callers was Mr. Alexander Johnson, who was a cowboy on my father's ranch thirty-five years ago.

Los Angeles, October 26, 1925. Eleven senators of Senate Committee on Reclamation began hearings on Colorado River problems. Senator Charles McNary of Oregon is chairman. Much hospitality extended to committee by citizens of Los Angeles. Senator Dill and Colonel Halsey of Senate and I dined with Mr. and Mrs. William G. McAdoo.

October 27, 1925. Tremendous enthusiasm in Los Angeles for Boulder Dam. I directed attention to the report on Colorado River by Engineer E. C. LaRue, just promulgated by Secretary of Interior, urging construction of Dam on the Colorado River, at a point higher up on the river than Boulder but Mr. LaRue's report was derided and ridiculed by Boulder Dam advocates.

San Diego, October 28, 1925. Motorcade of the committee, to San Diego. Outriders on motorcycles preceded our motorcade to San Diego and blew sirens to keep the road clear. Senator McNary, chairman, asked me to speak at banquet at Hotel Grant here tonight. With misgivings I consented but as I proceeded the audience became sympathetic. I pointed out that Colorado River flows hundreds of miles through Arizona and that Arizona furnishes many tributaries to the river.

October 29, 1925. At El Centro; Hotel Barbara Worth. All senators spoke and my speech was an anticlimax after my effort in San Diego last night.

El Centro, California, October 30, 1925. During the testimony of Mr. J. C. Allison who is now clearing much land in Lower California, Mexico, preparatory to irrigating the same from waters of Colorado River, I demanded that further withdrawals of water from Colorado River for use in Mexico cease, and I served notice that Arizona would not deprive herself of water in order to irrigate lands in Mexico placed under irrigation after date; whereupon the audience to my amazement and delight, broke forth with peals of cheers and shouts of approval.

October 31, 1925. Committee came to Yuma per autos from El Centro and spent day examining the levee. Senator Cameron received ovation when he spoke at banquet. I could not get a room at hotel, so I slept in the committee's Pullman car in the railroad yards and no one but the porter and I occupied the Pullman.

Phoenix, November 2, 1925. All witnesses but one, urged that dam be built at a site higher up the river than Boulder. On the list of witnesses the name of Mr. Heard, editor of the *Daily Republican* had been omitted, but at my invitation he addressed committee and said that the Colorado River Compact should not be ratified.

November 4, 1925. I employed a man to shovel a path through the snow from our car to the depot at Prescott. Breakfast at Yavapai Club and visited Veterans Hospital. All senators spoke. I presided. John Renoe took charge of the committee at Prescott and through his able direction everything went off well and our committee is now on train, bound for Las Vegas, Nevada.

November 5, 1925. Writing this near midnight in a stateroom on a train out of Las Vegas, Nevada, bound for Flagstaff, Arizona. The committee spent this day examining Boulder Dam site and attended banquet in evening. Governor Schrougham of Nevada was toastmaster. Our committee has dwindled in membership until only Senator Jones of Washington and myself remain. The other members recoiled from the hardships of the trip to Glen Canyon, Arizona, and being irremediably committed to a dam at Boulder, they declined to go elsewhere. The Colorado River touches seven states viz., Wyoming, Colorado, New Mexico, Utah (called upper basin states), Arizona, Nevada, and California (called lower basin states) and the upper basin states fear that the lower basin states (in *the absence of compact*) will appropriate all the waters of the River and that under the decision of the U.S. Supreme Court, *Wyoming vs. Colorado, Vol. 259 U.S. Reports, pp. 419 and 496,* those upper basin states might be required to send Colorado River water down to the lower basin. The California senators and representatives insist that any storage dam legislation proposed shall name Boulder

as the damsite. I have proposed that the damsite shall be selected by a board of engineers. Colonel E. A. Halsey, assistant
sergeant-at-arms of the Senate and Mr. Walter Clauson of the
Associated Press will go with us to Glen Canyon.

November 7, 1925. Citizens at Flagstaff disappointed that
our committee had dwindled to two senators. I carefully examined to make sure that adequate supplies and blankets had
been provided for our auto trip through the snow to Lee's Ferry
one hundred sixty miles distant. Roads muddy, progress slow.
At intervals we met wagonloads of Navajo Indians, men, women,
and children, proceeding to Flagstaff to sell pinyon nuts. Their
ramshackle wagons were drawn by weak, scraggly ponies. The
squaws wrapped in dirty blankets were huddled in the wagons
and the papooses stared at us from their scant wrappings as their
large black eyes stoically concealed their discomfort. It is absurd
to say that the Indians gain hardihood from such exposure. Long
after dark, Senator Jones, Colonel Halsey, and I reached the
bright campfires on the river bank, near Glen Canyon. Upon
leaving Flagstaff, this morning, I asked Governor Hunt to invite
Mr. Delph Carpenter of Colorado to ride with him, but the
Governor would not do so as Mr. Carpenter aided in drafting
the Colorado River Compact, and therefore Governor Hunt
would not fraternize with Mr. Carpenter.

November 8, 1925. Breakfast — fried eggs, bacon, hot cakes,
tea, syrup, and biscuits. Senator Jones, Governor Hunt and myself per gasoline launch went to the Glen Canyon damsite. We
were three hours proceeding upstream to the site but returned
to our camp in thirty minutes so swiftly does the Colorado River
flow.

Glen Canyon damsite is, by the meanderings of the river,
about four miles from Lee's Ferry although in a direct line it
is only 3500 feet away from the Ferry as the river here describes
a horseshoe.

Lee's Ferry is the point where many of the Mormon pioneers
crossed the Colorado River as they entered Arizona. Years ago
the emigrants cut a road into the mountainside, and travelers to
this day, dread this "dugway."

This is a silent lonely land; a country of vast deserts and giant cliffs. No wonder the Indians here cling to their religion of appeasing evil spirits, rather than accept a positive religion based upon the bounty of a generous God.

Senator Jones, Colonel Halsey and I started for Flagstaff. All afternoon we shivered, but when we saw the barefoot Navajo Indian women herding sheep on snow-covered hills we were silent. Mud, snow, and auto trouble prevented our reaching Flagstaff until midnight.

Washington, November 14, 1925. The field investigation of Lower Colorado River Basin, by our committee, is finished. A few persons in Phoenix are angry at my silence at the Phoenix hearings. The excitable ones expected me to bandy epithets and shout blue-blazes. It was not my time to talk. I was in good temper but many years ago I wrote in this journal that public servants should cultivate bad tempers. Amidst an excited crowd, a calm quiet politician is suspected as insincere. Arizona newspapers criticize the committee for their failure en bloc to proceed to Glen Canyon, and I am exempted from this criticism as I went to that damsite.

December 10, 1925. Secretary of Commerce Hoover was before our Irrigation Committee and urged construction of Boulder Dam. Replying to my suggestion that board of engineers should locate the damsite Mr. Hoover said too much emotion was "involved" in the Colorado River problems to allow a damsite to be selected on technical lines.

December 15, 1925. Mr. Delph Carpenter of Colorado addressed the committee and opposed any development on Colorado River until compact shall have been ratified by all states of the river basin. Governor Dern, Utah, disclaimed intention of Utah to interfere with the allocation of hydroelectric power or to share in any revenue derived from such power generated in Lower Basin of Colorado River, if compact were ratified.

December 16, 1925. Yesterday I argued to committee that Arizona may in lieu of taxes collect revenue upon all hydroelectric energy generated on Colorado River in Arizona, and that neither the federal government nor any other authority could construct a dam or maintain a reservoir in Arizona without the consent of Arizona. In reply, Senator Shortridge pointed out that under the Arizona Enabling Act and the Constitution of Arizona, all power sites on the Colorado River were subject to the exclusive control of federal government.

December 19, 1925. Some representatives from *upper* basin states before Irrigation Committee announced they would oppose the Coolidge Dam on the San Carlos Project on Gila River, Arizona, unless and until Arizona ratified the seven-state Colorado River Compact. My reply was, "Arizona scorns all bribes and wears no chains." Over four-fifths of the waters of the Gila River arise in Arizona and none thereof could reach the states of the upper basin.

December 23, 1925. My life-time friend, Mr. Ostora Gibson, Mayor of Tombstone, Arizona, died last night. He was one of the seven pupils present when my sister Eva, my brother Billie, and I entered the log schoolhouse in Flagstaff in 1883. Mr. Gibson was poet, one-armed cowboy, clergyman, and lawyer. On January first, 1892, he and I and some other cowboys were camped on Canyon Diablo, Arizona, when he "swore off" tobacco, liquor, and profanity, and thenceforth he was clean-spoken, chivalrous, a teetotaler and non-smoker. At the age of fifteen years, the accidental discharge of a shotgun destroyed his right arm. He was clerk of the court at Flagstaff whilst I was turnkey at County Jail.

Is death a curtain of darkness and oblivion where the lights never come on again? Is the soul a fiction invented to relieve man from contemplating utter extinction? Is there a survival of personality? The Self — whatever that may be — seems permanent and persists all through bodily changes; it is not the mind, not the brain, not the will, not the feelings, and is not the body.

It is improbable that mankind shall ever ascertain definitely what will be his lot after his death, and this improbability is, in and of itself, evidence of a Great Wisdom. If we had proof beyond doubt that those who once lived are now following our movements with alarm or affection, the result would be confusion. Suicide would be at a premium; the hand of man against himself would not be withheld by conscience or timidity if he were certain of an immediate and satisfactory resurrection. Man's dazzling ingenuity and his audacious efforts to remove the indefiniteness as to the future, are mercifully in vain under the law of the Great Wisdom.

Whilst nine out of every ten persons believe in some sort of existence after death, such a belief is not pleasant to all, as there are a few persons to whom the thought of life after death is horrid, but too many incomprehensible phenomena float in the universe for one dogmatically to assert that there can be no such phenomenon as an immortal soul in a mortal body.

Camden, New Jersey, January 7, 1926. Addressed the tenth anniversary banquet of the Camden Real Estate Board, at Hotel Walt Whitman.

The other speakers were Dr. Samuel Grafflin of the New York City YMCA and Mr. Con McCole of Wilkes-Barre, Pa.

January 11, 1926. At White House with Senator Cameron and Representative Hayden and urged that Paradise Verde Irrigation Project, Arizona, be granted further time to construct dam and canals.

Question by President Coolidge: "You say Arizona wants this dam but Arizona does nothing for me?"

HFA: "What do you want us to do, Mr. President?"

President Coolidge: "I want that Colorado River Compact ratified."

HFA: "The leading Republicans in Arizona are against ratification."

January 20, 1926. Senate debated American adherence to Permanent Court of International Justice, World Court, created by League of Nations Covenant.

Senators Borah, Reed, and Johnson opposed American adherence and their speeches were largely rescripts of their speeches against League of Nations. Senator Blease of South Carolina denounced ex-President Wilson for advocating League of Nations.

January 22, 1926. Young Senator LaFollette, who succeeds his late father, spoke, opposing American adherence to World Court at this time.

His speech was well documented and well delivered.

Although Mrs. Woodrow Wilson was in the gallery, La Follette criticized her late husband for attempting to take the U.S. into the League of Nations.

January 27, 1926. Senate by seventy-six yeas to seventeen nays, with reservations, adopted the resolution to adhere to the protocol of the World Court.

February 18, 1926. My brother William arrived here from Phoenix to attend the National Education Association.

February 19, 1926. Called to State Department by Secretary of State Kellogg who said he was formulating a treaty apportioning to Mexico some of the waters of the Colorado River. Told Secretary Kellogg that Arizona Senators would oppose such treaty. In my opinion we have had too many Secretaries of State who have surrendered American rights.

February 22, 1926. Spoke at Carnegie Hall, New York, yesterday under auspices of Sons of the Revolution.

March 12, 1926. Last evening addressed banquet at Paint, Oil, and Varnish Club at Hotel Biltmore, New York.

March 15, 1926. Last evening addressed Knights of Columbus at their auditorium in Brooklyn.

March 18, 1926. Last evening addressed banquet of St. Patrick's Society of Brooklyn at Waldorf-Astoria Hotel, New York.

April 12, 1926. When Senate recessed two days ago Senator Brookhart of Iowa, whose seat is contested by Mr. Daniel Steck, had upon a count of senatorial noses, four majority, but within the past twenty-four hours the Republican National Committee and the Democratic National Committee (both organizations anxious to oust Brookhart) switched four votes from Brookhart to Steck, and upon roll call today Mr. Brookhart was unseated and Mr. Steck was seated by four majority.

June 25, 1926. I have been too low-spirited, if not despairing, to write. What has caused this? Hypochondria? Over-work? Colorado River? I know not. I have a sensible and devoted wife, good health, a loyal constituency, freedom from financial worry, yet am impressed by the emptiness and futility of my efforts.

It may be that "writing pains" or the refusal to concentrate explains my failure to write.

June 26, 1926. My amendment to pay $50 per month to any ex-service person who has had a tuberculous disease of a compensable degree and has reached an arrest of the disease, adopted to veterans' bill.

July 5, 1926. Spoke at open-air meeting at Passaic, New Jersey.

Flagstaff, July 18, 1926. Called upon Mr. Saxton S. Acker, an old pioneer and cowhand who came to Arizona fifty years ago. Many a night have I "stood guard" and ridden herd with him on the rodeos. He is now bedridden and will never walk again.

Santa Monica, California, July 26, 1926. Met Mr. J. J. (Sandy) Donahue, once the local celebrity at Flagstaff, Arizona, where he gathered objets d'art, kept a carriage, drank vintages, wore clothing cut à la mode, was sheriff of his county. Of his revenues derived from his Senate Saloon and his gaming tables, he gave bountifully to the needy and helpless. Now, in his declining years, he labors hard for coarse fare, sleeps in bunkhouses, and travels in street-cars.

I asked him to talk of his fabulous days and he replied: "I have put them entirely out of my mind; I try to forget them."

Destiny is a mighty magician. In Williams, Arizona, thirty years ago, there lived Mr. Jacob Salzman, opulent merchant and Mr. Abe Caufman, who, in homely indigence, delivered milk from a small dairy, to Mr. Salzman. Today, they both live in Los Angeles and Mr. Salzman, now poor, delivers milk from a small dairy to opulent Abe Caufman. Fortune, fame, power, and reputation vanish at the beckon of a shunless fate.

St. Anthony, Idaho, August 17, 1926. Senators Stanfield, Kendrick, Gooding, Norbeck, and myself and Representative Smith of Idaho, Sinnott of Oregon, and Winters of Wyoming and about one hundred local citizens motored to Bechler Ranger Station as the first stop.

Here we left the autos and traveled by white-top stage-coaches which had for years been stored in barns and sheds. These horse-drawn vehicles creaked and "chuckled" as we proceeded, but recourse to them was necessary as automobiles could not negotiate this terrain. After a "dinner" cooked by campfire, the Congressional party proceeded on horseback to Colonnade Falls and Iris Falls. Our inspection was to ascertain if Bechler Meadows was of scenic value comparable to its value as a reservoir in which to store water for farmers along the North Fork of the Snake River who are in need of water.

St. Anthony, Idaho, August 18, 1926. To tailor, where the dried mud of yesterday's trip was brushed from my clothing. Hearings of committee held in Latter-Day Saints Tabernacle. Governor Moore of Idaho argued that Bechler Meadows should be eliminated from Yellowstone Park and utilized as reservoir site.

Portland, Oregon, August 23, 1926. On revenue cutter from Portland to Astoria to determine ownership of Sand Island, Columbia River. Senator Dill of Washington, practical idealist of smooth rhetoric, joined us.

August 24, 1926. Crossed Columbia River from Astoria to Ilwaco, Washington, and held hearings as to Sand Island. Said goodbye to Astoria — beautiful, romantic, soft, fresh Astoria where the Columbia River enters the Ocean.

August 25, 1926. Left train at Medford, Oregon, and went per auto-stage to Klamath Falls where I spent evening with my brother Edward and his family.

August 26, 1926. Left Klamath this morning and am now at Weed, Calif. where I have waited five hours for southbound S.P. train. As I write these lines, Mount Shasta in its grandeur, is in full view.

Greenville, Michigan, September 23, 1926. Luncheon with Mr. Brinton Ball at his home in Belding, Michigan, and spoke at Greenville Country Club at banquet of Michigan bankers.

Prescott, Arizona, October 2, 1926. Spoke at Wickenburg in support of Democratic nominees. Left Wickenburg in John

Renoe's auto and after proceeding about ten miles, I concluded to ride for a time with my brother William who was following us in his auto. So I alighted from John's car expecting to hail my brother's car, but he did not see me and sped by leaving me alone on the dark desert road.

I had walked an hour in the darkness when I was picked up by an auto carrying three young men, Anderson, Borden, and Medlock, bound toward Prescott on a deer-hunt. No sooner was I seated in their auto when one of the young men in the auto allowed his rifle to go off accidentally and the bullet narrowly missed me. Finally met John Renoe, who, overtaking my brother and discovering that I had been left on the dark road, was returning for me.

October 14, 1926. Spoke at banquet tonight at Phoenix Chamber of Commerce to celebrate arrival tomorrow of the first *main-line* passenger trains to reach Phoenix. Heretofore Phoenix has been served by two branch-line railroads but the Southern Pacific Company will run its passenger trains through Phoenix on its newly completed main line.

October 15, 1926. Thousands of citizens at Union Station. Passenger trains from east and from west, simultaneously drew into Phoenix over the main-line railroad. I delivered extended speech at Rotary Club. These speeches follow one another so closely that I am a bifurcated, peripatetic talking-machine. Senator Cameron is campaigning with immense energy for re-election to the Senate but many Republicans have bolted him, and I do not perceive how he can defeat Representative Hayden who is the most popular man in Arizona.

October 18, 1926. Delivered highly oratorical speech in Library Park, Phoenix, in support of Democratic ticket.

October 25, 1926. Left Phoenix to fill speaking engagements tonight. After proceeding about fifty miles eastward, I became so sleepy that John Renoe parked the auto on the roadside and I slept for one-half hour on the desert sand.

Washington, D.C., November 5, 1926. Mr. Hayden defeated Mr. Cameron for senator in Arizona. Luncheon with Mr. Ira

Bennett, editor of *Washington Post,* and we then attended funeral of our late friend, Mr. Arthur Wallace Dunn, who for years guided the Gridiron Club.

November 10, 1926. Senate sat as Court of Impeachment, the managers on the part of the House announced that the respondent, U.S. District Judge, George W. English, had resigned his judicial office. Managers requested that the Senate proceed no further.

Easton, Pennsylvania, December 5, 1926. Accompanied by Mr. Lanman, my secretary, I came from Philadelphia per auto, plowing sixty miles through a heavy snowstorm, and in afternoon addressed Elks Memorial.

March 4, 1927. On February 18 last, the Senate began considering the Swing-Johnson bill, which proposed a high dam at Boulder Canyon on the Colorado River.

On February 26, advocates of the bill (under the leadership of Senator Johnson of California) upon roll call failed to secure the two-thirds vote necessary to apply cloture, and the bill was laid aside.

Palmer House, Chicago, Illinois, March 7, 1927. Spoke at banquet of K of C in this hotel last evening. Mayor Dever delivered address of welcome.

Erie, Pennsylvania, March 9, 1927. Quartered at Hotel Lawrence; motored through Erie and its environs with Sir Henry W. Thornton, K.B.E. President, Canadian National Railways. Spoke at banquet at Masonic Temple; Sir Henry, the last speaker at banquet, was of pungent wit.

Hotel Astor, New York, March 18, 1927. Spoke last evening at the one hundred forty-third annual dinner of the Friendly Sons of St. Patrick of New York City. Other speakers were ex-Senator Gore of Oklahoma and Mr. Claude G. Bowers of the *New York World.*

Agua Caliente Springs, Arizona, April 20, 1927. Visited ruins of the ranch-house once occupied by Honorable King S. Woolsey, a distinguished early Arizona settler who was five times a member of the Territorial Legislature. His old adobe house is ruined, but the large palo verde tree hard by, from a limb of which he and his followers hanged at one time six outlaws condemned by Judge Lynch, is spreading its shade over the yard, and the fig trees which he set out are still flourishing.

Phoenix, April 23, 1927. Spoke at Fair Grounds at the athletic meet, in honor of the memory of General John G. Greenway.

Nogales, May 2, 1927. Spent day on local problems. In evening a public dinner was tendered to me by Nogales Chamber of Commerce, at which work sufficient to keep me busy for next year was projected.

Flagstaff, May 17, 1927. Spoke in Ashurst Auditorium at State Teachers College upon invitation of Honorable Grady Gammage, president of that institution. The faculty was pleased when I said that success comes only from constant endeavour and long-sustained effort and that most failures were those persons who were unwilling to pay the price in the toil and sacrifice success demands.

Luncheon at Rotary Club as guest of my boyhood friend. Mr. William Switzer.

May 22, 1927. Mr. Theodore Mossler, whom I knew in Flagstaff forty years ago, called. Mossler then went by the nickname of the "Sheeney" and was an expert gambler. He is now bent from the weight of years and is broken and faded from alcohol and narcotics. I gave this penniless derelict one dollar and told him to come tomorrow when I shall buy him a pair of new shoes. Forty years ago how well-groomed he was, how vital he then looked, how blithe then, how tragic today.

Phoenix, May 23, 1927. Mr. Heard, publisher of the *Daily Republican* of Phoenix, asked me to come to Phoenix to aid in drafting a bill which he says should be introduced by Arizona delegation as a counterpoise to the California (Boulder Dam) plan of Colorado River development.

Query: Will California abandon her *own plan* and adopt Arizona's plan when California, owing to her immense prestige, can pass her own bill?

Nations and states are not altruistic; they take all and what they can.

May 25, 1927. Called upon ex-Senator Towne at Methodist Hospital, Tucson. I tried to comfort him but departed knowing that this brilliant and scholarly man would soon pass to the realm of silence.

Spoke to high school graduating classes at Willcox.

May 26, 1927. At Bisbee spoke to Rotary Club at noon. In evening spoke to graduating classes at Bisbee; large classes and large audience.

Phoenix, May 27, 1927. At Willcox, Bisbee, and Mesa, respectively, the school superintendents offered me a handsome honorarium for my address which I declined in each instance.

Great Britain has severed relations with Soviet Russia and Europe is agog with war scares.

Phoenix, May 28, 1927. To Florence where I spoke to high school graduating classes.

May 30, 1927. At Glendale in forenoon I addressed convention of Rural Letter Carriers, in afternoon addressed Veterans of Foreign Wars, and in evening spoke to graduating classes at Chandler.

June 1, 1927. Addressed Junior Chamber of Commerce at Tempe.

June 2, 1927. Spoke to Chamber of Commerce at Gilbert.

June 3, 1927. Spoke at Phoenix Indian School. Friends suggested that my remarks might go over the heads of the Indian students, some five hundred in number, but the suggestion did not disturb me as I knew how well the Indian understands the forest, desert, mountain, stream, and all wild life, and how beautiful the sun, moon, and stars are to his race, so I spoke of the physical world.

Phoenix, June 6, 1927. Benito Mussolini, Italian Prime Minister, on May 26 last, spoke for two and one half hours to the Chamber of Deputies and reports say that Italy has witnessed no such scene nor heard a comparable oration since the days of antiquity when classical Roman senators shook the forum. In his

May 26 speech, Mussolini announced that Italy will enormously increase her army, navy, and air-craft. This at a time when attempts are made elsewhere to reduce armaments.

San Francisco, June 8, 1927. Mrs. Ashurst and John Renoe and I called upon the Mayor, Honorable James Rolph, Jr., who placed his motor-car at our disposal.

Mr. Rolph has been mayor since January, 1912; he has executive ability and personal charm. Mr. Edward Rainey, who has been his secretary since his inauguration as mayor, came to Arizona to aid in my first senatorial campaign.

San Francisco fascinated me in my youth-time and when the wanderlust brought me here, I was not disappointed. So gay, so clean, so romantic, so clothed with dignity is San Francisco that she has always been to me the city of delight.

My old cowboy friend, Mr. Charles Stanley, called.

June 9, 1927. Colonel Bash from Fort Mason sent his auto for us and we sailed on the "Chateau Thierry" for Honolulu.

Honolulu, June 15, 1927. Quartered at Young Hotel where luncheon was tendered us by City Club. Rode with Mr. Milton through city and its environs. Since my previous visit here, ten years since, Honolulu has improved and is now a metropolitan city. Called upon Governor Farrington at Capitol and then called at Washington Place, once the private residence of Queen Liliuakalani, now the governor's mansion.

June 16, 1927. Inspected Schofield Barracks which for reasons I shall not write down, is now our most important garrison.

Attended singing contest of Hawaii church choirs at Princess Theatre. Understood not a word but nevertheless, in this singing, heard rustle of leaves and wind and wave and recognized the funeral-chant, the vibrant war-song and the plaintive love-notes of Hawaii's once careless and free pagan days.

June 17, 1927. Banquet at Royal Hawaiian Hotel where Governor Farrington delivered address of welcome. I spoke thirty minutes. Governor Farrington placed a motor-car at our disposal.

The mesquite tree, not indigenous to Hawaii but transplanted hither from Arizona where it never reaches great size, grows to large proportions here and is here called the Algaroba.

Swam at Waikiki Beach, which ten years ago was dirty and teethed with sharp coral, but is now clean and the coral removed.

More than one thousand years ago primitive men without charts, without aid from science, and without a written language came here from Polynesia sailing two thousand miles in open canoes. They knew nothing of longitude but had some knowledge of the position of the moon and the constellations and had a crude sextant, made of calabash.

June 20, 1927. Visited the royal cemetery where are entombed the sovereigns and High Chiefs of Hawaii.

Curwensville, Pennsylvania, August 23, 1927. Spoke at Rotary Club banquet here tonight.

Washington, August 28, 1927. We dined last evening with Mr. and Mrs. Will Rogers, thence to the National Press Club Frolic at the Auditorium, where I introduced Mr. Rogers, actor, author and ex-cowboy to an audience of six thousand guests of the National Press Club. During his speech, Mr. Rogers called upon General Pershing and Secretary of Commerce, Herbert Hoover, each of whom "took a bow" and was much applauded.

Niagara Falls, September 24, 1927. At City Hall attended ceremonies whereat were dedicated memorials to the pioneers of this region and in evening addressed the Niagara Falls Historical Society. Other speakers were Dr. Flick, New York state historian, and Mr. Alex Porter, scion of old family here.

Washington, September 29, 1927. Mrs. Ashurst, Mr. Pickford, and I attended the Centenary Exhibition, or "Fair of the Iron Horse" near Baltimore. Replicas of all types of locomotives ever built steamed by the grandstand. Those with perpendicular boilers were the objects of much curiosity.

October 9, 1927. Wife and I this evening attended a reception given by the Egyptian Minister, Mr. Samy Pasha and Madame Pasha.

Minister Pasha, an engineer, is a member of an opulent Egyptian family and is worldy-wise. The éclat and frequency of the receptions which he and Mme. Pasha give are not eclipsed by any other social functions in Washington.

Detroit, October 18, 1927. To reception at Book-Cadillac Hotel in honor of His Eminence, Patrick Cardinal Hayes of New York, and later Admiral Benson and I delivered speeches at banquet. My nephew Harvey Pitts of Ann Arbor came into banquet room and said he was "entertained" by my speech, but I have my doubts.

October 22, 1927. Mrs. Ashurst and I are guests of President and Mrs. Coolidge on the President's yacht, "The Mayflower" for a cruise down Chesapeake Bay. Other guests on board are Senator Smoot, Senator Curtis, Senator and Mrs. Oddie, Assistant Secretary of War and Mrs. MacNider, and Mr. and Mrs. Roland Smith of New Orleans.

On board "The Mayflower," October 23, 1927. After morning worship, the newspapers were brought by hydroplane from Washington. The table is well supplied, and the President leads the procession into the dining room. He is not a valiant trencherman. He listens to sustained conversation and his countenance lights up at any witticism or short human-interest story. When he speaks, which he rarely does, it is but three or four words. He is inscrutable, calm, courteous, and silent. During the motion pictures last night, the President sat alone several feet from his guests.

When the guest-ladies thanked Mrs. Coolidge for her courtesy in tendering them the social honor which this cruise implies, she rejoined that their thanks should go to the President, who *alone,* and without consulting her or anyone else always selected the guests who come aboard "The Mayflower" and that until she steps aboard, she never knows whom the President has invited to go on a cruise.

November 5, 1927. Luncheon at Wardman Park Hotel tendered by Dr. O. C. Kiep, the German chargé d'affaires. No ambassador from Germany has yet been named to succeed the brilliant Baron Ago von Matzan, late Ambassador of Germany, who was killed two months ago in an airplane accident. Upon Baron von Maltzan's death, German-American relations lost an able interpreter.

Trenton, New Jersey, November 18, 1927. From my window of the Stacy-Trent Hotel, I descried a portion of the barracks captured from the Hessians by General Washington on Christmas in 1776. The structure while weatherbeaten is still substantial and not ramshackle.

I addressed the Nobles of the Mystic Shrine here in Trenton last evening.

November 24, 1927. On yesterday Soviet Russia astounded the Preparatory Disarmament Commission of the League of Nations at Geneva, by proposing through Mr. Maxim Litvinoff, abolition of all war forces whether land, marine or air; also dismantling of all forts, arsenals and munition factories; in other words, armies and navies and the industries and materials for equipping them are to be abolished and hereafter prohibited.

The Commission, although amazed, diplomatically refrained from ridiculing the proposal but speedily made it known that they regarded it as Utopian and entirely inpractical for our realistic, brass-tack world. American press regards the proposal as disingenuous and in *mala fides*.

Wilkes-Barre, Pennsylvania, December 3, 1927. Quartered at Hotel Sterling, here to address Elks. What relief even temporarily to escape from the vanities, banalities, and clumsy intrigues of the politicians now assembling at Washington.

*...the Democratic fragments
are shattered.*

December 5, 1927. Congress convened today. Among the new senators sworn in was Carl Hayden of Arizona.

Public opinion in Great Britain, France, and the United States believes that the disarmament proposal made at Geneva by Soviet Russia is thinkable in Russia which country, by virtue of her geographical situation, her great man-power, and her land-locked, self-sufficient and self-subsisting entity, is less than any other nation in danger of armed invasion, and that Russia might be reasonably secure in a disarmed world whilst Great Britain's food supply would be at the mercy even of privateersmen.

Mr. David Lloyd George, sometime British Prime Minister, says in an authorized interview that the Russians proposing such disarmament are either insincere or insane.

December 13, 1927. Senator Hayden and I sat silent in our seats all day ready to defend an item of three and one-half million dollars to complete Coolidge Dam on Gila River; we had been advised that senators from states of upper basin of Colorado River would attack the appropriation but no opposition was offered.

December 18, 1927. Senators Willis, Ohio, Copeland, New York, Thomas, Oklahoma, and I went to a small brick meeting-house in Froggy Bottom on Potomac River to hear John Sims preach. Sims, colored, is eighty-four years old, is now foreman of Senate barbershop, and was a slave in his youth.

January 17, 1928. Irrigation Committee commenced hearings on Senator Johnson's Boulder Dam bill. Governor Hunt of Arizona and Mr. Winsor, president of Arizona State Senate, spoke against the bill.

January 19, 1928. On yesterday, Senator Heflin of Alabama, denounced the Roman Catholic Church and when Senator Robinson of Arkansas in replying to Heflin, eulogized the character and sacrifices of Catholic nuns, Senator Heflin demanded that Senator Robinson be removed as Democratic Minority Leader, whereupon caucus of Democratic members was called this morning and by a vote of thirty-eight ayes to one *no,* a vote of confidence in Senator Robinson was carried.

At Boulder Dam hearings Governor Dern of Utah and Governor Emerson of Wyoming opposed Dam at Boulder Canyon unless and until *all* states of Colorado River Basin ratify Colorado River Compact.

In addition to Governor Hunt, the other gentlemen from Arizona who spoke against Boulder Dam, were Messrs. Winsor, Maddock, Gust, and McCluskey. The opponents of the Boulder Dam bill in the House are superbly led by Representative Douglas of Arizona.

January 24, 1928. Attended dinner at Hotel Mayflower given by Mr. Smiddy, the Minister of the Irish Free State, in honor of Mr. William T. Cosgrave, president of Executive Council of Irish Free State. Ninety-two guests present. Diplomatic folk were in full regalia.

Hotel Hollenden, Cleveland, Ohio, February 8, 1928. Addressed banquet of the Cleveland Real Estate Board. Mr. Charles Newcomb delivered the "funny" speech. At the speakers' table, amongst others, was ex-Senator Pomerene of Ohio.

February 14, 1928. Dispatches say that the Earl of Oxford and Asquith (Herbert H. Asquith) will not survive this day. When he dies there will be extinguished a lamp of idealism, not soon to be re-lumed in English politics. After the fall of his Ministry he stood honorable and helpless, but with dignity, as "exquisite gentleman, and the last of the great Victorians."

February 17, 1928. Maple syrup breakfast with President Coolidge. Sixteen senators present.

A politician's fate is pathetic. After years of labor (which would secure a competency for his old age were such efforts employed in a gainful occupation) he may reach a place of high responsibility, then comes defeat and he glides into obscurity, poverty, neglect, and decrepitude.

I have seen this fate overtake many worthy men who for a time were leaders of parties.

February 24, 1928. This is a Presidential year and all other issues are over-shadowed by the "wet and dry" question. Neither flood control, farm relief, tax reduction, tariffs, merchant marine, Muscle Shoals, Boulder Dam, nor all of these issues rolled into one, arouses such interest now as does the liquor question.

Some persons look upon the prohibition laws as their grandparents looked upon the Fugitive Slave Law, that is to say, as immoral and unenforceable. There are *two* views in the U.S. concerning beverage-alcohol, or what is known in the nomenclature of chemistry as ethyl-alcohol. One is the view held by a group of citizens who believe that alcoholic liquor as a beverage, breeds vice, crime, and poverty and that it undermines man's physical and mental powers.

The other is the view held by a group of citizens who believe that alcoholic liquor as a beverage, ameliorates and softens the hardships and asperities of life and that similar to the theatre, music and sports, it permits persons to whom life is drab and heavy, to escape from themselves at intervals.

In the medical profession there seem to be two groups of physicians: one group convinced that beverage-alcohol serves no remedial purpose and another group convinced that beverage-alcohol in moderate quantities is a tonic. This division of opinion was once so sharp that for a time it banished ethyl-alcohol from U.S. pharmacopia.

There are in truth two kinds of worlds, one is the world of fancy and imagination, the other a world of reality wherein we struggle for livelihood. Many persons are hard put to endure life's toil and routine and are unable to escape into the world of fancy and imagination without the aid of beverage-alcohol.

The question of use of beverage-alcohol is an issue upon which men's intellects do not yield to argument as it is an imponderable which like racial and religious questions may not be argued except by philosophers.

February 29, 1928. Senate Committee on Irrigation in session daily. Messrs. Tally, Favour, Murphy, McCluskey, Winsor, and Maddock, members of Arizona's Colorado River Commission, ably assisted by Senator Hayden and Representative Douglas, each evening review my notes of the Committee's discussions. The Arizona commissioners, however, are so often in disagreement, that I am obliged ultimately to rely upon my own judgment.

March 1, 1928. The Nevada Senators and myself, at Senate Committee on Irrigation, argued for an amendment to Boulder Dam bill to provide that annually, after the federal government deducts its own amortization costs, interest, and expense of operation and maintenance, from the avails of the sales of electrical energy generated by government at Boulder Dam, there shall be paid to the states of Arizona and Nevada jointly 37 per centum of remaining avails as equitable compensation to Arizona and Nevada in lieu of the taxes which those two states could have levied and collected were the power plant constructed and operated by private capital. The California senators, Johnson and Shortridge, opposed the amendment.

March 16, 1928. Senate Committee on Irrigation adopted the Arizona-Nevada amendment to Boulder Dam bill proposing that 37 per centum of the net avails of sales of electrical energy generated at Boulder Dam shall be paid annually to Arizona and Nevada jointly and the bill was ordered reported favorably.

Hotel Ten Eyck, Albany, New York, March 17, 1928. Addressed the Friendly Sons of St. Patrick at their banquet in this hotel tonight.

Washington, D.C., March 20, 1928. Banquet at Willard Hotel in honor of Mr. Joseph Schiavoni, president of the International Exchange Bank. Senators Walsh of Massachusetts and Edwards of New Jersey and I were the speakers.

March 22, 1928. Spoke at banquet at Hotel Commodore in New York, of Savings Bank Division of American Bankers Association.

April 3, 1928. Completed my Minority Report opposing those features of the Boulder Dam bill which would tend to deprive Arizona of an equitable share of the waters and potential electrical energy of the Colorado River.

April 10, 1928. Had as guests, at dinner at my house last evening, eleven senators, four representatives and three private gentlemen.

April 14, 1928. Had as my guests at luncheon Mr. McCluskey, Mr. Ira Bennett, editor of *Washington Post,* and Mr. George Rothwell Brown, the brilliant paragrapher.

April 18, 1928. Had as guests at dinner at my house last evening seven senators, four representatives and two private gentlemen.

April 30, 1928. Senator Smoot and Senator Hayden spoke against Boulder Dam bill. Senator Walsh of Montana read extracts from Hearst newspapers charging that "Power Trust" was opposing the Boulder Dam bill.

Mrs. Ashurst and I dined at the British Embassy.

May 9, 1928. Eleven gentlemen to dinner at my residence. Amongst the guests were Governor Hunt of Arizona and General Vijitavongs, Minister from Siam.

During the past year I have entertained at stag dinner-parties at my residence some of the senators and other gentlemen toward whom I have already too long delayed hospitality. To constitute an approach to a perfect dinner there should be not only an abundance of choice viands elegantly served, but also an adaptation amongst the guests so that none will be embarrassed.

There were present at one of my dinners the two senators from Iowa (Messrs. Steck and Brookhart), and it never occurred to me until the guests were assembled that these two senators are enemies, but everything went well as I had placed them far apart at the table.

May 13, 1928, Hartford, Connecticut. Delivered Mother's Day address. Thence to Farmington Avenue to see the house where once lived Mark Twain, master of mankind's widest estate, humor.

May 21, 1928. At dinner at our residence last evening were Governor Hunt, Senator Robinson of Arkansas, Senators Fletcher, Pittman, Shortridge and Walsh of Massachusetts, the Siamese Minister and Colonel Halsey of the Senate.

May 29, 1928. At six o'clock yesterday evening I began speaking against the Boulder Dam bill, and after speaking for six hours a quorum was called for but was not obtained until five o'clock this morning, whereupon I resumed my speech and spoke until ten o'clock this A.M. when Senator Hayden took the floor and spoke two hours. Senator Curtis, Republican leader, presented resolution for final adjournment, this evening and this motion was carried by eleven majority, whereupon Senator Johnson of California asked that the Boulder Dam bill be made the "unfinished business" for the Senate next December. I entered no objection but Senator Bruce of Maryland without my consent objected to Senator Johnson's request and a storm of disapproval fell upon him. Many senators shouted savage imprecations toward Mr. Bruce. I feared that the Senate would, in resentment, reconsider its adjournment motion and would enter a cloture motion to pass the Boulder Dam bill.

Mr. Lewis W. Douglas, representative in Congress from Arizona, of superb intellect, in his able speech opposing Boulder Dam insisted that the damsite be selected by competent engineers, and the Arizona delegation in Congress is now content as Congress has passed a joint resolution authorizing the President to appoint a commission of five engineers of large experience to investigate and report as to the feasibility of the Boulder site for a high dam.

June 12, 1928. Mrs. Ashurst and I visited Old Manse, the birthplace of Grover Cleveland at Caldwell, New Jersey. The Old Manse is now the property of the Cleveland Memorial Association.

In the house are the spinning-wheel and the candle-moulds.

Detroit, June 17, 1928. To Ann Arbor where I lunched with my nephew, Harvey Pitts. In evening, at invitation of Rev. Father E. J. Taylor, I delivered address to graduating classes at Saint Rose's School, Detroit.

Rev. Father Taylor performed the marriage ceremony of myself and wife in Ann Arbor in March 1904.

Washington, July 3, 1928. Senator James A. Reed of Missouri, who desired Democratic Presidential nomination, made a poor showing in the recent Democratic National Convention and will leave public office, March Fourth next. Senator Reed is learned, eloquent, and ambitious. Like most politicians, he wastes little time on issues where he may not become the "star" but he has nobly spoken for truth and justice. With courage he opposed the federal and state snoopers who, during recent years, have been prying into the citizen's closet, trunk, pantry, apartment, cellar, and bottle.

Rapid City, South Dakota, July 28, 1928. Senators Nye (Chairman) and Kendrick, Norbeck, McMaster, Dale and myself (of Public Lands) have finished our field investigation of the proposal to add one hundred square miles of wilderness area to the Yellowstone Park, and the proposal to establish the Bad Lands National Park.

At Yellowstone Park, the wildlife in its sanctuary approached us without fear. We spent one night at Old Faithful where the Geyser, near to nature's laboratories, spouts nearly every hour. We visited the Black Hills, rich in timber, minerals, and romance. From their slopes and crests, large needles of stone arise, singly and in clusters. We went into the Bad Lands where upstand large tubes of petrified clay.

Deadwood, South Dakota, July 29, 1928. Fifty or more years ago this town, Deadwood, was the crossroads of the Wild West and the rendezvous of many gunmen. Wild Bill Hickok and Calamity Jane are buried in Mount Morial Cemetery hard by. Wild Bill, fearless but *not* quarrelsome, was a quick and sure pistol-shot. The old song goes:

> *Thirty-seven men will never breathe again,*
> *Wild Bill beat them to the draw,*
> *But as he cut a poker-pack,*
> *They shot him in the back,*
> *In a manner quite 'agen' the law.*

Calamity Jane, a woman who drifted into Deadwood in its tough days, was sometimes an army scout and teamster; she wore men's clothes, gambled, drank liquor, and deported herself as a "bad-man." She was an expert with firearms but died a natural death.

Whilst we were at lunch here "Deadwood Dick," Richard Clark, a survivor of that motley throng of those wastrel and hard-bitten Wild West days, came in, shook hands with all. He was clad in his buckskins of early times and appeared ancient. His eyes startled us; terrible eyes — sharp, fierce, blazing like a panther about to spring upon its prey.

Flagstaff, August 3, 1928. John Renoe, Bill Ashurst, and I motored to Long Valley, sixty-five miles south of Flagstaff, to a rodeo. Bill and I were surprised to meet Mr. George Blodgett, who, forty-two years ago was our father's top cowboy. Mr. Blodgett was today the factotum of the rodeo and in spite of his weight of years, he sat jauntily upon his horse and directed the cowboy events. We assumed that he died a decade ago.

Prescott, August 16, 1928. Spoke at Kiwanis Club, and gave my sixteenth annual assurance that Prescott would secure a Federal Building "next year."

August 18, 1928. My existence is broken into incoherent fragments and I am so whirled from place to place and from speech to speech that I am a peripatetic phonograph.

Flagstaff, August 19, 1928. My wife and John Renoe and I motored to Mrs. Isabella Greenway's ranch at Bill Williams' Mountains. My brother, William, was born at that ranch in 1876. Pine, cedar, juniper, and oak trees abound, but my parents left there in 1877 because of the drouth. Mrs. Greenway is the Democratic national committeewoman.

Prescott, August 26, 1928. Governor Hunt and I spoke at the dedication of the Prescott Airport.

Orators and editors are urging the electorate to vote for or against the respective Presidential nominees upon such issues as prohibition, prosperity, farm-relief, tax reduction, flood-control, high-tariff, low tariff, Boulder Dam, Muscles Shoals, etc. and not to vote for or against either Mr. Hoover or Mr. Smith for some reason which the voter would not publicly avow, but in *this* campaign, far down in the depths of emotion is an issue – religious bias and prejudice – never brought to the surface as it is deep and primal.

September 10, 1928. Arizona Gazette wired me for pre-primary statement, and I gave out the following: "I have tried to give the people a devoted and constant service. I have walked humbly and hope I have grown in grace. I claim but two virtues; industriousness and freedom from prejudice."

September 11, 1928. At 10:00 P.M. the primary election returns indicated my nomination.

Ex-Senator Ralph Cameron is the Republican nominee for United States senator. Frequently a voter is met who declines to vote for Mr. Smith because Smith is a Roman Catholic, and frequently a voter is met who declines to vote for Mr. Hoover because Mr. Hoover is a "Quaker." In my speeches, I try to point out that the liberty upon which our nation is founded assumes that political life and religious life shall travel on parallel roads that never meet in any functional manner; that the state has no ecclesiastical function and that the church has no civil function.

October 10, 1928. Raw abuse smote me heavily all day. I have been insulted on the streets a score of times.

This furor arises because in my speech at Mesa City last evening anent prohibition I stated that:

I voted for the Eighteenth Amendment and for the Volstead Law and voted to pass the Volstead Law over the veto of President Wilson; I regarded the dry Constitution of Arizona as the indication of the will of my constituents upon the Prohibition question, and that I should not vote to repeal national prohibition unless and until the people of Arizona by a referendum vote, repealed their own prohibition organic law.

This seemingly innocent statement, made me as thoroughly discredited a politician as my opponent would wish to see. The furor is not a bubble but a billow.

October 11, 1928. The repercussion of my Mesa City speech is sharp. A vehement critic of my speech is Mr. Sidney Osborn, a man much respected. He was the first Secretary of State after statehood, and with whom, in all my previous campaigns, I was on terms of political comradeship.

During Governor Hunt's primary campaign for the gubernatorial nomination in 1924, Mr. Osborn was his opponent and I gave an interview in favor of Mr. Hunt, whereat, Mr. Osborn took deep offense, although I said nothing against Mr. Osborn who has much ability. It appears as if the rupture of our once friendly relations shall be permanent.

October 12, 1928. The furor aroused by my Mesa City speech has swollen to large volume. About twenty Democrats at the State Central Committee took me severely to task. I said that I had tried to promote Governor Smith's campaign; at which statement they guffawed raucously.

Phoenix, October 20, 1928. Whilst I was speaking, Mrs. Marshall, widow of the late Vice-President Marshall, was escorted to the platform amidst much applause. I shortened my speech so that she might address the audience, which she did with ability and grace.

My speech tonight was as big a success as the Mesa City speech was a fizzle.

It is interesting to observe that one of the exploits of Colonel Aaron Burr, who died in 1836, is playing some part in this campaign. Governor Smith, of New York, the Democratic Presidential nominee, is a member of Tammany Hall (Columbian Order) and some Republican orators and editors are charging that Tammany Hall is an organization of unsavory record; and these editors and orators assert that (although Tammany was founded in 1789 as a benevolent, charitable, and patriotic society) Colonel Burr, in the elections in 1800, transformed Tammany into a political organization and became its first "boss."

Tombstone, October 23, 1928. Enthusiastic rally here tonight. In the late seventies and early eighties, Tombstone was famous, or notorious rather, as the town where pistols were as much of a man's wardrobe as his boots, and he who was slow in drawing his pistol "died with his boots on."

Indeed, in Boot Hill Cemetery hard by, are men sleeping in nameless graves, who were "slow." Tombstone is the county seat of Cochise County but its population is under one-thousand persons. Some of its once widely known "dance-halls" and saloons are now heaps of rubbish and mouldering walls.

October 28, 1928. Governor Hunt and I motored to Globe where, at the Governor's request, I was quartered at a third-rate rookery. Sentiment controlled the Governor for he laid the foundation of his fame and fortune here in Globe, and this old bedbug hatchery was the tavern in bygone days where the celebrities put up.

October 29, 1928. Trod upon a carpet tack which this morning pointed upright and pierced my left foot. Oh, this old rooming house.

October 31, 1928. Governor Hunt, seventy years old, delivered four speeches today.

This campaign is the *cloaca maxima* of Arizona politics, and throughout the nation, Governor Smith's opponents have adopted the apothegm of the French dramatist Beaumarchais, "Calumniate, calumniate, calumniate. Something is sure to stick."

November 1, 1928. I was serene this morning as I viewed the improvements that have lately come to Phoenix. Skyscrapers, mansions, villas, and parks now cover the spaces where but a handful of years ago the giant cactuses upthrust their thorns, but my serenity evaporated when I learned that the Anti-Saloon League, which had several times assured me of its support, had suddenly become "savagely" neutral.

November 8, 1928. Mr. Hoover has broken the "Solid South" and has 444 Electoral Votes while Mr. Smith has 87. I am re-elected to the Senate, but the landslide would have swept me out had not three thousand leading Republicans bolted my opponent, Mr. Cameron. Governor Hunt is defeated. He was born in Huntsville, Missouri in 1859, was christened George Willie Paul Hunt and came to Arizona in 1881. He has traveled much in Europe and was sometime our Minister to Siam. Behind his gold-rimmed spectacles are steady, Oriental eyes. He is corpulent — stone-bald, with not a hair on his large, domed head. A fresh boutonniere every day. His clothing is costly and out à-la-mode. The wings and flanges of his huge moustache drooped sadly until he went to Siam, but he returned with this mustache so waxed that it resembled a Spanish Bayonet protruding from either side of his mouth. Although without a college education, he has by absorption and select reading become well informed, and discusses problems, both American and European, with enlightment.

Washington, November 15, 1928. Mr. Thomas Downs, my assistant secretary, left me today to begin law practice in Chicago.

Clarksburg, West Virginia, December 1, 1928. Quartered at the Waldo Hotel owned by Senator Guy D. Goff of this state. I served six years with his father in the Senate. I am to address the B.P.O. Elks here tomorrow.

December 4, 1928. President Coolidge's annual message, today announced that the special board of engineers appointed to consider the Boulder Dam project reported that a dam was feasible at Boulder. The message declares that while flood-control, irrigation, and domestic water purposes are governmental functions, there is no need for the government to go into the field of generating electrical energy for sale and that such field should be left to private enterprise.

December 14, 1928. The Boulder Dam bill passed the Senate yeas sixty-four, nays eleven. By this bill the Gila River of Arizona is exempted from making contributions of water for distribution to the main stream of the Colorado River, and California is limited to the exclusive, beneficial, consumptive use in perpetuity of not to exceed 4,400,000 acre-feet of water, annually, from the water allotted to the Lower Basin by the Colorado River Compact of 1922.

Dined with Chief Justice Taft at his residence. He is planning for a monumental building for the U.S. Supreme Court.

December 16, 1928. Mr. Theodore E. Burton was today sworn in to serve the unexpired term of Senator Willis of Ohio deceased. Mr. Burton served in the House, then in the Senate, then again in the House and now comes again to the Senate. Another interesting man of this short session is Senator Octaviano Larrazolo of New Mexico, a full-blooded Mexican who was born in Old Mexico, a bi-lingual orator.

December 17, 1928. On the sixth of April, 1927 (the tenth anniversary of the entry of the United States into the World War) Monsieur Briand, foreign minister of France, proposed that France and the United States respectively should denounce and abolish war as a method of deciding disputes.

Events, later proving to be great, are often almost unnoticed when they occur. This is probably due to the fact that creative thought, although ultimately of imperial authority, is so serene in its realm that it does not attract attention as does a dramatic act. In other words, the politics of Peace lack the color, excitement, and pageantry of War.

Very few journals gave M. Briand's proposal much attention, but Doctor Nicholas Murray Butler, president of Columbia University, called attention to the enormous importance of Briand's proposal, and after diplomatic interplay, a treaty now called "the Pact of Paris" or Multilateral Treaty, renouncing and outlawing war as a method of deciding disputes and settling national policies, was signed at Paris in August, 1928, by the following governments: Germany, The United States, Belgium, France, Great Britain, Canada, Australia, New Zealand, The Union of South Africa, The Irish Free State, India, Italy, Japan, Poland, and Czechoslovakia. Other governments were invited to join.

The operative parts of this treaty (omitting the preamble), the provisions for signatures, and the methods of ratification, are as follows:

Article I

The High Contracting Parties solemnly declare in the names of their respective peoples that they condemn recourse to war for the solution of international controversies, and renounce it as an instrument of national policy in their relations with one another.

Article II

The High Contracting Parties agree that the settlement or solution of all disputes or conflicts of whatever nature or of whatever origin they may be, which may arise among them, shall never be sought except by pacific means.

The Senate today, ordered this treaty to be the unfinished, executive business of the Senate for January 3, 1929.

The human race has reached a crisis in its career where it must, owing to the achievements of science, choose whether it shall run the risk of the destruction of civilization, *or* attempt to secure the safety and peace of nations by agreeing to abolish and outlaw war as an instrument and method of settling disputes.

December 31, 1928. After the defeat of Mr. John W. Davis, the Democratic Presidential nominee in 1924 I wrote *inter alia:*

"The Democratic forces are shattered," today I write:

"The Democratic fragments are shattered. The Republicans are united, whilst the Democrats are quarreling over Religion and Whiskey."

January 15, 1929. The Senate by eighty yeas to one nay, ratified the Pact of Paris (Kellogg Multilateral Treaty) which renounces war as an instrument of national policy.

Of the various attempts in the past to outlaw war, none ever had such magnitude and such powerful advocacy as this Pact of Paris.

January 19, 1929. Senator Walsh of Massachusetts gave a banquet at Brooke-Manor, near the Baltimore Pike, to Senator Peter G. Gerry who was defeated for re-election last November. Mr. Gerry, a scion of a wealthy family of Revolutionary War fame, is cultured and modest. One of his ancestors, Honorable Elbridge Gerry, was Vice-President under the second Madison administration. The mansion at Brooke-Manor was built about 1727 and has a fireplace so large that an auto could be parked therein.

January 21, 1929. My bill granting an annuity to Mrs. Marshall, widow of Vice-President Marshall, passed the House at $3000 per annum. This bill was passed solely through the efforts of my wife.

January 23, 1929. Senator Larrazolo sent for me and upon reaching his office, I found him suffering from heart failure. I put in a few hours helping this brilliant bilingual orator arrange his affairs so that he might leave here tonight and go home to New Mexico, to die.

February 14, 1929. Senator Moses, New Hampshire, asked me to give to Senator Reed of Missouri my place on the joint committee which will adopt plans for a monumental building for the United States Supreme Court. Senator Reed is eager for this place as it would bring him to Washington at intervals and keep him in touch with public affairs.

It is a dreary world for ambitious men when they retire from the theatre where for years they were stars of the first magnitude. Reed's public career ends with a bitter draught, for not only did he lose the Presidential nomination but his *bête noire* (Herbert Hoover) was elected President.

February 16, 1929. Wife and I dined with General Vijitavongs, Minister of Siam, who leaves to represent his government at Paris.

February 19, 1929. Joint Resolution passed Senate making Senator Reed of Missouri eligible for membership on commission to construct building for United States Supreme Court. Although I outranked Reed on the building committee, I waived, in his favor, membership on this commission which gratified him immensely.

March 4, 1929. Herbert Hoover inaugurated. Vice-President is Senator Charles Curtis, of Indian ancestry. The fiery Dawes in his valedictory, again denounced the Senate rules which (except when cloture is applied) permit unlimited debate, adverting to his speech of this day, four years ago, against unlimited debate, he shouted, "I take back nothing."

Time's prospective will appraise Calvin Coolidge, but with certainty it may *today* be said that he restored the White House to a symbol of dignified and moderate living. During his presidency, extravagance was the order of the day but neither Calvin Coolidge nor his wife was tainted by this corroding vice. By example they taught thrift. Coolidge defeated foreign debt cancellation and defied politicians who advocated nostrums.

During his administration, America had an attack of enlargement of the wallet, but this Vermonter of nasal drawl remained steady.

Andrew W. Mellon, Secretary of the Treasury, and James J. Davis, Secretary of Labor, in the Coolidge Cabinet, retain their respective portfolios in President Hoover's Cabinet.

The dice of destiny in March, 1921, summoned Mr. Andrew W. Mellon, the least known of our American multimillionaires, from the cloister of his Pittsburgh bank and plunged him into the arena of national politics.

Mr. Mellon, over seventy, is slender, frail, gentle, enigmatic, no speech-maker, no spoilsman, no political maneuverer, and yet he was the Richelieu of Republican officialdom during the Harding and Coolidge regimes. President Hoover knew that to let Mr. Mellon go, would have sent all securities, including government bonds, downward.

What are the sources of Mellon's power? What armour does he wear that turns aside the javelin and spear-thrust of criticism? Answer: He is one of the world's soundest bankers; he is a man of candor, thrift, and industry, and is clear-headed.

Cincinnati, Ohio, March 16, 1929. Addressed the Friendly Sons of Saint Patrick at Hotel Sinton.

Mr. Edward Babbitt of the Arizona firm of Babbitt Brothers, merchants and cattlemen, was present.

April 13, 1929. When Senator Harding became President he appointed Mr. Judd Welliver as research secretary to assemble the data and turn the phrases of the Presidential speeches. Mr. Coolidge, although of pride approaching vanity as to his own literary style, appointed Mr. Stuart Crawford, research secretary, to aid in making the epigrams shine, and Mr. Hoover has appointed Mr. French Strother to give Attic salt to the Presidential speeches.

April 15, 1929. Congress convened in extra session today. When, Oh when, will Presidents learn to avoid extra sessions?

April 16, 1929. Senate by acclamation confirmed the nomination of ex-Vice President Dawes to be ambassador to Great Britain. President Hoover's message *inter alia* recommends that a bill re-apportioning representatives be passed. This duty was evaded by the House in 1920.

Of all the men who have held the Vice-Presidency, none of them enjoyed the office so much as does Mr. Curtis and he is a good presiding officer.

May 20, 1929. Attended reception at Cuban Embassy to celebrate anniversary of independence of Cuba and spent the evening at the Persian Legation.

May 25, 1929. Spoke at Commodore Hotel, New York City, at banquet tendered by Mr. Harrison Burdick to the Harbor Marine Steel Corporation.

June 2, 1929. We motored with Attorney E. S. Clark of Phoenix and his granddaughter. Mr. Clark is here to urge an increase in the tariff on manganese, a metal used in making steel. Arizona miners are demanding this tariff and much manganese is found in Arizona.

June 13, 1929. Conference report on apportionment bill adopted by Senate, and thus Congress after nine years of "dodging" sends an apportionment bill to the President. That the Senate discharged its constitutional duty on reapportionment is due to the energy and ability of Senator Arthur H. Vandenberg of Michigan.

June 18, 1929. Called upon President Hoover and recommended ex-Governor Tom Campbell of Arizona for membership on the Hoover Farm Board.

Neither President John Quincy Adams nor President Benjamin Harrison could have refrigerated callers more quickly than President Hoover.

Senator Burton, Ohio, urges me to go to Geneva, Switzerland, to attend Inter-Parliamentary Union but I shall decline to go, for if I were absent in Europe whilst this tariff bill is considered by the Senate, those of my constituents who desire *free trade* on tomatoes imported from Mexico, and those who desire high tariff on hides, manganese, wool, cotton, etc., would fill my nostrils with burning sulphur.

Des Moines, Iowa, June 26, 1929. Addressed the Iowa Bankers Association here. The new paper money appears today and is one-third smaller in size than the old currency.

Flagstaff, Arizona, July 14, 1929. My brother William took me in his motor-car to the old Ashurst Ranch, a visit to which, I note in this Journal ten years ago.

On this ranch, my brother William was my companion, and on our long rides whilst cowherding, we talked as forest-folk and desert-folk do, of the enigmas of human destiny and the mysteries of the universe.

During our boyhood days on this ranch the summer sun splashed its heated brilliancy, and the lure of the free range so filled our hearts that, whilst indeed we perceived the tragedy of our family, we were so buoyant and resilient, that it made almost no impression upon us then; but now that life has swallowed up those times and for us youth is no more, our thoughts trail back into those bygone days on the ranch and we seem to be fumbling through some confused dream.

As we wandered around the ruined log cabin, we came here and there upon rusted objects which brought memories of happenings of the long ago. William found a wrench which our Father used nearly fifty years ago, and I found two ax-blades which chopped the wood during our boyhood.

The staccato barking of an "engine of the sky" filled our ears; it was a car of the Air Transport from New York bound for Los Angeles. Its occupants, doubtless, glanced at the greenery and the rugged landscape beneath them and sailed on oblivious to the ranch and its poignancy to us.

July 20, 1929. Dispatches say that the chancelleries of Great Britain, France, and the United States are trying to avert war in Manchuria between China and Russia and that the Kellogg Multilateral Treaty, ratified by the United States Senate, last January, was the medium through which the friendly advices were being offered.

July 21, 1929. Yesterday I wrote of the tension between China and Russia, and I was not accurate, as "Russia" is merely a state in the Union of Socialistic Soviet Republics. The state of

Russia has no more diplomatic relations with other countries than has the state of Prussia in the German Republic.

The Union of Socialist Soviet Republics consist of six republics, of which the Russian Socialist Soviet Republic is one state. The other states are: Ukrainian Socialist Soviet Republic, White Russia Socialist Soviet Republic, Transcaucasian Socialist Soviet Republic, Uzbek Socialist Soviet Republic, and Turcoman Socialist Soviet Republic. These Republics are united into one central authority, viz., the union of Socialist Soviet Republics. It *is*, therefore, the *Union of Socialist Soviet Republics* that is in dispute with China.

Washington, D.C., July 24, 1929. In the White House, today was promulgated the Kellogg Multilateral Treaty, Pact of Paris, denouncing recourse to war as a method of settling international disputes. Ex-President Coolidge took part in the ceremonies incident to the treaty's promulgation, and there was also present Mr. Frank Billings Kellogg, sometime Secretary of State under Coolidge.

I have hereinbefore written of the strange fashion by which destiny deals with men and events, and Mr. Kellogg's career illustrates how by sorcery or legerdemain, fate reinstates the vanquished.

Mr. Kellogg, who was a successful lawyer in Minnesota, came to the Senate in March, 1917. From his eminence at the bar, we believed he would achieve fame as a senator, but it would be difficult to name a man whose service in the Senate brought him less distinction than did the half dozen years Mr. Kellogg futilely spent in the Senate. Senator Brandegee dubbed him "Nervous Nellie;" Senator Norris smothered him beneath a weight of sneers and insinuations. In Senate debate he was ridiculed, chopped, slashed, and fricasseed like an Indian at the stake, until he finally shrivelled into such obscurity that even the Senate radicals deemed him too unimportant further to torture.

When he stood for re-election in 1922, Minnesota turned thumbs down on him in favor of thoughtful Mr. Henrik Shipstead, a huge-framed dentist.

Mr. Kellogg left the Senate with unpleasant memories, trembling hands, a glass eye, stooped shoulder, hoary hair and with his colleagues taking it for granted that he was headed for oblivion.

Soon after Calvin Coolidge acceded to the Presidency, he took up Mr. Kellogg (for reasons worthy but indelicate to mention now) and made him ambassador to Great Britain, where he served acceptably; and he then served as Mr. Coolidge's Secretary of State, in which Department he won world-wide renown from the Kellogg Multilateral Treaty outlawing war.

Today Mr. Kellogg is serene, mellow, happy, healthy, and famous. Many of the senators who derided him whilst he was in the Senate, were yet members when the Multilateral Treaty was considered; and thus last January, they voted for his treaty thereby giving him far-shining fame. In view now of Mr. Kellogg's niche in history, these senators would today exchange places with him, obsidian optic and all.

August 15, 1929. We spent the day in Montreal and then took steamer down the River St. Lawrence.

August 16, 1929. Breakfast in Quebec, an important city in the annals of North America. There are really two cities to be seen in Quebec, viz., the old French city of more than two centuries ago and the modern Quebec which is the provincial capital. These two cities, distinct yet united, form a centre of art, architecture, and history, both sacred and secular. Here, in an attempt to capture Quebec, fell General Richard Montgomery, a brave soldier of the American Revolution, and here by a curious freak of fate, Benedict Arnold and Aaron Burr under General Montgomery's command, fought gallantly in behalf of the American patriot cause.

September 10, 1929. Premier Briand of France, who inspired the Pact of Paris, known in Washington as the Kellogg Multilateral Treaty outlawing wars, announced at Geneva yesterday a project to form a grand confederation to be known as the United States of Europe. Mr. Briand looks upon Europe as an economic unit and he wants trade barriers removed. He advocates one monetary system and one general postal system for Europe.

I was toastmaster last evening at Hotel Mayflower at banquet of the American Manganese Producers.

September 27, 1929. Debate of elevated character in progress in the Senate over the so-called flexible feature of the pending Tariff Bill, which proposes that hereafter tariff rates shall be fixed by the President instead of by Act of Congress.

The Supreme Court of the United States, in the case of Hampton vs. the United States (276 U.S. 394) held it to be constitutional to grant to the President, as was done in Section 315 of the Tariff Act of 1922, the power to raise or lower, within some limitations, a tariff rate fixed by Act of Congress.

Senators Borah, young LaFollette, Walsh of Montana, and McKeller opposed remitting the rate-fixing to the President whilst Senator Fletcher advocated the plan.

Tom Connally, the new senator from Texas, opposed the flexible feature of the tariff bill. Senator Connally is an attractive speaker and said that "the power of Congress to fix tariff rates, surrendered by the Tariff Act of 1922, to the Executive, should be recaptured by Congress and re-deposited where it belongs, viz., in Congress."

October 6, 1929. Wife and I to the Persian Legation and met the Maharajah of Kapurthala, one of the largest states in India. One hundred guests present, and I was edified by a talk with Mr. Faik Konitza, the Minister from Albania. Mr. Kanitza is an accomplished linguist; he speaks seven languages and can think in six of them.

October 7, 1929. Honorable J. Ramsay MacDonald, the Prime Minister of Great Britain, here to promote naval disarmament, addressed the Senate. When he grew animated, his Scot *bu-r-r* rolled out. He has the Asquithian habit of pressing his clenched hands upon his chest while speaking.

Dined at the Egyptian Legation.

October 11, 1929. Attended at the Court House where Albert B. Fall, aged and infirm, is on trial charged with accepting a bribe when, as Secretary of the Interior, he leased the Elk Hills Oil Reserves to Edward L. Doheny.

October 12, 1929. Captain Hewitt of Silver Springs, Maryland, took me by motor car to Baltimore, where Governor Ritchie, Mayor Broening, and I addressed K.C. banquet.

October 22, 1929. I listened to the attorneys arguing for ex-Secretary of Interior, A. B. Fall. How terribly have his fortunes shrunk since that day when together he and I were inducted into the Senate! From scanty and arduous beginnings, he wrestled a fair education from a reluctant desert; he farmed, he mined, read law, soldiered, became a judge, then a senator, then a cabinet member and was influential in the Harding regime; today old, penniless, harried, wan-faced, looking mayhap into a prison cell, he is deserted by all save a few New Mexico cronies, and the doughty Irish millionaire, Mr. Doheny. None of these who here fawned upon and flattered Mr. Fall when he had power will speak to him now.

October 25, 1929. Jury found ex-Secretary of Interior Fall guilty of accepting a bribe from Mr. Doheny. I was not present when the verdict was rendered, having no desire to witness such distress as I knew would come (and did come) to his family from this verdict.

October 26, 1929. Senator Bingham, Connecticut, speaking to a question of personal privilege, charged that Senator Norris, Chairman of the Senate Committee on the Judiciary, in selecting the Lobby Committee, had "packed" the Lobby Committee against himself — Bingham.

Senator Bingham was born in Honolulu in 1875 and has seven sons. He taught at Harvard, Princeton, and Yale. He is an aviator and has explored faraway lands; he is cultured and imperturable.

October 29, 1929. Wife and I attended a reception at Turkish Embassy celebrating the anniversary of establishment of the Turkish Republic.

October 30, 1929. Funeral of Senator Burton, Ohio, in the Senate Chamber.

November 7, 1929. I spoke supporting amendment by Senator Oddie proposing an import duty of one cent per pound on manganese. Amendment adopted. Senator Barkley, Kentucky, charged that a lobby for manganese infested the Capitol.

November 10, 1929. The only writing I do today in this book is to copy the following entry which Lord Byron made in his journal on December 6, 1813.

This journal is a relief. When I am tired – as I generally am – out comes this and down goes everything.

But I can't read it over; and God knows what contradictions it may contain. If I am sincere with myself (but I fear one lies more to one's self than to anyone else) every page should confute, refute, and utterly adjure its predecessor.

November 11, 1929. Delivered Armistice Day address at Woodbury, New Jersey and was the guest of the American Legion Post there.

Washington, November 12, 1929. President Hoover urges that in time of war, ships carrying food supplies only, shall be exempt from hindrance or capture.

This idea comes to the President out of his experience as U.S. Food Administrator during our participation in the World War, and he points out that the rapid advance of industry has subjected vast populations to a dependence for food upon seaborne commerce, of which England is an example.

*...it is the birthright of every citizen
to have a fair opportunity
to* earn *a livelihood.*

November 14, 1929. The catastrophe in the stock market which three weeks ago brought the most drastic securities deflation in the world's history (shrinkage in stock of sixty billion dollars) has filled business with fear and alarm.

Financial ruin has fallen upon thousands of persons who one month ago were opulent, but who did not resist the temptation to gamble in stocks.

At the Chevy Chase School I heard Mr. Hamlin Garland lecture on "American Authors."

When I met Mr. Garland in London, six years ago, his shock of hair and his shaggy eyebrows were only iron-gray, but are now snow-white. He is our classic liaison man, connecting the authors of forty years ago with those of today. Mr. Garland personally knew William Dean Howells, Charles Dudley Warner, James Whitcomb Riley, Joaquin Miller, Mark Twain, Bret Harte, Richard Watson Gilder, Edwin Booth, and Robert G. Ingersoll, men whose fame in literature, art, histrionics, and eloquence, near the close of the nineteenth century sent out far-shining beams.

November 24, 1929. Senator Francis Emroy Warren of Wyoming, after a service in the Senate of thirty-six years, eleven months and twenty-four days, died here today. General Pershing, his son-in-law, was at his bedside when he died. Senator Warren was past sixty-four years of age and was the Senate's last Civil War veteran.

Hon. Roscoe Conkling, incorruptible, master of satiric invective, learned, domineering, sensitive, austere, athletic, prince of pyrotechnic eloquence, proud to a degree which approached vanity, with the front of Jove himself, a senator from New York during the two decades immediately following our Civil War, was one of the noted men of his time.

Although he received from the public during his political ascendency an adulation rare in our annals, his fame is today a dim tradition; but, to remind us of how he was adored half a century ago, we now have with us Senators Roscoe Conkling Patterson of Missouri, and Roscoe Conkling McCulloch of Ohio.

Newark, New Jersey, December 4, 1929. Addressed the New Jersey Lenders Association at their annual convention at the Robert Treat Hotel here.

December 7, 1929. The town of Tombstone, for fifty years the county seat of Cochise County in Arizona, once known as the "toughest" village of the wild and young Southwest, has lived up to its prophetic name and will soon be a ghost-town. A canvass of the returns of the recent special election shows that the County Seat will be moved from Tombstone to the city of Bisbee.

History and fiction have combined to give to Tombstone a romantic tradition of the pioneers, cattle-wars, mining adventures, duels, and forays of "gunmen" of Tombstone's bygone days. In the Tombstone courthouse to be abandoned, there was in early times often to be heard, speaking for law and order, the rich voice of my former senatorial colleague, Marcus Aurelius Smith, who began his political career in Tombstone.

December 19, 1929. Attended reception to the British Ambassador, Sir Esme Howard and Lady Isabella Howard, given by Mr. and Mrs. Peter A. Drury.

January 13, 1930. General Jan C. Smuts, soldier and ex-premier of South Africa, was received by the Senate today.

January 15, 1930. Wife and I dined at German Embassy with the Ambassador and Mrs. Von Prittwitz-Gaffon.

January 17, 1930. Senator Hayden was today appointed by Governor Phillips as advisor to Arizona's Commission on the Colorado River and he will leave tomorrow for Reno, Nevada, to attend a conference looking toward an agreement with California on the Colorado River problems.

February 3, 1930. Chief Justice Taft in failing health resigned his judicial office and Hon. Charles Evans Hughes was nominated to succeed him.

February 8, 1930. Senator Hayden returned from the River parley at Reno and reports that no agreement with California was reached.

February 11, 1930. Senators Borah and Glass today opposed confirmation of Mr. Hughes, as Chief Justice of the U. S. Their speeches were so severe that no man could read such utterances against himself without distress.

February 12, 1930. Senator Dill, excoriated President Hoover for the Hughes' nomination. Mr. Hughes will be confirmed, but he has been subjected to the most savage assault ever made upon a nominee for Chief Justice of the U. S. Supreme Court.

February 13, 1930. Senators Norris, George of Georgia, LaFollette, and Blaine opposed Mr. Hughes. The protests against Mr. Hughes seem to carry an implication that courts have interfered with the power of the states to regulate monopolies, but how Mr. Hughes is *involved* is not made clear. The debate on the Hughes nomination is an anthology of invective.

On roll call Mr. Hughes was confirmed by a large majority. The opposition to Mr. Hughes is symptomatic of the discontent now raging. Prosperity is a solvent for discontent, but prosperity evaporated last autumn when the stock market collapsed.

March 11, 1930. In a cold and blustery rain storm, the body of William Howard Taft, statesman, teacher, diplomat, and jurist was taken from the rotunda of the Capitol to All-Souls' Unitarian Church for services of the faith in which he lived. There was no sermon, no eulogy; and the body of him who rose to be President and later Chief Justice was then borne on a caisson to Arlington.

Consideration for others and fidelity to duty, were touchstones of his life. He met both extremes of political fortune and was serene in each.

March 20, 1930. The Earl of Balfour, philosopher-statesman died yesterday. Beneath his polished surface there was a tenacity of purposes and trenchancy of speech. When he was here in 1917 and in 1921, official and social Washington was attracted by his personal charm and his metaphysical subtleties.

March 22, 1930. The trial jury acquitted Mr. E. L. Doheny of the charge of bribing former Secretary of the Interior Fall on the oil leases.

April 26, 1930. Attended Gridiron Club dinner where the news-scribes let fly satirical shafts at President Hoover and various leaders in Congress.

The rollicking was put aside while John Philip Sousa, the March King of world-wide fame, swung his baton over the Welsh Fusileers of the Marine Corps. President Hoover and Dr. Glenn Frank, president of the University of Wisconsin, were the speakers.

May 2, 1930. Dined with the Ambassador of Turkey, Ahmed Mouftah Bey, at the Turkish Embassy.

May 24, 1930. I was master of ceremonies today at the unveiling of the statue of General John C. Greenway in Statuary Hall in Capitol Building. This statue, made by sculptor Gutzon Borglum, was presented to the nation by the state of Arizona. Speakers were Senators Robinson of Arkansas, Senator Hayden, Representative Douglas of Arizona, Representative Connery of Massachusetts, and Major General James G. Harbord, U. S. Army, retired.

June 14, 1930. Upon invitation of the Brazilian ambassador, Mrs. Ashurst and I were among the guests at dinner at Pan-American Union in honor of President and Mrs. Hoover, on the occasion of the visit of Senor Julio Prestes, the president-elect of Brazil.

June 17, 1930. Here ends this journal which began twenty years ago this day. No conceivable energy could have recorded more than an insignificant fraction of the events which came within my orbit since the first entry herein.

The all-too-frequent intrusion of the personal pronoun "I" in this book is disagreeable, and yet much could not have been avoided. To write objectively in works of history, is not mere literary form, it is unavoidable; to write autobiographies, journals, diaries and memoirs, *subjectively* and in the first person is inevitable.

June 28, 1930. Representative A. J. Montague of Virginia, chairman of the American Group of the Inter-Parliamentary Union, appointed me to attend the session of the Union at London, in July. I believed on June 17 that I had forever done with diaristic writing, but habit holds one in thralldom.

June 30, 1930. The French Line which on last Saturday sold us passage to London on the S. S. "Rochambeau," notified me that they sold me passage by mistake and that all accommodations on the "Rochambeau" were sold some days since.

New York City, July 5, 1930. The French Line transferred us to the S.S. "Minnewaska" of the Atlantic Transport Line, but before we could reach the "Minnewaska" she had lifted her gangplank and it appeared that we would be left, but she lowered the plank and we went aboard.

London, July 14, 1930. Quartered at Park Lane Hotel in Picadilly, a hostelry projected by Mr. Harry Wardman of Washington, D.C., before his fortune slipped from his once competent hand.

In London I seem oblivious to its commerce and its busy traffic. My imagination gallops back to those remote times when our own language and our law were here taking form.

To the House of Commons but the M.P.'s who extended courtesies to me seven years ago, to wit: Mr. T. P. O'Connor and Brigadier John Sanctuary, are now in their graves.

London, England, July 16, 1930. The twenty-sixth conference of the Inter-Parliamentary Union met in the Royal Gallery of the House of Lords. The delegates are four hundred in number; thirty-two governments are represented, and some delegates are here representing the League of Nations.

His Grace, the youthful Duke of Sutherland of the British group, was chosen presiding officer. The Duke in his speech, reminded his audience that (twenty-four years ago) in 1906, the I.P.U. met in London and that the then Prime Minister, Sir Henry Campbell-Bannerman, opened the conference. The Duke went on to recite a history of the formation and work of the Union. He concluded by saying that another World War in Europe would pull us all down into the flames of ruin, and that the facade of civilization would crack and crumble under the strain of universal bankruptcy.

Lieutenant Commander J. M. Kenworthy, M. P. of the British group, gave a dinner this evening at the House of Commons to the American group. Commander Kenworthy proposed a toast to the American group to which Representative Montague of Virginia, chairman of the American group, responded, and then at Mr. Montague's request, in a five-minute speech, I proposed a toast to the British group to which the Duke of Sutherland replied.

July 17, 1930. In the evening my wife and I and Mr. and Mrs. Ellinwood of Phoenix, Arizona, attended a reception given by Viscountess Astor and met Mr. George Bernard Shaw around whom were clustered a throng of admirers relishing his polished shafts of wit.

We moved from the Park Lane Hotel to the Strand Palace.

July 18, 1930. Upon invitation of Dr. Sherwood Eddy of the United States, Senators Barkley, Connally, Tydings, Wheeler, and I went to a small room in Old Queen Street where to an audience not exceeding sixty persons, Mr. David Lloyd George, ex-Prime Minister, replied to questions. Mr. Lloyd George said that free trade was making *no* headway in England; that neither Great Britain nor France but the United States rather, was receiving the benefits of the moneys paid over by Germany as reparations. He further said that unemployment remained acute until twenty years after the close of the Napoleonic wars and that he did not expect the present problem of unemployment to improve for some years more. He eulogized England as a leader for peace and said that the League of Nations could have *no* great authority unless the U. S. entered. He explained his reasons for recognizing Soviet Russia while he was Premier by saying that the Russians are a brave, numerous, and sensitive people and when aroused are a dangerous people. He said he admitted Russia's misbehavior but added that all nations at times misbehave and that it is wise to emulate Admiral Lord Nelson's example and put our telescope to our blind eye. Mr. Lloyd-George's replies, which really were extended speeches, justified his wide reputation as a man of mental power, humor, and eloquence. Ruddy of countenance, stockily built, with long-ish white hair and a white tab toothbrush of a mustache, he radiated vitality.

I took Mr. and Mrs. Ellinwood of Phoenix with me to hear Mr. Lloyd George.

The American Ambassador and Mrs. Dawes gave a dinner tonight to the American group of the I.P.U. and their ladies.

July 19, 1930. With the Duke of Sutherland as our guide, the 400 delegates to the I.P.U. and their ladies went by *charabanc* to Windsor Castle, the most royal of all the residences of British monarchs.

July 21, 1930. All the Delegates to the I.P.U. and their ladies attended a "Conversazione" given at Guildhall by the Corpora-tion of London (City of London). The Right Honorable Lord Mayor of London and the Lady Mayoress, accompanied by the Sheriffs of London and their ladies, were present in full regalia.

July 22, 1930. The American group of the I.P.U. called this morning upon Prime Minister Mr. Ramsay MacDonald at No. 10 Downing Street.

Mrs. Ashurst and Representative and Mrs. Montague and I lunched at the Cheshire Cheese, a restaurant off Fleet Street frequented by Mr. Boswell, Dr. Sam Johnson, and other cele-brities of past days.

The twenty-sixth Inter-Parliamentary Union adjourned. It is a polylingual assemblage which discusses imminent ques-tions and champions the parliamentary system of government.

In this conference are many delegates who hold, or have held, great places in their respective countries, e.g. Prince Toku-gawa, president of the Japanese Chamber of Peers; Count Car-ton de Wiart, some time prime minister of Belgium; and M.

Fernand-Bouisson, president of the French Chamber of Deputies. Amongst the American delegates is Mrs. Ruth Bryan Owen, daughter of the late W. J. B. and now a representative in Congress from Florida. One of the vivid personalities is Sir Maneckjee Dadabhoy who, in the English language, spoke in behalf of India, and said that theretofore the Union had limited its old world activities to Europe but should extend its membership to the Far East.

His Majesty's government gave a dinner tonight at Connaught Rooms to all the I.P.U. delegates. The speakers were the Lord Chancellor (Lord Sankey), Prince Tokugawa of Japan, Senator La Fountaine of Belgium, and Mr. Montague of the U.S.A. The toastmaster (Mr. Harry Orchard) was a tall lank blonde who, with a small ivory gavel held between his thumb and forefinger, poised above his head, remained standing directly behind each speaker, respectively, and now and then smiled benignly and said, "Pray order." In his introduction of the various speakers, he said in each instance, with a drawl, "Your Excellencies, Me Lords and Gentlemen" and then gave the name of the person whom he presented, but said not a word more, except that when he presented Lord Sankey (the Lord Chancellor) he announced that dignitary's title.

Dublin, Ireland, July 23, 1930. About 190 delegates to the I.P.U. are here as guests of the government of the Irish Free State.

Dublin, July 24, 1930. The Executive Council of the Irish Free State on behalf of the government, gave an elaborate luncheon at the Mansion House to the I.P.U. delegates and their ladies.

The Vice-President of the Executive Council (Mr. Blythe) and the Speaker of the Dail (Mr. Hayes), welcomed the delegates.

Senator La Fountaine of Belgium was first up and said that Belgium and Ireland had each tenaciously clung to liberty; Doctor Merlin of France saluted Ireland as a nation bound to France by ancient ties of race and culture; Mr. Montague of the United States eulogized Ireland's contribution to America, and then spoke Honorable Rennie Smith, M.P. of the British group, who said that Ireland had trodden the path of tragedy; that the Irish Race had a rich culture in the days of antiquity and had known every vicissitude.

July 25, 1930. All delegates and their ladies went thence by motorcoach to Glendalough, the site of a sixth-century university where we heard a lecture on the round-towers of Ireland.

At our hotel (the Gresham) we found ex-Senator and Mrs. James A. Reed of Missouri and ex-Representative and Mrs. Rodenberg of Illinois.

All delegates and ladies attended a reception at the Leinster House given by the Speaker of the Dail and the Chairman of the Irish group of the I.P.U.

July 27, 1930. All I.P.U. delegates went to the Valley of Boyne and visited the most remarkable prehistoric mounds of Northern Europe, i.e., the Royal Cemetery of the Middle Bronze age of Ireland. The mounds were plundered during the Scandinavian invasions.

London, August 4, 1930. Visited Hampton Court, a glorious Tudor Palace, once the favourite residence of monarchs. It was given by Cardinal Wolsey to Henry VIII in 1526.

August 7, 1930. To Stratford-on-Avon and as I entered the house where Shakespeare was born (not a squalid one, but a house made of wood and plaster, well-built and well-kept) I seemed to be touching memorials of an immortal. The house adjoining the birth-house was once used by Shakespeare's father as a storeroom for the agricultural produce in which the father dealt but is now a museum in which are exhibited books, pictures, reliques, and other authentic mementoes of Shakespeare and his day. Those who suspect that Lord Bacon wrote Shakespeare's works should examine the evidence of Shakespeare's authorship in this museum before rendering final judgment. At the village of Shottery we saw the home of Ann Hathaway, Shakespeare's wife. Thence to Holy Trinity Church where he and his wife are buried. We visited Warwick Castle which now, as in the fourteenth century, closes its portcullis at night.

Although the rain was falling fast, we visited the ruins of Kenilworth Castle referred to by Sir Walter Scott as "that lordly palace where princes feasted and heroes fought, now in the bloody earnest of storm and siege, and now in the games of chivalry where beauty dealt the prize the valor won."

I now take my leave of England, island of endurance. Myopic must be the one who cannot see that things are not going well in England. She has a rising tide of unemployment and taxation and a falling away of trade and commerce.

The "dole" system in England gives encouragement to shirkers and idlers.

A willingness to endure unpopularity for a time (mayhap for a long time) if exhibited by the English politicians of today, would immensely aid England.

For several years after the close of the World War, Great Britain attempted to resume her kingly game of playing at "continental politics," but the results were so perilous and expensive that the imperial privilege she once possessed of deciding European affairs has passed away from her.

Great Britain has too many mandates, and to avoid ruin she must surrender many of them. She has a mandate over the little Arab state of Iraq which mandate has cost her one billion dollars since she assumed it and not a shilling in return has she received.

Opulent with ironies as are human affairs, it is nevertheless strange to observe that Germany, defeated in the World War, now without an army, bereft of navy, destitute of money, stripped of colonies, and loaded with debts, holds the balance of power in Europe, whilst Great Britain, victorious in the World War, gives up that balance of power which she held for nearly three-hundred years. The reasons seem to be economic.

The industrial expansion of Great Britain's former allies and of her former enemies, coupled with her dependence upon foreign trade to feed herself, have brought this shifting of balance of power.

Washington, August 25, 1930. Telegram advising of the death of Mr. Andrew J. Bogard, my last surviving uncle. He crossed the plains in an ox-team seventy years ago and was sometime sheriff of Tehama County, California.

November 11, 1930. Honorable George W. P. Hunt, vital and cheerful, elected Governor of Arizona six times (defeated for Governor in 1928) has, in the nomenclature of politics "staged a come-back" and has been elected to his seventh gubernatorial term.

Among the factors origining the repulse of the Republicans at the recent Congressional elections, none was more powerful than the demand for cheaper electrical current.

As a part of its effort during the World War, the government constructed a dam and power plants at Muscle Shoals on the Tennessee River, and at the end of the War there developed, regarding Muscle Shoals, two blocks of public opinion; one block demanding that the Government operate the power plants at Muscle Shoals and the other block demanding that these plants be leased to private industry. These two blocks have been deadlocked for the past ten years.

Washington, December 2, 1930. Mr. James J. Davis (who served as Secretary of Labor in the Cabinet of Presidents Harding, Coolidge, and Hoover) was sworn in as senator from Pennsylvania over the objection of Senator Nye who charged illegal primary campaign expenses by Senator-elect Davis, but as Mr. Davis' credentials were regular on their face, the Senate by roll-call vote seated him.

December 3, 1930. Mr. Dwight W. Morrow, father-in-law to Colonel Lindbergh and sometime our ambassador to Mexico, was sworn in as a senator from New Jersey.

Altoona, Pennsylvania, December 7, 1930. Addressed the Altoona Lodge of Elks at their memorial exercises.

December 10, 1930. President Hoover, in a special message, laid before the Senate three protocols covering the statutes of the Permanent Court of International Justice and he urged American entry into the Court.

The creation of this World Court was provided by the Covenant of the League of Nations, and the Court was established in December, 1920, by the adoption of the protocol containing the World Court Statute, written by a committee of jurists appointed by the Council of the League of Nations, of which committee Honorable Elihu Root, of the United States, was a member.

Although the document establishing the World Court is called a protocol, it is, in fact, a treaty, so far as the United States is concerned, as the United States has never become a party to the Covenant of the League of Nations.

In January 1926, the Senate, by seventy-six yeas to seventeen nays, adopted the World Court resolution with five reservations. Four of these reservations were acceptable to the Court; the fifth reservation, which in effect, declared that: the Court shall render no advisory opinion without due notice to all signatories, and shall render *no opinion* on any dispute in which the *United States has or claims an interest,* was unacceptable to the Court. The proponents of our entry into the Court now announce that all objections have been ironed out and that all American interests have been safeguarded.

December 16, 1930. Of the "Lame Ducks" in this session who will soon no longer be englamoured with the authority and distinction of a toga, none is more dejected than the orator, Senator Tom Heflin of Alabama. In support of the Ku Klux Klan, he "talked" himself out of the Senate. He has no private income and has been away from the bar so long that he has no law practice to which he may return.

On Train, December 27, 1930. Senator Nye, Chairman of Lands Committee, with Senator Walsh of Montana, Oddie of Nevada, Norbeck of South Dakota, Glenn of Illinois, and myself, as members of the Committee, are on the Seaboard Airline Railroad going to inspect the area to be embraced within the proposed Everglades National Park in southern Florida.

With us are Dr. Roy Sexton, naturalist; Mr. Ernest Coe of the Everglades Park Association; Doctor Gilbert Pearson, president of the American Audubon Association; Mr. Morris Legendre and Mr. A. B. Cammerer of the National Park Service.

Washington, January 14, 1931. The Senate is now almost unable to function. This condition has, intermittently, prevailed in the Senate since Mr. Hoover became President. In the House of Representatives there is a *clear* Republican majority, whilst the Republicans have only a "paper majority" in the Senate.

This "paper majority" served to distribute the committee chairmanships and perquisites to the Republican senators, but no sooner had these "loaves and fishes" been distributed amongst the fifty-six Republican senators, than thirteen of these distributees (although elected and carried on the Senate rolls as Republicans) cooperated with the Democratic senators in efforts to paralyze President Hoover's program. Thus, chaos reigns in the Senate as this coalition (radical Republicans and Democrats) has not and could not have any definite program, except criticism, and thus persists, in the Senate, the paradox that its only majority is a negative one.

These radical Republican senators are filled with theories; they have contempt for Senate rules and precedents, and they have neither historical connection nor political sympathy with the radical Republicans led by Ben Wade, Charles Sumner and Thaddeus Stevens of post-Civil War days.

These radical Republican senators of today are suspicious of big business; they have no sympathy with protective tariffs; they oppose United States membership in the Permanent Court of International Justice (World Court) and look upon the hydroelectric industry as an industrial octopus with tentacles that should be amputated. These radical Republican senators of today, although arrogant, have a zeal for public affairs and an ability which may not be gainsaid. All of these radical Republican senators are able, and some of them are of high-grade intellect notably Borah, Johnson of California, Norris, Couzens, Nye, Brookhart, Blaine, LaFollette, and opulent, scholarly young Bronson Cutting, the editor from New Mexico.

January 18, 1931. Last evening I spoke at the dinner tendered by Mr. Joseph Schiavonne to Senator Dwight Morrow of New Jersey, at the Racquet Club.

January 21, 1931. Honorable George Wickersham, who was Attorney General under President Taft, as chairman of a Commission to Investigate Prohibition, after months of labor and the expenditure of a quarter million dollars, has reported to the President, who, in turn has laid the report before Congress. The report is ambiguous, equivocal and evasive and has infuriated the "Drys" and enraged the "Wets."

The press asked me for a statement on the report and I said, "The Members of the Commission are ardently disagreeing upon the issues they are 'straddling'."

January 23, 1931. Mrs. Ashurst and I were at the dinner last evening at the White House given by President and Mrs. Hoover in honor of the Supreme Court.

January 26, 1931. Speaking in the Senate on the Fourth and Fifth Amendments to the Constitution, I went on to say that there is no feature of our Constitution around which clusters more romance or the memorials of which give us more fascinating glimpses of vanished days than do these same Fourth and Fifth Amendments, and that, notwithstanding their apparent nonchalance, they sustain and protect civil liberty, repose and the privacies of life which are the natural rights of persons.

January 30, 1931. Yesterday Secretary of State Stimson transmitted to the Italian government an apology on behalf of the United States for the "discourteous and unwarranted utterance" by Major General Smedley Butler of the U.S. Marine Corps, toward the Italian Premier, Mussolini.

February 8, 1931. Attended a reception given by Senator and Mrs. Hawes of Missouri at their residence, in honor of Mr. Jack Lee and wife, singers of cowboy songs. Mr. Lee sang one entitled "The Silver Stallion of Ashurst Lake" which with its reference to the Ashurst mesa country in Arizona recalled memories of the herds of wild horses which, unmatched for strength and speed, once roamed that section.

February 9, 1931. Major General Smedley Butler of the Marine Corps wrote to Secretary of Navy, Adams, expressing regret for his (Butler's) "indiscreet" reference to Premier Mussolini and Secretary Adams, after reprimanding General Butler, ordered the court martial trial of General Butler to be abandoned.

February 10, 1931. The Treasury Department placed an embargo on lumber and pulpwood imported from Russia, the production, loading, and transportation of which has been done by "convict labor." The burden of proving that such labor was used is placed upon the importer.

February 13, 1931. Mr. Thomas H. Pickford, whose sagacity and judgment have been adverted to in this chronicle, gave me the disquieting information that some securities in which I have been investing my savings were not worth above ten cents on the dollar.

February 14, 1931. Senator Copeland, large-hearted, tried unsuccessfully to pass a bill with an item of five hundred thousand dollars to revamp the Senate Chamber, the better to preserve the health of senators. I descanted upon the happy hit in architecture of the Senate and House wings of the Capitol.

On Pennsylvania train leaving Detroit, near midnight, February 22, 1931. Spoke this evening at the Hotel Statler in Detroit at banquet of the Knights of Columbus. At this banquet I met upward of two-score of men who intimately knew my brother, Charles, who practiced law in Detroit many years ago.

February 24, 1931. Spent several hours examining report of Senate Judiciary Committee proposing repayment to the state of California of six million dollars expended by that state to aid the government during the Civil War.

March 1, 1931. Representative Henry Allen Cooper, aged, scholarly, insurgent Republican from Wisconsin who for years was a thorn in the flesh of the regular Republican party, died last night.

March 2, 1931. As this Congress reaches its end, white-haired, ruddy-faced, able Senator Elmer Thomas of Oklahoma is trying to pass a bill laying an embargo against further importations of crude oil into the U.S.A.

March 3, 1931. President Hoover vetoed the Muscle Shoals bill and sent us a message bristling with arguments opposing the entry of the federal government into gainful business in competition with citizens. He asserted that the government by going in business would destroy the equality of opportunity amongst the people. Senate sustained the veto.

March 4, 1931. President Hoover has now served one-half of his term. His victory in 1928 almost "wiped out" the Democratic party, but the Hoover prestige has ebbed and the myth of his "efficiency" seems exploded. Destiny is now weary of befriending him. Unemployment, prostration of business, and strokes of perversely weird and uncanny "bad luck" have afflicted his administration.

March 5, 1931. With what macabre sequence is this entry made, after my scribblings herein yesterday where I descanted upon Republican ill-luck. Today the Democratic National Committee met at the Mayflower Hotel at the call of its chairman, Mr. Raskob, to discuss ways and means of paying its half-million dollar debt.

A large audience was present. Out popped the liquor question; leading Democrats excitedly flayed one another hip and thigh, and adjourned.

March 14, 1931. Many, if not most persons, look upon our national political conventions as quadrennial sporting events of grand proportions, but alas, I am denied the exhilaration which uncertainty as to convention results furnishes, as it is now obvious to *me* that President Hoover will be renominated by the Republicans and that Governor Franklin Roosevelt will be nominated by the Democrats at the respective national conventions next year.

East Chicago, Indiana, March 26, 1931. Addressed high school students here one thousand in number and then addressed the Chamber of Commerce. Last year the Nobel Prize in Literature was awarded the American novelist, Mr. Sinclair Lewis, and a controversy still rages as to whether Mr. Lewis' talents and labors justify the award to him of this famous prize $40,000 cash. Mr. Lewis is the first American to receive this Nobel Prize in Literature. In my address to the Chamber of Commerce I defended this award to Mr. Lewis who has drawn an accurate but not a pleasant picture of the pollyanna-ism pervading America during the past twenty years.

March 28, 1931. Wife and I at New York embarked on the S.S. "California" of the Panama Pacific Line bound for Los Angeles. At our table are Mr. Charles Dana Gibson, the artist, and Mrs. Gibson, who is a sister of Lady Astor.

March 31, 1931. Havana, Cuba. Dr. Pedro Diego took us to breakfast and then with his wife and son by motor-car into the country and to luncheon at the Yacht Club.

April 3, 1931. Cristobal, C. Z. Transit through Panama Canal accomplished in six hours.

Captain Payne of the Panama Pacific Line, placed motor-car at our disposal, and we rode about Balboa and Panama City.

Attended services at the Church of the Golden Altar.

San Diego, California, April 10, 1931. Radio says that Honorable Nicholas Longworth, Speaker of National House of Representatives, is dead. A gallant gentleman gone.

Dined with Mr. and Mrs. Roy Pickford and met Ida Belle Thomas, daughter of Mr. Henry Thomas, my friend of Bay City, Michigan, days of long ago.

Los Angeles, April 11, 1931. Luncheon with my brother Charles and his wife at their residence at Coronado Terrace where I met my mother's niece (my cousin) Mrs. Della Seroy, who is beautiful and looks as my mother did fifty years ago; and then at my hotel met James Rolph, Governor of this state.

April 12, 1931. Brother Charles and his wife, Emma, and five of her young relatives, with large motorcar took me to see Mr. James Pitts at Upland; thence we visited Mother's grave, and then I called on my brother Andrew, near Azusa, who descanted upon Dr. Einstein's theory of relativity.

Yuma, Arizona, April 16, 1931. Sub-Committee of Senate's Indian Affairs held hearings at the Fort Yuma Indian Reservation, and our entourage through Arizona will be: Senator Frazier, chairman, Senator Wheeler, Senator Thomas of Oklahoma, and myself, and Mr. Henry Scattergood, assistant commissioner of Indian Affairs; Dr. Carson Ryan, director of Indian Education; Mr. Grorud, our attorney; Mr. Mason, our bursar; and Mr. Milburg, our reporter.

Phoenix, April 17, 1931. Spent the day with hearings at the Phoenix Indian School and dined with Senator Hayden at Casa Vieja (Old House) in which he was born in Tempe.

April 18, 1931. With Committee to old Fort McDowell, thirty-five miles from Phoenix; thence to Sacaton on the Pima Indian Reservation and held hearings. The Pima Indians centuries ago by irrigation ditches diverted water from the Gila River and upon regular fields they produced cotton, wheat, corn, pumpkins, melons, and beans. Being exposed on their immediate north and east to some warlike Apache tribes, they became warriors under necessity and performed prodigies of valor in defending themselves. Later they gave timely assistance to the immigrants traversing Arizona to California.

Tucson, April 18, 1931. The Committee entourage and Hon. Seymour Lowman, Assistant Secretary of the Treasury, were tendered a luncheon at the "Cave" in Nogales, Mexico, by the Nogales, Arizona, Chamber of Commerce; many speeches.

In the motor-car in which I went to Nogales was Tucson's mayor, my boyhood chum, Mr. George K. Smith, born in England. The president of the state university, Dr. Shantz, called in the evening.

April 20, 1931. Hearings in Federal Building, Tucson. Thence went to San Xavier del Bac Mission, "The Cathedral of the Papago Indians." (Bac means "where the water oozes from the sands.")

In 1692, the Jesuit explorer Padre Eusebio Kino made his first visit to this Indian village. Franciscan missionaries entered Arizona for the second time in 1768 and Fray Francisco Garces was appointed to take over the San Xavier del Bac. His successors and the patient Papagos labored for fifteen years on erecting this church. From Bac our committee motored to Sells Agency on the Papago Reservation and were the guests of Mr. and Mrs. Ben McKinney.

April 22, 1931. Motored from Tucson to Casa Grande Ruins, where a people of antiquity built temples and commodious dwellings, spun and wove cotton and flax, fashioned chieftains ornaments and queen's girdles, irrigated this desert by water canalized in ditches almost as durable as our modern concrete, and then vanished leaving no memorial as to who they were or whither and why they departed. Thence to Globe, where we were honored with a banquet. According to our custom, I acted as toastmaster, and owing to the frequency of these functions we are developing some post-prandial speakers. Every place I visit, someone hands me a copy of a speech recently delivered by Honorable Hoval Smith urging a tariff on raw copper. Mr. Smith is an able citizen and is a crusader for a copper tariff.

In our speeches tonight Senators Wheeler, Thomas, and I endorsed an import duty on raw copper, and Mr. Scattergood of Pennsylvania in his address taunted us for "out-pensing Pennsylvania" in advocacy of tariffs.

White River Agency, April 24, 1931. Held hearings at this agency. Visited old Fort Apache, a post established during the days when the Apache Indians fiercely resisted the advance line of the pioneers.

Fort Apache is now an Indian school.

Winslow, April 26, 1931. By motor-car to Flagstaff, where we visited Lowell Observatory which discovered the planet Pluto last year; thence to residence of Dr. Harold Colton, savant, where Dr. A. E. Douglass spoke on the age of the pine trees hereabout. Thence to the extinct volcano, Sunset Crater, where are several recent lava flows amid the two hundred craters in this immediate locality. The word "recent" employed here in its geologic sense, means not over a thousand years ago. Thence to the "Meteor" where a giant meteorite, or possibly the head of a small comet, struck the earth about 40,000 years ago.

April 27, 1931. Held hearings at the Leupp Agency on the Little Colorado River. Five hundred Navajo Indians present; almost all of them, male and female, were clad in parti-colored garments and were adorned with large earrings and heavy necklaces of turquoise, whilst most of the males wore large silver bracelets and had belts of silver discs around their waist.

The Commissioner of Indian Affairs, Honorable Charles Rhoades, has joined us and was at hearings today. There was also present Mr. Chee Dodge, livestock man, wise, subtle, opulent, and reflective, a supreme product of this Navajo tribe. The Navajos made demand that one million additional acres of land be added to their reservation to which I objected unless the consent of the governor of the state and the boards of supervisors of the various counties in which such proposed extensions would lie, be *first* obtained as 70 per cent of the area of Arizona is now within some sort of reservation and, therefore, is not bearing any of the burden of maintaining state and county government. I went on to say that inasmuch as the Navajos already possess ample lands, the federal government should not leap them out of bounds and that if the government would develop the water resources of the reservation, its present lands would support four times its present population.

Winslow, April 28, 1931. At hearing here it was inquired why Indians on reservations did not vote? I replied that the federal government held these Indians under guardianship and cited the decision of Arizona Supreme Court in 1928, holding that, under the Arizona Constitution, persons under guardianship could not vote, and I went on to say that neither the Indian Bureau nor a Senate committee had authority to suggest qualifications for voters in the states.

Flagstaff, Arizona, April 29, 1931. My Flagstaff of the pioneer times of the early 1880's is gone; scarcely a trace thereof may now be found.

True, here are the San Francisco Mountains which in winter thrust white fangs into the sky; here indeed are Elden Mountains, a gigantic "squeeze-up" of lava and scoria which came up as leisurely as toothpaste from a tube; here are the same hills, some of the pine trees and two tumbled-down shacks of prerailroad days, but the rude Flagstaff "settlement" has evolved into a sophisticated town. Events and issues which stirred the community here when the country was new and all its people were "late arrivals," have dwindled in importance. The founders of the town are in their graves or have retired from "developing."

I meet some of the pioneers' children, but they cannot live in the past; it means nothing to them that on this spot stood the log schoolhouse of 1883, or that on *that* spot stood the town Calaboose, where by decree of "Jedwood" justice, two brothers (Hawks boys) were shot to death in jail by a mob.

In new communities here in the Southwest, conditions change swiftly; things happen in large unhampered fashion, and the trail-blazers soon grow old and tired as on the border a life-time of experience is packed into half a score of years.

Prescott, May 4, 1931. Visited the Pioneer's Home here where infirm men with long gray whiskers revisit on the wings of memory, the ashes of their camp. When I was a lad they were men of physical endurance and dexterity, ready for any emer-gency, cool in shooting scrapes and faithful to their own rough code.

Visited the log house where during the early sixties the first Arizona Legislature assembled. Miss Sharlot Hall, historian, has stored in this building many relics of the epic border days when daring men rode the trails, accepted danger, hunger, thirst, and sacrifice with amiability and lived lives of color, romance, and high adventure. How drab our own day appears in contrast with those eventful times! Yet this drabness is only apparent, *not real.* Future writers will tell of the achievements of the first thirty years of the twentieth century which almost lifted the earth with the lever of Archimedes, made a whispering gallery of the skies, used the highway of the eagle as a highway of commerce, and in the laboratory tickled nature until she revealed some of her deeply hidden treasures.

Phoenix, May 7, 1931. I often wonder what is this Journal all about? And yet, in after years only the memory of events is left to us. Years glide swiftly into the background, and unless we look with some understanding upon the experiences we have had, the places we have visited, and the persons we have met, there is no romance or fascination in retrospection.

May 8, 1931. Called upon Governor Hunt who is crusading for a tariff (import duty) on raw copper imported into the U.S.

Low prices of raw copper have thrown thousands of men out of employment in Arizona.

Dozens of callers. Many persons (some of them once prominent, and not a few of them, eighteen months ago, well-to-do) importuned me for employment.

It is the birthright of every citizen to have a fair opportunity to *earn* a livelihood and it is the duty of government, nation, and state to furnish the citizen a *fair chance* to earn such livelihood. Have we estranged ourselves from nature, and is she now taking revenge by making us the slave of our own inventions?

Fort Defiance, Arizona, May 15, 1931. This Indian Agency, Fort Defiance, was established as a military post when Arizona was Doña Ana County, New Mexico. Seven hundred Navajo Indian bucks present at conference. Their high chiefs and fellow tribesmen exhorted them to engage in goat-raising rather than sheep-raising, and they exhibited many valuable blankets made, by their squaws, from goat-hair.

May 17, 1931. Left Fort Defiance early, but owing to recent rains, our motor cars bogged down, axle-deep, several times in the mud. Saw Cañon de Chelly where, high above the base of the red sandstone cliffs in the protected caves and crevasses, are found records of cultural progress covering a longer period than almost any other tribe in the Southwest.

Cañon de Chelly is a box canyon whose enclosing walls of red sandstone rise sheer from the stream bed to a height of one thousand feet, and in most places these walls are absolutely perpendicular.

Thence to Ganado where Don Lorenzo Hubbell established a home in 1874 and where he resided continuously until his death last November. Don Lorenzo was one of the Arizona grandees; he treasured friendships above life itself and he made hospitality an art.

Over one thousand Indians, with their *high chiefs* and members of the various chapters of the Navajo Tribal Council, were present at the Ganado hearing. Chairman Senator Frazier, called the meeting to order. I announced that the item of

$100,000 charged against the Navajo tribe as a part of the cost of the bridge across the Big Colorado River at Lee's Ferry, should be revoked and cancelled; whereupon the Navajo chiefs shouted, "Yot ta," meaning "very fine," and the Hopis quietly murmured "lolomi," meaning "good." We were then shown a large relief map made on the level ground by Navajo skill. On this map, mountains were indicated by small stones; twigs of pine denoted the pine timber; cedar twigs denoted the cedar and piñon timber; grazing lands were marked by blades of green grass; black sand represented deposits of coal; twine strings indicated roads and trails; water-holes by a pinch of green sand whilst the "quick-sands" with their fatal embrace, were shown by small crosses of red sands. The object of this relief map was to illustrate to the committee the vast area of potential grazing lands which the Indians cannot utilize until more water is developed. We saw Indians shearing sheep and goats, then we saw the washing, the carding, the dyeing and spinning, and finally we came to a woman weaving at a loom on which was a partially completed blanket. A moccasin maker was at work making moccasins; a silversmith was making bracelets and belt discs. One Indian was shaping bows and another was straightening arrows according to their immemorial custom; an old saddle-maker was making a saddle such as they used before the advent of the American cowboy saddle.

Thence we went to a large hogan on the floor of which was a beautiful "sand painting" representing the Sun, the Moon, and the Gila Monster. These "sand paintings" are begun after sunrise and must, owing to the Indian superstition, be completed and destroyed before sunrise of the following day. The "paintings" are drawn by allowing the impalpable sand to trickle between the end of the thumb and the crease inside the second joint of the first finger. It is as if a fine paint brush were used. Among the rugs suspended from the wall was one sixteen feet long by fourteen feet wide, which was a reproduction of a "sand painting" taken from the Shooting Chant and represented thunder and lightning. A bell sounded; it was the call to dinner with the Hubbells who came to the table *en famille* and the grandmother was waited upon first; age is honored in this house of courtesy and chivalry. The meal was served in the large hall of the Hubbell home, and among other viands was savory Angora kid flesh. On the walls of the home are many paintings, pastels, drawings, and etchings, together with a valuable collection of old blankets representing many tribes, some of them prehistoric.

At dark a huge bonfire was lighted and a Navajo squaw dance was soon under way. Whilst standing at the hem of the crowd which encircled the enormous bonfire (which rose to a height of forty feet) a buxom squaw, strong as a python and lithe as a panther, wearing at least fifteen pounds of turquoise and silver ornaments, seized me, drew me near the fire and whirled me around until I grew dizzy and fell down.

A thousand or more Indians, with their vari-colored velveteen shirts, silk bandanas, and silver, coral, shell, and turquoise ornaments, danced around this fire to the music of tomtoms and the chant of fifty voices.

May 18, 1931. Held hearings at Keams Canyon (the Hopi Agency) and also at Torea where Mr. Ralph Murphy of Phoenix argued for a definite marking of the exterior boundary lines of the Hopi Reservation.

Oraibi, May 19, 1931. At the hearing here Mr. Otto Lomavitu, a Hopi, who has translated the New Testament into Hopi language, said that his tribe was making blankets long before the Navajos adopted that art. In Hopi-land the men make the blankets whilst in Navajo-land they are made by the women.

Tuba, Arizona, May 20, 1931. Tuba, now in the Navajo Reservation, was founded over half a century ago by the Mormons under the leadership of Mr. Lott Smith, a high dignitary in his church. He was born for command, was aggressive, and fearless. He traversed dreary lands, met the perils of the border and fought savage beasts. He wore long white whiskers and was a philosophic empire-builder. When I was a boy I saw him at Mormon Lake, Arizona, emerge from the wilderness, preach eloquently to his people, mount his trusty mule, and then disappear into the forest.

When the days of oppression came upon him he once took sanctuary in our Flagstaff home. He was shot and killed thirty-nine years ago here at Tuba, during a dispute with a Navajo.

His body rested here ten years and was then re-interred at Salt Lake City, Utah.

Tomorrow, I shall leave this enchanted domain — the Navajo and Hopi Indian reservations — where dwell *43,000* Navajos and *2800* Hopis.

I shall carry with me vivid impressions of this land of the Corn-Chant and the Rain-Bringers' Song — of the Snake Dance and the Antelope Dance — this land of sunshine, of far-flung sand-hills, mirages, and rich colors; land of high mesas heavy with cedar, juniper, piñon and pine; land of painted deserts and treacherous quick sands, of blankets and baskets woven, and red clay pots and jars moulded by handicraft born of artistic skill and long-enduring patience; land of patriarchal natives with leathery faces silently going about their concerns; Indian families on sun-scorched hills herding their flocks; — a land opulent with *mythological lore* where most of the adults are afraid of the dead, are superstitious, wear much turquoise and silver ornament, and retain their dances, customs, and songs which were old when the first Witangemote assembled in England; — a land of few surface springs but with much water flowing underground.

The Indian is being slowly moulded into a self-supporting citizen, learning the inviolability of contracts, the rewards of industry and justifying (and in not a few instances repaying) the expense to which the government has been put in his behalf.

Flagstaff, May 23, 1931. The Supreme Court of the U.S. in the Boulder Dam case, decides, without euphony or reticence, that the Court will not upset nor go behind a declaration made by Congress that one of the purposes of a particular law is to improve navigation of a river. Congress having declared the Colorado River to be navigable, the river therefore becomes navigable, *at least in law.*

5

The New Deal

That law cannot be a sound one
which deals with the past and the
future in the same way...

Demosthenes

XIII   June, 1931–November, 1932

I have been a laggard
in recognizing the justice of nature
and the dignity of mankind...

Washington, June 20, 1931. Message from Mr. Theodore
Joslin, the President's secretary, to come to the White House at
once. Arriving there, I found President Hoover conferring with
Mr. Ogden Mills, the under-secretary of the Treasury. President
Hoover said that Europe faces industrial and financial bankruptcy unless a moratorium on war debts and reparations is
arranged.

Mr. Mills' plan is to postpone for *one* year the payments
due *from* Germany *to* Great Britain, France, Italy, Belgium,
Poland, *et al.;* and that if and when these countries agree to
such postponement, the U.S. will postpone for a like period our
demand for the moneys due to the U.S. from those countries
during that same year. The President then said, "Will you help
me?" He said that he would consult as many senators and representatives as possible so that he might assure Great Britain,
France, Italy, Belgium, Poland, *et al.* that when the Congress
met next December the eligible legislation for the one-year holiday on debts and reparations would be enacted.

June 22, 1931. President Hoover made public his plan for
moratorium of a one-year holiday on war debts and reparations,
and the stock market (low for months) shot upward.

The American press in praising Mr. Hoover for this action
drifted into eloquent cadenzas.

June 30, 1931. The Allied powers, *except France,* have accepted President Hoover's proposed moratorium of a one-year
holiday on war debts and reparations. The French Premier, M.
Laval, says that France has reached the limit of concessions of
war debts and reparations.

In three major instances in which the Washington government, during the past ten years, attempted to take part in European affairs, we approached France, clumsily and with disappointing results; witness; the arms parley here, the naval parley at London, the results of which were restricted to a three-power treaty with an escalator clause, and now French opposition may block the Hoover moratorium proposal.

No matter how trivial the elaborate diplomatic mien and usage may appear to us, the fact remains that prestige, etiquette, manner, and form in Europe, and especially in France, are important; and unhappily for us, in the cases above mentioned, our approaches to France were made with indifference.

France embodies qualities, attractive and otherwise, that have sustained that Gallic race through centuries of mutations. Pepins, Charlemagnes, czars, Bonapartes, wars and dynasties, Sedan disasters, Kaisers, Hapsburgs, and Hohenzollerns come and go, but French courage and realism, shrewdness and alertness, deftness and intellectual power, survive.

July 2, 1931. The Washington government has notified the French government that the failure of moratorium for a one-year holiday on war debts and reparations would entail indefinite delay in bringing order out of the world's economic dislocation.

The "notice" issued by the Washington government was labeled "Memorandum" and is unique in diplomatic annals. It is unsigned and was addressed to no government in particular. It bore no signature. The personal pronoun, I, appears in the first part of the memorandum, and later on the pronoun, we, is used. Diplomatic Washington says that it recalls no communication parallel to this one.

July 6, 1931. The New York *Tribune* telephoned me that France (rather than bear the blame which might follow from an European upset if she refused to yield) had agreed to the proposed moratorium of one-year holiday on war debts and reparations.

London, England, July 27, 1931. Wife and I arrived here on the S.S. "Minnetonka." Captain James P. McGovern, Washington attorney, whom I met in Flagstaff, Arizona thirty-three years ago, is with us.

Newspapers say that the court of last resort having refused to reverse the judgment against him, Mr. Albert Bacon Fall, on last Tuesday entered the prison at Santa Fe, New Mexico, to begin service of his sentence of a year and a day for accepting money from Mr. Edward Doheney, regarding oil land leases, made to Doheney by Fall, when Fall was Secretary of Interior in the Harding Cabinet.

Mr. Fall, sometime judge of the New Mexico Supreme Court, U.S. senator, cabinet minister, aggressive and authoritative, the personal friend of leading statesmen, is *now* penniless, old, imprisoned, ill, his hopes ruined, and his wife desolate.

July 28, 1931. Attended court at Old Bailey where Lord Kyslant, factotum of the Royal Mail Steam Packet Co., was on trial for publishing misleading statements anent his company's finances.

The jury looked like an American jury, but the judge, and the attorneys for the Crown and for the defense were wigged and gowned. Famous Sir John Simon was chief counsel for the defense.

The judge entered the court room carrying a bouquet of flowers, a custom coming down from the time when English prisons were pesthouses of vermin, filth, and disease, and the court officials in the unhappy days of the terrible London plague, thinking to arrest its ravages, spread sweet herbs upon the floors in prisons and court rooms, and carried bouquets of flowers believing their fragrance would repel the plague.

July 29, 1931. With Captain McGovern and Mrs. Ashurst into the Kent Country. Luncheon at the Royal Oak Hotel at the city of Seven Oaks.

England is a land where umbrellas, heavy underwear, Bank-Holidays, Big Ben, Rugby, tea, marmalade, thick-soled shoes, cricket, clotted (clouted) cream, aquatic-sports, reserve, repression, and "muddling through" rub elbows with Simon De Montfort, Evesham, Runnymede, Oxford, Richard III, the Tudors, Anne Boleyn, Canterbury, Shakespeare, Milton, Dr. Sam Johnson, Lady Jane Gray, Warwick, and the grandeur and power of the royal courts of bygone days. England is "a nation of shop-keepers" yet so poetic that it produced Shakespeare, Milton, Pope, Keats, Byron, Tennyson, and Kipling; a nation of ideals yet practical enough to acquire one-quarter of the earth. Here in England are customs and cathedrals that long ago negotiated a perpetual Treaty with Time. Here are echoes of a valorous past, where the scarlet threads of romance and history are shot through the dull drab of everyday routine; here are fat cattle and sheep feeding on the nutritious grasses beneath their feet, and here may be heard the midnight minstrel of the nightingale.

In this journal, eight years ago, I wrote of the English people, their habits, customs, tempo, and their outlook upon life.

July 30, 1931. The jury convicted Lord Kyslant, and he was at once taken to (of all names) Wormwood Scrubbs Prison.

Gresham Hotel, Dublin, Ireland, August 1, 1931. To the Library of Trinity College where, amongst other books and manuscripts on antiquity, we saw three books, each one nearly twelve hundred years old, viz., The *Book of Kells,* the *Book of Armagh* and the *Book of Durrow,* whose colors are as warm, fresh, and lustrous as if made *only* yesterday. They were written in non-perishable ink, with pens made of goose-quills or crow-quills. The vast extent of these writings and their extraordinary neatness and nicety, their symmetry, shadings, and tintings, have led some antiquarians to the opinion that they were written by some sort of machine, but the dexterity of touch, the manual skill, delicacy, and precision of the goldsmiths and the scribes and illuminators of parchments, were developed to perfection in Ireland during the sixth and seventh centuries.

In the Museum of the Royal Irish Academy we saw the bell of St. Patrick, probably the oldest authentic Irish relic of Christian metalwork.

Cork, August 5, 1931. Visited Blarney Castle, now a ruin, but once the residence of Irish high chiefs. In *a wall of* this castle is the stone which when kissed is supposed to sear the lips with Promethean fire and endue them with eloquence.

Ireland is romantic and fanciful; it is a land of hallowed vales and eerie monuments.

History, religious faith, valor, legend, sacrifice, and the fine arts, present such varied memorials and relics of the past that a tourist seems to become associated with, or an actor in, Ireland's stupendous mutations.

August 6, 1931. Train to Macroom, thence by charabanc over the Prince of Wales Highway to Glengariff on Bantry Bay, thence to Kenmare, and thence continuing on the Prince of Wales Highway to Killarney. I would require artistry of expression and wizardry of language to describe this Killarney country: Cataracts; silvery mists; green swards and deep glades; dense forests, spangled with lovely flowers; a variety and vigor of vegetation; mountains; foliage; rainbows; cloud-colorings; crystal waterways; pellucid lakes in which are anchored small islands crowned with vivid greenery.

Edmund Spenser, in his *Faerie Queene,* and Wordsworth, Thackeray, Lord Macaulay, and Lord Tennyson, made heavy drafts upon their literary resources in describing Killarney. What they found difficult, I shall not attempt.

Quartered at the Muckross Hotel near Killarney. A few rods distant is Mickross Abbey, a ruin "full of dignity and frigid beauty." In the centre of its cloister is a yew tree, four feet in diameter, planted six hundred years ago when the Abbey was building.

Queenstown (Cobb), August 14, 1931. Captain McGovern sailed for Bremen. My wife and I sailed for New York on the S.S. "George Washington," and before nightfall the ocean's salty and energizing breath (ethereal cordial) was pouring into our nostrils whilst our ship plows the "opalescent, the plentiful, and strong" as Emerson called the sea.

Washington, October 14, 1931. Trouble between China and Japan over Manchuria. Whether Japan has invaded Chinese sovereignty may be a question remote to an American citizen busy earning a subsistence; likewise the killing in 1914 of an Austrian Archduke by a Serbian, seemed too remote for our attention, but it ultimately brought the World War.

October 18, 1931. Thomas Alva Edison, inventor of inventions and the world's most famous physicist, died today. His incandescent lamp bathed civilization in a flood of light.

October 23, 1931. The Premier of France, M. Pierre Laval, is here and held conversations with President Hoover, presumably discussing world recovery. Senator Borah, chairman of the Senate Foreign Relations Committee (in an interview with French journalists) denounced the Versailles Treaty and said that peace would not come to Europe until the Versailles Treaty was revised, war debts cancelled, reparations abandoned, the Polish Corridor adjusted, and Austria and Hungary largely restored to their pre-war status. Premier Laval then said, "I have not come to Washington to indulge in polemics with Senator Borah."

December 7, 1931. The Seventy-Second Congress convened. Representative John Nance Garner of Texas was elected Speaker of the House.

Mr. Garner is of short stature, of ruddy complexion, and has white hair. He is practical and industrious and is now beginning his fifteenth term as a representative.

Colonel Thompson of Phoenix arrived here per airplane bringing Arizona-grown olives and dates and other gastronomic delights for the Arizona congressional delegation.

December 8, 1931. Mrs. Hattie Caraway, upon appointment of the governor of Arkansas, was inducted into the Senate to succeed her deceased husband.

The Republicans have a "paper" majority in the Senate, but the radical Republicans opposed Senator George Moses of New Hampshire for President Pro Tempore and scattered their votes. Senator Moses will, however, continue to be President Pro Tempore until his successor shall have been elected.

December 13, 1931. Senators Walsh and Coolidge of Massachusetts tendered a luncheon at Hotel Carlton to Governor Ely of that state. I sat next to Speaker Garner who commented with startling freedom upon public affairs and public men.

December 17, 1931. Great Britain, Japan, *et al.*, have quit the gold standard. The stock market this week reached new bottoms. Rails, coppers, and industrials skip their dividends and there are fears that the U.S. will go off the gold standard. This is the fiercest financial storm that ever blew.

Wife and I attended exercises at Smithsonian Institution where Chief Justice Hughes as chancellor of the Smithsonian presented through the Research Corporation of New York a purse of twenty-five hundred dollars to Dr. Andrew E. Douglass of the University of Arizona for his studies and discoveries with respect to tree-rings in Arizona. Thence, we went to hear the coloratura soprano, Miss Helen Donofrio of Arizona.

December 22, 1931. Senator Johnson of California spoke two hours yesterday and two hours *today* opposing the one year moratorium for our foreign debtors. With the aura and romance of a great career about him, the eloqent Johnson was at his best. He was severe but *not* unparliamentary; he lashed President Hoover and the senators who as he declared had "signed on the dotted line." The Moratorium Bill passed Senate: sixty-nine ayes to twelve noes.

December 24, 1931. A snowstorm of Arctic ferocity has fallen upon the Navajo Indian Reservation in Northern Arizona. Many Navajo Indians have perished in the snowdrifts or frozen in the frosts.

I spent the day at Indian Bureau in arranging relief for them.

January 3, 1932. Senator Byrnes of South Carolina and I spoke at the banquet in honor of Mr. Theodore F. Schuey and Mr. Reuel Small. Mr. Schuey for the past sixty-four years has been an official reporter of the House.

January 25, 1932. Senator Wheeler spoke supporting his bill to remonetize silver. The silver question (paramounted in 1896 by the late Colonel W. J. Bryan) is to the front again.

Honorable Huey Pierce Long, some time Governor of Louisiana, was inducted into the Senate. Mr. Long is englamored by more fame (mayhap notoriety) than has surrounded a senatorial recruit for some years. Handsome and vital, he provokes and attracts with equal indifference. He entered the Chamber with a fat black cigar in his lips and laid the smoking cigar on my desk when he advanced to take the oath. He then took his seat beside Mrs. Caraway but soon began a nervous tour of the Senate Chamber, whispering to this one and nodding to that one.

January 27, 1932. President Hoover and the director of the Bureau of the Budget today reversed their previous action and approved my item of $75,000 to relieve stormbound Navajo Indians in Northern Arizona, and both houses of Congress agreed to the item.

Army bombing planes, winged almoners, are dropping down to these Indians one hundred pound bundles containing bacon, chocolate, tea, coffee, bread, matches, and clothing.

January 29, 1932. My wife and I were amongst the guests at a large dinner party at the White House last night tendered by the President and Mrs. Hoover to the Chief Justice and the associate Justices of the U.S. Supreme Court.

February 4, 1932. China and Japan are at war. True, they have not "declared war" but warships have fired upon land forts; bombing planes have shelled cities; all weapons of warfare are being employed and thousands of persons have been killed or wounded within the past fortnight.

Both China and Japan are signatories to the Briand-Kellogg Treaty outlawing war which treaty contains the following: "The high contracting parties agree that the settlement or solution of all disputes or conflicts of whatever nature or of whatever origin they may be, which may arise among them, shall never be sought except by pacific means."

February 23, 1932. This day was spent trying to induce various architects to use copper for roofing on our federal buildings.

Have I become a salesman, a hawker of wares? Still I must try to restore the copper industry as 50 percent of the taxes paid in Arizona are paid by the copper industry and one-third of Arizona's people depend upon copper mining for a livelihood. Copper miners and smeltermen are unemployed, and American copper industry is prostrate before the copper produced in Africa and South America, by cheap labor.

February 24, 1932. I spoke a few minutes on copper tariff, and my impatient constituents will soon perceive that under the Constitution, the House, not the Senate, originates revenue (tariff) bills.

Secretary of State Stimson, in a letter to Senator Borah, accomplished objects of much importance viz., he re-affirmed the "open door" policy as to China; he declared that Japan was violating the Nine-Power Treaty to which treaty both the U.S. and Japan are signatories, and he gave notice that refusal would be made by the U.S. of any right, title, privilege, or claim which Japan, in violation of treaty, might hereafter assert in China.

March 2, 1932. Tremendous tragedy. The twenty-month old child of Colonel and Mrs. Charles A. Lindbergh was kidnapped from their home in New Jersey. Not since Booth shot President Lincoln has such a nation-wide "man hunt" been known in the U.S. as is now going on.

Mrs. Lindbergh is the daughter of Senator Dwight Morrow, who died last October.

March 8, 1932. I spoke on "bugs" and went on to say that *only* the optimistic person is assured that mankind and not insects might ultimately inherit the earth's food. There are about 400,000 different kinds of insects, and they are all aggressive competitors of mankind for the world's food supply.

April 1, 1932. The House in a desperate attempt to balance the federal budget, passed the tax bill after a fortnight of tumult. Short, fat, volatile Representative La Guardia, Republican of New York, and tall, lanky, dour Representative Doughton, Democrat of North Carolina, led a bolt from their respective parties. With the shibboleth "soak the rich" they struck the sales tax from the bill. The press criticised the "revolt" and charged that the defeat of the sales tax was evidence "that the Democratic party was not fit to rule." In vain did the proponents of the sales tax argue that historically the sales tax is the product of the study and researches of the economist and that its strengh is its universality.

April 2, 1932. Just reached my office from the hospital at Mount Alto where Doctors Fuller and Cook operated upon me and removed from the back of my neck a lymphoma, "tumor" weighing one pound.

April 5, 1932. Destiny inexorably weaves her designs. The Spinner's hand is not to be stayed.

I have heretofore written in this journal of the splendid but unavailing efforts of the Democratic hosts from 1918 to 1930, a space of time during which the Republican party's faux pas, no matter how grievous, could not stay the Spinner's hand when her motif was Republican victory.

Every reflective Republican knows that his party will renominate Mr. Hoover and that Mr. Hoover will be defeated in the elections. The question is asked, why nominate the sincere Mr. Hoover when he is certain to be slaughtered? The answer is that the Spinner's *motif* this year is to nominate Mr. Hoover in June and defeat him in November.

In this Diary, I have frequently employed the words: "Kismet," "Spinner," "Destiny," "Fate," but they do not here-in imply any cabalism for I seem to use them as synonyms for *"Law of Compensation," "Law of Reaction,"* and *"Logic of Events."* Fatalism appears to be a doctrine of indolence or timidity in as much as man possesses reason and the power of selection.

April 21, 1932. Senate began consideration of the contest against the seat of Senator Bankhead of Alabama brought by ex-Senator Heflin.

Senator Bratton of New Mexico, one of our leading legal lights, defended Mr. Bankhead's right to the seat.

April 28, 1932. The Senate seated Senator Bankhead. Ex-Senator Heflin, the contestant, stunned by the result, slowly walked out of the Chamber.

Mr. Bankhead's father was senator from Alabama for about thirteen years and died whilst in service, in 1920.

May 13, 1932. The millions of unemployed persons are growing desperate and their numbers increase daily; business men are afraid to venture; capitalists are frightened by the mulcting of the tax-gatherer, and a gloomy picture is presented.

May 20, 1932. The "combination" of senators, including eighteen Democrats, demanding tariffs on imported oil, coal, lumber and copper, sustained the oil and coal items today amidst denunciations from low tariff Democratic senators who expected to make tariff "extortions" a major feature of the coming Presidential campaign. Senators Hull, George, Walsh of Massachusetts, Harrison and Costigan, low tariff Democrats, are much disappointed.

July 1, 1932. President Hoover addressed the Senate yesterday and urged reduction of government expenses; adoption of sales tax and passage of the tax bill restoring national solvency. The Senate sat until 12:30 A.M. this day passing the tax bill but rejecting the sales tax feature thereof.

I broadcast, supporting a five billion dollar prosperity loan, to wit: from avails of sales of government bonds, begin needful public works.

June 3, 1932. Wife and I attended a garden party at British Embassy given by Ambassador and Lady Lindsay.

The people are tax-conscious. Extravagances of municipal, county, state, and federal officials have enormously increased taxes and Congress may consider some economies. There is a national demand for the repeal of the Eighteenth Amendment.

June 21, 1932. Senator Bingham, tall, white-haired, scholarly senator from Connecticut, announced that Mrs. Amelia Earhart Putnam, the first woman to make a solo flight across the Atlantic Ocean, was in the V. P.'s room, whereupon Amelia, the curly-haired, willowy, lissome sylph was escorted into the Chamber.

June 29, 1932. Senate considered House bill proposing Philippine independence.

Altruism, idealism, and natural rights have for a generation argued in vain for Philippine independence, but the American demand for markets and profits is now arguing.

American farmers are seeking protection from Filipino competition and workmen are demanding exclusion of Filipino immigrants. Demands for markets may bring to the Filipino that freedom which ideals did not bring to him.

Even the most sang froid man *cannot* keep his face straight and argue for our retention of the Philippines whilst at the same time we are applying to the Filipino our stringent immigrant exclusion laws and our high tariff laws. In other words, if

we refuse independence to the Filipino, we must in good conscience, allow the Filipinos and the products of their islands to
come here.

July 1, 1932. The Senate, weary and tortured by the heat
wave, laid aside the Philippine bill until next December.

Hot weather and voracious flies hurried adoption in 1776
of the American Declaration of Independence but did not aid
the Filipino today.

July 6, 1932. Many Arizonians here, and they called Senator
Hayden and me into Senate reception room and informed us
that Arizona demanded the repeal of prohibition.

They went on to say that we had both been here so long
that we did not know the true sentiments of Arizona on the
liquor question.

July 9, 1932. Since Uncle Sam has turned banker and is
lending money through his Reconstruction Finance Corporation, dozens of Arizonians are here trying to borrow money
from him.

July 16, 1932. Mr. Fergus Hume died this week in Essex,
England. His name means nothing to this generation, but it was
a famous name when I was a boy. He standardized the art of
detective fictions and forty-five years ago he wrote *The Mystery
of a Hansom Cab* which was read by millions of persons and
became the "best seller" of its day. My father's cowboys carried
this novel in their saddlebags and it was *one* subject to discuss
which, the cowboys around the campfire would suspend their
Rabelaisian ribaldry. I got this novel from the library today;
it is now nearly midnight, and for the past three hours I have
been reading its yellowed and brittled leaves. Mr. Hume wrote
137 thrilling detective novels, yet his name does not appear in
any history of literature. What fickle jades are fame and fortune.

July 16, 1932. Congress adjourned *sine die.*

An analysis which someone will make in the future of the
laws we passed at this session in an attempt to lift ourselves by
our own bootstraps, will awaken dormant risibilities.

An avalanche of telegrams came today demanding to know
how soon bankrupt counties, "busted" cities, dubious schemes,

and Pollyanna promoters may borrow money from the Federal Reconstruction Finance Corporation. Question: May we reclaim a ruined spendthrift by filling his pockets with money?

July 24, 1932. Senator Borah, who has prevented three Presidents—viz., Harding, Coolidge, and Hoover—from even discussing cancellation of World War debts due the U. S., broadcast a speech warning all nations that no "international accord" on armament reduction is possible unless war debts are revised.

July 26, 1932. Mr. James A. Farley, chairman of the Democratic National Committee, conferred with Democratic senators and asked the conference if Governor Roosevelt, the Democratic Presidential nominee, should go on a speaking tour? Senators were of opinion that since Governor Roosevelt was certain to win he could gain nothing if he went "Swinging Around the Circle."

July 27, 1932. Many men are here to borrow federal monies. When the day comes to repay these loans, Uncle Sam will be denounced as a Shylock for trying to collect.

Hotel McAlpin, New York, July 29, 1932. En route here lost my portmanteau containing, amongst other papers, a letter from Mr. George Arliss, thespian.

Mrs. Ashurst, John Renoe, Helen, and I to Music Box Theatre and saw musical comedy, *Of Thee I Sing,* a caricature of Washington officialdom. It fits nicely into the iconoclasm of the times with not a dismal nor boresome line. The light operas by Gilbert and Sullivan of fifty years ago, portraying the primness and smugness of the mid-Victorian days, do not excel this musical comedy.

New York, July 30, 1932 Hotel detective restored my lost portmanteau; none of the letters is missing.

Washington, August 1, 1932. Governor Hunt of Arizona has applied for loans to the tune of millions of dollars from Federal Reconstruction Finance Corporation. The Governor is conducting a primary campaign for renomination and many voters are protesting against the RFC canalizing money through his office during his campaign and thus facilitating one outfit at expense of the other.

August 13, 1932. It is, I suppose, a human tendency to try to advance one's self, and even eminent philosophers seem to desire a social order fitted to the skills and qualities they possess. Plato's preference was for a rule by the philosophers; Jefferson, a man of virtue and learning, favored a government by the virtuous and learned. The unlearned, incompetent ones, would seek equality by reducing all to mediocrity.

It is becoming obvious as the years roll on that I and the other diarists who are so "truthful" in telling tales about others rarely, if ever, write of our own mean, petty, and contemptible doings but seldom omit recording our own generous and virtuous actions. My opponents derisively say that I have flattered Neptune out of his trident yet Senator J. Hamilton Lewis recently said to me, "Why, dear Prince Hal, you have by making immaterial concessions to human vanity, stimulated many persons into worthy action."

Be that as it may, it is nobler to be truthful and resolute than to be eloquent, lubricous, and socially and politically eligible. I have been tardy in divining that no matter how meagre, obscure, and indigent a particular human life may be, romance inheres in that life.

To my misfortune, from my earliest sentience, I accepted existence as a futility more honorably endured by complaisance than by resentment; and my failure accurately to appraise and evaluate life was a ghastly mistake, difficult of correction now. I have been a laggard in recognizing the justice of nature and the dignity of mankind. In order to live a worthwhile life, indeed, in order to enjoy even a moderate measure of graceful and felicitous existence, it is requisite that one shall approach life realizing that the universe is operated according to "a good and great plan" and that in harmony with this plan mankind, endowed with reason and conscience, may direct his affairs beneficially if his goal be justice and righteousness. To achieve any durable success one must have a fixed and settled realization that demonstrable truths do exist and that mankind is capable of applying these truths to this life.

Las Vegas, Nevada, August 29, 1932. Senators Kendrick, Oddie, Howell, Dill, Carey, and Chairman Thomas of Senate's Reclamation Committee arrived.

Citizens of Las Vegas had expected to reap not a little profit from the federal monies expended in constructing the project and they operate their own commissary at Boulder City. After midday meal at Boulder City (which for variety, quantity and excellence of food surprised the Committee, being the same as is served to all the workmen) we inspected progress of the work on the project.

The dam could not be built except by diverting the Colorado River and to divert it, four tubes or tunnels (two on either side of the river) each over four thousand feet long and fifty-six feet in diameter, have been bored through the solid rock.

The work on Boulder project is being done under contract let by the Secretary of the Interior to "The Six Companies." To translate the immensity of the operation here into understandableness; take for example the largest irrigation project ever built, and then multiply its features, problems and potentialities by ten.

The workmen on the project number thirty-three hundred and each shift of eleven hundred men works eight hours of every twenty-four.

Los Angeles, California, August 30, 1932. Senators Thomas, Howell, Carey, and I visited the studio of the Metro-Goldwyn Mayer talking picture producers. Met Mr. Lionel Barrymore. Lunched with Mr. Mayer, president of the Company. Called upon my brother, Charles, and he and his wife and I motored to Upland, and called upon Mr. and Mrs. James Pitts. Thence to Azusa and called upon my brother Andrew's family.

Fresno, California, August 31, 1932. Breakfast at Bakersfield, thence our Committee formed a motorcade to Visalia to lunch.

When my father was a cattleman in Arizona, his saddles were made in Visalia, and any vaquero who came riding a Visalia saddle found no difficulty in securing a job at his ranch.

To Fresno for banquet where Senator Dill's speech "clicked." I rode all day with Mr. Arthur Tarpey.

Mr. Phil Thornton and Mr. Butler Minor of my Williams, Arizona, days called.

September 1, 1932. Motored from Fresno to Merced with Mr. and Mrs. Thornton and Mr. Minor; public luncheon at Merced where I spoke in good postprandial form.

Arriving at Stockton I wandered about nostalgically and found the old school building of the business college whose portals I left thirty-seven years ago, at the corner of East Channel and California Streets and there hard by, now a ramshackle, stood the house, once the mansion, where resided Duke Ramsey, the principal of the business college. I viewed the stairway upon which, for kissing a girl, nameless here, I was almost rusticated, but was saved when she argued to the principal that she was not annoyed by my oscular activity.

Hotel Tremont, Red Bluff, California, September 2, 1932. During my speech at the public dinner at Red Bluff I adverted to the fact that my parents were married in this town sixty-two years ago this month and that sixty years ago they left here in an *uncovered* wagon to commence their gypsying (to my mother endless and agonizing) which took them per wagon across the Sierra Nevada Mountains, thence through the state of Nevada crossing the Colorado River into Arizona at Stone's Ferry, swallowing the desert's bitter dust, stopping for *two years* near Hell's Canyon south of the Bill Williams Mountains, and thence jolting wearily to what was known later as the "Old Ashurst Ranch." My father had the wanderlust; he was a pilgrim, not truly a settler; he was never anchored.

At the banquet tables tonight were several persons whose parents "crossed the plains" with my parents in the covered wagon days.

Clio's iron pen or a Macaulay's genius for sustaining a gorgeous narrative, will, at the proper place on the stream of time write of the nineteenth-century-westward migrations in America.

Those argonauts who plodded less than twenty miles per day their difficult trail into Arizona, Colorado, Idaho, Montana, New Mexico, Nevada, Utah, Wyoming, and on to the Pacific

Ocean States, found the journey bristling with hardships and perils. They and their dauntless women fought savage men and savage beasts. They were scorched by desert heat, stung by reptiles, and maddened by thirst. Hunger gnawed their vitals; their tongues were swollen and their lips and eyes were blistered by hot alkali-desert dust. Mirages lured them to their doom and all-too-frequently, the water they at last found, ironically enough, was bitter or poison and not to be drunk by man or beast. Their trailside was littered with household articles which at the outset they had expected to use in a home at their journey's end. Their livestock starved, dropped dead from exhaustion, or perhaps, smelling water, bolted and fled never to be seen again. Wagons had to be abandoned; food supplies too bulky to carry, had to be cached and were never recovered. Children cried, "When will this end?" How many persons perished en route can never be known, but all along the trail men and women exhibited courage and endurance to a grand degree, and many left their bones to bleach in the fury of a desert sun.

Romance, heroism, and high-endeavour were woven through those migrations like a scarlet thread, along with sacrifice, disappointment, and tragedy.

Hotel Barton, Willows, California, September 3, 1932. Committee went to Kennett damsite where it is proposed to build a dam on the Sacramento River for flood-control, irrigation, navigation, and development of hydro-electric energy. To inspect this damsite and to learn first-hand the problems and possibilities of this river is the object of our trip.

Mr. Wayne Taylor took me per state car back to Red Bluff, and there I walked through the cemetery where lie sleeping three of my uncles and two of my aunts. Thence Mr. Taylor and I went to Willows to supper with my cousin, Mrs. Carrie Neilson.

Hotel Senator, Sacramento, California, September 4, 1932. Cousin Carrie and her husband, Mr. Neilson, and I motored from Willows up Stoney Creek and called upon numerous kinfolk. Thence to Stoney Creek Cemetery where sleep two of my aunts and my paternal grandparents.

Hotel El Tovar, Grand Canyon, Arizona. September 6, 1932. The National Park officials took me per auto to inspect the new roads. Over opposition in my own state, I secured in 1919 the passage of an act creating this National Park.

Prescott, September 10, 1932. Mrs. Greenway, Democratic national committeewoman for Arizona and I spoke at a Democratic rally held here.

Some of Governor Hunt's over-zealous appointees are sour toward me because I declined to announce that the Governor had secured many loans from the Reconstruction Finance Corporation.

I am weary of eating toadstools to find out if they really are mushrooms!

Visited Pioneers' Home here to greet men and women who contributed in making the border days in Arizona tolerable.

Saw here many men who were once prominent or opulent, now penniless, palsied, or blind; yet, they seemed cheerful. The faces of the old were serene. They appear to have found peace at the end of a long trail, without any hangover of bitterness from the hardships of frontier life. What memories whirl in their brain, only themselves know!

Met at the Pioneers' Home Mr. and Mrs. J. B. Tappan, both of whom I knew in Flagstaff forty-five years ago when he was a prosperous sheepraiser and she was Miss Laura Fulton. She is now helpless; one of her eyes was hooked out years ago by a wild cow. She was a sister of Mr. Harry Fulton who, when I was six years old, was my tutor on the old Ashurst Ranch.

Washington, D. C. September 24, 1932. Dispatches say that France refuses to recognize the "new" state of Manchukuo (Manchuria) and thus, on this question, the French view concurs with the American view.

Japan has seized Manchuria in violation of the Covenant of the League of Nations and of the Treaty to Outlaw War (Paris Pact) to both of which treaties Japan and China are signatories. Our Secretary of State, Mr. Stimson, is deservedly praised for refusing to countenance Japan's tearing Manchuria out of the living body of China.

New York, September 26, 1932. Today the Democratic headquarters here breathed easily as Governor Roosevelt has canvassed the West without stubbing his toe. It appears that the Governor's trip to California was a brilliant success.

Santa Fe Depot, Chicago, October 1, 1932. Large audience at Democratic rally at Greenville, Ohio, last night. I spoke in a barn where livestock are auctioned every Thursday. Colonel North, an auctioneer, was my chairman.

Supper at the home of young Mr. Bosserman who took me by auto to Union City, Indiana, to catch Pennsylvania train to Chicago. Having to wait at Union City three hours for my train and disrelishing sitting alone in the dark and cold depot, I went into a ramshackle fourth rate rookery (the only hostelry I could find), secured room, no sleep. An old man who was acting as night clerk told me he received one dollar for working all night, that he dared not ask higher wages, as ten men were ready to take his place the moment he quit, and that a family was dependent upon him.

Phoenix, October 5, 1932. Called upon Democratic State Central Committee; its coffers are empty and no subscriptions coming in. Congratulated Committee that whilst they have no money, they will have plenty of votes on election day.

October 7, 1932. My callers number about seventy persons daily, and the telephone is always ringing. Amongst my callers today was Mr. William Marks who years ago at Flagstaff was professional gambler and who without a tremor would bet large sums of money on the turn of a card. He was then a Beau Brummel and was the darling of three or four of the demi-monde. How tragic was he today, emaciated, hungry, ragged, and I suspect, an addict of drugs. A filthy hat crowned his matted hair, and shoes with uppers but without soles, enclosed his fetid feet. I gave him what I could spare. He discussed the old days with a humor that was not pretended. He said that a true gambler must meet either extreme of fortune without "batting an eyelid" and so he must.

October 12, 1932. After my luncheon of lettuce and oatmeal and cream, I was seized with cramps in my stomach. It seemed as if a giant with iron claws was rending my "innards." My wife gave me hot water and soda whereupon I grew better. Although weak, I did not skip my speaking date.

October 14, 1932. Met at Democratic headquarters today, Mr. Charles Dillaha, cowboy whom I knew at Flagstaff forty years ago; he is sixty-seven years old, has black hair, black mustachios, flashing eyes, and is erect as a lamppost.

Bisbee, October 15, 1932. Came here today from Phoenix on steam cars. On the train about noon, the giant with the iron claws again seized my "innards," but the conductor brought me hot water and soda.

Phoenix, October 17, 1932. Told Senator Hayden and Representative Douglas they were certain to be re-elected. Ex-Senator Ralph Cameron (who has often appeared on these pages) is Senator Hayden's opponent.

Large audience tonight. I attempted to speak, but only a hoarse and raucous roar issued from my throat. I discovered that by inclining my head forward I could talk, if I spoke slowly. It required two hours to deliver my speech.

October 30, 1932. These are halcyon days for me. The politicians and a segment of the general public are displeased because I am nonchalant. Critics say that I glide along indifferent to the campaign now in progress.

There is no complaint that I have slacked in any task or skipped any speaking engagement. My serenity derives from the fact that I never again expect to be a candidate for office, hence, I am freed from the tyranny of faction; to be misquoted or to be the subject of canards is humorous, and I am not intimidated by the fear that some phrase (I have a penchant for phrase-making) will rebound to inpale me. I now say what I please, go where I choose, and am neither gagged nor gyved.

Mirable dictu—this very independence, this very freedom, promptly and vigorously to say no, this alacrity in withdrawing from the company of bores and in rejecting the overtures of schemers is a source of political strength, a reservoir of power and prestige upon which I have not heretofore drawn.

Should public men ever learn what a valuable political asset such demeanor is, and how fervently it is admired, a new and better breed of public men (taking counsel of courage instead of timidity) may come forth. It is probable that an element contributing to my *sang froid* in this campaign is the realization that nothing could defeat the Democratic Presidential nominee.

Whilst no person can make a laboratory of oneself that will analyze one's own motives, or will discover the reasons why one believes and says thus and so, the ultimate fact in my own case is that I have reached the "envied estate" acquired by so few political men, that is to say, willing to reject joyously the cup of office and power when it is actually at the lip and to choose instead the quieter abstinence which health and a well-rounded plan of life require.

November 2, 1932. During the past thirty-six years, I have, without requiring security, loaned (as accommodations) to various persons (probably three hundred persons in number) sums of money ranging in amount from one dollar to fifteen hundred dollars, which sums of money so loaned by me now aggregate seventy-three thousand dollars and out of this total sum of money thus loaned, there has been repaid to me only five hundred and twenty dollars, and these repayments were made by nine persons.

Some of these "loans" I made when I myself was in straitened circumstances, but believed (how shallow-pated I was) that the borrowers would repay me. They served me right in not repaying me, for, I blush to write that the form of flattery to which, until lately, I always yielded, was the implied compliment from the borrower that he believed me to be financially independent.

My father was susceptible to the same sort of flattery; his weakness in this regard ruined his fortune, and my own weakness on this same point has cost me a pretty penny.

This entry in this Journal is not made with any expectation that I shall receive back as much as one per centum of my hard-earned seventy-three thousand dollars, but *the entry is made* because a Mr. Bondurant called at my hotel today and astounded me by repaying five dollars which I loaned him in Washington, D. C., long ago.

Phoenix, November 5, 1932. Addressed Democratic rally at Emerson School. My "last" speech of this campaign? Will the day ever come when I shall say for all time "this is my *last* political speech?" Politicians, philanderers, and drug-addicts seldom reform.

November 6, 1932. How ironical the Journal entry of yesterday appears wherein I wrote of my "last" speech of this campaign for I was today "compelled" to motor to Cave Creek, thirty miles distant, and speak at a Democratic barbecue and then to dash back to another Democratic barbecue at West Phoenix and speak there. Yes, indeed, a politician quits "politicking" only when he is dead.

November 7, 1932. I took early train for Tucson where Colonel Thominson, the commanding officer of Fort Huachuca, met me and took me by auto to the Fort, where I inspected the Fort and conferred with the Committee of Citizens from Bisbee.

Phoenix, November 9, 1932. Democratic landslide. My hotel is crowded with applicants for federal appointments, and my wife and I had to "muscle" our way through them to breakfast; yet it is probable that many in the throng have legitimate reasons for an interview.

At the Democratic turnover twenty years ago (1912) I was dismayed by the truculent demands of place-hunters, but I have learned to make *no* promises.

On Train, November 10, 1932. Although a Republican defeat was not surprising, no one expected so general a repulse of Republican leaders as was that of last Tuesday. Veteran Republican senators, viz., Smoot, Jones of Washington, Bingham, Watson, Moses, Oddie, and Glen were defeated. The defeat of President Hoover confirms the Republican tenet that only politicians (using that word in its high sense) should be nominated for the Presidency.

The Republican experiment of a President from the world of economics instead of from the world of politics will not soon be tried again. President Hoover, sincere citizen, able economist, ran afoul of a depression. Another lethal potion to his regime was his refusal to attempt to liquidate the tremendous objection to national prohibition.

During the last sixty days of the campaign, President Hoover fought with courage and energy, and some of his campaign speeches will be charts to guide those who desire to remain in the paths of Constitutional government. With 11 million willing workers idle, with wheat lower than ever before, with five thousand defunct banks, with the savings of the people swept away, with our foreign trade gone, with industry collapsed, with taxes (federal, state, county, and municipal) piled high upon an already crushing load of private debts — ugly things which no political party could promote or prevent — all that remained for Mr. Hoover to do was to meet his fate with becoming fortitude, which he seems to be doing.

XIV

November, 1932 – January, 1935

President Roosevelt, during the special session,
sent Congress so many messages
that we grew dizzy.

Washington, November 14, 1932. I gave statement to the press that the Democratic National platform having declared for the repeal of the Eighteenth Amendment, and the voters in Arizona having repealed Arizona's anti-liquor laws, the mandate to Arizona's senators was clear and that I would respect it. I went on to say that the Democrats would be "embezzlers of power" if they refused to observe their platform pledges.

November 15, 1932. My formal statement issued yesterday anent repeal of prohibition appeared in many dailies. Reporters are inquiring if the phrase "embezzlers of power" is original with me? I directed attention to the fact that in my statement the phrase was in quotation marks. I do not recall whence I obtained the phrase; it cannot be original with me as it come trippingly to my pen, whereas my original phrases are accompanied with pains of parturition.

November 22, 1932. Lunched at Senate Restaurant with Senator Pat Harrison. Present, twelve senators and twelve representatives, also present Admiral Cary Grayson, and Mr. Bernard Baruch, the cultured, silver-haired New York capitalist; also present the erudite Brigadier General Hugh S. Johnson, U. S. A. retired, noted for his research work in federal fiscal affairs. General Johnson spoke on agriculture, foreign debts, and economy in government. Mr. Baruch opposed cancellation of foreign debts and said excessive taxes might ultimately wreck the government.

Upon telephone from Governor Roosevelt (President designate) I went to Mayflower Hotel, where I found also waiting to call upon him Speaker Garner, (Vice-President designate), six senators, ten representatives and Professor Raymond Moley of Governor Roosevelt's "brain-trust." I had not seen him since the banquet of the Dutchess County Society at the Hotel Astor, New York City, in February 1921. He has recovered from his attack of infantile paralysis so far that, with a cane and with his legs supported by iron braces, he walks. He has the habit of nicknaming persons and referred to Secretary of the Treasury, Mr. Ogden Mills, as "Oggie."

December 22, 1932. Introduced joint resolution proposing Constitutional amendment prohibiting issuance hereafter of tax-exempt securities by federal or state governments. Senators Gore and Connally assailed my proposal as hampering federal and state credit.

January 1, 1933. Attended luncheon given by Senator Walsh of Massachusetts to forty guests at Hotel Carlton in honor of Most Reverend Pietro Funasoni-Biondi, Apostolic delegate. Many of Senator Walsh's guests were of the diplomatic corps. I sat beside Mr. Faik Konitza, envoy from Albania who speaks seven languages and can, upon a given set of facts, divine what action a particular diplomat will assume. He has wide knowledge of history, and his philosophy has reconciled him to this comic world. He rescues fellow-diplomats from embarrassment and smoothly softens down macabre incidents. He seems unattached, but I have never pumped up the temerity to ask him whether he is bachelor or widower.

January 4, 1933. My secretary, Mr. Lanman, has been with me twenty years today. I told him that anyone who could endure him twenty years is a philosopher, and that anyone who could endure me twenty years is a saint.

January 4, 1933. Spoke in Senate upon seventy-fifth birthday of Senator Glass, and my concluding paragraph was as follows:

> Senator Glass is one of the few men in American public life who would be at ease in the company of, and who would understand the plans and purposes and the processes of thought of the Olympian philosophers, the tragic poets, and the comic dramatists who in the days of antiquity made Attic Greece immortal.

January 5, 1933. Ex-President Calvin Coolidge died at Northampton, Mass. Few of our eminent men had as much individual quality of manner and habit as he. He was prosaic, indeed almost dull, amidst glamorous events. He was rustic and plain at the crest of dazzling success. Momentous problems, some of them of world-wide import, he solved by "horse-sense" or by laissez-faire. He appeared sour, but was not of lofty mein, and at times he seemed almost insentient. He believed that youthful poverty, obscurity, and humility were good for the soul and that they breed virtues. He believed that the right to acquire and to hold property, both large and small, was true personal liberty.

On the special train en route to Washington, D. C., January 7, 1933. The Vice-President, yesterday upon motion of Senator Walsh of Massachusetts, appointed a committee of senators to attend the funeral of ex-President Coolidge. This special train, carrying President Hoover and Mrs. Hoover, Vice-President Curtis, Secretary of State Stimson, Chief Justice Hughes, the Senate committee and the House committee, left Washington last night, arriving at Northampton, Massachusetts at 10:00 this A.M., but the street was so crowded that our autos could not approach the Jonathan Edwards Congregational Church where the funeral services were held; hence, the senators abandoned autos and elbowed through the throng into the church. Only by police action opening a path through the crowd, could the Presidential party enter the Church, whilst some of the Presidential party, blocked by the throng, returned to the train.

Youthful Rev. Albert J. Penner, pastor of the Edwards Church, conducted the services. There were prayers and hymns but no sermon, no eulogy.

The President and Mrs. Hoover and Vice-President Curtis called at the Coolidge residence to express to the bereaved family the nation's sorrow. The special train with its official dignitaries started for Washington, whilst the cortège, in a drizzling rain, started for Plymouth, Vermont, to the homestead of the boyhood of Calvin Coolidge, where, late this evening, the sod will open for him to enter into rest with his ancestors.

I invited into my stateroom ex-Governor Andrew Montague of Virginia.

Mr. Montague is one of the erudite members of the House of Representatives. He admires the character of Grover Cleveland, and we fell into a discussion of that departed statesman. Mr. Montague went on to say that he had tried vainly to find some man who personally knew Mr. Cleveland when Cleveland was a young lawyer. I replied, "Alas, I too have tried in vain to find someone who knew Mr. Cleveland intimately before he was sheriff." Within a few minutes Mr. Thomas V. O'Connor, president of the U. S. Shipping Board, came in and we related to him our conversation, whereupon Mr. O'Connor replied: "I'm your man. Over fifty-five years ago I blacked Mr. Cleveland's boots six days each week, he paid me thirty cents per week for my work, and paid me every Saturday morning." He said that Mr. Cleveland smoked "cheroots," that stale beer was his beverage, and that he drank it only when seated in a beer-garden with sawdust on the floor.

January 11, 1933. I had ten reporters to luncheon (terrapin) at Senate Restaurant. The luncheon was an act of courtesy toward these press representatives, already too long deferred. One of my guests, Sir Wilmott Lewis of the London *Times*, anent the Washington whirligig said, "Everything is moving mysteriously and simultaneously in all directions."

January 14, 1933. President Hoover vetoed the Philippine Independence Bill. The House of Representatives overrode the veto and the New York *Herald-Tribune* today, in denouncing the House action, carries editorially a savage criticism of the House.

January 17, 1933. The Philippine Independence Bill became law today when the Senate overrode President Hoover's veto. Scholarly, opulent Senator Cutting, progressive Republican of New Mexico, in criticising the veto message, went on to say that probably for the first time in history, a powerful nation, of its own volition and without external pressure, is proposing to grant freedom to a people whose domain is under the jurisdiction and authority of the *powerful* nation.

January 31, 1933. Senator "Ham" Lewis spoke today and warned President-Elect Roosevelt against making executive commitments on war debts. Senator Lewis revealed that he (Lewis) urged President Wilson, not to attempt personally to negotiate the peace treaty following the World War. Senator Lewis' suggestions were approved by the learned Senator Reed of Pennsylvania who said Europe does not realize that an executive commitment does not bind the Congress.

February 3, 1933. Senator Hawes of Missouri resigned and Colonel Bennett Champ Clark, son of Speaker Champ Clark, was sworn in as Mr. Hawes' successor.

Copies of a magazine, *New Outlook*, drifted into the Chamber, containing an article written by Mr. David Barry, Senate Sergeant-at-Arms, charging that some members of Congress "sell their votes." The irate Senate brought Mr. Barry to the bar, questioned him and suspended him from his office, upon his admission that he had no evidence to sustain his charge.

Mr. Barry, aged seventy-four, stern-faced, with large white bristling moustachios, made a poor showing under the cross-fire of questions from senators. Fifty-eight years ago he was a page in the Senate.

February 7, 1933. Sergeant-at-Arms Barry removed from his position by the Senate. Are we thin-skinned?

February 9, 1933. The economy wave has struck the Senate full abreast. It is now proposed to close the Senate Barber Shop, in existence for eighty years, and to eliminate funeral expenses of senators. This move is led by Senators Walsh of Massachusetts, Hayden and Byrnes.

February 11, 1933. If one-tenth of the time wasted by senators in listening to the pleas of spoilsmen and spoilswomen were expanded in the public interest, our country's weal would be promoted. The timorousness with which I dealt with spoils-hunters twenty years ago, humiliates and mortifies me, and the memory of my shiftiness at that time on this subject now shames me. Painful as that memory is, it has made me strong to resist this raid. I make no promises and hold out no appeasement to place-hunters.

February 16, 1933. Although Senators Shepphard and Brookhart had threatened to *"die in the last ditch"* filibustering against a final vote on the resolution proposing a submission to the states of the repeal of the Eighteenth Amendment, they did not carry on a filibuster and the resolution today passed the Senate, yeas sixty-three, nays twenty-three. The resolution refers this Amendment to "Conventions in the States." All amendments heretofore have been referred to "Legislatures of the States."

The courage and ability of Democratic leader, Robinson of Arkansas, drove the resolution through the Senate. No matter how able a Congress or an army may be, it is but a mob if not led by a dauntless leader.

February 20, 1933. The House of Representatives today, by more than the required two-thirds vote, adopted the resolution proposing repeal of the Eighteenth Amendment.

February 21, 1933. President-Elect Roosevelt has drawn heavily upon the Senate for Cabinet material. Senator Hull of Tennessee will be Secretary of State, Senator Walsh of Montana will be Attorney General, and Senator Swanson of Virginia will be Secretary of the Navy. Senators Johnson of California and Cutting of New Mexico — each in turn declined the Interior portfolio.

February 22, 1933. During the incumbency of Mr. Henry Lewis Stimson, the Hoover Premier, momentous events in world affairs transpired. Financial panics afflicted most nations: revolutions were so common that expert observers were baffled in trying to keep abreast with the tempo and policies of the new governments but this quiet, shy Mr. Stimson held to his purpose, viz., Justice, Equity, and Peace amongst the nations. He assembled and translated "moral disapproval" of governments that violated their treaties.

Born to opulence, Mr. Stimson could have had an easy life, but he chose hard work. He was a U.S. Attorney under T. R., was sometime Secretary of War under President Taft, and was once Governor General of the Philippine Islands.

He has a prominent nose, stubby moustachios, and bangs his hair like Honorable Elihu Root, his life-time friend.

Like Mr. Bainbridge Colby (sometime Secretary of State under W. W.), Mr. Stimson was one of the Premiers who realized that our State Department exists *primarily* to make known to one nation the policies of another.

The débâcle of the Hoover regime occluded Mr. Stimson's fame, but his talents and his zeal for his country's ideals are known. He did *not* treat the signature of the Japanese to the Kellogg-Briand Anti-War Pact as a mere gesture. He believed that the Nine Power Treaty imposes upon its signatories the obligation to respect the sovereignty, independence, and territorial integrity of China.

Mr. Cordell Hull, who will be Roosevelt's Premier, entered the Senate two years ago, after serving many years in the House. He was a farmer's boy, is tall, dark, lanky, reserved, modest, and has studied tariff and finance. When walking he bends forward as Lincoln did, and like Lincoln likewise, he is more nearly a dyspeptic than a eupeptic.

Mr. Hull gained national prominence when he sponsored the federal income tax and the federal estate or inheritance tax. He was Chairman of the Democratic National Committee in 1924.

No other senator with whom I have served has clung more perseveringly to the orthodoxy of Jefferson than has Mr. Hull.

He favors the World Court and believes that signatures to treaties are more than a mere collection of autographs.

For learning, wisdom, moderation, and prudence he will, his health permitting, rank with our famous premiers.

February 26, 1933. Senator Walsh of Montana (Attorney-General designate) married yesterday at Havana, Cuba to Señora de Truffin.

Although Walsh and I have been deskmates in the Senate for years, he gave me no inkling of his intention to marry.

February 28, 1933. Financial panic now rages in Washington.

Senator Smith of South Carolina, a cotton planter, now carries his remaining cash resources in a belt strapped around his waist.

March 1, 1933. Washington is now in full regalia for the inauguration; hostelries are filled, and the number of visitors may reach one hundred and fifty thousand.

My wife and I will have ten house-guests.

Amongst the numerous Arizonians here is Mr. Wirt G. Bowman, the Democratic National Committeeman. He desires appointment as our ambassador to Mexico — and is *more* than merely *persona grata* with the Mexican government, for its present rulers have put forth every effort compatible with diplomacy to have him appointed.

Mr. Bowman was once interested in the resort in Agua Caliente, Lower California, which by comparison, made the Casino at Monte Carlo seem commonplace and prosaic.

March 2, 1933. Senator Walsh of Montana, aged seventy-three years, died on a train bound thither from Florida. The Senate was expecting to welcome him and his wife here tomorrow morning.

March 4, 1933. Vice-President Charles Curtis, after forty years of service in the Capitol building, delivered a brief address of farewell in a voice choking with emotion, and then Mr. Garner, the new V.P., delivered a yet briefer address of salutation. Mr. Hoover, weary and worn, entered the Senate Chamber. The years of his Presidency are the years that the locust hath eaten. Forty-eight months ago, with exalted hopes he was joyously acclaimed, and today he quits office forever.

Unsophisticated well-wishers and not a few sycophants built him up and heralded him as a superman, but he could not (no man could) live up to the dizzily-high standard they set for him. Destitute of the politician's skill he never united the Republicans in Congress.

Roosevelt's Inaugural Address was in part an indictment of the stock-gamblings of the "spendthrift years," and after reviewing the parade, he convened his Cabinet (confirmed at a special session of the Senate) and at once considered the catastrophic posture of affairs, for it appears as if the U.S. may go off the gold standard.

The Inaugural Ball tonight was a vortex of "milling" humanity; hats, coats, and cloaks were strewn over the floor, but we left early and escaped the confusion.

March 5, 1933. For some days I had meditated making an entry in this book anent the strange conduct of place-hunters, but no language could portray the fury of the applicants. Other Democratic senators tell the same tale, therefore, the mania is not peculiar to my section. The place-hunters seem to have eaten of some noxious root which has driven them mad because they will not eat regularly unless appointed to an office.

Many of the letters demanding appointments are so imprecatory that I do not permit even my own secretaries to read them.

March 6, 1933. The casket containing the body of Senator Thomas J. Walsh of Montana was brought into the Senate Chamber. The President, the Supreme Court Justices, the members of the House of Representatives and the ambassadors, ministers and envoys from foreign powers were present. The funeral service was conducted by the Most Reverend Michael J. Curley, Archbishop of Baltimore.

March 8, 1933. Attended Democratic Steering Committee and inherited the chairmanship of the Senate Committee on the Judiciary. I am hopeful that the able Senator Walter L. George of Georgia will be placed upon this committee. Senator Pittman of Nevada became chairman of the Committee on Foreign Relations and Senator Harrison of Mississippi became chairman of the Committee on Finance.

Thousands of place-hunters who expected to remain here many days are returning to their homes, as checks and drafts cannot be cashed. Some of them luckily came here on round-trip railroad tickets.

March 9, 1933. The Seventy-Third Congress convened in special session. Colonel Edwin A. Halsey of Virginia elected Secretary of Senate and Mr. Chesley W. Jurndy of Texas elected Sergeant-at-Arms.

Colonel Halsey has been an employee of the Senate since December, 1897, whilst Mr. Jurndy was sometime secretary to Senator Culberson and later was secretary to Senator Copland.

Messrs. Halsey and Jurndy are cultured, courteous men, of elegant deportment.

Representative Henry T. Rainey of Illinois was elected Speaker of the House.

Before nightfall the two Houses passed a bill giving the President authority to decide which banks may open their doors and which banks shall remain closed.

This bill also grants President the power to decide how and when the currency may be expanded, and the Secretary of the Treasury is authorized to prosecute persons who fail to deliver their gold to the Federal Reserve System.

March 13, 1933. Owners of gold coin are delivering it to the Federal Reserve System, and some persons, fearing arrest, have delivered up their gold watches, rings, chains, buckles; and some persons have deposited with the government even their gold teeth, so poignant is their fear of federal prosecution.

June 16, 1933. The special session of the Seventy-Third Congress adjourned today. If this "depression" shall continue its ravages, the blame may not be laid upon a paucity of laws.

President Roosevelt, during the special session, sent Congress so many messages that we grew dizzy. Before we could analyze one message from the White House, swiftly upon that message would come another and yet another, and so on, until Senators and Representatives became whirling dervishes. Each House had from ten to twenty committees in session by day and by night.

We ground out laws so fast that we had no time to offer even a respectful gesture toward grammar, syntax, and philology. We counted deuces as aces, reasoned from non-existent premises and, at times, we seemed to accept chimeras, phantasies and exploded social and economic theories as our authentic guides.

During this Special Session, place-hunters and pot-house politicians, like an obscene brood of harpies, screeched at and clawed and pecked Congressmen and department heads and bureau chiefs. President Roosevelt, through his sagacious patronage dispenser (Postmaster General Farley) notified Congressmen that there would be *no* appointments for their ravenous henchmen, unless and until the Roosevelt recovery program was fully completed. President Hoover lost control of Congress during the special session he called in 1929, and he never regained it; but President Roosevelt, during the special session, was backed by that force which, when aroused, is authoritative viz., public opinion; and public opinion demanded that Congress follow President Roosevelt.

Congress, during this Special Session, behind the facade of fear and need, made experiments on a grand scale and temporarily transmuted our way of life from individualism into regimented state socialism.

History is not definitely written by persons contemporaneous with the event, and it is only by the flight of time and the test of decades that events may be observed with an approach to a true perspective. For aught we know, this Congress may have done what Russia did by her bloody revolution i.e. nationalized labor, commerce, agriculture, capital, and industry. Economic pressure is the Great Reformer. Shocking and sour as this philosophy may appear, it is true.

Under our new laws (some of them half-baked) many of the tested standards, methods and principles such as thrift, prevision, industriousness, capability, and responsibility (which made the American citizen his own master, eligible to succeed according to the measure of his own talent, merit, ability, and luck) may be jettisoned; initiative mayhap be shackled and incentive to individual endeavour and high emprise cancelled. Social control over competitive and economic enterprise may be on the way. Who knows? Yet it is but natural, during the worst financial storm that ever blew, the most crushing panic in history, for the citizen to look to the government for relief, when the government is the only source of employment, credit, and commerce.

June 17, 1933. Furiously beset, Senator Hayden and I, followed by a troop of our impatient constituents, besieged the departments, in an endeavour to secure *plums* for some of these job-hunters. As we proceeded we saw tortured senators and representatives, captaining squads of avid "pie-hunters." When I returned to my office, I was amazed to find waiting for me, Mr. Richard E. Sloan, sometime associate justice of the Supreme Court of Arizona Territory, and also sometime Governor of Arizona Territory.

Twenty-one years ago President Taft nominated Mr. Sloan for U.S. District Judge for Arizona, but Senator Mark Smith and I prevented his confirmation by the Senate. Today, mellow and uncomplaining, Mr. Sloan seems to have forgiven me, but I have not forgiven myself; remorse, like a festering arrow, has for years troubled me over the fact that Mark Smith and I could have had such malignant heart and such beefy brain as to reject this scholar and jurist.

June 20, 1933. Received frantic telegrams from constituents demanding that, inasmuch as the Roosevelt recovery program has been "put through," I begin now to deliver "appointments." Luckily for me, I have made no promises.

June 24, 1933. Quartered at Hotel McAlpin, New York City, having come here under a Senate resolution to investigate the reported failure last year of the Department of Justice promptly to prosecute the alleged violations of law by the Harriman National Bank.

Willis Cheatham, assistant Sergeant-at-Arms of the Senate, has been busy here for two days subpoenaing witnesses to appear before my sub-committee.

New York, June 26, 1933. It was fortunate that Willie Cheatham and I went early to the Old Post Office Building, at Broadway and Park Avenue, to inspect the room for our Senate committee hearing, for we found that a small, poorly-lighted, vilely-ventilated room (a thermos bottle) had been assigned for our use.

Appealing to District Attorney Medalie, to U.S. Marshal Mulligan and to District Judge Knox, the judge's courtroom was granted for our use. Senators Neely, McCarran, and Hasting, with myself as chairman, began the hearing early and drove steadily until we finished.

Mr. Nugent Dodds, ex-assistant attorney general, assumed all responsibility for the delayed prosecution of Mr. Harriman, of the Harriman National Bank. During Mr. Dodds' testimony, he seemed to reflect upon Senator Neely, whereupon Neely seized a large carafe (water jug) and was on the point of hurling it at Mr. Dodds, when I seized Neely's hand and restrained him, while Senator Pat McCarran restrained the lunging Mr. Dodds. After that episode, all was serene. Young Tom Cullen of the Department of Justice, from Washington, helped Willie to round up the witnesses.

June 30, 1933. Returned to Washington and resumed answering demands of place-hunters.

Callers numerous; five stenographers grappled all week with the mail.

Is there really some lycanthorpy whereby place-hunters and politicians become werewolves? Members of Congress and department heads are beginning to believe there is.

July 5, 1933. Mr. Charles Addams, member of Arizona Highway Commission, and I called upon Postmaster General Farley; and then Senator Hayden and I presented him to President Roosevelt in behalf of the Paradise Verde Irrigation Project in Arizona.

July 7, 1933. In the springtime of 1892 (over forty-one years ago), one of my father's cowboys Mr. William H. Pitts, brought to the Old Ashurst Ranch a volume of the works of Edward Bulwer Lytton (Lord Lytton). After the other cowboys were under their tarpaulins, Pitts would sit candle in one hand and cigarette in the other, reading Lytton's novel, *Ernest Maltravers.*

After Pitts had finished the story of Ernest, I commenced to read it. The volume was a thick book ten inches long by seven inches wide, and I read probably 150 pages thereof when suddenly we were notified that the round-up (rodeo) would begin. This news meant that there would be no more reading until December. When the rodeo ended and all the mavericks had been branded, we returned to the ranch, but Lord Lytton's novel had disappeared, and I resolved never to finish it unless and until I could secure an exact copy of the volume which we had upon the ranch; and so today, while passing a bookstore, there on sale for ten cents was a well-bound volume, identical in format, size, shape, and type with the one I had begun forty-one years ago. I purchased the book, and thus tonight instead of the theatre, I shall find out what happened to Ernest, to Alice, to Valerie, to Lumley Ferrers, the light cynic, to Frederick Cleveland, and all the others.

Chicago, July 2, 1933. Visited the Century of Progress. That an exposition so rich in our national memorials could be held in these hard times, is a tribute to the courage of its projectors.

Jackson, Teton County, Wyoming, August 7, 1933. Our sub-committee, composed of Senators Nye, Norbeck, Carey, Adams, and myself, all members of Land Committee, convened here. We came hither in obedience to a resolution of the Senate, directing us to ascertain if the National Park Service or the Snake River Land Company has discouraged citizens from settling upon public lands and national forests in the region of the Yellowstone and the Grand Teton National Park.

Some citizens of this county assert that the further inclusion of public lands into reservations will make it impossible to maintain Teton County, whilst other citizens assert that the county should become wholly a reproduction of a pioneer settlement and that, owing to the sublime scenery hereabout, the revenue derived from tourists and "dude ranchers" would exceed the revenues derived from farming and stock-raising.

Jackson, August 8, 1933. I was in Jackson in July, 1928 and it was then a sprawling ramshackle village, but it is now clean, has many buildings of rustic western frontier construction, and many log cabins with bath and electricity.

Jackson, August 9, 1933. Senator Norbeck, champion of the National Park Service, is just out of the hospital, hence is impatient with prolix witnesses. Senator Carey alleges that Mr. John D. Rockefeller, Jr., acting through the medium of the Snake River Land Company, has purchased much land here, and intends to purchase more, with a view of transferring all these lands to the U.S. for park purposes, thus by reducing the taxable area extinguish the county.

This locality is an elk refuge, and thousands of elk are fed here in the winter. The questions is which shall survive here, elk or people? Senator Norbeck is on the side of the elk and Senator Carey on the side of the people. These two senators clash daily.

August 11, 1933. Sub-committee heard witnesses until midnight and concluded hearings at Jackson. Heavy-eyed and weary, we retired to our several log cabins, only to be called about 5:00 A.M. to make auto trip to some of the lands in question. Luncheon at the home of Mr. and Mrs. Struthers Burt, fiction writers, and just before dark Mr. Roger Toll landed us per auto at the Canyon Hotel. Mr. Toll is a nephew of the famous Edward O. Wolcott, who served twelve years as a senator from Colorado.

Washington, August 15, 1933. After examining about three hundred letters, I gave over the task. Most of them were savage in tone and upbraided me for not securing more appointments of Arizonians to office.

August 23, 1933. Long talk with Senator McAdoo who has one of the best intellects that ever functioned in the Senate. He is sour toward Eff Dee and says that he, McAdoo, at the National Convention, gave Eff Dee the 100 votes Eff Dee needed to win the nomination; but that he McAdoo, as Democratic senator from California, is ignored on appointments, and that no social amenities have been extended to him by Eff Dee. I told him that his lamentation was an old story to me; that for eight years many Democratic senators chanted similar Jeremiads against Wilson, his, McAdoo's, famous father-in-law.

August 24, 1933. Dr. Shantz, President of the University of Arizona, called. Says his budget is cut, and many of the faculty must go. Says that when prosperity returns he will go ahead fullsteam with added members of the faculty and new buildings. Told him no person was ever cognizant of prosperity while it was reigning; only when prosperity has evaporated do we realize that it ever existed.

August 29, 1933. The Paradise Verde delegation from Arizona presuming upon my coming campaign for re-election, are daily harping upon the string, "You must get this loan (millions) for us if you expect to be reelected" – "If you fail to get this loan, for us, you will be defeated," etc.

September 3, 1933. Mr. Lanman, my secretary, received a letter from a Mr. A. H. McFarland, automobile manufacturer, now of Phoenix, volunteering the statement that he would *not* support me for re-election to the Senate, for the reason so Mr. McFarland assigns, that while I possess learning, scholarship, training, foresight and diplomacy, I have wasted my talents and have employed my time with empty gestures, gracious demeanor, brilliant but useless rhetoric, and (a new charge) philandering frivolity.

September 5, 1933. Wife and I dined with Secretary of State and Mrs. Hull at the Carlton.

September 6, 1933. Paradise Verde delegation here howled like wolves on Unalaska's shore when told I was going to Arizona within a fortnight. They asked me to remain in Washington until loan (millions) is granted to them.

September 7, 1933. Many telegrams urging me not to come to Arizona until Paradise Verde loan is approved here.

September 14, 1933. Some weeks since, Senator McAdoo of California urged me to sign petition to Eff Dee requesting him more speedily to displace Republican officials. I declined to sign it, believing that except for cause, officials should serve terms to which appointed. About thirty Democratic senators had signed when I refused. Press discovered this round-robin and smeared it on front page, hence many letters are coming strafing me for not signing the round-robin asking that more patronage be dealt to Democratic senators by Eff Dee.

September 15, 1933. At the hearing at Interior Department Judge Richard Sloan of Phoenix, on behalf of Roosevelt Irrigation Project, opposed granting of loan to Paradise Verde project. Attorney Laney of Phoenix, and Senator Hayden and I urged the loan. Twenty Arizonians were present opposing Verde loan, and twenty-five Arizonians were present favoring the loan.

September 16, 1933. Upward of a dozen proposed irrigation and flood control projects in Arizona have filed with the Administration of Public Works, application for loans. Although the officials of these proposed projects write or wire me almost daily, demanding haste in securing these loans, none of them has been able to "maintain" such a delegation in Washington as has the Paradise Verde.

September 21, 1933. My old friend, Ray Stevens, is home from Siam, where for some years he was financial adviser to the King of Siam. He and I are of opinion that our mutual friend, ex-Senator Hollis of New Hampshire, now residing in Paris, is unhappy there because he so inverately writes us that he *is* happy.

Even this giant government will reach — all too soon — an end to its policy of dealing with unemployment through relief work.

Conditions must be created under which agriculture, commerce, and industry may thrive and pay wages and taxes. No government can feed all the people by gifts, bounties, and largesses from its treasury.

Mail filled with letters criticising me for not urging Eff Dee to "displace Republicans at once."

September 28, 1933. Paradise Verde delegation called, and I gave them the doleful news that Secretary of Interior, Mr. Harold Ickes, and Secretary of Agriculture Mr. Henry Wallace, in order to get rid of the surplus of agricultural products, were distributing federal funds to farmers as a *reward* for plowing their crops under.

October 10, 1933. Governor Moeur of Arizona and Mrs. Isabella Greenway, Arizona's new representative in Congress, arrived and many Arizonians met them at the Willard for conference anent Arizona's demands that federal projects be speeded up.

October 12, 1933. Senator Hayden, Mrs. Greenway and Govenror Moeur and I called upon the President and remained with him one hour, urging approval of Paradise Verde project in Arizona.

Over 500 Arizonians are here to secure political appointment or allocations of money from the federal treasury, to their pet projects. It is no small task to interview these people. Although many of them are courteous, most of them are irritated by the prolixity in passing out appointments to office and the delay in handing out federal cash.

I had as guests to dinner this evening at the Hotel Lafayette, Governor and Mrs. Moeur, Mrs. Greenway, Mr. Tom Pickford, Mrs. Greenway's little son Jack and her secretary, and Miss Heardt, my assistant secretary.

October 17, 1933. Attended banquet given by the Arizona State Society to Governor Moeur and Mrs. Greenway; amongst the two hundred Arizonians present were Mrs. Cameron, wife of the ex-Senator from Arizona, and Mrs. Jennie Zuck, the latter of whom went to Holbrook, Arizona, over fifty-two years ago. Mrs. Zuck, now ninety years of age, jauntily addressed the banqueters. Surely she has made a truce with *Anno Domini.* Mr. Leon Kneipp of Prescott was toastmaster. Governor Moeur spoke five minutes. Mrs. Greenway spoke ten minutes.

October 18, 1933. Rauscher (caterer in Washington) served a buffet lunch in my office, whither I invited such Arizonians as I could reach.

Douglas, Arizona, October 23, 1933. Senators Bill and Carey of Irrigation Committees arrived. Motorcade to Bisbee. Senators Bill, Carey, and I addressed the citizens from the Court House steps in Bisbee. Motorcade to Tombstone, which town was gaily bedecked — not for us but for its Helldorado, a gala day which annually reproduces Tombstone as it was when the West was "wild."

At Tombstone, a man came in from the desert exhibiting the largest rattlesnake ever captured hereabouts. It was the size of a python.

Mr. Jack Flynn of Bisbee drove my auto and Mr. Bill Mathews, able publisher of the *Daily Star* of Tucson, rode with Mrs. Ashurst. Mr. Mathews has for years opposed me, and I abashed him not a little today by advising him that if re-elected to the Senate it would be only by the follies of my opposition.

Sub-committee examined on the San Pedro River the dam site near the site of the now vanished town of Charleston, which fifty years ago contained five thousand persons. Thence we went to St. David for barbecue. Rain stopped the speech-making. The San Pedro River rises in Mexico but has many affluents from the mountains in Arizona, and it flows into the Gila River above Winkleman.

Phoenix, October 25, 1933. In forenoon, accompanied by Mr. Sanford of Reclamation Bureau, I inspected the irrigable lands of Paradise Valley.

I issued a statement to the presses distributing to Governor Moeur, Senator Hayden, Mrs. Greenway, and Mr. Lewis Douglas the credit for securing the Verde project loan from the Federal Emergency Administration of Public Works. It is futile to prophesy and I'll be ridiculed if this loan should be denied, but before leaving Washington I was assured by highest authority that this loan would be granted. Callers came in a steady stream until near midnight. Disappointed place-hunters were bitter and inprecatory. Nothing can mollify a disappointed applicant for office, so I ignored their abuse and their threats. What else could I do? It is no very great philosophy to endure that which may not be cured.

Los Angeles, October 28, 1933. Quartered at Hotel Biltmore in Los Angeles, whither I have come as chairman of a special committee to investigate receivership and bankruptcy proceedings and appointment of receivers and trustees. Senator Van Nuys of Indiana, Senator Hebert of Rhode Island, and Senator Austin of Vermont, of the special committee, are already here, and Senator McAdoo, vice-chairman of the committee, arrives tomorrow. Long conference with Colonel Neblett and Mr. John Sokieski, counsel for our special committee.

October 30, 1933. Went early to Federal Building to make ready for hearings of our sub-committee. With enormous volume of work already piled upon me, I should have declined to serve as chairman of this committee.

Happily, our committee's labors have been lightened by the assistance of the U.S. district attorney and the U.S. marshal of this district, and by Mr. Myerson and Mr. Findley of the Federal Bureau of Investigation. Colonel W. N. Neblett and Mr.

John Sobieski of this city have assembled a multitude of documents and are serving as attorneys for our committee without compensation.

October 31, 1933. Among the spectators at our hearing was Mr. John J. Hawkins, sometime associate justice of the Supreme Court of Arizona during territorial days. When I was turnkey at the county jail at Flagstaff he sat at *Nisi Prius.*

November 2, 1933. Scores of ex-Arizonians call daily. Many of them are aggrieved that I do not give them more of my time. I try to give five minutes to each person. Senator McAdoo's secretaries, together with Mr. Harold Hogan whom I brought here from Phoenix, are aiding me.

November 3, 1933. Special committee suspended its labors, and with our ladies, we motored to Culver City, where we were entertained at luncheon tendered at the M G M studios by Mr. Louis B. Mayer, president of that company. We heard the young baritone, Mr. Nelson Eddy, sing Kipling's "Mandalay." Few voices are as rich and under such control as Mr. Eddy's. His diction is clear, and he has personal charm. After luncheon, I met the publisher, Mr. William R. Hearst, whom I had not seen for over twelve years. He is now fat and baldish and was cordial.

November 5, 1933. Brother Charles and I called upon Mr. Abe Caufman, opulent ex-cowboy from Arizona. Of all that gay and reckless throng of Knights of the Lasso, who years ago, for meagre wages, rode hard in the inclement winters around Williams, Arizona, gathering the "dogies," only Abe Caufman acquired a fortune. Even during those raw and wastrel days Abe neither drank nor gambled nor philandered.

November 8, 1933. As our special committee grinds out its grist, it is obvious that the fees, salaries, and expenses of receivers, attorneys, auditors and appraisers, incident to equity receiverships here, have been disproportionately large.

November 9, 1933. Members of the committee and our ladies attended a dinner given by Mr. Louis B. Mayer, president of the M G M Studios, to cinemactress Marie Dressler in honor of the sixty-second birthday anniversary. We met fourscore famous thespians, amongst whom were Lionel Barrymore, Norma Shearer,

Will Rogers, Jimmy Durante (Schnozzle), and Mary Pickford; and again we heard the rich-voiced baritone, Mr. Nelson Eddy.

November 11, 1933. The special committee lunched with Dr. Rufus von KleinSmid, president of the University of Southern California, at its Memorial Library, where were present ex-President and Mrs. Herbert Hoover and Mr. Edwin Markham, the octogenarian poet.

Dr. von KleinSmid called me up to introduce my party and after doing so, I went on to say that we were honored to break bread with Mr. Hoover. I spoke with felicity of phrases, whereupon the guests, numbering over two hundred, broke into long-continued emotional applause. The Hoovers came here for the football game between Stanford and the University of Southern California.

November 12, 1933. Our eyelids are heavy from lack of sleep. From sundown last evening until early this morning, a gang of several hundred persons, male and female, many of whom were celebrating the football game of yesterday, stormed through the lobbies and hallways of every floor of this hotel.

Entering the rooms, they ripped open the pillows and sifted the feathers into the streets. They threw empty bottles from the hotel windows, and not a few pedestrains below were injured thereby. They pounded at our door, threatening to crash through unless I gave them liquor, of which I had none. Twice it seemed they would force the door, and had they done so they would have hurled my wife and me to the streets below. Chandeliers were shattered and elevators were abandoned. I was infuriated — not at them but at myself, for being caught in such a contemptible situation. I searched my room for a suitable object to make defense, in case they should crash the door. I telephoned the police, but it was useless. The police simply warned the pedestrians not to approach the hotel. I planned to put my shoes on my hands and thus make a sort of "knuckles" with which to fight. This experience may teach me to carry in my luggage a pistol with which to resist such threats. Before sunset, the hotel authorities, realizing what was coming, removed all furniture from the hallways and lobbies.

All senators and their ladies went today to Mr. Will Rogers' ranch to luncheon. Mr. Rogers has in his ranch-museum a sample saddle, bridle and a pair of spurs from every land where horses are ridden.

November 14, 1933. The committee were guests at a stag dinner tendered to us by Mr. Kyle D. Palmer, reporter of the *Los Angeles Times.* I was the only speaker.

Flagstaff, Arizona, November 25, 1933. Resolving never again to be defenseless in a perilous plight such as the one into which we were thrust a fortnight ago at the Hotel Biltmore in Los Angeles, when bounders tried to force our door, I today purchased from my old-time friend, Mr. William Switzer, a pistol and cartridges of 45 calibre. I shall carry this weapon in my luggage to repel such murderous assaults as were attempted upon us two weeks ago.

Washington, D.C., December 6, 1933. National prohibition ended yesterday when the thirty-sixth state (Utah) ratified the repealing amendment. The State Department issued a formal certification that three-fourths of the States had ratified, whereupon President Roosevelt issued a pronouncement, viz., a proclamation and exhortation in which he eloquently urged the people to temperance, moderation, and restraint in their restored liberty, and he inveighed against the excessive drinking of alcoholic liquor.

December 14, 1933. Wife and I attended state dinner last night in White House, in honor of Chief Justice and the associate justices of the U.S. Supreme Court. Amongst the guests were Mrs. Woodrow Wilson and Mrs. Alice Longworth.

December 17, 1933. This afternoon upon invitation of Dr. Leonide Pitamic, the erudite Minister of Yugoslavia, we attended a reception at Yugoslav Legation in honor of birthday anniversary of that nation.

April 11, 1934. Last night my wife and I attended a reception given by Ambassador Troyanovsky at the Russian Embassy on Sixteenth Street, near our house.

For the past thirteen years, the windows of this embassy have been boarded up and the doors locked, but after a renovizing which occupied the past fortnight, the doors were opened and this reception was as brilliant as any ever held here by an ambassador. He has added the Soviet hammer and sickle in the balcony grille.

Ambassador Troyanovsky and his wife greeted their guests, about six hundred in number, at the top of the grand-stairway in the salon.

The Ambassador speaks English, is smooth shaven, youngish, stout, and squat. His eyes are deeply set into his head and his yellow teeth are firm. He wore a tuxedo and his wife wore an evening gown (not low-cut) of pale salmon pink, with no jewelry of consequence.

The guests were refected in the state dining room by an elaborate buffet of viands, exceeding in variety and abundance the refreshments served at the usual state functions. On the long tables were choice and rare products of American, French and Russian culinary art. Among the Russian dishes were purushock (a thin, flaky, flourpaste, baked and filled with fish, meat, jam, and cheese) and the plump tasty blini (pancakes drenched in melted butter or cream). Here were also balyk (back of the sturgeon, smoked) and large dishes full of caviar. Amongst the beverages was vodka in fantastically shaped bottles.

Members of the embassy staff aided in welcoming the guests who represented the various official, diplomatic, and resident society folk here. Amongst the out-of-Washington guests was a sprinkling of authors, savants, and radical-intelligentsia. Secretary of State Hull introduced us to Mr. James Truslow Adams, the historian, and here we also met General Adolphus W. Greely who more than fifty years ago starved for months in the Arctic.

April 12, 1934. Attended dinner at Mayflower Hotel last evening, to Governor Moeur of Arizona, given by Mr. and Mrs. Spillsbury of Arizona.

May 2, 1934. Argued before a sub-committee of the House Committee on Ways and Means, the right of husband and wife to make separate and individual income tax returns in the various community property states.

May 19, 1934. Speaker of the House, Mr. Rainey, took me in his automobile to Bay Ridge on Chesapeake Bay, to luncheon given by Washington Board of Trade.

New York City, June 25, 1934. Senator Hebert, Rhode Island, Senator Austin, Vermont, and I are here to investigate the receivership of the Interborough Rapid Transit Co. Captain McGovern, attorney from Washington, is counsel for the committee.

Washington, August 3, 1934. My wife and I shall take train for Arizona to begin my campaign for renomination to the Senate. The primary elections will be held on September eleventh next.

In times of depression and distress, constituencies are critical and quickly find fault with sitting members of Congress; but in Arizona, I am assailed with ferocity I never expected to meet.

Flagstaff, August 8, 1934. My old cowboy friend, Mr. William Roden, now of independent means, took me in his high-powered motor-car to Winslow and Holbrook.

As Mr. Roden and I zizzed along the smooth road, we passed (at the highway bridge across Canyon Diablo) the ruins of the "horse-camp" where forty-four years ago, he and I and other Knights of the Remuda easily endured what now appear to have been meagre and bleak days, although such hardships at that time were not noticed by any of us and were common to the country.

Williams, August 9, 1934. Too weak to walk, I employed Mr. William Nagiller to convey me in his auto, and pass in front of every house in the town.

Prescott, August 13, 1934. During the past few days many citizens have called to assure me of their support. All of them say that I have a difficult contest with the outcome doubtful.

Luncheon at Rotary Club as guest of Mr. Stuart, publisher of the *Daily Courier.*

Miss Susan Murphy, who was my stenographer when I practiced law here before entering the Senate, will be my stenographer during my campaign. My wife went to Phoenix today to establish my campaign headquarters.

My opponents in this primary election are Mr. Sidney P. Osborn, now the collector of internal revenue for Arizona, Attorney Renz Jennings, Colonel Charles Rutherford, who ran against me in the primary election in 1928, and Mr. William Cozon, who years ago named one of his sons for me, but who now says he will go to court to relieve the youth of such a handicap.

Kingman, August 14, 1934. My brother William and I set out last evening from Prescott for a two hundred mile drive to Kingman in his Buick, arriving here at 5:00 this A.M.

Upon a stretch of the dark road many miles from any habitation, we encountered an auto parked crosswise on the highway. The occupants of this parked car attempted to halt us and for no good purpose. I was alarmed, but my brother was calm and whizzed around the parked car, which at once righted itself and gave pursuit; but William drove furiously for ten miles until we found refuge behind a clump of cedars in the dark, as the pursuers passed on.

Phoenix, Arizona, August 16, 1934. Visited campaign headquarters which my wife has established, and I found that through her executive ability, events are progressing smoothly and my campaign is gathering momentum.

Nogales, August 18, 1934. Here to welcome Senator and Mrs. Key Pittman of Nevada. Governor Moeur and Mrs. Greenway also here.

The Republic of Mexico today presented to Senator Pittman a large, silver plaque bearing the ancient Aztec calendar, in recognition of Senator Pittman's services at the London Economic Conference in 1933 in behalf of the coinage of silver. Senator Pittman accepted the plaque in an appropriate speech whereupon about three hundred dignitaries (American and Mexican) went to the "cave" in Nogales, Mexico, to luncheon. There was much postprandial oratory. The speeches were translated from English into Spanish and vice versa.

My speech was translated by a young Mexican scholar who supplied grace to my remarks. In speaking of the plaque I said that the Aztec calendar was older than the Pyramids, and my interpreter transformed my sentence into a polished and glowing classic.

Douglas, Arizona, August 20, 1934. My political prospects seem so poor that I have told "sportsmen" that it was a good "two-to-one" bet that I would not be renominated.

The chief complaints against me are that I am not sufficiently radical; that too few Arizonians have been appointed to federal office; that I have failed to secure protective tariff on copper, and that I have been to Europe three times.

Bisbee, August 21, 1934. I was cheered when a delegation of twenty ladies of Bisbee called and encouraged me with offers of support.

August 25, 1934. Mr. Frank Stewart took me to a barbecue near Tempe to speak at an afternoon rally.

As we drew near the platform, Mrs. Greenway was concluding her address, and just before I was called up, Mr. Stewart told me that I was now to "address the most radical audience ever assembled in Arizona." He was correct; I had scarcely begun to speak when a pelting hail of questions struck me; — "You voted against fiat money" shouted one man, "You did nothing for free silver" yelled another, "You have a government printing press there in Washington, why don't you print some money and send it to us" sagely spoke another. One man howled like a wolf: "We want a commodity dollar." Scores of question relating to specie and currency were fired at me. I called out for a roast beef sandwich and shouted "I want the meat rare, indeed, blood raw, if possible." Whereupon a plate of sandwiches was handed to me, and I ate until quiet was restored. At the close of my address which lasted two hours, many questions, some friendly, were asked me.

Yuma, August 27, 1934. Mr. E. F. Sanguinetti, leading merchant here, took a day off from his business to escort me about town.

Tucson, August 31, 1934. Willie Tresnon of Phoenix brought me here per auto.

Mr. McKinney and other friends arranged my speaking engagement here, and no candidate could have asked for a more courteous audience.

After the speaking, Mr. and Mrs. McKinney tendered me a dinner at their home at which about ninety of principal citizens of Tucson were present, including Dr. Homer Shantz, president of the state university, and Mr. William R. Mathews, editor of the *Arizona Star*. Mr. Lewis Douglas, director of the budget, has resigned, and the government will no longer have the services of this superb official.

Bisbee, September 1, 1934. For months the citizens of southeastern Arizona have been preparing to celebrate on Labor Day the opening to tourists of the Chiricahua National Monument. Some men of national reputation were expected to be the chief speakers; but the Committee telephoned me tonight that their speakers were unable to be present, and they invited me to "pinch-hit" and deliver the principal address, whereupon, I accepted their invitation.

Faraway Ranch, September 2, 1934. Six hundred persons are tonight camped near this ranch in the Chiricahua Mountains. I was handed copy of an editorial favorable to myself, published this morning in the *Arizona Daily Star* at Tucson.

September 3, 1934. Nine thousand persons were present at the celebration in the Chiricahua Mountains. I was scheduled to speak for one hour, and when I began speaking I realized that I would soon be baked by the scorching sun. To speak with hat on would be discourteous; to hold an umbrella would be ludicrous, therefore I plugged away uncovered, and at the end of the hour was like a boiled lobster. A physician treated me, bandaged my head and face, and Willie Tresnon and I then set out for a fourteen-hour auto ride to Phoenix. At Safford another physician treated my burns.

Phoenix, September 5, 1934. Spoke at high school stadium to three thousand persons. Although I did not organize this speech so well as the Tucson speech of last Friday, I am of opinion that tonight's speech turns the tide in my favor. Restraint was its strong feature.

The circumambient atmosphere resounds with canards launched by persons who have yet to learn that eleventh-hour tales are futile and are frequently a "boomerang" which rebounds to strike the umbilicus of him who launched it.

September 6, 1934. To Miami where a public dinner was tendered to me by the principal citizens of the town. Mr. Cleve Van Dyke was toastmaster and over a score of citizens responded to toasts.

Prescott, September 10, 1934. For the past year, signs indicated that I would *not* be renominated, but it now appears that I shall be victorious. I have the inclination but have neither the time nor the strength to record here the incidents and factors that reversed the public sentiment so sharply against me five months ago.

My campaign was ably managed by my wife, and she brought Miss Susan Murphy of Prescott into headquarters to handle the correspondence. Miss Murphy was my stenographer during all the time I maintained a law office in Prescott. My opponents *overdid* their criticisms of myself. Had they employed a gentle, temperate malice toward me they might have fared better.

Prescott, September 11, 1934. Voted and then spent the day reading the plays of Aristophanes, the Greek comic dramatist.

Prescott, September 12, 1934. At 3:00 this A.M. I was aroused from sleep by telephone from my wife at Phoenix announcing that I was nominated.

September 14, 1934. On Santa Fe train bound for Washington to attend departmental matters.

I cannot write. I do not read. I cannot think. I have no appetite. I sit here in the Pullman, a lumpish leaden, tired, weary man.

Washington, September 20, 1934. Reached here last Monday; quartered at our big lonely house on K Street, no one with me but the faithful Julia and husband Harry.

October 1, 1934. Heretofore in state campaigns, the Democratic nominees divided into two groups, thus requiring two rallies in every town. I suggested abandoning the two-group plan and argued that if all Democratic candidates traveled together, they would develop the comradeship of "troupers" much needed now as some gaping wounds inflicted by the late primary campaign must be healed before election day. I further pointed out that the local committees could not now bear the expense of two rallies. My plan was adopted.

Prescott, October 6, 1934. All Democratic nominees spoke here tonight. Argentiferous-tongued Attorney Pat O'Sullivan presided and eloquently lauded all the candidates.

October 7, 1934. All candidates to lunch at Mrs. Greenway's cattle-ranch south of Bill Williams' Mountain near Hell Canyon: My brother William was born at this ranch on a bleak Christmas morning in 1876. My parents abandoned this place in 1877 because of drought.

When, during my address to the audience, I glimpsed but a few feet away the ruins of the hut which in the long ago sheltered my father and mother, I almost lost composure. I realized how harsh and meagre was their life here, and when I compared my shining entourage and my creature-comfort to their homely indigence and to the unavailing sacrifices they made on this very spot, I felt like a whelp unworthy of the lioness from whose loins I sprang.

Holbrook, October 9, 1934. Upon reaching Holbrook, about one hundred constituents called upon me. I skipped supper and held interviews until time to go to speaking.

Winslow, October 10, 1934. My brother William and I traversed some of the country west and south of Winslow over which Bill, as a cowboy, rode hard when he was a youth.

Flagstaff, October 11, 1934. Here I met my Republican opponent, Colonel J. E. Thompson, a generous-minded gentleman of pulchritude and ample stature.

I am almost tempted to write of the speeches delivered in this campaign, but all campaign speeches are of the same tenor. Audiences seem to expect, yea, seem to demand extravagant promises from candidates. The candidate who champions firmness, efficiency, and economy in the federal government sounds a sour note. Constituencies demand huge appropriations and lower taxes.

My brother William too ill to accompany me further. Governor Moeur, who is a physician, took him to Phoenix.

Phoenix, November 3, 1934. Mrs. Ashurst and I dined with Governor Moeur and Senator McAdoo, the latter of whom during the evening addressed a large audience.

November 6, 1934. Mrs. Ashurst and I and Chief Justice and Mrs. Henry D. Ross were dinner guests at the residence of Attorney and Mrs. E. E. Ellinwood. During dinner the radio announced that I was reelected and that Mrs. Greenway had defeated Mr. Hoval A. Smith for representative in Congress.

The radio then blared out the announcement that Senator David A. Reed, Republican of Pennsylvania had been defeated by Mr. Joseph F. Guffey, a Democrat.

Hotel Chancellor, Los Angeles, California, November 11, 1934. We answer no telephone calls and receive no visitors, except Mrs. Felicia Grannen, formerly of Flagstaff. I have not the strength to meet callers.

Washington, D. C. November 19, 1934. Arrived in Washington today, and the state of my health required me to go to bed immediately. Mrs. Ashurst is answering all correspondence.

December 12, 1934. I presided this evening at the conference, called by Attorney General Cummings, on the prevention of crime.

December 26, 1934. The Department of Justice has told me that the President would appoint me to the circuit judgeship to fill the vacancy on the ninth circuit caused by the death of Circuit Judge William H. Sawtelle of Arizona. I requested the Department to notify the President that I valued this mark of his confidence but would decline the appointment.

January 2, 1935. At caucus of Democratic senators today, Senator Joe T. Robinson of Arkansas, truthful, diligent and dependable, was unanimously re-elected majority leader. He is a debater of severe logic and would acquit himself well in any assemblage of parliamentarians.

In the long list of our Presidents,
none, but a scarce half-dozen,
was either versatile or subtle.

January 3, 1935. I was today sworn in for my fifth term in the Senate.

To dinner with Mr. Justice Van Devanter of the Supreme Court. Guest of honor was the Chief Justice of Canada.

January 5, 1935. Mrs. Ashurst and I dined with the Chief Justice of the United States and Mrs. Hughes.

January 20, 1935. Attended at the Carlton Hotel this evening a dinner given by Hon. Joseph P. Tumulty to ninety of his friends. Amongst his guests were senators, representatives, judges, librettists, lawyers, artists, and authors.

February 2, 1935. For some weeks the nation has been nervously awaiting the outcome of the "Gold Clause Cases" pending in the Supreme Court of the United States. States wherein that Court is to decide whether Congress had the constitutional power to invalidate the "Gold Payment Promises" of bonds and contracts and to order payment thereof at face value in the present devalued currency.

The Gold Clause Cases arise out of a series of acts of Congress, executive orders and proclamations between March 5, 1933 and January 31, 1934. Banks and stock exchanges for the past fortnight have been bracing themselves to meet any shock that might come, and the Securities and Exchange Commission was ready to act if hysterical trading resulted from the Court's decision.

February 7, 1935. My work in the Judiciary Committee is of such volume that I resigned my chairmanship of and my membership on the Special Committee to Investigate Appointment of Receivers, etc. and Senator McAdoo of California was made chairman.

February 18, 1935. The Supreme Court of the United States today by five to four, decided that the so-called "Gold Clause" is valid. The market immediately "upped," and stocks and bonds soared. Chief Justice Hughes delivered majority opinion and Associate Justice McReynolds delivered minority opinion.

February 21, 1935. Mr. and Mrs. Clifford Berryman were hosts to Mrs. Ashurst and myself to dinner this evening at the University Club. Mr. Berryman is a famous cartoonist who for more than forty years past, has drawn cartoons recording the dramatic march of national events.

August 31, 1935. Representative George Burnham of California, telephoned me yesterday, and on behalf of the California Pacific International Exposition at San Diego, invited me to deliver the Constitution Day Address, to be broadcast to the nation on September 17, next. Thus on yesterday opportunity — it will not return — came on luminous wings to my door but found me unready, doubting and hesitating.

From the time of my accession to the chairmanship of the Senate Committee on the Judiciary, I have been repeatedly asked if there exists Constitutional authority for the federal government to take from the law-observing, industrious person that which he has earned and to give it, even indirectly, to the thriftless person who lacks prevision and who cannot or will not earn his keep. I owe the nation truth and faithful service and should have accepted this invitation and pointed out that to "regiment" and "straight-jacket" the citizen was never in the mind of the framers of the Constitution.

Public men who sustain civil liberty are those who are audacious and ready, and there is no agony more sickening than when remorse drives its fangs deep because of a grand opportunity unembraced.

Chicago, September 9, 1935. Pullman conductor told me that U. S. Senator Huey Pierce Long of Louisiana was at death's door, having been shot through the body by a fanatic last night in Baton Rouge.

Topeka, Kansas, September 10, 1935. Pullman conductor told me that Senator Long of Louisiana was dead.

Concho, Arizona, September 15, 1935. Spending the night with my brother William who is principal of the public school here.

Concho is a Spanish-American village where for past seventy years grandees have flourished.

September 16, 1935. Mrs. Candelaris, a member of one of the old Spanish families of Concho, brought me back to Flagstaff in my brother William's Buick.

Hotel Escalante, Ash Fork, Arizona, September 17, 1935. After declining Representative George Burnham's invitation on August 30 to broadcast to a nationwide audience on Constitution Day, my intuition tortured me with a gnawing uneasiness over the sublime opportunity I had failed to grasp.

Ex-President Hoover spoke in my stead and his speech was broadcast from the California Pacific International Exposition at San Diego. If Mr. Hoover were not already irretrievably out of the political picture, his speech of today would go far toward aiding him to secure the Republican Presidential nomination next year.

In declining this invitation to broadcast, I was under no illusions as to the importance of the occasion. Had I not been exhausted from my arduous labors as Chairman of the Senate Committee on the Judiciary, with anti-gangster and bankruptcy legislation, I would have accepted and would have pointed out that American citizens have a far better opportunity to earn dignified livelihood and to achieve economic independence and social security under that balance of power between federal and state governments than they (the citizens) would have were all power centralized in the federal government for thus all-too-soon the citizens, as in Germany, would exist only for the government.

At Sea, October 17, 1935. Last summer, in Washington, D. C., Honorable Manuel Quezón who will be the first president of the Commonwealth of the Philippines, called upon me and invited me and my wife to attend his inauguration into the presidency on November fifteenth next, in the city of Manila. We accepted his invitation and yesterday we sailed from Seattle, on the SS "President Grant," bound for the Philippines. A. O. Lustie, U.S.N.R. is the SS "President Grant's" commander.

During the long procession of centuries in which ships have sailed the ocean, all kinds of galleons and argosies have plowed the waves and all sorts of cargo have been carried. These persons now sailing on the SS "President Grant" will stand in history as witnesses voyaging to a newly-created altar of liberty there to testify to the blessing of freedom. By this voyage of the SS "President Grant" America keeps her word and redeems her promise of ultimate independence to the Filipino.

A special niche in ocean lore seems to have been reserved for some ships: the ship "Argo" built from the pine trees of Mount Pelion which, in the days of remote antiquity, set sail with fifty oars under the command of Jason in search of the Golden Fleece; the little ship which carried the Apostle Paul from Asia across the isles of Greece and thus to Europe; the "Santa Maria," Columbus' flagship; the "Mayflower" — these were ships that achieved as romantic a fame as any craft in all the annals of the ocean, and so inspiring was their voyage that they almost became nautical mythology. An aura of mystery clings to the smallest ship and to the humblest sailor because ships and sailors have to do with the sea, its magic, its manifestations of power, and its stories of adventure and heroism.

The Congressional party aboard the SS "President Grant" is composed of: the Vice-President and Mrs. John N. Garner, the Speaker of the House and Mrs. Joseph W. Byrns, seventeen United States senators, twenty-seven representatives in Congress, many prominent publishers, editors and reporters, some attachés from each House of Congress, together with a dozen or more guests specially invited by the Philippine authorities. In all, these voyagers (to the Philippines, including the ladies) number about 150 persons.

Last evening at the Empress Hotel at Victoria, a public dinner was tendered to our party and its entourage by the high officials of the province of British Columbia.

October 22, 1935. This is the day that, for *our* ship, never was. We went to bed Monday evening, October 21, and the next morning it was Wednesday, October 23, for us.

Yokohama, October 28, 1935. Ford Motor Company placed autos at our disposal and the afternoon was spent sightseeing and shopping in Tokyo, eighteen miles from Yokohama. In evening returned to our ship to dress, thence back to Tokyo where party was entertained at a soiree and buffet-supper given by the American-Japan Society.

Ex-Senator Harry Hawes loaned me his top-hat as I forgot to bring mine.

October 29, 1935. To Tokyo to Japanese luncheon tendered to our party by the American-Japan Society. All guests removed their shoes before entering the restaurant.

All attended a reception at the American Embassy. Our Ambassador, Mr. Joseph Grew, was absent "on leave" but we were entertained by chargé d'affairs, Mr. Edwin Neville and his staff.

The Vice-President and the Speaker of the House had audience today with the Emperor of Japan.

October 30, 1935. Landed at Kobe. Went shopping in rickshaws. The Consulate and American Association gave our party a reception at the Hotel Oriental. Boston baked beans formed the pièce-de-résistance at the buffet-supper. General Motors Corporation placed autos at our disposal.

Japan proper is not as large in area as the state of California and in all Japan there are only 2100 Americans resident.

Shanghai, November 2, 1935. All quartered at Hotel Cathay in Shanghai and shopped during morning. Luncheon at City

Government Hall tendered by Wu Te Chen, the Mayor of Greater Shanghai and Madame Wu Te Chen. Chopsticks—no knives, no forks.

Tea with Minister of Finance of the Chinese National Government and Madame H. H. Kung and then to formal dinner at Park Hotel tendered by our Ambassador to China, Honorable Nelson Johnson, and our Consul General at Shanghai, Mr. Edwin Cunningham. Cutlery, no chopsticks.

Madame Wu Te Chen, wife of the Mayor of Greater Shanghai, was my dinner partner and Madame Wellington Koo at my left was Vice-President Garner's dinner partner. Madame Wu spoke no English but Madame Koo is an English scholar. When I adverted to the negative and placid philosophy of China, Madame Koo replied: "It may have been beautiful and great for the China of antiquity but the China of today should cohere and advance nationally." Madame Koo is a student of palmistry and adverted to the subject several times, but of it I know nothing.

November 5, 1935. City of Victoria on the Island of Hong Kong. The men of our party went to tailor for white tuxedos and black surcingle sash to wear on formal occasions. In afternoon we motored around the Island which is in the estuary of the Pearl River. Superb road for miles—not blasted but chiseled out of living rock.

At the Peninsula Hotel in the City of Kowloon, our consul general, Mr. Charles Hoover and Mrs. Hoover, and the members of the American community here gave our party a formal dinner.

November 6, 1935. Donned cutaway coats and top-hats to attend an investiture whereat titles were announced to five British subjects here.

In afternoon a garden party at the peak, on Island of Hong Kong eight hundred feet above City of Victoria, was tendered by Sir Robert and Lady Ho Tung, wealthy British subjects of Chinese ancestry. Sir Robert has several residences and has two hundred house servants at this particular one.

November 8, 1935. Landed at Manila amidst the thunder of saluting guns, much band music, and the welcoming shouts of the multitude.

Party quartered at Manila Hotel, a large five-story structure of steel and concrete, facing Manila Bay; a palm-bordered, grass-lawned park on the waterside.

This hotel has large modern tiled bathrooms, cool verandas opening off each apartment, and all floors are made of wide planks of polished Philippine hardwood. Manila is "a many-hued opal in a setting of emerald" and hard by is the walled city (Intramuros) of the Middle Ages, of grim bastions and heavy battlements with glimpses of medieval Spain.

All called upon Governor General Frank Murphy. In the evening a reception was given by the Governor General at Malacanan Palace in honor of party.

November 10, 1935. Those of our party who went to Baguió returned here to Manila to attend the reception given by the President-elect and Mrs. Quezón in honor of Governor General Murphy.

November 11, 1935. Attended review of the Philippine Division of the U. S. Army at Fort William McKinley. This Philippine Division composed entirely of Philippine Scouts, is commanded by Brigadier General Alfred Smith. These troops owe allegiance only to the United States and are part of the Army of the United States.

After review, buffet luncheon tendered by the commanding general and officers of the Fort.

November 12, 1935. Attended special (joint) session of Philippine Legislature where Vice-President Garner and Speaker of the House, Joseph Byrns, each delivered appropriate—yes, superb speeches.

Many groups of non-Christian tribes from Mindanao, Sulu, and the Mountain Province, some of them carrying long spears, are arriving for the inauguration. They have, as requested, brought their complete native costumes as well as their war arms and implements. The costumes will be worn during the inaugural parade, and the arms are to be displayed when the native dances are performed.

November 13, 1935. Some of our party went to Corregidor Island which is called "The Tadpole," thanks to the happy penchant of soldiers, sailors, and marines for applying apt nicknames.

This tadpole-shaped island, separated from the Bataan Peninsula by a three-mile stretch of water, dominates Manila Bay and is, for the most part, sheer rock rising abruptly out of the water, with its tail, a low sandy beach, curving into the bay.

After his victory in May 1898 over the Spanish Fleet in this Bay, Admiral George Dewey notified the Washington government that he could at any time take, but had insufficient men to hold, the city of Manila.

By this notice to his government, Admiral Dewey, it would appear, gave a hint or warning, rather, to statesmen and empire builders not to swallow more than they may digest.

Students of geopolitics are of the opinion that in grappling with the problem of the Philippine Islands, the Washington government has fallen between two stools, in that after Dewey's victory in which he sank the Spanish fleet, we should either have sailed away and notified interested powers that we declined any and all responsibility for the Islands or, as an alternative, we should have announced a permanent occupation and authority sustained by an ample force to be maintained at any cost.

The black beetle in our amber is the fact that we never truly follow either plan but give an intermittent half-hearted support to each plan (occupying and abandoning) at one and the same time.

The Filipino, when questioned, with airy complacence jauntily declares his belief that Japan does not intend to gobble up the Philippine Islands, but all this jauntiness is apparent only, not real. In the Filipino there is quite artfully concealed a message from his subconscious, in the form of the gnawing *fear* of Japan.

This fear is strictly tabu and is not to be mentioned in polite circles in Manila.

November 15, 1935. Arose at 6:00 A.M. to be ready for the exercises which began at 7:30 in a cool, radiant morning. After the invocation by the Archbishop of Cebu, Governor General Murphy, at the request of Honorable George H. Dern, the Secretary of War, then read the proclamation of President Roosevelt.

The President of the Commonwealth, Honorable Manuel Quezón, delivered his inaugural address which for rhetoric and comprehension of duties and obligations has not been excelled by any chief magistrate ever inducted into office. Amongst the many gems of President Quezón's address were the following:

I shall tolerate neither corruption nor inefficiency in public office . . .

I am a firm believer in the institution of private property . . .

The experience of centuries shows that the one sure way to protect society against class-war, is to secure to wage-earners their due . . .

And this sublime, yet harsh truth:

Liberty and independence can be possessed only by those who are ready to pay the price in life or fortune . . .

By 10 o'clock a tropical sun scorched those of us who were silk-hatted, frock-coated, and starched-collared and drove us to the white linens before viewing the parade. The Philippine Islands made an approach to their debut into the society of nations with an insignificant debt and with that asset which no other nation today possesses, viz., "a balanced budget."

President Quezón is in poor health, is emaciated. At dinner at his palace last evening, he did not take a morsel of food or sip of wine. Mrs. Ashurst and I went to Los Pinas Church to see the hundred year old bamboo organ made of 950 bamboos.

November 16, 1935. Ex-Senator Hawes, who for past sixty days has been ill from heart trouble, arose from his bed today and in a dignified speech at Malacanan Palace, presented to the Philippine government an oil portrait of the late Senator Bronson Cutting of New Mexico.

November 17, 1935. Mrs. Ashurst ill from Dengue (breakbone) fever.

November 25, 1935. Again in Shanghai, Mr. William P. Hunt (who a dozen years since was an elevator boy at the U. S. Senate and who is now a tycoon (magnate) here in Shanghai) was host to our party.

Shanghai is really three cities, i.e., the International Settlement, the French Concession, and the "Chinese Cities."

Shanghai is the New York City of China and is on the Whangpoo River, about sixteen miles above the point where the Whangpoo flows into the yellow muddy estuary of the Yangtze Kiang River.

Most of the news from China is filtered to the world through Shanghai. In the Cathay Hotel, the Palace Hotel, and the other hotels along the International Settlement's bund, numerous reporters are busy gathering facts for their dispatches and reaching conclusions from small data dropped in the lounges and at the bars of these large hotels. Toward evening the reporters begin to winnow and sift the varied rumors, verify and check them and then send out their news stories.

From that long-ago day in antiquity when (contemporaneous with the beginnings of Egypt, Assyria, Babylon, and Damascus) civilization dawned in China, down to the present time, China has never had a national unified currency and until she does have, China will be futile in world affairs.

China currency has always been the most involved of any in the world, and even now American visitors to China are amused or annoyed by her currency. For example: Shanghai money is not good outside of Shanghai.

Probably the most tragic breakdown in the statesmanship of this century, was the failure of Sir John Simon, Great Britain's Secretary of State for Foreign Affairs in 1932, to back up our

Secretary of State, Hon. Henry L. Stimson, who announced anent the puppet state of Manchuko, that recognition would not be accorded as to territory acquired by Japanese aggression.

Honolulu, December 8, 1935. Lieutenant Commander Thomas Ross whom, years ago, I nominated to Naval Academy, met us at dock.

To church and then to residence of Mr. E. W. Greene, Manager of the Chau Sugar Company where, under a large marquee, our entire party lunched.

Upon descrying the vast extent of cactus on the hillsides nearby, I was not surprised when informed that this plantation of 12,000 acres planted to sugar cane, is dependent upon irrigation.

Reception at residence of Princess Kawananskoa who would be the Queen now, had the monarchy here continued.

In evening our party was tendered a dinner at the Royal Hawaiian Hotel. Native songs and native dances.

December 9, 1935. Military review and luncheon at Schofield Barracks; then sailed for Seattle.

Washington, May 5, 1936. The Department of Justice having lately received notice from Fred C. Jacobs, one of the U. S. district judges in Arizona, that he has retired, I have been bombarded for the past six days with telegrams from the various gentlemen, twenty-six in number, who desire to succeed Judge Jacobs.

I have recommended David W. Ling, now and for some years past, Superior Judge of Greenlee County, Arizona, for U. S. Judge to succeed Judge Jacobs, having known Mr. Ling since his birthtime.

May 20, 1936. So fierce is the controversy over Judge Jacobs' successor, that some of the applicants have telegraphed me demanding that I accept them "as my second choice for this judgeship." To which telegrams I sent the following reply: "I have no second choice. I shall neither trade nor bargain nor maneuver."

May 28, 1936. The President today nominated Judge Ling for District Judge to succeed Judge Jacobs, who has retired.

Night, May 30, 1936. I am sitting in silence on board a train, bound for Flagstaff, Arizona. At breakfast this morning, Mr. Joseph C. Duke, one of my assistant secretaries, telephoned me that a telegram had arrived from Governor Moeur of Arizona, expressing condolences on the sudden death of my brother, William. This news stunned me, but I recovered my strength and telegraphed to my brother's widow that I would leave for Flagstaff at once. The Senate confirmed the nomination of Mr. Ling for District Judge before I left Washington.

Flagstaff, June 1, 1936. Arrived here tonight. My brother William's son, Thomas, met me at the depot and told me that William, about four days ago, fell against a bathtub, breaking some ribs, and that pneumonia and pleurisy set in, to which he succumbed, with calmness and courage.

Flagstaff, June 2, 1936. My lifetime friend, Mr. William H. Switzer, assembled six "old timers" who had known my brother since his childhood, to serve as pall bearers. Reverend Ragsdale, of the Federated Churches, conducted brief and dignified funeral services. William was born on a ranch now owned by Representative Greenway, near where the town of Williams, Arizona, later grew, and he would have been sixty years old next Christmas. Although two years younger than I, he was a world-weary old gentleman. He always carried in his luggage testaments written in Greek and in Latin and read these two languages with facility.

With his interment there was buried the companion of my boyhood days, who knew as no one else knows, the intimate incidents of my young life. His widow and his son and my sister Maude and her husband, Mr. West, and I motored to the Old Ashurst Ranch, and saw the ruined log cabin in Padre Canyon, where our family for years lived the meagre life of pioneers.

On board Santa Fe Train, June 3, 1936. My brother William's widow, and his son and I, motored to Representative Greenway's ranch where William was born. Entering the train at Williams, to return to Washington, the radio announced that Honorable Joseph W. Byrns, Speaker of the House of Representatives had just died from heart failure. He seemed vital and jocund, last autumn, on our voyage to the Orient.

Senaca Falls, N. Y., September 17, 1936. Luncheon with Democratic Club at Hotel Gould, thence to County Fair, and thence I proceeded per auto through the Finger Lake Country passing the towns of Romulus, Ovid, Lodi, Hector and on to Watkins Glen, where I spoke one hour.

Mr. Leffingwell took me per auto to Elmira. Although it was dark when I reached Elmira, I insisted that Mr. Leffingwell take me to see Mark Twain's grave in Woodlawn Cemetery.

Grand Canyon, Arizona, September 26, 1936. Mr. Joe Duke brought me and my wife here in his auto from Williams. During the day, I arranged for my father's body to be removed to the local cemetery here and I ordered an appropriate headstone.

San Diego, California, October 20, 1936. Came here yesterday with Mr. Fred Williams, from Los Angeles per auto placed at my use by Messrs. O'Boyle and McDonald of Monrovia. Spoke last night at Roosevelt Junior High School auditorium; many ex-Arizonians in the audience.

Los Angeles, October 22, 1936. Addressed a Democratic rally here last night at the Philharmonic Auditorium. I prepared with much care my speech for this occasion, and it was the most successful of all my political speeches.

October 24, 1936. Last evening I addressed the Presidential dinner at the Hollywood Roosevelt Hotel and many of the Democratic leaders of Los Angeles were present. After the dinner I went to the Hollywood High School auditorium and delivered a political address. A pleasant episode at the auditorium meeting was that I met Professor Harry L. Weems who was my school teacher in Flagstaff, Arizona, forty-five years ago.

Washington, D. C., February 5, 1937. Yesterday, Colonel Marvin McIntyre, assistant secretary to the President, telephoned that the President wanted me at the White House at ten thirty A.M. today.

This morning at the Cabinet Room of the White House I found present only Representative Sumners of Texas, Chairman of the House Committee on the Judiciary. We went into a huddle — each asking the other, "Why are you here?" Each divined that we might be asked something (we knew not what) as to judicial matters. Cabinet members carrying portfolios began drifting in and soon there were present the following: Secretary of State Hull, Secretary of War Woodring, Attorney General Cummings, Secretary of Navy Swanson, Secretary of Interior Ickes, Secretary of Agriculture Wallace, Secretary of Commerce Roper, Secretary of Labor Perkins, Vice-President Garner, Speaker Bankhead, Senator Robinson, Democratic Majority Leader in Senate, Representative Sam Rayburn, Democratic Majority Leader in House, Representative Sumners, and myself.

The President then came in and greeted each by his first name. All took seats whereupon the President said that on January twelfth last he sent a message to Congress recommending reorganization of the Executive department of the government and that he now had an important message recommending reorganization of the Judicial branch which he would send to Congress today. He read a letter dated February 2 addressed to him by the attorney general inveighing against delays in the administration of justice in the U. S. Courts and then read the message he proposed to send to Congress. His reading required an hour as he frequently ad libbed. He recommended, *inter alia,* a law permitting justices of the Supreme Court of the United States to retire at seventy years of age on full pay, and he further recommended that if any Supreme Court justice upon reaching seventy did not retire, the President might in such event, appoint an additional justice to the Supreme Court of the United States for every Justice who refused to retire within six months after reaching seventy, until the total number of the Supreme Court Justice aggregated fifteen.

During his reading he went on to say that he had "attached to the message something (draft of the bill) into which Henry and Hatton (Mr. Sumners) can sink their teeth." When the President concluded his reading, he said, "I must now go to the press conference and give this message to the reporters," whereupon he immediately left the Cabinet Room.

It is my opinion that no member of the Cabinet, except the Attorney General, knew aught in advance of the President's proposal.

Although I have introduced and passed bills providing for additional justices of the circuit courts and additional judges of the district courts, I have never urged an increase in the number of justices of the Supreme Court. Indeed, personally, once within the past two years and once per telephone last January, I advised the President to make no attempt to increase the membership of the U. S. Supreme Court and on each occasion I did *not* omit to say to him, "Father Time, with his scythe, is on your side. Anno Domini is your invincible ally."

Chucking a copy of the message and bill into my pocket, I motored to the Capitol with Vice-President Garner where I found a tremendous sensation raging, and then set to work at once to verify the statement attributed to the late William Howard Taft (sometime President and also sometime Chief Justice) that justices should retire at the age of seventy.

February 6, 1937. Much excitement over the President's proposal to reorganize the Judicial Branch of the government. This excitement may simmer down to a billow, even to a bubble, but an angry ocean of adverse opinion is now rolling over Eff Dee. Some observers believe that he has been toppled from his dizzy peak of popularity and that his prestige is gone. He is denounced as attempting to "pack the Court" in order to validate New Deal laws. His proposal is condemned by the press as "indirect," "immoral," and "too clever."

February 8, 1937. Senate Committee on the Judiciary at its meeting today requested me *not* to appoint a subcommittee to consider the President's Judiciary Reorganization Bill but to lay the bill before the entire committee for consideration.

At White House to luncheon; Senator Wagner of New York and Representative Sumners, Chairman of House Committee on the Judiciary, were present. An electrically heated oven with trays containing food was brought in; whereupon the President, sitting in his chair, handed us plates, cups, and cutlery and he then carved a baked pheasant. He ate but little, and for an hour he argued for his Judiciary Reorganization Bill.

I urged him to put his strength behind the bill already favorably reported to the House by Representative Sumners, allowing Justices of the Supreme Court to retire at the age of seventy at full pay as that bill would assure them of their compensation without interference from Congress, as is now the law for retirement of judges of the Circuit Courts and of the District Courts.

February 14, 1937. Mr. Thomas Corcoran, attorney for the Reconstruction Finance Corporation and one of the President's advisers, phoned that the President wished to see me at three o'clock this afternoon.

At the White House I found Representative Sumners of Texas. The President was disappointed because I had postponed until February twenty-second the meeting of the Senate Committee on the Judiciary that had been scheduled for tomorrow. I replied that I would avoid haste, would go slowly, and give the opponents of his bill ample time and opportunity to explore all its implications. He received this statement with disrelish. I then went on to say that the opposition was searching avidly for some shred of evidence tending to show that he was "hurrying" the bill.

The President said he was opposed to any attempt at this time to amend the Constitution in order to secure authorization of the needed social legislation as an amendment would have to be ratified by the legislatures of three-fourths of the states and that in his opinion such an amendment could not be ratified within the next five years.

Eff Dee's quarrel with the Judiciary is as acute as were those of Jefferson and Jackson.

The President, during the week, sent for a dozen or more of the members of the Senate Committee on the Judiciary to discuss his plan with them.

February 19, 1937. Today in the Senate I discussed Eff Dee's plan to reorganize the Judicial Branch of the government, the implementing bill for which plan I have introduced formally and as a courtesy to the President, thus following the long-established practice of the various committee chairmen regarding legislation urged by the head of a department. During the course of my remarks, Senator Josiah Bailey of North Carolina said:

> I wish to ask the Senator if, as reported in the newspapers, he spoke the following words?"
>
> And among the unjust criticisms which have been uttered, or printed, rather, about President Roosevelt was that he intended at some time—nobody knows when or where—to increase by some legerdemain—nobody knows when or where—the membership of the Supreme Court of the United States, so that his policies might be sustained.
>
> I desire to ask the Senator from Arizona whether that is an accurate quotation from the newspaper of his remarks?

To this I replied:

> It is obvious from the rhetoric that that is my utterance.

And I then continued as follows:

> My faults are obvious. There can be no doubt I have my full share. I suffer from cacoethes loquendi, a mania or itch for talking, from vanity, and morbidity, and as is obvious to everyone who knows me, an inborn, an inveterate flair for histrionics.
>
> But there never has been superadded to these vices of mine the withering, embalming vice of consistency. Whoever in his public service is handcuffed and shackled by the vice of consistency will be a man not free to act as various questions come before him from time to time; he will be a statesman locked in a prison house the keys to which are in the keeping of days and events that are dead. Let me quote Emerson: "A foolish consistency is the hobgoblin of little minds, adored by little statesmen."
>
> I spoke of my vice, cacoethes loquendi. There is another vice called cacoethes carpendi, the mania to find fault, to carp against everything that somebody else proposes, but never suggesting a remedy yourself. Such is cacoethes carpendi, a vice not wholly unknown in this Senate Chamber!

February 20, 1937. Within past fortnight I have declined several invitations to speak per radio anent the Judicial Reorganization Bill. To White House at 5:00 P.M. where I found Vice-President Garner; Senator Robinson, Arkansas; Senator Harrison, Mississippi; Senator Byrnes, South Carolina; Senator Barkley, Kentucky; and Senator Black, Alabama.

The President amazed me by asking our opinion as to a Constitutional amendment which would grant to Congress (when the Supreme Court declared an Act of Congress invalid) the power to override the Supreme Court and thus allow the law to stand.

Vice-President Garner favored the plan. Senator Robinson and I opposed the plan and argued that it would transfer the judicial power from the Supreme Court to Congress, to which proposal we were opposed. Senator Byrnes suggested that Eff Dee assure the country by message or otherwise that the "sit-down strike" was illegal and Vice-President Garner in burning earnestness said that the "sit-down strikes" would, if unchecked, destroy the Roosevelt administration.

Eff Dee deplored the lack of progress on his Judiciary Reorganization Bill. Now before my committee I chanted "There must be no haste, no heat, no hurry, no worry on that bill."

As we were leaving the President said: "When in January, 1941, I retire to private life, I hope to turn over to my successor this government intact, and we have no time to waste in approaching these problems that must be solved."

February 22, 1937. Senate Committee on the Judiciary today set Tuesday, March 9, next, as the date upon which our entire committee will begin hearings on Eff Dee's Judiciary Reorganization Bill.

February 26, 1937. A familiar voice from the White House (not Eff Dee's) telephoned that Eff Dee would broadcast a "Fireside Chat" next Tuesday evening and requested that I postpone until Wednesday, March 10, the committee hearing on Eff Dee's Judiciary Reorganization Bill. All the members of my committee consented to such postponement.

February 28, 1937. Wife and I dined last evening with Chief Justice of the U. S. and Mrs. Hughes at their residence on R Street. Among the guests were Messrs. McReynolds, Butler, Van Devanter, Roberts, and Cardozo, associate justices of the Supreme Court, and there was not even a remote reference to the Judiciary Reorganization Bill.

Near Midnight, March 9, 1937. Just returned from Hotel Mayflower where I presided as toastmaster at a banquet tendered by former Senator Harry Hawes of Missouri to Honorable Manuel Quezón, President of the Philippine Commonwealth. As toastmaster I limited all speeches (except that of President Quezón) to five minutes.

Senator Hawes' guests (in addition to Senator and Mrs. Pittman of Nevada) comprised the Congressional party and the editors, publishers, and reporters who sailed on the SS "President Grant" in October, 1935, to the inauguration of the Philippine Commonwealth.

Realizing that this banquet would be attended by a large number of sophisticated persons, I spent two hours yesterday and many hours today arranging the details as to what public characters should have precedence at the tables and in what order the various post prandial orators should be called up.

March 10, 1937. Up early for turkish bath so that notwithstanding the banquet of last evening I could be ready to preside at the public hearings which began this morning before the Senate Committee on the Judiciary on the President's bill to reorganize the judicial branch of the government.

The eighteen members of the committee viz., William H. King, M. M. Neely, Patrick McCarran, Frederick Van Nuys, M. M. Logan, William H. Dieterich, George McGill, Carl A. Hatch, Edward R. Burke, Key Pittman, Tom Connally, Joseph C. O'Mahoney, James H. Hughes, William E. Borah, George W. Norris, Warren R. Austin, Frederick Steiwer, with myself as their chairman, met in an ante-room and marched in procession into the adjoining "caucus room," a large room in the Senate Office Building, with marble-tiered walls and damnable acoustics. Five hundred spectators, one hundred newshawks, also many senators not members of the Judiciary Committee, were present.

Attorney General Homer Cummings who occupied one hour in presenting his argument in support of the bill, parried many sharp questions thrust at him by senators opposing the bill.

This proposal to reorganize the judicial branch of the government is now and since February 5 has been a torrid topic of conversation in Washington.

Even in the dignified Senate Committee on the Judiciary the feeling is high, and it is ironical that most of my time and nervous energy are spent in becalming and besmoothing the tense situations that crop out during the hearings.

March 22, 1937. Senator Burton Wheeler of Montana came before the Senate Committee on the Judiciary and for one hour denounced the bill which proposes to reorganize the Judicial Branch of the government, but his own argument was overtowered by a letter asserting *inter alia,* that:

The Supreme Court is fully abreast of its work . . .

An increase in the number of Justices of the Supreme Court apart from any question of policy, . . . would not promote the efficiency of the Court. There would be more judges to hear, more judges to confer, more judges to discuss, more judges to be convinced and to decide. The present number of justices is thought to be large enough so far as the prompt, adequate and efficient conduct of the work of the court is concerned.

April 2, 1937. Having this day accomplished twenty-five (25) years as senator, I examined records as to my correspondence and ascertained that during this quarter century period I have composed and signed about 183,000 letters and have dispatched about 36,500 telegrams.

This volume of correspondence averages twenty (20) letters and four (4) telegrams daily for each and every day including Sundays and holidays of this twenty-five year period.

Dined this evening at the Chinese Embassy. His Excellency, Honorable Manuel Quezón, President of the Philippine Commonwealth, was guest of honor.

April 23, 1937. The hearings before the Senate Committee on the Judiciary on the President's plan to reorganize the judicial branch of the government ended today. Eighty-four witnesses were heard by the committee, one million words of testimony were taken and during the hearings the committee was assisted by our scholarly and diligent Clerk, Mr. Dix W. Price, of Arizona.

April 26, 1937. Eff Dee leaves tomorrow for a two-weeks' fishing cruise in the Gulf of Mexico. At the White House today the mercury of his manners toward me registered zero as he suggested that his bill for judicial reorganization be reported from the Senate Committee on the Judiciary to the Senate *without recommendation,* and he handed me a memorandum containing some data he desired should be used in such proposed report. He requested me to show the memorandum to Senator Robinson, Democratic Majority Leader, which I did during the afternoon and upon exploring the situation, Senator Robinson and I ascertained that to report the bill *without recommendation* was not feasible.

I was not surprised this evening when a "Friendly Voice," nameless here, came over the telephone warning me that Eff Dee believes that I have killed his Judicial Reorganization Bill by Fabian tactics and delay and postponement, in that although he submitted his plan to the Senate on February fifth last, I did not commence the hearings before my committee until March 10 and then strung the testimony out.

Beyond doubt my refusal to pass his Judicial Reorganization Bill through the Senate has alienated him from me and has also damaged my prospects for re-election to the Senate in 1940 as a majority of my constituents are intensely pro-Roosevelt and, similar to other constituencies suffering from an economic depression, are torridly radical and favor this bill.

May 18, 1937. Honorable Willis Van Devanter, for past twenty-six years associate justice of the Supreme Court, announced his retirement, effective June third next. Senate Committee on the Judiciary, by a vote of ten Yeas to eight Nays, ordered the President's Judiciary Reorganization Bill reported to the Senate with the recommendation that the bill *not* pass.

This rejection by the Senate Committee on the Judiciary of the President's plan to reorganize the Judicial Branch of the government has occurred because he could not overcome an "imponderable" which for generations has emotionally and mystically invested the Supreme Court of the United States with symbolism as the power which protects the security and personal liberty of the citizens.

Even many persons who believe in President Roosevelt opposed his bill because they were haunted by the terrible fear that some future President might, by suddenly enlarging the Supreme Court, suppress free-speech, free assembly, and invade other Constitutional guaranties of citizens.

In the long list of our Presidents none but a scarce half-dozen was either versatile or subtle. All but this half dozen clung to fixed principles, insisted upon commitments that could run the gantlet of the courts.

June 1, 1937. The Supreme Court of the United States, lately the subject of acrimonious controversy in and out of Congress, adjourned today until its regular term next October.

During its term which ended today this Court, rendered some far-reaching decisions, the full implications of which are beyond the ken of the clearest seer.

Only the future can reveal the extent of the changes that may come in the life and economic system of the American people as a result of the decisions rendered during this late term, which interpreted the "Commerce Clause" of the Constitution and broadened its "General Welfare" clause beyond the expectations of the New Dealers.

It is asserted in some circles that during this late term, the Supreme Court (under the leadership of Chief Justice Charles Evans Hughes) in order to circumvent the threatened increase in its membership, reoriented itself, executed a *volte-face* and validated all the New Deal laws coming before it during the late term. On these points I have no information; the results speak for themselves and are as follows:

During Eff Dee's first Presidential term, the Supreme Court of the United States voided, wholly or in part, the following

New Deal laws: NRA, AAA, Guffey Coal Act, "hot oil" regulation, building association charters, farm mortgage moratorium, original railway pension act, processing AAA tax refunds, right to withdraw securities before registrations, municipal bankruptcy act, rejected the Humphrey dismissal and sustained the following New Deal laws: original gold devaluation, and the sale of TVA surplus power.

Thus far, during Eff Dee's second term, the same Court has sustained all the important New Deal laws coming before it as follows: Chaco arms embargo, shipment of prison labor goods, silver purchases, gold bullion contracts, second farm mortgage moratorium, collective bargaining for railway labor, Wagner Labor Act, Philippine coconut oil tax, restrictions on process tax refunds, unemployment insurance, assignment to the United States of assets of pre-Soviet corporations, and the old-age pensions.

Eff Dee's bill to rejuvenate the Judicial Branch of the government is now moribund as a result of these late decisions for they go as far to the so-called "left" as any justice appointed by Eff Dee could possibly go.

July 12, 1937. Senator Josiah Bailey of North Carolina delivered a philippic against Eff Dee's plan to reorganize the Judicial Branch of the government.

In the Senate reception room, Senator Robinson of Arkansas, Democratic majority leader, told me he had a sharp pain in his breast. I immediately dispatched two colored boys to give him hot water and common soda which appeared to relieve him.

July 13, 1937. Senator Robinson of Arkansas, Democratic majority leader, at a conference of thirty Democratic senators at his office, went on to say that the opposition was "cutting to pieces the President's bill to reorganize the Judiciary." Senator Robinson then *seriatim* asked the senators present to speak in support of the bill. Turning to me he said, "Henry, when will you speak?" I replied, "My physician will tell you when I may speak and you, Joe, should not speak unless your physician permits."

July 14, 1937. Telephone rang whilst I was at breakfast; Mrs. Ashurst answered and gave me the shocking news that Senator Robinson of Arkansas, Democratic majority leader, had been found dead in his apartments in the Methodist Building.

Apparently he was seized with heart attack about one o'clock this morning. Mrs. Robinson is in Arkansas because of her brother's illness.

Little Rock, Arkansas, July 18, 1937. Special train, made up of ten Pullman cars and carrying the body of the late Senator Robinson, reached here early this morning. This funeral party is composed of forty senators and twenty representatives, also Mr. Harvey Couch of Arkansas, Mr. Bernard M. Baruch of New York, Postmaster General Farley, Assistant to the Attorney General Mr. Joseph B. Keenan, and many others of Senator Robinson's close friends.

Large concourse of people went to State House where Senator Robinson's body lay in state.

As the cortege approached the cemetery, peals of thunder and flashes of lightning set in, and before the senator's body was interred, a downpour of rain drenched everyone.

Met Mr. J. N. Heiskell, editor of *The Arkansas Gazette,* with whom I served in the Senate in 1913. He asked if I remembered him. I replied, "I not only remember you, but I shall now repeat to you extracts from the speech you made in the Senate over twenty-four years ago."

Vice-President Garner who had been vacationing at his home in Uvalde, Texas, came here to attend the funeral and will return to Washington.

Washington, July 21, 1937. At Democratic caucus today Senator Alben W. Barkley of Kentucky was elected majority leader over Senator Pat Harrison of Mississippi by one vote.

Vice-President Garner telephoned me to come to his office immediately saying, "Important." At his office I found Senator Barkley, the new Democratic majority leader, also Senator Burton K. Wheeler of Montana, Senator Josiah Bailey of North Carolina, and Senator Harry Byrd of Virginia, the three latter of whom are opponents of the President's plan to reorganize the Judiciary. The Vice-President said that the time had come to render a great service; that the President's plan to reorganize the Judiciary was now a plague to the country, to the Senate, and to the Democratic party, and that it ought to be within the resources of my commitee's statesmanship to bring in a bill for judicial reform and relief without increasing the membership of the Supreme Court of the United States.

Upon suggestion of the Vice-President I called a special meeting of the Senate Committee on the Judiciary to convene tomorrow morning, and I invited Senators Barkley and Wheeler and Vice-President Garner to appear and discuss the details of a new bill for judicial reform.

This evening the "Friendly Voice" again came over the telephone advising me that Eff Dee's opinion that my attitude during the judicial reorganization contest was fatal to his bill had been *confirmed* by an article lately printed in the *Daily News* of Washington, as follows:

> Ordinarily a filibuster is a pretty nasty affair. And this one has all the makings of a bad-tempered row.
>
> But there is one cheering thought that brightens the dark picture. It is that HENRY FOUNTAIN ASHURST as chairman of the Judiciary Committee, has nominal charge of the legislation. And certainly he is one who measures up to Kipling's standard — one who can keep his head though all about him are losing theirs. Though other debaters hurl bitter invectives, he can be depended upon to remain serene.
>
> This long and purple controversy over the Supreme Court has tried many senator's souls, but the gentleman from Arizona has not lost an inch of his hide, nor shed a drop of blood, nor a bead of perspiration.
>
> When it is all over, even though he be trampled in the dust of defeat, we expect to see HENRY FOUNTAIN ASHURST rise and, with engaging smile and courtly bow, sigh that he regrets the conclusion of the friendly tête-a-tête, but rejoices in a glorious triumph.

July 22, 1937. Senate Committee on the Judiciary assembled in special meeting. All members thereof present except Senator Norris, absent because of illness. Also present Senators Barkley and Wheeler who are not members of the Committee. Vice-President Garner, also present.

After long discussion it was decided that Senator M. M. Logan of Kentucky, Democrat, member of the committee, should today move to recommit to the Committee on the Judiciary the President's bill to reorganize the Judicial Branch of the government and the agenda of a new bill was agreed upon by the committee and ordered to be reported to the Senate as follows:

No increase in the Supreme Court membership.

No roving or ambulatory judges of the lower courts, and no proctor to assign them from district to district.

Provision for direct appeal to the United States Supreme Court when the constitutionality of a federal statute is challenged.

Authority for the Attorney General to intervene in lower court proceedings when the constitutionality of a federal statute is challenged.

Provision for the reassignment of judges of the lower courts by the senior judges of the individual district.

New judges to be appointed on a basis of need and not of age.

These agenda were agreed to by the committee (only Senator Hatch of New Mexico and Senator Hughes of Delaware dissenting). Today the Senate, upon motion of Senator Logan, Kentucky, by a vote of seventy "ayes" to twenty "noes," *recommitted* to its Committee on the Judiciary the President's plan for increasing membership in the Supreme Court and this question is now no longer imminent.

July 27, 1937. Senate Committee on the Judiciary today ordered favorable report on the bill for judicial reform along the lines of the agenda desecribed in this diary of July twenty-second.

I now lay down my diaristic pen. My duties as Chairman of the Senate Committee on the Judiciary (not to mention my other tasks as senator) require me to spend several hours daily in examining the bills coming to my committee. Many of these bills make refined distinctions and require careful consideration and enormous research, as a phrase — yes, merely a word — if improvidently employed, could cause protracted litigation.

To perform these tasks and also keep a journal, calls for an expenditure of time and energy not conceivably within the compass of any man.

Some of the persons who know of this diary, have exhorted me to go on with it, but for reasons of weariness and press of official duties, I here quit my entries.

In looking over these pages, it is observed that numerous events with which I was connected are not mentioned and that no reference has been made herein to many persons who played important parts during the space of time between the beginning and the conclusion of this diary. These omissions are not occasioned because such unrecorded events and unnoticed persons were not deemed worthy of mention but because they did not happen to be in my attention when I sat down to write.

It is a comforting assurance that nothing in this diary will cause pain to any living person or bring reproach to the memory of anyone who is dead.

PERSONAE

ADAMS, CHARLES FRANCIS (1866–1954), Secretary of the Navy during Hoover's Administration, 1929–33.

ADAMS, JAMES TRUSLOW (1878–1949), American historian. Pulitzer Prize-winner in 1922.

ADAMSON, WILLIAM M. (1862–1920), Mayor of Douglas, Arizona three times. Organizer of Douglas street railway, ice plant, city waterworks and telephone company.

ALEXANDER, JOSHUA W. (1852–1936), Democratic representative from Missouri, 1907–19. U. S. Secretary of Commerce, December, 1919 to March, 1921.

ASQUITH, HERBERT HENRY (1852–1928), British statesman, liberal leader, and Prime Minister of England from 1908 until 1916.

ASTOR, VISCOUNTESS, Nancy Witcher (1879–   ), First woman to sit in House of Commons. Hostess at Cliveden Estate. Leader in gradual reform measures of "Tory Democracy."

AUSTIN, WARREN ROBINSON (1877–   ), Republican senator from Vermont from 1931 until 1946 when he became United States representative on the United Nations Security Council, 1946–53.

AYER, EDWARD EVERETT (1865–1927), Railroadman, lumberman, and bibliophile who donated his entire collection of books to the Newberry Library in Chicago in 1911.

BABBITT, EDWARD (1908–   ), Flagstaff, Arizona businessman and director of the Valley National Bank.

BACON, AUGUSTUS OCTAVIUS (1839–1914), Democratic senator from Georgia, 1895–1914.

BAILEY, JOSEPH WELDON (1862–1929), Democratic representative from Texas, 1891–1901, United States senator, 1901–13.

BAILEY, JOSIAH WILLIAM (1873–1945), Democratic senator from North Carolina, from 1930 until his death.

BAKER, NEWTON D. (1871–1937), Secretary of War under Woodrow Wilson during World War I, strong advocate of League of Nations, unsuccessful candidate for Democratic Presidential nomination.

BALDWIN, STANLEY (1867–1947), Three times Prime Minister of England: in 1923 after resignation of Bonar Law; from 1924 to 1929; and from 1935–37, during abdication crisis of Edward VIII.

BALFOUR, ARTHUR JAMES FIRST EARL, (1848–1930), Conservative opponent of Irish home rule, First Lord of Admiralty, 1916–19, and author of Balfour Declaration expressing Britain's approval of a Jewish homeland in Palestine. First British delegate to League of Nations.

BALL, LEWIS HEISLER (1861–1932), Republican representative from Delaware, 1901–03, and senator, 1903–05 and 1909–25.

BANKHEAD, JOHN HOLLIS (1842–1920), Democratic representative from Alabama, 1887-1907, and senator, 1907-20. Father of senators John and William Bankhead.

BANKHEAD, JOHN HOLLIS II (1872–1946), Democratic senator from Alabama, 1931–46. Outstanding New Deal legislator.

BARKLEY, ALBEN L. (1877–1957), Democratic representative and senator from Kentucky. Resigned from Senate in 1949 to become Vice-President of the United States until January, 1953.

BARRYMORE, LIONEL (1878–1954), Actor on American stage, screen and radio.

BARUCH, BERNARD MANNES (1870–   ), American financier and statesman who served as unpaid adviser for every President from Woodrow Wilson through Eisenhower.

BAYARD, THOMAS FRANCIS JR. (1868–1942), Democratic senator from Delaware, 1922–29.

BENSON, WILLIAM SHEPHERD (1855–1932), American admiral and chief of naval operations during World War I.

BENTON, THOMAS HART (1782–1858), Senator from Missouri from 1820 until 1850. Early advocate of "Manifest Destiny" and free homestead lands.

BERNSTORFF, JOHN HEINRICH (1862–1939), German ambassador to United States, 1908–April, 1917. Member of Democratic party during Weimar Republic, left Germany during Hitler rise.

BEVERIDGE, ALBERT JEREMIAH (1862–1927), U.S. senator from Indiana, supporter of Theodore Roosevelt, and an organizer of the Progressive Party. Author of distinguished four-volume biography of John Marshall.

BILIKE, A. C. (?–1915), Tombstone hotel owner in the late 1880's, later owned hotels in Los Angeles. Died on the Lusitania.

BINGHAM, HIRAM (1875–1956), Republican senator from Connecticut, 1924–33.

BLACK, FRANK S. (1853–1913), Republican governor of New York, 1897–99.

BLACK, HUGO LAFAYETTE (1886–   ), Democratic senator from Alabama, 1927–37, and Associate Justice of the U.S. Supreme Court since 1937.

BLAINE, JOHN JAMES (1875–1934), Wisconsin Republican senator, 1927–33.

BLEASE, COLEMAN LIVINGSTON (1868–1942), Democratic senator from South Carolina, 1925–31.

BLENNERHASSET, HARMAN MRS. (1765–1831), Wife of conspirator with Aaron Burr in the plot to separate the Western states from the United States.

BLISS, TASKER (1853–1930), Graduate of West Point, 1875, President of Army War College, 1903, Chief of Staff, 1917, and later part of U.S. delegation to Versailles.

BORAH, WILLIAM EDGAR (1865–1940), Republican senator from Idaho, 1907–40. Unsuccessful candidate for Republican presidential nomination, 1936.

BOWERS, CLAUDE G. (1878–1958), Indiana newspaperman who became ambassador to Spain, 1933, ambassador to Chile, 1939, and author of books on Jefferson, Reconstruction, the Jackson Period, etc.

BOWMAN, WIRT G. (1874–1949), Arizona rancher, politician, and delegate to the Democratic convention in 1924. One of the developers of the resort at Agua Caliente, Baja California.

BRADY, JAMES HENRY (1862–1918), Republican senator from Idaho, 1913–18.

BRANDEGEE, FRANK BOSWORTH (1864–1924), Republican representative from Connecticut, 1902–05. Senator, 1905–24.

BRATTON, SAM GILBERT (1888–   ), Democratic senator from New Mexico, 1924–33. Circuit judge of the U.S. Circuit Court of Appeals.

BRISTOW, JOSEPH LITTLE (1861–1944), Kansas Republican senator, 1909–15.

BROOKHART, SMITH WILDMAN (1869–1944), Progressive Republican senator from Iowa, 1922–26; 1927–33.

BROUSSARD, EDWIN S. (1874–1934), Democratic senator from Louisiana, 1916–33.

BROUSSARD, ROBERT F. (1864–1918), U.S. representative from Louisiana, 1897–1915. Senator from 1915 until his death.

BRUCE, WILLIAM CABELL (1860–1946), Democratic senator from Maryland, 1932–39.

BRYCE, JAMES (1838–1922), British statesman, jurist, and author. British ambassador to the United States, 1903–13.

BUCKINGHAM, GEORGE T. (1864–1940), Illinois attorney, defense lawyer in a number of trust cases.

BURCHARD, SAMUEL (1812–1891), Presbyterian minister in New York who played critical role in the election of 1884, with denunciation of "Rum, Romanism, and Rebellion." Author of a book by that name.

BURGOYNE, JOHN FOX (1782–1871), British general and field marshal, in Napoleonic and Crimean wars.

BURKE, EDWARD R. (1880–   ), Democratic representative from Nebraska, 1933–35; senator, 1935–41.

BURLEIGH, EDWIN CHICK (1843–1916), Republican representative and senator from Maine, 1897–1913.

BURLESON, ALBERT S. (1863–1937), Texas attorney and member of U.S. House of Representatives. Postmaster under Wilson 1913–21.

BURNHAM, GEORGE (1868–1939), Republican congressman from California, 1933–37.

BURR, AARON (1756–1836), New York Democrat who served in U.S. Senate, 1791–97, Vice-President of the United States, 1800–04. Killed Alexander Hamilton in a duel, July 7, 1804. Tried for treason for attempting to form a new republic, but acquitted.

BURTON, THEODORE E. (1851–1929), Republican representative from Ohio, 1880–91; and senator, 1921–28.

BUTLER, NICHOLAS MURRAY (1862–1947), American educator, president of Columbia University, 1901–45. Republican candidate for Vice-Presidency, 1912. Nobel Peace Prize-winner, 1931.

BUTLER, PIERCE (1866–1939), Associate Justice of the United States Supreme Court, 1923–39.

BUTLER, MAJOR SMEDLEY (1881–1940), Marine Corps general twice awarded the Congressional Medal of Honor. Director of Public Safety for Philadelphia, 1924–25.

BYRD, HARRY FLOOD (1887–), Democratic senator from Virginia, 1933–

BYRNES, JAMES FRANCIS (1879–), Democratic representative from South Carolina, 1911–25; senator, 1931–41; associate justice of Supreme Court, 1914–42; Secretary of State, 1945–47.

BYRNS, JOSEPH WELLINGTON (1869–1936), Democratic representative from Tennessee, 1909–36.

CALAMITY JANE (1852–1903), Martha Jane Canary, frontierswoman associated with the Black Hills Gold Rush of 1875.

CALDER, WILLIAM MUSGRAVE (1869–1945), Republican representative from New York, 1905–15; senator from 1917–23.

CAMERON, RALPH H. (1863–1953), Delegate from Arizona to the Sixty-First Congress, 1909–11. Defeated by George W. P. Hunt in 1914 race for governor of Arizona. Republican senator, 1921–27.

CAMPBELL, THOMAS (1878–1944), Republican governor of Arizona, 1917–22.

CAMPBELL-BANNERMAN, SIR HENRY (1836–1908), British liberal and member of Parliament, 1905–08.

CANNON, JOSEPH G. (1836–1926), Republican representative from Illinois; Speaker of the House, Fifty-Eighth through Sixty-First Congresses.

CAPPER, ARTHUR (1865–1951), Republican senator from Kansas, 1919–49.

CARAWAY, HATTIE WYATT (1878–1950), Democratic senator from Arkansas, 1932–45.

CARAWAY, THADDEUS HORATIUS (1871–1931), Democratic representative from Arkansas, 1911–21, and senator, 1921–31.

CARDOZO, BENJAMIN (1870–1938), Associate Justice of the U.S. Supreme Court, 1932–37.

CAREY, ROBERT DAVIS (1878–1937), Republican senator from Wyoming, 1930–37.,

CARNEGIE, ANDREW (1835–1919), American steel industrialist and philanthropist whose benefactions totaled about $350,000,000 including over 2800 free libraries across the United States.

CARRANZA, VENUSTIANO (1859–1920), Governor of state of Coahuila, Mexico, at the time of President Madero's assassination, 1913. President of Mexico, 1917 until death, May 21, 1920.

CASTLEREAGH, ROBERT STEWART, SECOND VISCOUNT (1769–1822), British statesman, diplomat, coordinator of British land and sea power and key figure in fashioning the Quadruple Alliance, 1815.

CATRON, THOMAS BENTON (1840–1921), Republican delegate to Congress from New Mexico, 1895–97. U. S. senator, 1912–17.

CHAMBERLAIN, AUSTEN (1863–1937), British statesman, eldest son of Joseph and brother of Neville. Forty-five years in Parliament; chief author of the Locarno Pact. Foreign secretary, 1924–29.

CHAMBERLAIN, GEORGE E. (1854–1928), Oregon Democratic senator, 1909–21.

CHINDBLOM, CARL RICHARD (1870–1956), Republican representative from Illinois, 1919–33.

CLANCY, ROBERT HENRY (1882–   ), Democratic and Republican representative from Michigan, 1923–26 and 1927–33, respectively.

CLAPP, MOSES EDWIN (1851–1931), Republican senator from Minnesota from 1901 to 1917.

CLARK, BENNETT CHAMP (1890–   ), Democratic senator from Missouri, 1933–45. Son of James Beauchamp (Champ) Clark. Biographer of John Quincy Adams.

CLARK, CLARENCE DON (1851–1930), Republican congressman from Wyoming, 1890–93. Senator, 1895–1917.

CLARK, E. S. (1862–   ), Arizona attorney. Territorial Attorney General, 1905–09.

CLARK, JAMES BEAUCHAMP (CHAMP) (1850–1921), Democratic representative from Missouri, 1897–1920. Speaker of the House under Woodrow Wilson. Defeated by Wilson in 1912 in race for Democratic Presidential nomination.

COCKRAN, WILLIAM BOURKE (1854–1923), Democratic representative from New York, 1887–89; 1891–95; 1904–09; 1921–23.

COLBY, BAINBRIDGE (1869–1950), Secretary of State in Wilson's Cabinet, March, 1920 to March, 1921.

COLLINS, MICHAEL (1890–1922), Irish politician, fighter for Irish freedom in the Sinn Fein, chief organizer of battle resulting in the breakdown of British government in Ireland. Assassinated after setting up the Free State with Arthur Griffith.

COLT, LE BARON BRADFORD (1846–1924), Republican senator from Rhode Island, 1913–24.

COLTON, HAROLD S. (1881–   ), Zoologist, archaeologist, author. Founder and retired director of the Museum of Northern Arizona.

CONKLING, ROSCOE (1829–1888), Republican representative and senator from New York in the years from 1859 to 1881. Appointed and confirmed as Associate Justice of Supreme Court, but did not accept.

CONNERY, WILLIAM PATRICK (1888–1937), Democratic representative from Massachusetts, 1923–37.

CONNOLLY, THOMAS TERRY (1877–   ), Democratic representative from Texas, 1917–29, and senator, 1928–53.

COOPER, HENRY ALLEN (1850–1931), Republican representative from Wisconsin, 1893–1919; 1921–31.

COPELAND, ROYAL SAMUEL (1868–1938), Democratic senator from New York, 1923–38.

CORCORAN, THOMAS (1900–   ), Assistant to Secretary of the Treasury, 1933; Special Assistant to the Attorney General of the United States, 1932–35.

CORWIN, THOMAS (1794–1865), Whig and Republican representative and senator from Ohio; U.S. Secretary of the Treasury from July, 1850 to March, 1853.

COSGRAVE, WILLIAM THOMAS (1880–   ), President of the Irish Free State executive council 1922–32, after the death of Arthur Griffith and Michael Collins.

COSTIGAN, EDWARD PRENTISS (1877–1939), Democratic senator from Colorado, 1931–37.

COUZENS, JAMES (1872–1936), Republican senator from Michigan, 1922–36.

COX, JAMES M. (1870–1957), Democratic Presidential nominee in 1920.

CREEL, GEORGE (1875–1953), Colorado editorial writer and politician who headed Committee on Information under Wilson and played major role in U.S. propaganda efforts during World War I.

CULBERSON, CHARLES ALLEN (1885–1925), Democratic Governor of Texas, 1894–98. U.S. senator, 1899–1923.

CULLOM, SHELBY M. (1829–1914), Republican representative from Illinois, 1865–71. Nominated General Grant for Presidency at the Republican National Convention in 1872. U.S. senator, 1883–1913.

CUMMINGS, HOMER S. (1870–1956), Attorney General of the United States from 1933 to 1939.

CUMMINS, ALBERT BAIRD (1850–1926), Republican senator from Iowa, from 1908 to 1926.

CURLEY, JAMES MICHAEL (1874–1958), Democratic representative from Massachusetts, 1911–14 and 1943–47.

CURTIS, CHARLES (1860–1936), Republican representative and senator from Kansas. Vice-President of the United States, 1929–33.

CUTTING, BRONSON (1888–1935), Republican senator from New Mexico, 1927–28; 1929–35.

DALE, PORTER HINMAN (1867–1933), Republican representative and senator from Vermont, 1915–23; 1923–33.

DANIELS, JOSEPHUS (1862–1948), Secretary of the Navy, 1913–18. U.S. ambassador to Mexico, 1933.

DAUGHERTY, HARRY M. (1860–1941), Directed Harding's Presidential campaign. Attorney-General, 1921–24. Biographer of Harding Administration.

DAULS, JAMES J. (1873–1947), Republican senator from Pennsylvania, 1921–30; Secretary of Labor, 1921–30; senator, 1930–45.

DAVIS, JEFF (1862–1913), Democratic senator from Arkansas, 1907–13.

DAVIS, JOHN W. (1873–1955), Democratic representative from West Virginia, 1911–13. Unsuccessful candidate for the Presidency of the United States in 1924.

DAWES, CHARLES G. (1865–1951), First director of the Bureau of the Budget, 1921–23, and Vice-President of the United States, 1924–28.

DE LESSUPS FERDINAND (1805–1894), French diplomat and engineer in charge of the construction of the Suez Canal. Also attempted a canal across the Isthmus of Panama, but was unsuccessful.

DENBY, EDWIN (1870–1929), Republican representative from Michigan, 1905–11; Secretary of the Navy, 1921–24.

DENEEN, CHARLES SAMUEL (1863–1940), Illinois Republican senator, 1925–31.

DENISON, EDWARD EVERETT (1874–1953), Republican representative from Illinois, 1915–31.

DEPEW, CHAUNCEY MITCHELL (1834–1928), Political orator and railroad official. Republican senator from New York, 1899–1911.

DERN, GEORGE HENRY (1872–1936), Democratic Governor of Utah, 1924–32. Secretary of War, 1933–36.

DEWEY, ADMIRAL GEORGE (1837–1917), American admiral and hero of the Battle of Manila.

DIAZ, VITTORIO (1861–1928), General, and Italian marshal in World War I. Rebuilt Italian army after the Battle of Caporetto.

DIETERICH, WILLIAM H. (1867–1940), Democratic representative from Illinois, 1931–33; senator, 1933–39.

DILL, CLARENCE CLEVELAND (1884–   ), Democratic representative from Washington, 1915–19; senator, 1923–35.

DILLINGHAM, WILLIAM PAUL (1843–1923), Republican Governor of Vermont, 1880–90. Elected to the United States Senate in 1900; served until time of his death.

DOE, EDWARD M. (1850–1919), First District Attorney of Coconino County, Arizona. Associate Justice of the Territorial Supreme Court of Arizona, 1909–12.

DOHENY, EDWARD L. (1856–1935), Oil industrialist credited with beginning the oil industry in Los Angeles in the 1890's.

DONOFRIO, HELEN (?–), Phoenix, Arizona-born coloratura soprano.

DOOLEY, DUNNE FINLEY PETER (1867–1936), American social and political commentator and humorist.

DOUGHTON, ROBERT LEE (1863–1954), Democratic representative from North Carolina, 1911.

DOUGLAS, JAMES S. (1837–1918), Developer of Copper Queen Mine in Bisbee and other mining interests in Southeastern Arizona. Father of Lewis Douglas.

DOUGLAS, LEWIS (1894–   ), Democratic representative from Arizona, 1927–33. Director of the Bureau of the Budget, 1933–34. U.S. ambassador to Britain, 1947–50.

DOUGLAS, STEPHEN A. (1813–61), Democratic representative from Illinois, 1843–47; senator, 1847–61. Democratic nominee for the Presidency, 1860.

DOUGLASS, ANDREW ELLICOTT (1867–   ), President of the University of Arizona, 1910–11. Founder of the science of dendrochronology, or research in tree-ring chronologies.

DRYDEN, ROBERT CRAIG (1857–?), Graham County physician and member of the Arizona Territorial Legislature, 1893–95.

DUPONT, THOMAS COLEMAN (1863–1928), Republican senator from Delaware, 1921–22; 1925–28.

EARHART, AMELIA (1898–1937), First woman aviator to fly alone across the Atlantic Ocean. She disappeared over the Pacific Ocean while attempting to fly around the world.

EDISON, THOMAS A. (1874–1931), American inventor and genius in the practical application of scientific principles. Among his inventions are the electric light, the phonograph, and talking pictures.

EDDY, NELSON (1901–   ), American singer and actor in motion pictures and radio.

EDWARDS, EDWARD IRVING (1863–1931), Democratic senator from New Jersey, 1923–29.

ELLINWOOD, EVERETT E. (1862–1943), Arizona newspaper owner and chief counsel for Phelps Dodge.

ELY, JOSEPH BUELL (1881–1956), Massachusetts Democratic Governor, 1931–35.

FAIRBANKS, CHARLES WARREN (1852–1918), Republican senator from Indiana. Vice-President under Theodore Roosevelt, 1905–09. Defeated Vice-Presidential candidate, 1916.

FALL, ALBERT BACON (1861–1944), Republican senator from New Mexico, 1912–21. Secretary of the Interior in Harding's Cabinet, but forced to resign in 1923 because of his part in the Teapot Dome scandal.

FARLEY, JAMES A. (1888–   ), American politician. Campaign manager for Franklin D. Roosevelt in 1932 and U.S. Postmaster General, 1933–40.

FARRINGTON, JOSEPH RIDER (1897–   ), Republican delegate from the Territory of Hawaii, 1943–49.

FAVOUR, ALPHEUS H. (1880–1939), Prescott attorney and banker. Authority on Colorado River water rights.

FESS, SIMEON DAVISON (1861–1936), Republican representative from Ohio, 1913–23; senator, 1923–35.

FISH, HAMILTON JR. (1888–   ), Republican representative from New York, 1920–45.

FLETCHER, DUNCAN UPSHAW (1859–1936), Democratic senator from Florida who served from 1909 to 1936.

FLOOD, HENRY D. (1865–1921), Virginia Democratic representative, 1901–21.

FLYNN, THOMAS A. (1872–1944), Flagstaff, Arizona attorney and U.S. Attorney from 1914 to 1922. An ardent Democrat.

FRANCE, JOSEPH IRVIN (1873–1939), Republican senator from Maryland, from 1917–23.

FRANK, GLENN (1887–1940), Magazine editor. President of the University of Wisconsin from 1925 to 1937.

FRAZIER, LYNN JOSEPH (1874–1947), Republican senator from North Dakota, 1923 to 1941.

FRÉMONT, JOHN C. (1813–1890), Western explorer, leader of expeditions in the 1840's. Aided Bear Flag Revolt in California in 1846. Promoted western railroads and became Governor of Arizona in 1878.

FUNSTON, FREDERICK, GENERAL (1865–1917), Congressional Medal of Honor winner in the Philippines during the Spanish-American War. Captured Aguinaldo, leader of the Filipino resistance to the United States. In command of border forces when Pershing led punitive expedition into Mexico.

GALLINGER, JACOB HAROLD (1837–1918), Republican representative from New Hampshire, 1885–89; senator, 1891–1918.

GARDNER, AUGUSTUS P. (1865–1918), Republican representative from Massachusetts, 1902–17, when he resigned to enter the U.S. Army.

GARLAND, HAMLIN (1860–1940), American novelist famous for his works on the Middle Border.

GARNER, JOHN NANCE (1868–   ), Democratic representative from Texas, 1903–33. Vice-President of the United States, 1933–41.

GARRISON, LINDLEY M. (1864–1932), Secretary of War during period prior to World War I.

GEDDES, AUCKLAND CAMPBELL (1879–1954), British politician and ambassador to the United States, 1920–24.

GEORGE, WALTER FRANKLIN (1878–1957), Democratic senator from Georgia, 1922 to 1957.

GERARD, JAMES W. (1867–1951), Corporation attorney elected to the New York Supreme Court in 1907, and in 1913 was made U.S. ambassador to Germany. With outbreak of World War I he was active in aiding individuals involved in wartime chaos. Leading candidate for Democratic Presidential nomination, 1920.

GERRY, ELBRIDGE (1744–1814), Anti-Federalist representative from Massachusetts, 1788 to 1793. Vice-President of the United States, 1813-14.

GERRY, PETER GOELET (1879–1957), Democratic representative from Rhode Island, 1913–15, 1917–29; senator, 1935–47.

GIBBONS, CARDINAL (1834–1921), Cardinal of Baltimore, 1887 until 1921. Believer in benefits of democracy for Catholic Church. Friend of Presidents Cleveland, Theodore Roosevelt, and Taft.

GIBSON, CHARLES DANA (1867–1944), American artist and illustrator. Creator of the "Gibson Girl."

GILLETTE, FREDERICK H. (1851–1935), Republican representative from Massachusetts, 1893–1925; senator, 1925–31.

GIRAND, JAMES B. (1873–1949), Texas-born engineer. As Territorial Engineer for Arizona, he designed the bridge across the Salt River at Tempe.

GLASS, CARTER (1858–1956), Democratic representative from Virginia, 1902–18; senator, 1920–46. Secretary of the Treasury in Wilson's Cabinet, 1918–20.

GLENN, OTIS FERGUSON (1879–   ), Republican senator from Illinois, 1928–33.

GOETHALS, GEORGE WASHINGTON (1858–1928), U.S. Army engineer in charge of the construction of the Panama Canal. As General of the Quartermaster Corps in World War I directed entire Army supply system.

GOFF, GUY D. (1866–1933), Republican senator from West Virginia, 1925–31.

GOFF, NATHAN (1843–1920), Republican representative from West Virginia, 1883–89; senator, 1913–19.

GOLDFOGLE, HENRY (1856–1929), Democratic representative from New York, 1901–15, 1919–21.

GOODING, FRANK ROBERT (1859–1928), Republican senator from Idaho, 1921–28.

GORE, THOMAS PRYOR (1870–1949), Democratic senator from Oklahoma, 1907–21; 1936–49.

GOULD, JAY (1830–1892), Early associate of Daniel Drew and James Fisk in manipulation of Erie Railroad stocks. Led attempt to corner gold market in 1869 (Black Friday). Controlled half of the railroad mileage in the Southwest, and the Western Union.

GREELY, ADOLPHUS W. (1844–1935), American soldier and explorer of the far north.

GREELEY, HORACE (1811–1872), American newspaperman and politician. Founder of the *New York Tribune,* Presidential candidate of the liberal Republican and Democratic parties in 1872.

GREENE, FRANK LESTER (1870–1930), Republican representative from Vermont, 1912–23 and senator, 1923–30.

GREENWAY, JOHN G. GENERAL (1872–1926), Arizona mining engineer who developed the New Cornelia Mines at Ajo, Arizona, and several other mines.

GREW, JOSEPH (1880–   ), U.S. ambassador to Japan prior to World War II, 1931–41.

GREY, VISCOUNT (1862–1933), Member of Parliament for 31 years. Foreign Secretary from 1905 to 1916. Advocate of a strong entente wtih France.

GRIFFIN, APPLETON P. C. (1852–1926), American librarian and bibliographer. Chief bibliographer of the Library of Congress, 1900–08. Chief assistant Librarian of Congress, 1908–26.

GRIFFITH, ARTHUR (1872–1922), Irish Nationalist leader elected Vice-President of the Irish Republic, 1919, and President, 1921.

GRONNA, ASLE JORGENSON (1858–1922), Republican representative from North Dakota, 1905–11; and senator, 1911–21.

GUFFEY, JOSEPH F. (1870–1959), Pennsylvania Democratic senator, 1935–47.

HAIG, DOUGLAS, FIRST EARL (1861–1928), Marshal in the Boer War, distinguished in battle on several occasions. Commanded First Army Corps in 1914, serving throughout World War I.

HALE, FREDERICK (1874–   ), Republican senator from Maine, 1917–41.

HALL, SHARLOT (1870–1953), Early historian and "poet-laureate" of Arizona.

HALSEY, THOMAS JEFFERSON (1863–1951), Republican representative from Missouri, 1929–31.

HARDWICK, THOMAS WILLIAM (1872–1944), Democratic representative from Georgia, 1903–14; senator, 1914–19.

HARRELD, JOHN W. (1872–1950), Republican representative from Oklahoma, 1919–21; senator, 1921–27.

HANNA, MARCUS ALONZO (1837–1904), Republican senator from Ohio, 1898–1904. Credited with great power during the McKinley Administration.

HARRISON, BYRON PATTON (1881–1941), Democratic representative from Mississippi, 1911–18; senator, 1911–18 and 1919–41.

HASTINGS, DANIEL OREN (1874–   ), Delware Republican senator, 1928–37.

HATCH, CARL A. (1889–   ), Democratic senator from New Mexico, 1933–49.

HAWES, HARRY B. (1860–1947), Democratic representative from Missouri, 1921–26; senator, 1926–33.

HAY, JOHN BREESE (1834–1916), Republican representative from Illinois, 1869–73.

HAYDEN, CARL (1877–   ), Arizonan, and senior member of U.S. Senate, Chairman of Senate Appropriations Committee. Held seat in House from 1912 when Arizona became a state to 1927 when he was elected to the Senate.

HAYES, PATRICK CARDINAL (1867–1938), Catholic leader of social and industrial reform. Bishop of armed forces during World War I.

HERBERT FELIX (1874–   ), Republican senator from Rhode Island, 1929–35.

HEFLIN, JAMES THOMAS (1869–1951), Democratic representative from Alabama, 1904–20; senator, 1920–31.

HENDERSON, CHARLES BELKNAP (1873–1954), Democratic senator from Nevada, 1918–21.

HEYBURN, WELDON BRINTON (1852–1912), Republican senator from Idaho, 1903–12.

HICKOK, "WILD BILL" (James Butler), (1837–1876), Frontiersman, scout, U.S. Marshal, and one-time showman with William "Buffalo Bill" Cody. Murdered in Deadwood, Dakota Territory.

HICKS, FREDERICK L. (1872–1925), Republican representative from New York, 1915–23.

HITCHCOCK, GILBERT M. (1859–1934), Democratic representative from Nebraska, 1903–05, 1907–11; senator, 1911–23.

HOGAN, FRANK J. (1877–1944), Washington, D.C. attorney distinguished for successful defense of individuals in suits brought by the federal government. Shakespearean authority and collector of rare books.

HOLLIS, HENRY FRENCH (1869–1949), Democratic senator from New Hampshire, 1913–19.

HOUSTON, DAVID FRANKLIN (1866–1940), President of Texas A & M. Secretary of Agriculture in President Wilson's Cabinet, 1912–20; Secretary of the Treasury, 1920–21.

HOUSE, EDWARD MANDELL (1858–1938), A Texas colonel. Adviser to President Wilson, 1912–19. Wilson and House split over the Versailles Treaty when Colonel House advised Wilson to compromise with the mild-revisionists in the Senate.

HOWELL, ROBERT BEECHER (1864–1933), Republican senator from Nebraska, 1923–33.

HOWLAND, LEONARD PAUL (1865–1942), Republican representative from Ohio, 1907–13.

HUBBARD, ELBERT (1859–1915), Founder, author, and editor of *The Philistine,* "a magazine of protest." Illinois native and founder of Roycroft Shop, East Aurora, New York.

HUGHES, JAMES H. (1867–1953), Democratic senator from Delaware, 1937–42.

HULL, CORDELL (1871–1955), Democratic representative from Tennessee, 1907–21, 1923–31; senator, 1931–33; Secretary of State, 1933–44.

HUNT, GEORGE WYLIE PAUL (1859–1934), First governor of the state of Arizona. Re-elected seven times. Formerly member of Territorial House and Senate. Appointed Minister to Siam in 1920.

HUSTING, PAUL O. (1866–1917), Democratic senator from Wisconsin, 1915–17.

ICKES, HAROLD LE CLAIRE (1874–1952), Secretary of the Interior, 1933–46.

INGALLS, JOHN J. (1833–1900), Republican senator from Kansas, 1873–91.

INGERSOLL, ROBERT G. (1833–1899), New York-born attorney, prominent in Illinois law and politics and famed as an orator for his agnostic speculation on Christian belief. Coined the term "Plumed Knight" for James G. Blaine in memorable Republican nomination speech.

IVES, EUGENE S. (1859–1917), Council member of Twenty-First and Twenty-Second Territorial Legislatures of Arizona.

JAMES, OLLIE MURRAY (1871–1918), Democratic representative from Kentucky, 1903–13; senator, 1913–18.

JELLICOE, JOHN (1859–1935), British admiral largely responsible for combating the German submarine campaign in World War I.

JENNINGS, RENZ (1896–   ), Elected Justice of the Arizona Supreme Court November 8, 1960. Took office December 12, 1960.

JOFFRE, MARSHAL (1852–1931), Marshal of France in World War I. Responsible for halting the Germans and saving Paris. Became Commander of the French forces on Western Front in 1914. In 1916 became technical adviser and chairman of Allied War Council.

JOHNSON, CHARLES FLETCHER (1859–1930), Democratic senator from Maine, 1911–17.

JOHNSON, HIRAM WARREN (1866–1945), Republican senator from California, 1917–45. Vice-Presidential nominee of Progressive Party in 1912. Republican candidate in 1924. Isolationist in two world wars.

JOHNSON, HUGH S. (1882–1942), American government administrator and soldier. Headed Selective Service in World War I and National Recovery Administration, 1933–34.

JOHNSON, MAGNUS (1871–1936), Farmer-Labor senator and representative from Minnesota. Served in the Senate, 1923–25; in the House, 1933–35.

JOHNSTON, JOSEPH FORNEY (1843–1913), Democratic senator from Alabama, 1907–13.

JONES, HOMER RAYMOND (1893–   ), Republican representative from Washington, 1947–49.

JONES, J. E. (1872–1929), First probate judge of Coconino County, Arizona. Also judge of Superior Court, 1918–29. One-time owner of the *Flagstaff Gem*, newspaper.

JONES, WESLEY LIVSEY (1863–1932), Republican representative from Washington, 1899–1909; senator, 1909–32.

JONES, WILEY EMMET (1856–1924), Democratic attorney from Graham County; Arizona Attorney General, 1914–21.

JUSSERAND, JEAN (1855–1932), French author and diplomat. French ambassador to the United States, 1902–25.

KELLOGG, FRANK BILLINGS (1856–1937), Republican senator from Minnesota, 1917–23. Secretary of State, 1925–29. Awarded the Nobel Peace Prize in 1929 for the Kellogg-Briand Pact. Judge of the Permanent Court of International Justice.

KELLY, GEORGE H. (1854–1929), Arizona State Historian, 1923–29. Formerly newspaperman with *Arizona Daily Star* and *Tucson Citizen*. At various times owner of *Valley Bulletin*, Clifton; *Bisbee Daily Review*, and *Douglas International*. Started *Arizona Historical Review* in 1928.

KENDRICK, JOHN BENJAMIN (1857–1933), Democratic senator from Wyoming, 1917–33.

KENYON, WILLIAM SQUIRE (1869–1933), Republican senator from Iowa, 1911–22. Resigned to become judge of the U.S. Circuit Court of Appeals, Eighth Circuit.

KERENSKY, ALEXANDER (1881–   ), Headed Russian provisional government from July to November, 1917, after playing prominent role in overthrowal of Czarist regime. Fled the Bolshevist onset and lives in California.

KERN, JOHN WORTH (1849–1917), Democratic senator from Indiana, 1911–17. Ran with Bryan for Vice-President, 1908.

KIBBEY, JOSEPH (1853–1924), Territorial Governor of Arizona. Attorney General, legislator, author of Kibbey Decision pertaining to water appropriation rights.

KING, ISABELLA GREENWAY (1886–1953), Democratic representative from Arizona, 1933–37.

KING, WILLIAM HENRY (1863–1949), Democratic representative from Utah, 1897–98; senator, 1916–41.

KIRBY, WILLIAM FOSGATE (1867–1934), Democratic senator from Arkansas, 1916–21.

KITCHEN, CLAUDE (1869–1923), Democratic representative from North Carolina, 1901–23.

KITCHENER, HORATIO HERBERT (1850–1916), First Earl. British statesman and military leader of British imperial expansion. Fought in Boer War and as Commander-in-Chief in India, 1902–09. Head of War Office, 1914.

KLUCK, ALEXANDER VON (1846–1934), German general in World War I. Took part in Battle of the Marne.

KNAPP, CLEON T. (1882–1953), Tucson attorney. Member Arizona Board of Regents, 1940–51.

KNEIPP, LEON F. (1880–   ), U.S. Forest Ranger in Arizona, 1900–04. Forest Supervisor in New Mexico, 1905–07. At time of retirement, 1946, assistant chief, Branch of Grazing, U.S. Forest Service.

KNOX, PHILANDER C. (1853–1921), Republican senator from Pennsylvania, 1904–09, 1917–21. U.S. Attorney General, 1901–04; Secretary of State, 1909–13.

KOSTERLITZKY, EMILIO (1852–1928), Commander of Mexican *rurales* who served to enforce will of Porfirio Diaz as president of Mexico. Played large part in putting down Cananea riots, 1906. In 1912 surrendered to Americans rather than be taken by Carranza and Villa. Later served U.S. Department of Justice.

LA FOLLETTE, ROBERT MARION (1855–1925), Republican representative from Wisconsin, 1885–91; senator, 1906–25. Unsuccessful candidate of Progressive Party for Presidency, 1924. Author of "Wisconsin Idea" for tax reform, railroad rate control, and direct primary.

LA FOLLETTE, ROBERT JR. (1895–1953), Progressive Repblican senator from Wisconsin, 1924–47.

LA GUARDIA, FIORELLO H. (1882–1947), Republican and Socialist representative from New York, 1923–33. Mayor of New York City, 1934–45.

LANE, FRANKLIN K. (1864–1921), Secretary of the Interior from 1913–20.

LANE, HARRY (1855–1917), Democratic senator from Oregon, 1913–17.

LANEY, LYNN M. (1883–   ), Phoenix attorney, currently head of the Arizona State Board of Regents.

LANSING, ROBERT (1864–1928), Authority on international law, U.S. counsel in Bering Sea and Alaska boundary disputes. Secretary of State in Wilson's Cabinet, World War I.

LARRATOLO, OCTAVIANO A. (1859–1930), Republican senator from New Mexico, 1928–29.

LAURENS, HENRY (1724–1792), South Carolina member of the First Provincial Congress, January, 1775, president of the Congress. Delegate to the Continental Congress, 1777. Minister to Holland, 1779, captured enroute, imprisoned in Tower of London. Released in exchange for Lord Cornwallis, Peace Commissioner to Paris Peace Conference.

LEA, LUKE (1879–1945), Democratic senator from Tennessee, 1911–17. Organized First Tennessee Field Artillery which he commanded in France.

LENROOT, IRVINE L. (1869–1949), Republican representative from Wisconsin, 1909–18; senator, 1918–27.

LEWIS, ERNEST WILLIAM (1875–1927), Republican lawyer and judge. Resident of Phoenix, Arizona.

LEWIS, JAMES HAMILTON (1863–1939), Democratic representative from Washington, 1897–99; senator from Illinois, 1913–19 and 1930–39.

LEWIS, SINCLAIR (1885–1951), American social critic and author of such novels as *Main Street, Arrowsmith, Elmer Gantry,* etc. Winner of Nobel Prize for literature in 1930.

LINDBERGH, CHARLES A. (1902–   ), American aviator who made first non-stop trans-Atlantic solo flight.

LING, DAVID W. (1890–   ), Judge of the Superior Court, Greenlee County, Arizona. Appointed by F. D. R. to U.S. District Court.

LING, REESE M. (1866–1916), First graduate of Arizona Normal School at Tempe, 1885; assistant U.S. Attorney, 1896. Defeated as Democratic candidate for United States Senate, 1911.

LINNEY, H. H. (?–?), Prescott lawyer and Speaker of the House in the special session of the First Arizona Legislature.

LITVINOFF, MAXIM (1876–1951), Russian politician and Soviet foreign minister, 1930–39.

LIVERPOOL, LORD (1770–1828), British Prime Minister, 1812–27.

LLOYD GEORGE, DAVID (1863–1945), Elected to Parliament as Liberal candidate in 1898. Became Chancellor of the Exchequer in 1908, Prime Minister of England in 1916. Took part in making of Versailles Treaty, 1919, resigned as Prime Minister in 1922. Active in Parliament and opponent of appeasement of Germany preceding World War II.

LODGE, HENRY CABOT (1850–1924), Republican representative from Massachusetts, 1887–93; senator, 1893–1924.

LOGAN, MARVEL (1875–1939), Democratic senator from Kentucky, 1931–39.

LONG, HUEY PIERCE (1893–1935), Governor of Louisiana, Democratic senator from 1932–35, a ruthless demagogue whose goal was the Presidency. Assassinated at Baton Rouge, 1935.

LONGWORTH, NICHOLAS (1869–1931), Republican representative from Ohio, 1903–13; 1915–31.

LEE, ARTHUR HAMILTON (Lord of Fareham), (1868–1947), British politician during World War I.

LORIMER, WILLIAM (1861–1934), Republican representative from Illinois, 1895–1901, 1903–09; senator, 1909–12, when his election was declared invalid by a Senate ruling that "corrupt methods and practices were employed in his election."

LOUD, GEORGE A. (1852–1925), Republican congressman from Michigan, 1903–13, 1915–17.

MC ADOO, WILLIAM GIBBS (1863–1941), Wilson's Secretary of the Treasury, 1913–18; Director-General of the Railroads. Contender for Democratic Presidential nomination, 1920 and 1924. Democratic senator from California, 1933–39.

MC ALLISTER, WARD (1827–1895), New York society leader who chose the original "Four Hundred" elite.

MC CARRAN, PATRICK A. (1876–1954), Nevada Democratic senator, 1932–57.

MC CLINTOCK, JAMES HARVEY (1864–1934), Arizona historian, newspaper editor, and politician.

MC CLUSKEY, HENRY S. (1887–?), Phoenix, Arizona attorney and one-time member of the State Board of Regents; Secretary to Governor Hunt.

MC CORMICK, MEDILL (1877–1925), Republican representative from Illinois, 1917–19; senator, 1919–25.

MC CULLOCH, ROSCOE C. (1880–1958), Republican representative from Ohio, 1915–21; senator, 1929–30.

MC CUMBER, PORTER JAMES (1858–1933), Republican senator from North Dakota, 1899–1923.

MC DONALD, J. RAMSEY (1866–1927), British Labor leader and Prime Minister of England, 1929–31. Leader of "The Great Betrayal."

MC GILL, GEORGE (1879–   ), Democratic senator from Kansas, 1930–39. Philadelphia-born Congressman from California, 1885–92. Attorney-General, 1897–98, and Supreme Court Justice, 1898–1926. Noted for conservative judgements.

MC KINLEY, WILLIAM BROWN (1856–1926), Republican representative and senator from Illinois. Served in the House, 1905–13, 1915–21; and in the Senate, 1921–26.

MC LEAN, GEORGE PAYNE (1857–1932), Republican senator from Connecticut, 1911–28.

MC MASTER, WILLIAM HENRY (1877–   ), Republican senator from South Dakota, 1925–31.

MC NARY, CHARLES L. (1874–1944), Republican senator from Oregon, 1918–44. Unsuccessful candidate for Vice-President on the Republican ticket, 1940.

MC REYNOLDS, JAMES CLARK (1862–1946), United States Attorney General, 1913–14, and Associate Justice of the U.S. Supreme Court, 1914–41.

MALONE, WALTER (1866–1915), Mississippian who became a New York attorney and literary man, especially interested in poetry.

MANN, JAMES ROBERTS (1856–1922), Republican representative from Illinois, 1897–1922.

MARCH, PEYTON CONWAY (1864–1955), Chief of Staff, U.S. Army, 1918–21.

MARKHAM, EDWIN (1852–1940), Poet, Oregon-born, California school principal and rancher until 1899 when he devoted full time to writing and lecturing. His famous works include "The Man With the Hoe," "Ballad of the Gallows Bird," "Lincoln and Other Poems."

MARLEY, JOHN W. (?–?), Operator of Flying V Ranch in the White Mountains of Arizona.

MARSHALL, THOMAS RILEY (1854–1925), Vice-President of the United States, 1912–20.

MARTIN, THOMAS STAPLES (1847–1919), Democratic senator from Virginia, 1895–1919.

MARTINE, JAMES E. (1850–1925), New Jersey Democratic senator, 1911–17.

MASON, WILLIAM ERNEST (1850–1921), Republican representative from Illinois, 1887–91; senator, 1897–1903; representative again, 1917–21.

MATHEWS, WILLIAM R. (1893–   ), Co-owner and editor of *The Arizona Daily Star* in Tucson.

MAXIMILIAN, PRINCE OF BADEN (1867–1929), From 1907–18, president of the First Chamber of Baden Diet. In 1918 appointed imperial chancellor. Initiated negotiations for the armistice and declared abdication of Kaiser Wilhelm, November 9.

MAYER, LOUIS B. (1885–1957), Movie producer and president of Metro-Goldwyn-Mayer.

MEANS, GASTON B. (1879–1938), Aided the Germans in learning about Allied purchasing and shipping in World War I. Claimed to have contacted kidnappers of Lindbergh child. Thereafter jailed for 15 years for grand larceny.

MELLON, ANDREW WILLIAM (1855–1937), Industrialist and Secretary of the Treasury. Donor of National Gallery of Art, Washington, D.C.

MERCIER, CARDINAL DESIRÉ (1851–1926), Belgian priest famous for pastoral letter, "Patriotism and Endurance," issued early in World War I, condemning the burning of Louvain. Resisted Germans publicly. Became Cardinal in 1907.

MEREDITH, EDWIN T. (1876–1928), American journalist. Secretary of Agriculture during President Wilson's last year in office.

MILLS, OGDEN L. (1884–1937), Republican representative from New York, 1921–27. Undersecretary of the Treasury, 1927–32, Secretary of the Treasury, 1932–33.

MOEUR, BENJAMIN BAKER (Doctor), (1869–1937), Democratic Governor of Arizona, 1933–36.

MOLEY, RAYMOND (1886–   ), Early New Dealer. One of advisers known as F.D.R.'s "brain-trust."

MONTAGUE, ANDREW JACKSON (1862–1937), Democratic representative from Virginia, 1913–37.

MORLEY, SIR JOHN (1838–1928), Prominent British Liberal and pacifist who resigned from the Cabinet with the outbreak of World War I.

MORROW, DWIGHT WHITNEY (1873–1931), American banker and diplomat. Served in Senate, 1930–31. Highly successful ambassador to Mexico, 1927–30.

MOSES, GEORGE HIGGINS (1869–1944), Republican senator from New Hampshire, 1918–33.

MURPHY, FRANK (1890–1949), Governor General of the Philippines, 1935–36; U.S. Attorney General, 1939–40; Associate Justice of the U.S. Supreme Court, 1940–49.

MYERS, HENRY LEE (1862–1943), Democratic senator from Montana, 1911–23.

NAVE, FREDERICK S. (1873–1912), District Attorney of Santa Cruz County, 1900. U.S. District Attorney, 1902–05; Justice of the Supreme Court of the Territory, 1906–09; president of Arizona State Bar Association at the time of his death.

NEELY, MATTHEW MANSFIELD (1874–1958), Democratic representative from West Virginia, 1913–21, 1945–47; senator, 1923–29, 1931–41, 1949–55.

NELSON, KNUTE (1843–1923), Republican congressman from Minnesota, 1883–89, 1893–95; senate, 1895–1923.

NEW, HARRY STEWART (1858–1937), Republican senator from Indiana, 1917–23. Postmaster General in Cabinets of Harding and Coolidge.

NEWBERRY, TRUMAN HARDY (1864–1945), Republican senator from Michigan, 1919–22. Secretary of the Navy, 1908–09.

NEWLANDS, FRANCIS GRIFFITH (1848–1917), Democratic representative, 1893–1903; senator, 1903–17.

NORBECK, PETER (1870–1936), Republican senator from South Dakota, 1921–36.

NORRIS, GEORGE WILLIAM (1861–1944), Republican representative from Nebraska, 1903–13; senator, 1913–42.

NORTHCLIFFE, LORD (Fred Charles William Hornsworth), (1865–1922), British journalist.

NUGENT, JOHN FROST (1868–1931), Democratic senator from Idaho, 1918–21.

NYE, GERALD PRENTICE (1892–   ), Republican senator from North Dakota, 1925–45.

OBREGÓN, ALVARO (1880–1928), Mexican general who became President in 1920 after death of Carranza. Re-elected, but assassinated in 1928.

O'CONNELL, DANIEL (1775–1847), Fought for repeal of laws placing civil disabilities on Catholics. In 1829 became leader of Irish party in House of Commons. In 1842 began agitation for separation from England.

O'CONNER, JUDGE W. A. (1863–1933), Judge of Superior Court, Santa Cruz County, Arizona, 1913–33; county attorney, 1906–12.

ODDIE, TASKER LOWNDES (1870–1950), Nevada Republican senator, 1919–33.

O'GORMAN, JAMES ALOYSIUS (1860–1943), Democratic senator from New York, 1911–17.

O'MAHONEY, JOSEPH C. (1884–   ), Democratic senator from Wyoming, 1934.

O'NEILL, EUGENE BRADY (1869–1917), Democratic representative from Maricopa County to Twenty-Fourth and Twenty-Fifth Territorial Legislative councils.

ORME, JOHN (1852–1936), Arizona pioneer who arrived in the Phoenix area around 1880.

OSBORN, SIDNEY PRESTON (1884–1948), Democratic Governor of Arizona from 1941–48.

OVERMAN, LEE SLATER (1854–1930), Democratic senator from North Carolina, 1903–30.

OWEN, ROBERT LATHAM (1856–1947), Oklahoma Democratic senator, 1907–25.

OWEN, RUTH BRYAN (1885–1954), Democratic representative from Florida, 1929–32.

PAGE, CARROLL S. (1830–1925), Republican Governor of Vermont, 1890–92. U. S. senator, 1908–23.

PARSONS, ALBERT F. (1852–?), Representative to 1910 Constitutional Convention from Cochise County, Arizona.

PATTERSON, ROSCOE C. (1876–   ), Republican representative from Missouri, 1921–23; senator, 1929–35.

PARNELL, CHARLES S. (1846–1891), Irish Nationalist leader.

PENROSE, BOIES (1860–1921), Republican senator from Pennsylvania, 1897–1921.

PERKINS, FRANCES (1882–   ), Secretary of Labor in F.D.R.'s Cabinet, 1933–45. First woman Cabinet member.

PERKINS, GEORGE CLEMENT (1839–1923), Republican senator from California, 1893–1915.

PERRIN, E. B. DR. (?-?), Involved in land grant cases of Babocomari, Arizona in 1920's.

PHELAN, JAMES DUVAL (1861–1930), California Democratic senator, 1915–21.

PHILLIPS, JOHN C. (1870–1943), Republican Governor of Arizona, 1928–30.

PINCHOT, GIFFORD (1865–1946), First head of U.S. Forest Service, 1905. Worked for conservation during Theodore Roosevelt's two terms, and after break with Taft aided in organizing the Progressive Party. Governor of Pennsylvania, 1922-26. Re-elected in 1930.

PIRTLE, ELMO (1868–1922), Real estate developer in Douglas, Arizona, area.

PITTMAN, KEY (1872–1940), Democratic senator from Nevada, 1913–40.

POINDEXTER, MILES (1868–1946), Republican senator and representative from Washington, 1909–11, 1911–23.

POMERENE, ATLEE (1863–1937), Democratic senator from Ohio, 1911–23.

POU, EDWARD WILLIAM (1853–1934), Democratic representative from North Carolina, 1901–34.

POWELL, WILLIAM DEMPSEY (1846–1936), Rancher in Flagstaff area who in 1885 helped build the Opera House and later the Flagstaff Teachers' College.

QUEZÓN, MANUEL LUIS (1878–1944), First President of the Philippine Commonwealth, 1935–44.

RAINEY, HENRY T. (1860–1934), Democratic representative from Illinois, 1903–21, 1923–34.

RAKER, JOHN EDWARD (1863–1926), Democratic representative from California, 1911–26.

RALSTON, SAMUEL MOFFETT (1875–1925), Democratic senator from Indiana, 1923–25.

RANKIN, JEANNETTE (1880–   ), Republican representative from Montana, 1917–19, 1941–43. First woman elected to the House of Representatives.

RASKOB, JOHN JAKOB (1879–1950), New York financier and chairman of Democratic National Committee, 1928.

RASPUTIN, GREGORY (1871–1916), A peasant monk, who through apparent uncanny ability to heal the heir to the Russian throne, gained great influence over Nicholas II and the Court. His interference in state affairs during World War I led to his assassination in 1916.

RAYBURN, SAM (1882–1961), Democratic representative from Texas, 1913 until his death. Served as Speaker of the House during several sessions of Congress.

RAYNER, ISIDOR (1850–1912), Democratic representative from Maryland, 1887–89, 1891–95; Senate, 1905 until his death.

REDFIELD, WILLIAM COX (1858–1932), Congressman from New York; Secretary of Commerce in Wilson's Cabinet, 1913.

REED, DAVID AIKEN (1880–1953), Republican senator from Pennsylvania, 1922–35.

REED, JAMES ALEXANDER (1861–1944), Democratic senator from Missouri, 1911–29.

RHODE, J. P. (?–?), Arizona rancher who shot and killed his brother-in-law, Lee Murphy, after a misunderstanding. Convicted and sentenced to prison for twenty years for second-degree murder.

RINEHART, MARY ROBERTS (1876–1958), American mystery story writer and playwright.

RIORDAN, MICHAEL J. (1865–1930), Flagstaff, Arizona businessman and Democratic representative from Coconino County to Twenty-First Legislature. Student of Catholic literature and philosophy.

RIORDAN, TIMOTHY A. (1858–1946), Flagstaff businessman, president of Central Arizona Railroad Company, Flagstaff Electric Light Company, and principal stockholder of the Howard Sheep Company.

RITCHIE, ALBERT C. (1876–1936), Governor of Maryland, 1920–35. Former professor of law at University of Maryland and practicing attorney.

ROBERTSON, ALICE MARY (1854–1931), Republican representative from Oklahoma, 1921–23.

ROBINSON, JOSEPH TAYLOR (1872–1937), Democratic senator and representative from Arkansas, 1903–37. Minority leader, 1923–33, majority leader, 1933–37. Democratic candidate for Vice-President in 1928.

ROCKEFELLER, JOHN D. JR. (1874–1960), American oil millionaire and philanthropist. Financed the restoration of colonial Williamsburg.

RODENBERG, WILLIAM AUGUST (1865–1937), Republican representative from Illinois 1899–1901, 1903–13, 1915–23.

ROGERS, JOHN JACOB (1881–1925), Republican representative from Massachusetts, 1913–25.

ROLPH, JAMES (1869–1934), Republican Governor of California, 1931–34.

ROOT, ELIHU (1945–1937), New York Republican who was Secretary of War, 1899–1904, and Secretary of State, 1905–09. Served one term in Senate. Awarded Nobel Peace Prize, 1912 for work in International Law.

ROPER, DANIEL C. (1867–1943), Secretary of Commerce from 1933–38.

ROSEBERRY, ARCHIBALD, P. P. (1847–1929), Leader of English Liberals in the early twentieth century.

ROSS, HENRY D. (1861–1945), Justice of the Arizona Supreme Court, 1912–45.

SANGUINETTI, E. F. (1867–1945), Pioneer Yuma, Arizona merchant.

SAPP, SIDNEY (1868–1938), Holbrook, Arizona lawyer and newspaperman. Judge of Navajo County Superior Court, 1911–19.

SAULSBURY, WILLARD (1861–1927), Democratic senator from Delaware, 1913–19.

SAWTELLE, WILLIAM H. (?–1934), U.S. District Court judge from Arizona, 1931–34.

SCOPES, JOHN T. (1901–   ), Tennessee biology teacher whose teaching of evolution resulted in the Scopes Trial of 1925.

SHAFROTH, JOHN FRANKLIN (1854–1922), Republican representative from Colorado, 1895–97, Democratic representative, 1897–1904; Democratic senator, 1913–1919.

SHANTZ, HOMER LE ROY (1876–1958), Distinguished soil and plant scientist who was president of the University of Arizona, 1928–36. Later became Chief, Division of Wildlife Management, Forest Service; principal investigator, African Expedition, 1956–57; honorary president, International Botanical Congress, Stockholm, 1950.

SHAW, GEORGE BERNARD (1856–1950), Irish-born British critic, playwright, and pamphleteer. Socialist, and founder of Fabian Society.

SHEPPARD, MORRIS (1875–1941), Democratic representative from Texas, 1902–13; senator, 1913–41.

SHERMAN, JAMES S. (1855–1912), Republican representative, 1887–91, 1893–1909. Re-elected Vice-President of the United States, 1908. Renominated in 1912, but died before the election.

SHIELDS, JOHN KNIGHT (1858–1934), Tennessee Democratic senator, 1913–25.

SHIPSTEAD, HENRIK (1881–1960), Farm-Labor and Republican senator from Minnesota, 1923–47.

SHIVELY, BENJAMIN FRANKLIN (1857–1916), National anti-monopolist member of House, 1884–85, Democratic representative, 1887–93, U.S. senator, 1909 until his death.

SHORTRIDGE, SAMUEL M. (1861–1932), Republican senator from California, 1921–33.

SIMMONS, FURNIFOLD MC LENDEL (1854–1940), Democratic representative from North Carolina, 1887–89; senator, 1901–31.

SIMON, SIR JOHN (1873–1954), Leader of British Liberal National party, 1930–40, Home Secretary, 1915–16, Foreign Secretary, 1931, Home Secretary, 1935–37, Chancellor of the Exchequer, 1937–40, Lord Chancellor, 1940–45.

SINCLAIR, HARRY (1876–1956), Involved in the Teapot Dome oil lease scandals during the Harding Administration. Convicted.

SINNOTT, NICHOLAS JOHN (1870–1929), Republican representative from Oregon, 1913–28.

SLOAN, RICHARD E. (1857–1933), Associate Justice of the Arizona Territory Supreme Court, 1888–94, 1897–1908. Territorial Governor, 1909–12. Appointed by President Taft as U.S. District Judge for Arizona, but his appointment not ratified by the Senate.

SMITH, ADDISON TAYLOR (1862–1956), Republican representative from Idaho, 1913–33.

SMITH, ALFRED E. (1873–1944), Democratic Governor of New York, 1918–20, 1922–28. Democratic nominee for the Presidency, 1928.

SMITH, ELLISON DURANT (1866–1944), Democratic senator from South Carolina, 1909–44.

SMITH, GEORGE (1870–1937), Mayor of Tucson, 1931–33.

SMITH, HOKE (1855–1931), Democratic senator from Georgia, 1911–21. Secretary of Interior in Cleveland's Cabinet, 1893–96.

SMITH, LOTT (1830–1892), Pioneer Mormon settler and prominent religious leader in Arizona.

SMITH, MARCUS A. (1851–1924), Longtime Arizona Territorial delegate to Congress; U.S. senator, 1912–1920. From then until his death served on International Joint Commission on use of boundary waters.

SMITH, WILLIAM ALDEN (1859–1932), Republican representative from Michigan, 1895–1907. Senator, 1907–19.

SMOOT, REED (1862–1941), Republican senator from Utah, 1903–33.

SMUTS, JAN CHRISTIAN (1870–1950), Leader of the Boers, highly skilled general in Boer war and prominent organizer of Union of South Africa. Loyal to England in World War I. Prime Minister of South Africa and among organizers of United Nations after World War II. Delegate to first meeting of UN at San Francisco.

SPENCER, SELDEN PALMER (1862–1925), Republican senator from Missouri, 1918–25.

STANFIELD, ROBERT NELSON (1877–1945), Republican senator from Oregon, 1921–27.

STEINER, FREDERICK (1883–1939), Republican senator from Oregon, 1926–38.

STEPHENSON, ISAAK (1829–1918), Republican representative from Wisconsin, 1883–89, senator, 1907–15.

STERLING, THOMAS (1851–1930), South Dakota Republican senator, 1913–25.

STIMSON, HENRY LEWIS (1867–1950), Secretary of War, 1911–13, 1940–45; Secretary of State, 1929–33.

STONE, WILLIAM JOEL (1848–1918), Democratic representative from Missouri, 1885–91, senator, 1903–18. Chairman of Senate Committee on Foreign Relations.

SUMNER, CHARLES (1811–1874), Free-Soil and Republican senator from Massachusetts, 1851–74. From 1857 on, a Republican. Caned by Representative Brooks of South Carolina.

SUMNERS, HATTON WILLIAM (1875–   ), Democratic representative from Texas, 1913–47.

SUN YAT SEN (1866–1925), Chinese Republican leader who led the successful revolt against the Manchu Empire.

SWANSON, CLAUDE AUGUSTUS (1862–1939), Representative from Virginia, 1893–1906, senator, 1910–1933 when he resigned to become Secretary of the Navy in F.D.R.'s Cabinet.

SWING, PHILIP D. (1884   ), Republican representative from California, 1921–33.

TALLY, ROBERT EMMET (1877–1936), President and general manager of United Verde Copper Company in Arizona; Chancellor, University of Arizona.

TAYLOR, ROBERT L. (1850–1912), Democratic representative from Tennessee, 1879–81, senator, 1907 until his death. Was Governor of Tennessee from 1887–91 and 1891 to 1899.

THOMAS, CHARLES SPAULDING (1849–1934), Democratic senator from Colorado, 1913–21.

THOMAS, JOHN WILLIAM ELMER (1876–   ), Democratic representative from Oklahoma, 1923–27, senator, 1926–51.

THOMPSON, MARK BAIRD (1881–1941), Phoenix, Arizona attorney who defended Albert Fall during Teapot Dome scandals and ensuing trial.

THOMPSON, WILLIAM HOWARD (1871–1928), Democratic senator from Kansas, 1913–19.

TILLMAN, BENJAMIN RYAN (1847–1918), Democratic senator from South Carolina, 1895–1918.

TRAMMELL, PARK (1876–1936), Democratic senator from Florida, 1917–36.

TUMULTY, JOSEPH PATRICK (1879–1954), Wilson's secretary, 1910–20.

UNDERWOOD, OSCAR WILDER (1862–1929), Republican representative from Alabama, 1895–96, 1897–1915; senator, 1915–26.

UPSHAW, WILLIAM DAVID (1866–1952), Democratic representative from Georgia, 1919–27. Prohibition Party candidate for the Presidency, 1932.

VAN DEVENTER, WILLIS (1859–1941), Associate Justice of the U.S. Supreme Court, 1910–37.

VAN NUYS, FREDERICK (1874–1944), Democratic senator from Indiana, 1933–44.

VARDAMAN, JAMES KIMBLE (1861–1930), Democratic senator from Mississippi, 1913–19.

VENIZELOS, ELEUTHERIOS (1864–1936), Greek statesman, member of Parliament, 1910, supporter of Allied cause, 1915. Established provisional government in Salonika, 1916. Took over government of Greece, June, 1917, after dethronement of King Constantine.

VIVANI, RENÉ (1863–1925), Algerian-born premier and foreign minister of France, 1914, succeeded by Briand, 1915, and became minister of justice. Retired in 1921, but accompanied Briand to Washington Conference of 1921.

VOLSTEAD, ANDREW JOHN (1860–1947), Republican representative from Minnesota, 1903–23. Author of Act providing for Prohibition.

VYNE, NICHOLAS ALBERT (1863–1951), Representative from Yavapai County, Arizona in Fifth State Legislature. Prescott attorney.

WADSWORTH, JAMES JR. (1877–1952), Republican senator from New York, 1915–27, representative, 1933–1951.

WAGNER, ROBERT FERDINAND (1877–1953), Democratic senator from New York, 1927–49.

WALLACE, HENRY A. (1888–   ), Secretary of Agriculture, 1933–40, Vice-President of the United States, 1940–44, Secretary of Commerce, 1944–46, unsuccessful Progressive candidate for Presidency, 1948.

WALSH, DAVID IGNATIUS (1872–1947), Democratic senator from Massachusetts, 1919–25, 1926–47.

WALSH, THOMAS JAMES (1859–1933), Democratic senator from Montana, 1913–33. Appointed Attorney General in 1933, but died before taking office.

WARREN, CHARLES BEECHER (1870–1936), Lawyer from Michigan who served as ambassador to Japan, 1921–23. In 1925 was nominated for Attorney General, but disapproved by Senate.

WARREN, FRANCIS EMROY (1844–1929), Republican senator from Wyoming, 1895 until death. Holder of Congressional Medal of Honor for activities in Civil War.

WATSON, JAMES ELI (1863–1948), Republican representative from Indiana, 1899–1909, senator, 1916–33.

WATSON, THOMAS (1856–1922), Democratic representative from Georgia. Served in House as Populist, 1891–93, in senate as Democrat, 1921–22. Peoples' Party candidate for the Presidency in 1904.

WEDEMEYFR, WILLIAM WALTER (1873–1913), Republican representative from Michigan, 1911–13. Accidentally drowned in harbor of Colon, Panama.

WEST, WILLIAM STANLEY (1849–1914), Democratic senator from Georgia, appointed to senate, March, 1914, and served until November election in that year.

WHEELER, BURTON K. (1882–   ), Democratic senator from Montana, 1923–47. Vice-Presidential candidate of the Progressive Party, 1924. Leading isolationist.

WHITE, EDWARD DOUGLASS (1845–1921), Chief Justice of the U.S. Supreme Court, 1910–21. Previously U.S. senator,, 1891–94, and Justice of the Supreme Court, 1894–1910.

WHITE, HENRY (1850–1927), American diplomat who was appointed ambassador to Italy in 1905.

WILLIAMS, JOHN SHARP (1854–1932), Representative from Mississippi, 1893–1909, senator, 1911–23.

WILLIS, FRANK BARTLETT (1871–1928), Republican representative from Ohio, 1911–15, senator, 1921–28.

WILSON, JOHN F. COL. (1846–1911), Democrat, member of Arizona Constitutional Convention of 1891. Territorial Delegate from Yavapai County, Arizona to Fifty-Sixth and Fifty-Eighth Congress.

WILSON, WILLIAM B. (1862–1934), Democratic representative from Pennsylvania, 1907–13, Secretary of Labor, 1913–21.

WINSOR, MULFORD (1874–1956), Prominent Democrat in Arizona political life. Editor, publisher, and founder Yuma *Sun*, 1896–1901. Manager and co-publisher *Daily Citizen*, Tucson. First Arizona Historian, 1909; executive secretary to first governor, 1912; chairman and organizer State Land Commission 1912–15. Member, State Senate 1917–28, president 1923–28; Director, State Department of Library and Archives, 1932–1956.

WINTER, CHARLES EDWIN (1870–1948), Republican representative from Wyoming, 1923–29.

WISE, RABBI STEPHEN S. (1874–1949), Rabbi who founded Free Synagogue, leader in liberalizing Judaism, eloquent speaker, and foremost Zionist.

WOLCOTT, EDWARD O. (1848–1905), Republican senator from Colorado, 1889–1901.

WOOD, HOMER R. (1869–1952), Came to Arizona from Michigan in 1891; Yavapai County Attorney, 1895; Yavapai County Treasurer, 1904. Delegate to Constitutional Convention, 1910, and state senator, 1912–13.

WOODRING, HARRY HINES (1890–   ), Democratic Governor of Kansas, 1931–33. U.S. Secretary of War, 1936–40.

WOOLSEY, KING S. (1832–1879), Pioneer Indian fighter, politician, and promoter in the Arizona Territory.

WORKS, JOHN DOWNEY (1847–1928), California Republican senator, 1911–17.

YANCEY, WILLIAM L. (1814–1863), Firebrand secessionist. Confederate Commissioner to France and England, 1861–62, member of Confederate Senate, 1862 until death.

YATES, RICHARD (1818–1873), Whig and Republican representative and senator from Illinois. Whig representative, 1851–55, Union Republican, 1865–71.

INDEX

Senator Ashurst's diary was set in type by Morneau Typographers of Phoenix, using ten-point Baskerville with two-point leading throughout the text, and heads in Bulmer. The book was printed by Tyler Printing Company on University Eggshell text paper manufactured by Warren, and bound by Arizona Trade Bindery in Joanna aqua-gray linen. Jacket and end papers are of Andorra stock, from the Hamilton Paper Company. The book was designed by the staff of The University of Arizona Press.